Study Guide

for use with

Law for Business

Ninth Edition

A. James Barnes
Terry W. Dworkin
Eric L. Richards
All of Indiana University

Ken Mark
Kansas City Community College

McGraw-Hill
Irwin

Boston   Burr Ridge, IL   Dubuque, IA   Madison, WI   New York   San Francisco   St. Louis
Bangkok   Bogotá   Caracas   Kuala Lumpur   Lisbon   London   Madrid   Mexico City
Milan   Montreal   New Delhi   Santiago   Seoul   Singapore   Sydney   Taipei   Toronto

McGraw-Hill Irwin

Study Guide for use with
LAW FOR BUSINESS
A. James Barnes, Terry M. Dworkin, Eric L. Richards

Published by McGraw-Hill/Irwin, an imprint of The McGraw-Hill Companies, Inc., 1221 Avenue of the Americas, New York, NY 10020. Copyright © 2006, 2003, 2000, 1997, 1994 by The McGraw-Hill Companies, Inc. All rights reserved.

1 2 3 4 5 6 7 8 9 0 BKM/BKM 0 9 8 7 6 5

ISBN 0-07-297615-2

www.mhhe.com

The McGraw-Hill Companies

Contents

CHAPTER 1
LAW, LEGAL REASONING, AND THE LEGAL PROFESSION

Outline

I. Introduction

II. The Nature of Law

    A. Definition of the Legal System is not a simple one. Law is an institution within American society that changes and evolves to reflect, influence, and interact with other social institutions within society.

    B. Functions of Law include keeping the peace, enforcing standards of conduct, maintaining order, facilitating planning, and promoting social justice.

III. Classifications of Law

    A. Substantive law and procedural law. Substantive law sets out rights and duties; procedural law establishes the rules under which substantive rules of law are enforced. Note, however, that the distinction is not always so clear.

    Example: Yahoo v. La Ligue Contre le Racisme et L'Antisemitisme: The U.S. District Court for the Northern District of California held that a U.S. court can issue a declaratory judgment holding a French order unenforceable in the United States.

    B. Occasionally, federal Constitutional rights conflict with state substantive law.

    C. Criminal law and civil law.

        1. Criminal law defines the duty of individuals to society. Breach of that duty results in prosecution by the government against an individual.

        2. Civil law defines duties owed by individuals to other individuals. (Examples include negligence and contract law.) Breach of the duty one individual owes to another may result in a lawsuit brought by the individual who was harmed by the breach.

IV. Constitutional Foundations

    A. Law and Government: The law in the form of a constitution, establishes the government and also limits the power of that government.

    B. Constitutional powers and limitations include the Bill of Rights (first 10 amendments to the U.S. Constitution), and the system of "Checks and Balances" between the three branches of government.

V. Sources of Law

    A. Federal and state sources include constitutions, treaties, statutes, administrative rules and decisions, executive orders, court decisions, and private law.

    B. Courts make law through interpretation, common law, and judicial review.

    C. Court Decisions—Nature of Common Law. The United States is a "common law" country, sharing the English common law system with other English-speaking countries. Under this system, court decisions have the force of law, and the decision of a court is binding on lower courts within its jurisdiction. The principle that a court should follow precedent (or a prior judicial decision on point in the present case) is called the principle of *stare decisis*.

    D. Judicial review: Courts have power to declare statute inconsistent with a state or U.S. Constitution.

VI.   Legal Reasoning

    A.   Courts use a process of legal interpretation by looking to the plain meaning of the language, examining the legislative history of the rule, considering the purpose to be achieved by the rule, and by trying to accommodate public policy.Example: <u>Twisdale v. Snow</u>: The court is asked to determine if Title VII's protection against retaliatory discharges should be interpreted to encompass retaliation against a manager who sided with an employer against the victim of discrimination. The court concluded that, although the manager's claim fell within the literal meaning of Title VII's language, it ran against the purpose and policies of the law. Thus, the company could retaliate against him without violating Title VII.

        Example: <u>In re Blanchflower</u>: The New Hampshire Supreme Court held that homosexual activity between two women is not adultery, despite the fact that one of the women was married. The court used the literal meaning of adultery to reach this conclusion. It found this meaning by referring to the dictionary. In reaching its result, the court rejected the legislative purpose argument that the rules relating to adultery were designed to promote marital loyalty. It also rejected the policy argument that finding homosexual activity to fall within the statutes promotes even-handed treatment between heterosexuals and homosexuals.

VII.   Law and Orderly Change

    A.   One of the important principles underlying the Common Law, and its principle of *stare decisis* is the belief that law should be predictable. However, the Common Law must also be <u>adaptable</u> in order to respond to changing social and political realities.

        Example: <u>Lawrence v. Texas</u>: The U.S. Supreme Court struck down a Texas sodomy statute that prohibited sexual relations between same-sex partners. In reaching its conclusion, the Court overturned *Bowers v. Hardwick*, a previous decision upholding a similar Georgia sodomy statute. The Court explained that its actions would not undermine respect for the judicial system, in part, because there was no individual or societal reliance on *Bowers*. Further, it believed that the rationale of *Bowers* was unsound, emphasizing that it was not correct today, and was not correct when it was decided.

    B.   Today, business managers must be familiar with basic principles of statutory and common law affecting business. Not only will this help them avoid costs associated with litigation or penalties associated with violating public law, it can also help managers minimize legal risks and consequences.

VIII.   Legal Jurisprudence

    A.   Legal positivism believes in enforcing the letter of the law.

    B.   Natural law holds that law and morality are not separate.

    C.   Sociological jurisprudence considers the legislative purpose of laws as well as perceptions of public policies. Example: <u>Carafano v. Metrosplash.com</u>: An unknown person, using an Internet dating service, falsely submitted a profile of a female television celebrity. As a result, she was bombarded with sexually explicit and threatening messages. Her invasion of privacy lawsuit against Matchmaker.com, the dating service, was dismissed by the court because the Communications Decency Act grants Internet services immunity from liability for information provided by third parties.

    D.   Legal realism believes that legal decisions are often attributable to the biases of decision makers.

IX.   The Legal Profession

    A.   The Adversary System: Justice will most likely prevail when each party involved in a dispute is represented by competent legal counsel.

    B.   Professional Responsibilities: Attorneys have a fiduciary relationship with their clients.

    C.   Confidentiality: The attorney-client privilege is an important part of the legal system in the United States. The work-product privilege is equally important to the justice system.

Example: <u>Rico v. Mitsubishi Motors</u>: The plaintiff's attorney improperly gained access to the notes of one of the defendant's attorneys. He used these materials to prepare his expert witnesses and to impeach the testimony of the defendant's witnesses. The court disqualified both the plaintiff's attorneys and the plaintiff's experts because of this violation of the work-product privilege.

Example: <u>United States v. Stewart</u>: Martha Stewart, under indictment for securities law violations, sent an e-mail to her attorney explaining her actions. She also forwarded a copy of the e-mail to her daughter. The U.S. attorney prosecuting her case sought access to the e-mail. The court concluded that Stewart waived the attorney-client privilege by sharing the e-mail with her daughter. However, it refused to compel disclosure of the e-mail's contents because it was protected by the work-product privilege.

    D. Competence and Care: Attorneys must act with ordinary skill and competence in representing their clients.

X.   Preventive Law

    A. The objectives of preventive law are to prepare business plans that avoid losses from fines and judgments, and reach business goals with enforceable contracts that avoid government prohibitions.

    B. Clients should have an awareness of the law as it affects them.

Learning Objectives

1. You should understand the basic functions law serves.

2. You should understand the differences between civil law and criminal law.

3. You should understand the basic idea of checks and balances and be able to give some examples of its operation.

4. You should know what the Supremacy Clause of the Constitution is and the effect it has on state law, as well as being able to identify constitutional powers and limitations.

5. You should be <u>thoroughly</u> familiar with the different sources of law.

6. You should understand the three ways in which courts make law.

7. You should be aware of the ways in which the law ensures predictability while still remaining adaptable to changing circumstances.

8. You should have an awareness of the legal reasoning process.

9. You should have an understanding of the various types of legal jurisprudence.

10. You should have an awareness of the legal profession in the United States and the duties and responsibilities of attorneys.

11. You should have an awareness of preventive law.

Learning Hints

1. Substantive law sets forth rules spelling out the rights and duties that govern citizens in our society. Procedural law sets forth the rules governing the behavior of our government as it establishes and enforces the rules of substantive law.

2. A civil action is a lawsuit between private parties (one of whom may be the government). In a criminal action, the government is basically acting in the prosecutorial role and is enforcing criminal law. Criminal law is a body of law set up to punish breaches of duty to society at large.

3. In a civil suit, the plaintiff is the party who is suing and the defendant is the party being sued. In a criminal suit, the party who is being prosecuted is the defendant. In criminal cases, however, the government (which always brings the criminal case against the defendant) is not usually referred to as the plaintiff.

4. The Constitution can limit Congress's law-making power in two ways: by specifically listing Congress's powers and saying that Congress shall have these powers and no others, and by imposing certain independent checks on Congress when it exercises its legitimate powers, such as the requirement that citizens be given due process of law.

5. The Taxing Power is a source of regulatory power because of the effect that taxation can have on socially disfavored activities. Therefore, it is often said, "the power to tax is the power to destroy." Also, various tax deductions and tax credits can have a regulatory effect by encouraging certain kinds of activities, and denying tax deductions discourages other kinds of activities.

6. Delegation is a process whereby the legislature effectively "hands over" some of its power to legislate to a subordinate body. The rules issued by the subordinate body are valid because the legislature has given that body power to issue them. Among the sources of law discussed in the text, administrative rules and decisions and executive orders clearly result from a legislative delegation of lawmaking power.

7. Law and equity used to be dispensed in separate courts, and the test for obtaining equitable relief was whether the plaintiff lacked an adequate remedy at law. Today, law and equity are usually dispensed within the same courts. Also, equitable remedies and equitable concepts are sometimes applied in what seem to be "law" cases.

8. As the text stresses, the doctrine of *stare decisis*, while appearing to be very rigid, actually permits considerable change in the common law. This is because it is theoretically possible to distinguish every past case, or precedent, from the case being decided. The power to determine what appropriate distinctions of past cases are rests with the courts.

9. Law is a means by which society attempts to control certain kinds of behavior. Rules of ethics and morality are concerned with questions of right and wrong. In many cases, law reflects a society's moral or ethical belief. However, there are cases where law may not. In these cases, should a person follow the law or his own ethical belief? What are the ethical and social ramifications of your answer?

10. A significant distinction between criminal and civil law is the purpose of the legal action. In a criminal case, the purpose is generally to deter certain conduct through punishment. In civil cases, the purpose is generally to compensate a person who has been injured by another's wrongful act.

True-False

In the blank provided, put "T" if the statement is True or "F" if the statement is False.

_____ 1. Common law is law created by the courts.

_____ 2. In deciding a case, the judge looks at earlier cases that are similar to the current case, finds the rule of law used in the earlier case and applies it to the current case. This is an example of *stare decisis*.

_____ 3. A natural law judge believes a law should be exactly enforced, despite the fact that the judge may feel that the law is unjust.

_____ 4. A client may be able to successfully sue his attorney for malpractice if the attorney fails to assert the correct defenses in representing his client.

_____ 5. Courts look to the plain meaning, legislative history, and purpose or public policy of a statute to try to interpret it.

_____ 6. A legal realist believes that a judge's decision may be influenced by the judge's biases.

_____ 7. Law is a set of principles that can be applied to society, were developed by a legitimate authority within society, and that may threaten sanctions against parties who fail to comply with the principles.

     8.   Courts may provide equitable remedies when strict adherence to the law would cause grave injustice.

     9.   Legal reasoning is a type of critical thinking that is useful in analyzing statutes.

   10.   Legal interpretation of statutes by the courts include considering the intended purpose of the law and how public policy can be furthered through application of the statute.

Multiple Choice

Circle the best answer.

1.   The school of jurisprudence known as legal realism:
   a.   Views law as a social ordering process reflecting current societies dominate interests and values.
   b.   Believes that an unjust law should not be enforced or obeyed.
   c.   Advocates obedience to any properly enacted law, regardless whether that law is just.
   d.   Defines law as the behavior of those charged with enforcing and applying the law rather than the law as it appears in written form.

2.   Which of the following statements is not true?
   a.   Common law is a law created by statutes.
   b.   Private contracts are unenforceable when they conflict with public policy.
   c.   The first step in interpreting a statute is to look at the plain meaning of the words.
   d.   When judges apply the doctrine of *stare decisis*, they look at rulings in prior cases that have precedents for the current case.

3.   Which of the following is not true of the doctrine of *stare decisis*?
   a.   *Stare decisis* helps achieve a level of consistency among court decisions.
   b.   Courts have some flexibility in selecting precedent cases.
   c.   Legislatures cannot overrule *stare decisis*.
   d.   A lawyer may apply rules from a precedent case narrowly or broadly.

4.   Judge Bean is known as a judge who looks at the plain meaning of the words and who enforces the law to the letter. Judge Bean is probably a:
   a.   Natural law judge.
   b.   A legal positivist.
   c.   A legal sociologist.
   d.   A legal realist.

5.   Legal positivists:
   a.   Are likely to consider their own sense of morality when enforcing the law.
   b.   Look to the plain meaning of words to follow the will of lawmakers.
   c.   Recognize equitable exceptions to strict enforcement of legal rules.
   d.   Do not value predictability in the enforcement of legal rules.

6. Judge Simpson lost his son in an automobile accident caused by a drunken driver. Some people feel that Judge Simpson is particularly harsh when dealing with driving under the influence cases because of the experience with his son. This view of Judge Simpson's decisions is known as:
   a. Natural law.
   b. Legal realism.
   c. Sociological jurisprudence.
   d. Legal positivism.

7. The common law:
   a. Exists only at the federal level.
   b. Exists only in situations that are governed by statutes or other positive law.
   c. Will prevail over a conflicting constitutional provision.
   d. Is judge-made law that develops through the use of *stare decisis*.

8. Trish is a member of a pro-life organization. She closely watches legal cases involving issues such as partial-birth abortion, funding of abortions, right to die cases, and stem cell research. Trish is hoping that each case moves society a little closer to the pro-life position. Trish would probably be best classified as:
   a. A legal sociologist.
   b. A natural law thinker.
   c. A legal positivist.
   d. Both a and b.

9. Which of the following statements is not true?
   a. The judicial process in the U.S. relies on the adversary system.
   b. An attorney who loses a case is liable to his client for malpractice.
   c. Perry, an attorney, has a duty not to divulge confidential information told to him by his client, Scott.
   d. Documents, notes, interviews, and other information gathered by Perry, an attorney, in representing his client, Scott, are privileged information.

10. In interpreting the law, judges may:
    a. Look at the plain meaning of the words in the statute.
    b. Look at how the law relates to public policy.
    c. Look at the legislative history as to how the law was created.
    d. All of the above.

Short Essay

1. Judge Dullard is a trial judge in State X. He is in a quandary over a recent case filed in his court. There are several state Supreme Court cases from the 1960s and 1970s applying a common law rule that is the opposite of a rule stated in a 1982 statute. He believes the rule contained in the statute is bad public policy and the common law rule is better. How should he decide this case?

2. Explain how the doctrine of *stare decisis* not only produces stability and predictability in the common law, but also enables the common law to evolve to meet changing social conditions.

3. Ben must appear before Judge Stone regarding a reckless driving charge. Ben's friend, Sam, has appeared before Judge Stone in the past. Sam tells Ben, "You need to hope he had a good breakfast that morning because that guy can be really moody." What legal philosophy is Sam applying to Judge Stone?

4. A woman in Florida has been in a vegetative state for years. Her husband wants to pull life support. The Judge who hears the case has strong pro-life feelings. He rules that the woman should remain on life support. What legal philosophy is the judge likely practicing in this case?

5. Tilly is seriously injured in a car accident. She consults with an attorney and sues the car manufacturer. Tilly loses the case, but then later finds out that her attorney probably used the wrong basis for the lawsuit. What are Tilly's rights in this case?

6. Karen is an attorney representing Jake in a murder trial. During her consultation with Jake, Karen learns that if he is released on bail, Jake plans to commit another murder. Does attorney-client privilege prevent Karen from divulging this information?

7. Bobby is an attorney representing Joey. Joey is suing the manufacturer of his car for negligence in the design of the air bags in the car. What doctrine would Bobby probably want to follow in gathering information for this case?

CHAPTER 2
DISPUTE SETTLEMENT

Outline

I.   Means of Dispute Settlement
    A. Negotiation
    B. ADR (Alternative Dispute Resolution)
       1. Mediation
       2. Arbitration

       Example: <u>Circuit City Stores, Inc. v. Saint Clair Adams</u>: The U.S. Supreme Court held that the Federal Arbitration Act includes private employee contracts and compels courts to enforce a wide range of written arbitration agreements.

       3. International Alternative Dispute Resolution
       4. Mini/Summary Trial
       5. Private Judging

II. The Courts
    A. Courts must have Jurisdiction

       Example: <u>System Design, Inc. v. New CustomWare Company, Inc.</u>: New CustomWare's interactive Web site met the minimum contacts test because the site was intended to reach potential customers in Utah, therefore Utah courts have jurisdiction to hear a case involving new CustomWare.

       Venue is where, within a jurisdiction, a suit must be heard.

    B. State Courts
       1. Inferior Courts: Not courts of record
       2. Trial Courts
       3. Appeals Courts
    C. Federal Courts
       1. Trial court is the District Court
       2. Special Courts
       3. Courts of Appeals
       4. U.S. Supreme Court

III. The Adversary System
       1. Functions of the Judge
       2. Functions of Procedure (The Pleadings and Discovery)
       3. The Trial
       4. The Appeal

Learning Objectives

1. You should understand dispute resolution techniques including arbitration, mediation, mini-trial, and international dispute resolution.

2. You must know what is required for the two types of federal court subject-matter jurisdiction: diversity jurisdiction and federal question jurisdiction.

3. You should be able to name and describe all of the procedural steps in a civil lawsuit.

4. You should know the difference between the burden of proof in a criminal case and the burden of proof in a civil case.

5. You should know the permitted grounds and procedures for appealing the decisions in civil lawsuits.

6. You should know the theory behind the adversary system, and how the judge and the lawyers function in this system.

7. You should understand the principle of federal supremacy and the U.S. Supreme Court's ultimate power to declare a federal or state law unconstitutional.

8. You should understand the principle of personal and subject matter jurisdiction and distinguish it from venue.

Learning Hints

1. Most cases are heard in state (rather than federal) courts. An important distinction between state inferior courts and state trial courts of general jurisdiction is the fact that inferior courts are not courts of record. This means that in many instances, an appeal from a state inferior court will result in a new trial at the state trial court level.

2. In most cases, there are two aspects to jurisdiction. The first is the ability of the court to hear a particular kind of case--this is referred to in the textbook as "subject-matter jurisdiction." For example, a state may set up special courts to handle only a certain type of case, such as special divorce, probate, and juvenile courts. The other aspect of jurisdiction is the territorial or geographical reach of the court. This issue arises mainly during discussions of the state courts, for federal courts have nationwide jurisdiction.

3. In federal cases brought under diversity jurisdiction, the amount involved must be at least $75,000. There is no minimum amount of money that is required for federal question jurisdiction to exist.

4. Many civil lawsuits may be brought either in a state trial court or in a federal District Court. For example, a lawsuit against a driver from another state for an amount over $75,000 can be brought in either state trial court or in federal District Court. The existence of this choice creates strategic questions for the plaintiff's lawyer. Keep in mind also that the defendant may ask to have a case filed in state trial court removed to federal District Court.

5. With very few exceptions, cases do not begin in appellate courts. Appellate courts are usually limited to correcting alleged errors of law (not fact) made at the trial court level.

6. Be aware of the ways in which the basic state court structure or hierarchy parallels the basic federal court structure or hierarchy.

7. The summons and the complaint, while often served on the defendant together, are not the same, and serve very different functions.

8. The motion to dismiss disposes of many cases. The most common form of the motion to dismiss goes to the legal sufficiency of the complaint, and states that even if the facts stated in the complaint are true, the plaintiff still cannot recover because there is no legal remedy for such a situation. For this reason, it is often said that the motion to dismiss amounts to saying "So what?" to the plaintiff's complaint.

9. The motion for a directed verdict and the motion for judgment notwithstanding the verdict are both ways of asking the judge to decide the case instead of the jury. Basically, both assert that no reasonable jury could decide in favor of the other party. The existence of these motions reveals the American legal system's ambivalence about juries, because if all juries were reasonable, the motions would not be necessary.

10. Generally speaking, the appellate courts only review legal errors that one party claims were made by the trial court--not errors in deciding questions of fact. Legal errors include at least the following: lack of jurisdiction, rulings during discovery, rulings on motions to dismiss, evidentiary rulings at trial, rulings on motions for directed verdict and motions for judgment notwithstanding the verdict, and the judge's findings of law (if there was no jury present at the trial).

True-False

In the blank provided, put "**T**" if the statement is True or "**F**" if the statement is False.

_____ 1. In some cases, a federal administrative agency decision may be appealed to the U.S. Court of Appeals.

_____ 2. Parties who want to change the place where their trial will be held ask for a "court of record".

_____ 3. The decision of a mediator is binding upon the parties.

_____ 4. The decision of a state court can never be appealed to the U.S. Supreme Court.

_____ 5. In the American legal system, a judge cannot overturn a jury verdict.

_____ 6. A mini-trial is conducted under the supervision of the court.

_____ 7. The Tax Court would have jurisdiction to hear appeals cases involving decisions made by the Internal Revenue Service.

_____ 8. A writ of certiorari is the most common way to appeal a case to the Supreme Court.

_____ 9. Cases heard in the federal courts must involve either a federal question or situations in which there is diversity of citizenship between the parties.

_____ 10. A motion to dismiss may be requested by the defendant if it is clear that the plaintiff does not have a case.

Multiple Choice

Circle the best answer.

1. Which of the following is not true of the appellate procedure?
   a. The appellate court hears witnesses and gathers new evidence.
   b. A transcript of the trial must be sent to the appeals court.
   c. The appealing party must show that material errors occurred in the trial.
   d. The appeals court may reverse and remand the decision.

2. If P sues D, and D wants to allege that P's own negligence caused her injury, D should allege this in:
   a. The complaint.
   b. The answer.
   c. The reply
   d. The counterclaim.

3. Venue concerns:
   a. Whether a federal court has jurisdiction.
   b. Whether a state court has jurisdiction.
   c. The most appropriate place for the action to be brought.
   d. Whether a defendant has been properly served with process.

4. Which of the following is not true of trials?
   a. Preponderance of evidence is the standard used in civil trials.
   b. Proof beyond a reasonable doubt is the standard used in criminal trials.
   c. The state can make a motion for judgment n.o.v. when the defendant is acquitted in a criminal trial.
   d. A directed verdict may be granted if the plaintiff's evidence is not sufficient to support her allegations.

5. Eve attempts suicide by locking herself inside the trunk of her car. Someone discovers Eve after several days. She is still alive. Eve sues the manufacturer of her car for a large amount of money because it did not provide for a latch inside the trunk. Which of the following may be a good course of action for the car manufacturer in this case?
   a. Make a motion to dismiss the case.
   b. Make a motion for a directed verdict.
   c. Make a motion of judgment n.o.v.
   d. Take the case to small claims court.

6. Which of the following is a type of alternative dispute resolution that is binding on the parties?
   a. Mediation
   b. Mini-trial
   c. Private judge
   d. Summary jury trial

7. Federal question jurisdiction:
   a. Is a type of jurisdiction possessed by state trial courts.
   b. Is the most common form of U.S. Supreme Court jurisdiction.
   c. Requires that the amount in controversy be at least $10,000.
   d. Is jurisdiction over questions arising under federal laws, treaties, and the U.S. Constitution.

8. Which of the following statements is not true?
   a. Bob, a resident of New Jersey, sues Ed, a resident of Florida, for $100,000 over a real estate deal. Bob must bring his suit in a Florida court.
   b. The conflict of laws may guide a federal court in deciding which state's laws to apply in a case.
   c. Federal courts have exclusive jurisdiction over bankruptcy cases.
   d. You are not required to be represented by an attorney in small claims court.

9. Johnson is a creditor of Barnes. Johnson wants to file a petition to have Barnes declared bankrupt. Which of the following statements is true?
   a. Johnson can file his petition in either state or federal court.
   b. Johnson should file his petition in U.S. District Court.
   c. Only a federal bankruptcy court can hear a bankruptcy case.
   d. Bankruptcy cases can be heard in Federal Tax Court.

10. Which of the following is not an inferior court?
   a. Justice of the peace
   b. U.S. District Court
   c. Small claims court
   d. Municipal court

Short Essay

1. Briefly describe some advantages and disadvantages of the adversary system.

2. Andrea and Tom are planning on a late June wedding. Several weeks before the wedding date, Andrea breaks things off with Tom. Tom learns that Andrea sold their shower gifts, withdrew more from a joint checking account than she deposited, and made a large amount of charges on Tom's credit card. Tom sues Andrea. Assuming Tom wins this case, what is one way that the court could enforce its judgment on Andrea?

3. What are the basic steps in a civil lawsuit?

4. The board and faculty of Happy College cannot reach a contract agreement for the school year. Under state law, the next step is for each side to present its case to a mediator. The mediator agrees with the board's arguments. Is the mediator's decision binding upon the two parties? Why or why not?

5. The "borderless" Internet has created a new wave of jurisdictional issues for our courts. Over the years, the use of "long arm" statutes helped courts ascertain jurisdictional boundaries when courts could find some minimal contact of doing business in a state for it to be able to assert its jurisdiction. How much Internet activity would you consider to be sufficient to satisfy the minimum contact rule?

6.   Briefly describe two types of discovery.

7.   Briefly discuss the standards for burden of proof in civil cases and criminal cases.

CHAPTER 3
BUSINESS ETHICS AND CORPORATE SOCIAL RESPONSIBILITY

I. Introduction

II. Ethical Theories

  A. Rights Theory

Rights theory emphasizes actions and not consequences, therefore it is also known as a deontological ethical theory.

    1. Kantianism. The morality of any action is determined by applying a categorical imperative. One imperative is to judge an action by applying it universally. Another imperative is to not manipulate others for our own self interests.

    2. Modern Rights Theory. Moral rules should be abided by unless a greater moral rule conflicts with it.

    Example: <u>Virginia v. Black</u>: The U.S. Supreme Court ruled that a cross could be burned at a rally on private property without there necessarily being an intent to intimidate any particular party.

  B. Justice Theory

This theory calls for a just distribution of the society's resources. The Greatest Equal Liberty Principle says that each person has an equal right to basic liberties. The Difference Principle argues that social inequalities are unacceptable unless these inequalities cannot be eliminated without making things worse for the worse-off class.

Example: <u>U.S. v. Virginia</u>: The U.S. Supreme Court ruled that a male-only admission policy at Virginia Military Institute violated the Equal Protection Clause and discriminated against females.

  C. Utilitarianism

An ethical decision must weigh the costs and benefits for each member of society. With this theory, the ends justify the means. Act Utilitarianism focuses on decision makers considering the costs and benefits of each action. With Rule Utilitarianism, the action is seen as part of a larger rule.

Example: <u>Illinois v. Lidster</u>: The U.S. Supreme Court found that a police checkpoint set up for appropriate criminal investigatory purposes does not violate liberties guaranteed under the Fourth Amendment.

  D. Profit Maximization

This theory believes that maximizing profits for businesses will lead to optimum social utility.

Allocation Efficiency holds that the primary objective for businesses is to maximize profits and that by doing so, the most efficient allocation of society's resources will take place.

Critics of profit maximization argue that social concerns may outweigh the need for profit maximization.

Justice Theory, Utilitarianism, and Profit Maximization are teleological theories. They focus on the consequences of ethical decision making and not just the actions.

III. The Law as a Corporate Control Device

  A. Limitations

    1. Corporate Influence on Content of the Law

      a) Try to head off risk of future unpredictable lawsuits

    b) Influence the nature of legislation and manage the risk of more extreme and costly regulations

    c) Ensure that all competitors are subject to the same constraints

  2. Conscious Lawbreaking

  Corporate disregard for unpopular laws

  Example: <u>Liu v. Amway</u>: The 9th Circuit Court held that the company violated the Family Medical Leave Act and improperly terminated the employee.

  3. Unknown Harms

  Time may pass before problems with products become known. (ex: Merck & Co., Inc. pulled Vioxx from the market because it became aware of heart problems caused by the drug.)

  4. Irrational Corporate Behavior

    a) Risky Shift

    Example: <u>Midwest Motor Sports v. Arctic Cat Sales</u>: The 8th Circuit Court found that attorneys for Arctic Cat used a private investigator for improper activities in researching the case.

    b) Groupthink

    Members of a group may minimize risks that conflict with the group's goals.

    c) Bad News Does Not Rise

    Information that conflicts with top management goals may not be reported.

    Example: <u>U.S. v. Park</u>: The Supreme Court held that a CEO was responsible along with his corporation for violations of the Federal Food, Drug, and Cosmetics Act.

IV. Defining Ethical Corporate Behavior

Ethical guidance for corporations may come from three sources.

  A. Values that Find Wide Acceptance

  Conflicting values may be present in our culture and in the cultures of other countries.

  B. Corporate or Industry Codes of Conduct

  The Sarbanes-Oxley Act and other laws may require companies to adopt and disclose a code of ethics.

  C. Constituency Values

  Most companies have a large number of stakeholders and their interests in the company may conflict at times.

  Example: <u>International Union v. Johnson Controls</u>: The U.S. Supreme Court held that the company's policies regarding fetal protection illegally discriminated on the basis of sex.

V. The Corporate Governance Agenda

Three recommendations to make corporations more sensitive to social concerns are mentioned. These recommendations are procedural in that they focus on the corporate decision making process rather than looking at details of corporate behavior.

  A. Giving Shareholders Greater Power

    1) Give shareholders greater power to nominate the board of directors

    2) Give shareholders power to adopt resolutions that bind the corporate directors

<ol type="a">
<li>many shareholders are mostly focused on profits and are not likely to recommend actions that are contrary to profit maximization.</li>
<li>most shareholders are not in a position to evaluate the non-economic performance of the corporation</li>
<li>a small percentage of people own stock, so the recommendations of shareholders do not necessarily reflect the values of society as a whole</li>
</ol>

B. Changing the Composition of the Board

Sarbanes-Oxley requires publicly traded corporations to have board audit committees. Many proposals emphasize the need for greater involvement of outside directors as a system of checks and balances on management power.

C. Changing the Management Structure

1. Several proposals have been made in an effort to generate more responsible corporate behavior.

<ol type="a">
<li>specified offices within certain corporations – watchdog in nature</li>
<li>licensing requirements for holding certain corporate positions</li>
<li>offices for ensuring relevant external information is received by the corporation</li>
<li>internal information flow procedures for ensuring that important external information gets to the proper internal corporate departments</li>
<li>documentation of certain internal findings before taking actions</li>
</ol>

2. The corporate reward structure needs to be changed so that focus is not so much on maximizing short term profits

VI. Guidelines for Ethical Decision Making

A. Control devices, such as the law, have shortcomings

B. Model for Making Ethical Decisions

1. Which course of action does the most good and the least harm?
2. Which alternative best serves others' rights?
3. What course of action is consistent with personal morality and basic values of the company?
4. Which course of action is feasible?

Learning Objectives

1. You should be able to distinguish deontological ethical theories from teleological ethical theories.
2. You should be able to understand Rights Theories and be able to distinguish between Kantianism and Modern Rights Theory.
3. You should be able to explain Justice Theory and to distinguish between Greatest Equal Liberty Principle and the Difference Principle.
4. You should be able to understand Utilitarianism and to explain the differences between Act Utilitarianism and Rule Utilitarianism.
5. You should be able to understand Profit Maximization and to explain Allocation Efficiency.
6. You should be able to explain how the law acts as a corporate control device.

7. You should be able to describe the limitations on the law's ability to serve as a corporate control device.

8. You should be able to explain the three sources of ethical guidance for corporate managers.

9. You should be able to describe the three recommendations for making corporations more sensitive to social concerns.

10. You should be able to describe the guidelines for ethical decision making.

Learning Hints

1. The four ethical theories are guides for decision makers to make ethical choices.

2. Rights theory emphasizes the rights of individuals in our society.

3. Kantianism and Modern Rights Theory are the two types of Rights Theories.

4. Justice Theory looks at the fairness of a decision maker's choices.

5. Ethical decisions are ones that produce more benefits than costs under Utilitarianism.

6. Profit Maximization theorists believe that managers should make decisions that maximize the company's profits. Maximizing profits results in efficient allocation of society's resources and therefore optimizes social utility. Critics of profit maximization would argue that maximizing profits results in employee layoffs, outsourcing, dangerous products, etc.

7. The law can only go so far in protecting society from irresponsible corporate behavior. Some managers may still decide to disregard certain laws that are contrary to corporate interest. Sarbanes-Oxley attempts to increase the likelihood that corporations that violate the law, including the obstruction of audits, will face felony charges and stiff penalties. However, the law cannot prevent seemingly good products from having potential problems that are unknown at the time they were placed on the market. Large, powerful corporations can still attempt to influence the law in their favor. Managers may still make decisions that later would appear to be foolish and unwarranted.

8. Some managers may be guided in their decision making by corporate codes of ethical conduct. Sarbanes-Oxley and other government regulations may require public corporations to adopt a code of ethics. Managers may also be influenced by widely accepted values and values of constituency groups. However, many different values exist in our society. Values among labor unions, employees, shareholders, customers, and other constituents will likely vary a great deal. Also, companies that do business in foreign countries may find that widely held values in these countries may be far different than those held by people in the United States.

9. Recommendations to improve corporate responsibility include increasing shareholder power, changing the composition of the corporate board, and changing the management structure. Many critics believe that the emphasis needs to shift away from short-term profit maximization in order for managers to focus more on long-term, ethically-based decisions. Often, salaries, bonuses, stock options, etc. are based on profitability in the short-term.

10. The Model for Making Ethical Decisions is a common-sense approach to making choices. The four questions comprising the model should be asked concurrently. As with any model, its main purpose is to serve as a guideline for making decisions.

True-False

In the blank provided, put "**T**" if the statement is True or "**F**" if the statement is False.

_____ 1. Justice theory subscribes to the view that human rights are fundamental.

_____ 2. Under Kantianism, human beings are to be treated as ends rather than means.

_____ 3. The Difference Principle says that each person has an equal right to basic rights and liberties.

_____ 4. Someone who subscribes to Utilitarianism would likely not have much of a problem with increased screening and security at airports.

_____ 5. A worker whose job was moved to India would likely agree with the Allocation Efficiency theory.

_____ 6. The tendency for group members to internalize group values and perceptions and to suppress critical thought is called groupthink.

_____ 7. Risky shift is a teleological theory based on the laissez faire theory of capitalism.

_____ 8. The Sarbanes-Oxley Act requires public corporations to disclose whether they have adopted a code of ethics for senior financial officers.

_____ 9. The values of various corporate constituencies are usually very similar.

_____ 10. Most proposals to make corporations more sensitive to outside concerns attempt to define ethical corporate behavior in detail.

Multiple Choice

Circle the best answer.

1. Which of the following is an example of rights theory?
   a. Kantianism
   b. Utilitarianism
   c. Justice Theory
   d. Risky Shift

2. The Difference Principle says:
   a. Each person has an equal right to basic rights.
   b. Treat human beings as ends, not means.
   c. Our moral compulsion is not to compromise a person's right unless a greater right takes priority.
   d. Social inequalities are acceptable only if they cannot be eliminated without making the worst-off class even worse off.

3. Which ethical theory most focuses on the outcome of the decision?
   a. Utilitarianism
   b. Justice Theory
   c. Rights Theory
   d. Profit Maximization

4. XYZ management honestly believes that moving some of their production to a third world country will provide more benefits than costs to our society. This thought process is an example of:
   a. Justice Theory
   b. Rights Theory
   c. Utilitarianism
   d. Profit Maximization

5. XYZ management believes that society here may suffer somewhat if some production is moved overseas, but they also believe that their shareholders will greatly benefit in the long run from such a decision. This decision would appear to be an example of:
   a. Utilitarianism
   b. Justice Theory
   c. Modern Rights Theory
   d. Profit Maximization

6. Which of the following is not a limitation on the law's ability to control irresponsible corporate behavior?
   a. Corporate influence on the content of law
   b. Unknown harms
   c. Sarbanes-Oxley Act
   d. Irrational corporate behavior

7. Which of the following is not a type of irrational corporate behavior?
   a. Risky Shift
   b. Ensure that all competitors operate under the same constraints
   c. Groupthink
   d. Bad news does not rise to the top

8. Which of the is not a recommendation to make corporations more sensitive to outside concerns?
   a. Giving the corporate board greater power
   b. Giving the shareholders greater power
   c. Changing the composition of the corporate board
   d. Changing the management structure

9. Which of the following is not a reason that giving shareholders greater power will likely not lead to greater corporate social responsibility?
   a. Most shareholders are more interested in profit maximization.
   b. Shareholders represent a narrow range of social interests.
   c. Shareholders are generally more informed of relevant issues than corporate management.
   d. Many shareholders will not have access to enough information to monitor non-economic performance of the corporation.

10. Which of the following is not part of the Model for Making Ethical Decisions?
    a. Which course of action does the most good and the least harm?
    b. Which course of action maximizes profits?
    c. Which alternative best serves others' rights?
    d. Which course of action is feasible?

Short Essay

1. The chapter describes four ethical theories: Rights Theory, Justice Theory, Utilitarianism, and Profit Maximization. Which of these four theories make the most sense to you? Why?

2.	Nike has been criticized for reaping great profits while manufacturing many of its products in third world countries where wages are low. Discuss this situation by considering the four ethical theories in this chapter. With each theory, discuss how Nike may have made the decision to manufacture its products in cheap labor markets.

3.	In this chapter, four limitations on the law's ability to control irresponsible corporate behavior are mentioned; corporate influence on the content of the law, conscious lawbreaking, unknown harms, and irrational corporate behavior. Think about the problems in recent years with the tobacco industry. Pick at least two of the limitations and describe how you feel these have played a role in what has happened with companies in the tobacco industry.

4.	XYZ Company has a large customer service department. Employees in this department handle customer orders by phone, mail, and the internet. This department also handles customer complaints and questions. XYZ management is seriously thinking of relocating this department to India in order to save costs. Use the Model for Making Ethical Decisions and analyze this decision making process.

5. Merck & Co. recently pulled the arthritis drug Vioxx off the market because of evidence that the drug causes heart problems. From what you have learned in this chapter, discuss the possible decision making process at Merck that led up to this conclusion.

6. Briefly discuss the three recommended ways to make a corporation more socially sensitive and responsible; giving shareholders greater power, changing the composition of the corporate board, and changing management structure.

CHAPTER 4
BUSINESS AND THE CONSTITUTION

Outline

I.   State regulation of business.

    A.   States retain the power to regulate intrastate commerce, but the U.S. Constitution gives the federal government power to regulate interstate commerce.

    B.   If Congress enacts valid interstate legislation and state law conflicts, the state law is preempted. States may regulate aspects of interstate commerce not preempted so long as that regulation does not place an unreasonable burden on interstate commerce.

        Example: Crosby v. National Foreign Trade Council: A Massachusetts statute was preempted by the federal Burma Act.

        Example: Washington v. Heckel: A Washington statute did not unconstitutionally burden interstate commerce.

II.   Federal regulation of business.

    A.   In order to apply, state action must exist for constitutional checks on governmental power.

        Example: Raich v. Ashcroft: The court found that the federal government could not apply a drug anti-trafficking law against California residents who were using marijuana for medical reasons because this was not an activity that Congress could regulate under the Commerce Clause.

        Example: Ridge Line v. United States: The appellate court overturned a decision of a trial court that no compensable taking had occurred when the federal government built a post office next to a privately owned shopping center and the resulting increase in storm run-off caused severe damage to the shopping center.

    B.   The Due Process Clause guarantees procedural due process and certain substantive rights.

        Example: National Council of Resistance of Iran v. Albright: The process of making foreign terrorist organization determinations denied the National Council of Resistance of Iran due process of law.

    C.   Certain state actions are unconstitutional because they are substantively unfair and violate substantive due process.

    D.   The Equal Protection Clause prohibits unfair discrimination against certain protected classes.

        Different tests are used to determine whether governmental discrimination is unconstitutional: rational basis and strict scrutiny tests.

        Example: Goodridge v. Department of Public Health: The court found that the Massachusetts state ban against gay marriages is unconstitutional. The court used rational basis analysis and rejected the state's argument that same-sex marriages would undermine marriage.

        Example: Ashcroft v. American Civil Liberties Union: Using strict scrutiny analysis, the court enjoined enforcement of the Child Online Protection Act. The court believed that there were less restrictive alternatives to the act.

    E.   The First Amendment protects commercial speech in some cases. The courts have given the highest degree of constitutional protection to noncommercial speech.

        Example: Mainstream Marketing Services v. Federal Trade Commission: The court upheld the national do-not-call registry. The registry's restriction of commercial speech passed the intermediate scrutiny test.

III.   Administrative agencies.

    A. Law establishes agencies. Their powers and duties are established by the enabling legislation creating the agency. Agencies may have legislative, judicial, and executive functions.

    B. The Federal Trade Commission Act created the FTC to enforce federal antitrust policies and prevent unfair competitive practices in the marketplace.

Learning Objectives

1. You should understand the evolution of government regulation of business from a 19th century *laissez faire* approach to business activity to today's increasingly complex regulatory environment.

    You should understand the various forces that have triggered the enormous growth in government regulation during this century, and should recognize why, despite deregulation movements in some quarters, many of these same forces will not permit a totally free market economy.

2. You should be familiar with basic constitutional principles affecting business. One of the most significant questions is whether business activity affects interstate commerce. If so, state regulation of that activity may be preempted by the commerce clause of the U.S. Constitution. You should understand the Commerce Clause and the restraints it imposes on state regulation, as well as the diminishing impact of the Commerce Clause as a restraint on federal regulation.

3. Even if federal action does not preempt state regulation of a business activity, state regulation is prohibited if it places an unreasonable burden on interstate commerce.

4. Several constitutional protections are significant for businesses. The 14th Amendment due process and equal protection clauses are among these. You should understand what is meant by the rational basis test and why the likelihood of invalidating legislation under this analysis is slight.

5. You should become familiar with the meaning of strict scrutiny and with the kinds of situations that will trigger this more stringent analysis of a government regulation.

6. You should develop an awareness of what suspect classes and fundamental rights are, and of what significance each has with regard to the application of the equal protection clause.

7. You should understand the development of the First Amendment, and in particular the different levels of protection given by it to commercial speech and political speech.

8. You should become familiar with the reasons for the tremendous growth of administrative agencies, and should understand the diverse functions the agencies perform, as well as the various limits on their powers.

9. You should understand why the FTC was created and be aware of its broad scope of authority.

10. You should understand the importance of enabling legislation in establishing an administrative agency's powers and duties.

Learning Hints

1. One of the most significant legal developments in this century for American business is the tremendous growth of administrative agencies. Agencies like the FTC (Federal Trade Commission) and EPA (Environmental Protection Commission) exercise enormous power and authority over business activities. These agencies are established by federal enabling legislation which establish their powers and duties, and which also limits their authority to act in some cases.

2. States also establish state agencies. State legislatures adopt enabling legislation establishing agencies with the power to adopt rules and regulations governing business activities. Significant state agencies include environmental protection agencies, state OSHA agencies (Occupational Safety and Health), and state Industrial Workman's Compensation Boards.

3. The tremendous growth of regulation is easily understood if one considers the economic notion of "externalities." Externalities are the things one does that have an impact on other people. Although in the abstract most people probably would favor more independence for themselves, they frequently lobby for regulation in order to control the behavior of others, when that behavior's external effects will have an impact on their lives. In a complex, interdependent world, one would expect these externalities to increase rather than decrease, meaning that regulation is not going to disappear.

4. The notion of externalities also explains the judicial interpretation of the Commerce Clause that has caused the clause to be a restraint on state acts. The activities of any state almost always affect the rest of the country. Hence, state acts having external effects that might undermine the solidarity of the nation, as a whole will be struck down. Likewise, this notion has reduced the negative influence of the Commerce Clause on the federal government. Instead, the federal government is viewed as the only body that can address the needs of the whole nation. It is, therefore, considered to be better suited to regulate in the areas that have the greatest likelihood of affecting the nation as a whole.

5. When studying the due process clause and the equal protection clause, it is important to understand that they only limit <u>government</u> action. They are not addressed to private persons or businesses. The vast majority of statutes and regulations confronting the business community are instead based upon the federal government's authority to regulate interstate commerce. Through such statutes and regulations, the activities of private persons and businesses clearly can be reached.

6. In cases in which a violation of the equal protection clause is alleged, the notion of strict scrutiny is used only when fundamental rights have been interfered with or suspect classes have been singled out for discrimination. Normally, the court would not indulge in such exacting analysis because the court is not ordinarily inclined to second-guess a legislative body. However, when the regulation discriminates against a suspect class (race, religion or national origin) or interferes with a fundamental right, the court feels compelled to act because the judiciary is the guardian of fundamental (constitutional) rights and of those persons against whom discrimination has been common throughout history. The strict scrutiny analysis is largely outcome-determinative, in that a decision by the court that strict scrutiny governs the case effectively determines what the result of the case will be most of the time, because the government is hard pressed to prevail under such a rigorous standard.

7. Equal protection cases involving a claim of discrimination on the basis of one's sex are given a special degree of analysis that falls somewhere between strict scrutiny and the lenient rational basis test applied in cases involving most economic regulations.

8. Do not forget that there is no violation of one's first amendment rights if no government action created the alleged deprivation. (Government action is also required in order for there to have been a violation of the due process clauses or the equal protection clause.)

9. Be certain to note the distinction between the constitutional protection given to commercial speech and the constitutional protection given to political speech. Commercial speech, though entitled to first amendment protection, does not receive the full panoply of protection given to political speech. Remember, too, that corporations cannot be denied, simply on the basis of their corporate status, the political speech rights that a natural person would have. The cases in which first amendment protection has been extended to commercial speech have tended to be based on the idea that the public (listeners) has a right to hear the views of these speakers. At least in part, a similar rationale has been utilized in the corporate political speech cases.

True-False

In the blank provided, put "**T**" if the statement is True or "**F**" if the statement is False.

_____ 1. Congress can enact legislation that will expressly preempt state laws.

_____ 2. The Commerce Clause of the U.S. Constitution prohibits state legislation that burdens interstate commerce.

_____ 3. A zoning ordinance is an example of a taking, therefore compensation to the landowner is required.

_____ 4. The First Amendment of the U.S. Constitution gives the highest level of protection to political speech.

_____ 5. The government must follow substantive due process whenever it interferes with people's economic rights.

_____ 6. The Due Process Clauses contained in the U.S. Constitution prohibit the federal and state governments from taking the private property of citizens.

_____ 7. The Supremacy Clause gives the states the authority to legislate to promote the health, safety and welfare of their citizens.

_____ 8. Legislation that discriminates on the basis of a suspect class will likely be reviewed under rational basis analysis.

_____ 9. The First, Fifth, and Fourteenth Amendments to the U.S. Constitution protect against infringements of certain basic rights.

_____ 10. Government regulation of business is a relatively new phenomenon that had its beginnings in the 1930's.

Multiple Choice

Circle the best answer.

1. Which of the following is not a true statement?
   a. Many government agencies have the authority to issue regulations that have the force of law.
   b. Arbitrary agency decisions may be overturned by the courts.
   c. Agency hearings usually involve juries.
   d. Persons who will be affected by agency actions should be given advance notice of agency proceedings and the opportunity to appear at a hearing.

2. Which of the following statements is not true regarding noncommercial speech?
   a. To be protected by the courts, noncommercial speech must be true.
   b. Restrictions on noncommercial speech must be reviewed under strict scrutiny analysis.
   c. Restrictions will be upheld if the government can show that the regulation is furthering a compelling government interest.
   d. Restrictions will be upheld if the regulation of the least intrusive means is used to promote the governmental interest.

3. Which of the following requires that statutes differentiating between similarly situated persons or groups must bear a "rational relationship" to a legitimate state purpose unless the statute involves a "suspect" classification?
   a. The Due Process Clause of the 14th amendment.
   b. The Equal Protection Clause of the 14th amendment.
   c. The commerce clause.
   d. The First Amendment.

4. Which of the following statements is true?
   a. Protection of commercial speech does not require that the speech be truthful.
   b. Commercial speech does not enjoy First Amendment protection.
   c. Misleading advertising enjoys First Amendment protection.
   d. Courts use intermediate scrutiny to analyze commercial speech regulations.

5. Which of the following statements is not true?
   a. Legislation involving non-fundamental (property) rights is subject to strict scrutiny.
   b. Legislation that denies people fundamental rights such as the right of free speech is subject to strict scrutiny.
   c. Under strict scrutiny, the government must show that it is achieving a compelling governmental interest in the least intrusive manner.
   d. If the government allows procedural due process in cases involving only economic rights, its actions will be constitutional.

6. Which of the following components of the Takings Clause is correct?
   a. A taking by the government must take place.
   b. The taking must serve a public purpose.
   c. The property owner whose property is taken is entitled to just compensation.
   d. All of the above.

7. Judicial interpretations of the Commerce Clause:
   a. Overall have greatly narrowed the reach of the clause since the 1930s.
   b. Consistently permit the states broad latitude to regulate interstate commerce.
   c. Have been expansive in the recent past, but recent cases indicate this could change.
   d. Consistently have prevented the states from regulating commerce in any respect.

8. Under the Due Process Clause, a court would be very likely to strike down state legislation that:
   a. Regulated the minimum age for employment.
   b. Regulated the maximum hours that employees could work.
   c. Dispensed with the right to a trial for criminal prosecutions.
   d. Did any of the above.

9. Which of the following are factors that will be considered in determining the validity of state legislation as it impacts interstate commerce?
   a. The legislation must further a legitimate state interest.
   b. The legislation must not favor local interests against out-of-state interests.
   c. The legislation must not impose costs on interstate commerce that are higher than necessary to achieve the state interests.
   d. All of the above.

10. Which of the following statements is not true?
   a. The federal government has the exclusive right to regulate foreign commerce in the United States.
   b. Federal legislation may impliedly preempt state laws.
   c. The federal government has the power to regulate intrastate commerce.
   d. Federal legislation may expressly preempt state laws.

Short Essay

1. George operates an auto parts store in Kansas City, Kansas. George sells his products mostly to consumers, but he also does sell parts to various garages in the area. Is George's business affected by laws regulating interstate commerce?

2. Bill wants to build a shop on his property at his residence so that he can build cabinets to sell to customers. The county ordinances do not allow Bill to operate a business such as a cabinet shop from his home. Does this situation fit under the Takings Clause? Is Bill entitled to receive compensation from the county in this situation?

3. River City is presented with an opportunity to have a NASCAR speedway built within its city limits. The speedway could likely spawn a large number of other businesses for the area. To build the speedway, the city must take over one hundred private residences through the power of eminent domain. The city proposes to pay each property owner the fair market value for his or her home. Is River City acting properly under the Takings Clause?

4. California has a large umber of international companies doing business within its borders. Under the California accounting rules for measuring income for its state income tax, California uses a unitary system of accounting, i.e., if the worldwide income of the organization is $100 million and 10 percent of its business is done in California, and then the state income would be measured by $10 million. A number of these international companies object to this accounting system because the actual level of profits or losses may greatly differ from their total worldwide operations. These companies claim that California cannot use that accounting system because it violates the federal government's power to regulate foreign companies. Does the Interstate Commerce Clause of the US Constitution preempt the California system?

5. Tim and Tina Freeman own a house across the street from a large acreage of land. The city is trying to change the zoning laws so that a casino/resort can be built on the land. The city's planning commission sent the Freemans and other property owners in the area notice of their meetings so that the property owners could hear arguments for and against the proposed casino and so that they could offer their opinions. The city leaders believe that this casino will generate revenues for the city that will far outweigh any potential negatives. After a long process was followed by the city, it decided to have the casino built on the property. The Freemans are very upset. Describe the type of analysys the local government needs to exercise in a situation like this.

6. California has had a long-standing problem with air pollution and has taken aggressive actions to cut down on its sources. One such action requires that automobile manufacturers sell a certain percentage of their cars as "zero emissions vehicles." Failure to do so will result in the state taking that manufacturer's license to do business in California. Manufacturers object to this plan because electric cars have failed in the marketplace and that this is a burden on interstate commerce. California argues that it is a legitimate exercise of its police power. Who wins?

7.   Give an example of a federal agency and how it may impact your life.

CHAPTER 5
CRIMES

Outline

I.   The Nature of Crimes: Crimes are public wrongs and the state rather than an individual party brings prosecutions.

   A. Kinds of crimes: Felonies and misdemeanors

   B. The Essentials of Crime: The state must prove a <u>criminal statute</u> existed at the time the act was committed, that defendant's acts <u>violated</u> that statute, defendant had the <u>capacity</u> to form a criminal intent, and formed that intent.

   Example: <u>Chaffee v. Roger</u>: The U.S. District Court in *Chaffee* finds the Nevada intimidation statute unconstitutionally vague and gives police officers too much discretion. Additionally, the court finds the Nevada statute to be overbroad. The court remanded the issue to the Nevada Supreme Court so that the court could narrow the meaning of "threat" and "intimidation."

   C. The state must prove every element of the offense charged against defendant beyond a reasonable doubt.

   D. The requirement of criminal intent is an element of most serious crimes.

   E. Criminal Procedure: Our system has procedural safeguards to protect the accused.

   Example: In <u>United States v. Kyllo</u>, scanning a home with thermal imaging devices to detect marijuana plants was unconstitutionally intrusive under the 4th Amendment.

II. Crimes and Business

   A. Personal liability for corporate executives has been imposed under the theory this will <u>deter</u> violation of laws.

   Example: <u>United States v. Hong</u>: Hong may not actually be a corporate officer, but he is found liable under the "responsible corporate officer" doctrine.

   B. Other issues include problems with individual liability, and application of RICO (Racketeer Influenced and Corrupt Organizations Act) to businesses.

   Example: <u>State of Connecticut v. Nanowski</u>: The state is not required to prove that Nanowski did not intend to pay his employees in order to successfully prosecute him.

   C. Other illustrations of a "get tough" attitude are recently adopted federal sentencing guidelines.

   D. Numerous white-collar crimes continue to be prosecuted under the Racketeer Influenced and Corrupt Organizations Act (RICO).

   Example: In <u>Cedric Kushner Promotions, Ltd. v. Don King</u>: The U.S. Supreme Court stated that RICO requires two separate entities, but those entities can be the corporate owner/employee, a natural person, and the corporation itself even if they are one and the same.

Learning Objectives

1.   You should be able to distinguish the parties involved in civil and criminal actions, the standard of proof, and the burden of proof required in each action.

2.   You should be familiar with the rationales for punishment underlying criminal law.

3.   You should know the essentials of crime and be able to explain constitutional protections that apply in criminal prosecutions.

4.   You should know the general difference between a felony and a misdemeanor.

5.   You should know the rules surrounding the three major types of criminal incapacity: intoxication, infancy, and insanity.

6. You should be familiar with the more important procedural protections that our legal system has developed to protect the accused.

7. You should understand the trends and problems for the criminal justice system as it deals with white-collar crime.

8. You should understand the purpose of RICO and its application to business and corporate executives.

9. You should understand the main features of the Sarbanes-Oxley Act.

10. You should understand the highlights of the Foreign Corrupt Practices Act.

11. You should understand the basic points of laws aimed at cybercrime.

Learning Hints

1. One important difference between criminal and civil law is the purpose or function of the action. An important purpose of criminal prosecution is to <u>punish</u> in order to deter similar activity in the future. The purpose of civil law, on the other hand, is to <u>compensate</u> the plaintiff for injury caused by the wrongful act of the defendant.

2. An essential requirement of a crime is that there be a statute in effect at the time the defendant's act occurred that prohibited that activity. A statute passed after the act occurred cannot be the basis of a criminal prosecution under the constitutional prohibition against <u>ex post facto</u> laws.

3. The postponement of trial or sentencing, or the acquittal of the defendant, on the basis of the defendant's insanity does not necessarily mean that the defendant will be released from custody. In many such cases, the defendant is committed to an institution for psychiatric treatment.

4. Remember that whether a given act is classified as criminal or not is a social question, and that only the legislature can criminalize behavior in the U.S.

5. The protections provided for persons accused of crime are designed to prevent innocent people from being convicted of crimes they did not commit, and also represent the appropriate role of government in a democracy.

6. White-collar crimes are usually characterized by non-violence and deceit, but they do cost the public billions of dollars a year, and often maim and kill.

True-False

In the blank provided, put "**T**" if the statement is True or "**F**" if the statement is False.

_____ 1. Crimes are defined as private wrongs against individuals for which compensation can be sought.

_____ 2. In order for someone to be convicted of a crime, the prosecution must prove beyond a reasonable doubt that the accused person committed a crime.

_____ 3. Congress or the state legislatures define crimes.

_____ 4. Voluntary intoxication is a complete defense to criminal liability.

_____ 5. The fourth amendment prohibits any search or seizure of a criminal defendant without a warrant.

_____ 6. The Federal Sentencing Guidelines mandate stiffer penalties for white-collar crime.

_____ 7. Many prosecutions of white-collar criminals are controversial because it is often difficult to prove criminal intent on the part of high-level corporate executives.

_____ 8. Some criminal statutes impose liability on a corporate executive for the acts or omissions of other corporate employees without requiring proof of criminal intent or knowledge on the part of any corporate employee.

_____ 9. Companies could face both criminal and civil liability under RICO.

_____ 10. A person who was insane at the time he committed a crime cannot use his insanity as a defense to absolve him from the criminal liability.

Multiple Choice

Circle the best answer.

1. Mary was arrested for loitering under the provisions of a statute that prohibited "being in the same general location for at least 15 minutes during which he had two or more face-to-face encounters that lasted no more than two minutes, while exchanging money." Her best defense to prosecution is:

    a. She lacked the capacity to commit the offense.

    b. Prosecution is prohibited under the constitutional prohibition against *ex post facto* laws.

    c. The statute violates the first amendment of the U.S. Constitution.

    d. None of the above is a good defense to prosecution under this ordinance.

2. Which of the following statements regarding insanity is not true?

    a. Modern courts may require a defendant to prove her insanity beyond a reasonable doubt.

    b. Under the irresistible impulse test, a defendant is not criminally responsible for his acts due to a mental illness.

    c. A trial cannot be delayed for an insane person who is not capable of assisting in his defense.

    d. Some courts have found defendants guilty, but mentally ill.

3. Which of the following statements concerning crime is not true?

    a. Misdemeanors are serious crimes that can result in disenfranchisement.

    b. Crimes are public wrongs committed against the state or federal government.

    c. As an example of an *ex post facto* law, once Prohibition became the law of the land, Al Capone could not have been convicted of selling liquor before the law had been passed.

    d. Rape is an example of a felony.

4. The Eighth Amendment to the United States Constitution:

    a. Protects persons charged with crimes by requiring that they be warned that they have the right to counsel.

    b. Protects persons against unreasonable search and seizure.

    c. Protects those accused of crimes by providing they have the right to confront and cross-examine their accusers.

    d. Prohibits excessive bail and fines and cruel and unusual punishment.

5. Which of the following is generally not essential for the state to convict someone of criminal behavior?

    a. That the accused person premeditated the crime.

    b. A prior statutory prohibition of the act.

    c. Proof beyond a reasonable doubt that the defendant committed every element of the criminal offense.

    d. Proof that the defendant had the capacity to form criminal intent.

6. Which of the following statements is not true?

    a. *Mens rea* is a necessary element for most serious crimes.

    b. Infancy relating to capacity for criminal intent is not rebuttable by evidence.

    c. Voluntary intoxication may prevent the formation of criminal intent.

    d. Premeditation may be necessary to convict someone of first-degree murder.

7. Which of the following statements is not true?

   a. A warrant for a search can generally be issued even without probable cause.

   b. Acquitted defendants cannot be tried twice for the same crime.

   c. Defendants in criminal cases have the right to remain silent.

   d. Accused persons have the right to a speedy public trial by jury.

8. Which of the following pieces of evidence is a court required by the Fifth Amendment to exclude from the evidence admitted at trial?

   a. Samples of the defendant's hair that were clipped from his head by the arresting officers without his consent.

   b. The defendant's confession to the commission of the crime, which occurred after he was arrested and advised of his <u>Miranda</u> rights.

   c. Fingerprints of the defendant obtained through governmental compulsion.

   d. None of the above.

9. Which of the following statements is not true?

   a. The Federal Sentencing Guidelines may cause stiffer penalties to be imposed on someone convicted of insider trading, such as Martha Stewart.

   b. RICO has been used even against legitimate businesses that are involved in white-collar crime.

   c. Persons injured by RICO violations may sue for treble damages plus attorney's fees.

   d. The Supreme Court has narrowed the application of RICO so that it no longer can be applied to legitimate businesses.

10. Which of the following is prohibited under RICO?

   a. Using income derived from a pattern of racketeering activity.

   b. Acquiring an interest in an organization through a pattern of racketeering activity.

   c. Conducting the operations of an organization through a pattern of racketeering activity.

   d. All of the above.

Short Essay

1. Jane was a passenger in her boyfriend's (Jack's) car when he was arrested for criminal trespass. The statute made it a criminal offense to knowingly or intentionally trespass upon the land of another. Jack had taken a short cut through the back of a neighbor's property in his car when the arrest occurred. Explain <u>two</u> defenses to prosecution that <u>Jane</u> may raise in this case.

2.   Briefly distinguish between misdemeanors and felonies. Give an example of each.

3.   The president of a local company was charged with criminally negligent homicide for the deaths of two workers killed while they were working in the company's boiler room. The conditions violated federal Occupational Safety and Health Administration (OSHA) regulations. The president has challenged the state charges against him on the ground that OSHA preempts state enforcement of workplace safety. Under the holding in Sabine v. Texas, will this argument be successful? Discuss.

4.   For a period of ten years, Ted stalked, raped, and murdered a total of 25 women. Do you think it is likely that Ted could be absolved from these criminal acts by stating a plea of insanity?

5.   Because of the events of September 11, 2001, a wide variety of new technologies are being adapted by government agencies to combat terrorism. One such device is a full-body x-ray screening device used to help detect weapons and/or explosives. The technology is very effective, but some have argued that it is effective because it results in a "strip search" where the machine can see through all clothing. Does this technology violate the 4th Amendment?

6.   Briefly discuss the balance in our legal system; the desire to prosecute those people who are guilty of criminal activity balanced against the protection of rights for people in our legal system.

7.   *Ex post facto* rules generally apply to offenses that are categorized as crimes. What about statutory provisions that have elements of both criminal and civil sanctions? For example, a number of tax laws are passed every year that have retroactive effects to dates before the passage of the tax act. Does this practice violate the constitutional prohibition against retroactive laws?

8.   Why do you think that there has been more of a get-tough attitude toward white-collar criminals in recent years?

9.   Briefly discuss RICO. Do you think Congress in 1970 intentionally drafted this law by using broad languge so that the law could be used against not only organized crime families, but also against legitimate business who engage in white-collar crime?

CHAPTER 6
INTENTIONAL TORTS

Outline

I.   Intentional Torts: Torts are private wrongs.

    A. Kinds of Damages include compensatory and punitive damages.

        .Example: <u>Mathias v. Accor Economy Lodge, Inc.</u>: The court found the hotel liable for both compensatory and punitive damages for knowingly renting a room infested with bedbugs to the plaintiff.

    B. Kinds of Torts include Intentional, Negligence, and Strict Liability.

    C. Standard on burden of proof in civil cases, including torts, is preponderance of evidence.

II.   Battery: Intentional harmful or offensive touching. Assault is putting another in apprehension of an imminent battery.

    Example: <u>Hutchison v. Brookshire Brothers, Ltd.</u>: The court found that forcing someone to suck and siphon gasoline from an automobile constitutes battery.

III. False Imprisonment: Wrongful confinement without the other's consent.

IV. Intentional Infliction of Mental Distress: Defendant's conduct must be outrageous and produce severe emotional distress.

    Example: <u>Roach v. Stern</u>: Use of decedent's remains for entertainment purposes, and against the family's expressed wishes, was sufficiently outrageous to trigger severe emotional distress.

V.   Defamation: Injury to a person's reputation by publication of untrue statement of facts.

    A. The U.S. Supreme Court has held that a <u>public figure</u> or <u>public official</u> must prove <u>actual malice</u> in the publication of the defamatory statement by a media defendant in order to recover damages for this tort.

        Example: <u>Evel Knievel and Krystal Knievel v. ESPS, Inc.</u>: The court found that a caption of Evel Knievel as a "pimp" is not defamatory.

        Example: <u>Carafano v. Metrosplash.com, Inc.</u>: The lawsuit against Metrosplash was prevented by the Communications Decency Ac.

VI. Invasion of Privacy: A relatively recently development in tort law protecting a persons reasonable expectation of privacy.

    Example: <u>Felsher v. University of Evansville</u>: The Indiana Supreme Court held that a corporation does not have a right to privacy in tort law.

    Example: <u>Rosa Parks v. LaFace Records</u>: Rosa Parks is allowed to sue the hip-hop group Outkast for the appropriation of her name.

VII. Malicious Prosecution/wrongful use of civil proceedings

    Example: <u>Brennan v. Tremco Inc.</u>: The California Supreme Court held that an arbitrator's decision cannot insist on a requirement of a successful outcome for malicious prosecution purposes.

VIII. Interference with Property Rights

    A. Trespass: Entry by a person onto land in the possession of another.

        Example: <u>H.E. Stevenson, et al v. E.L. DuPont de Nemours</u>: The court found that contamination by airborne particles constitutes trespass to land.

    B. Trespass to personal property may constitute <u>conversion</u>.

C. Other intentional torts may include interference with economic relations, disparagement, and interference with contract.

Learning Objectives

1. You should distinguish a civil action from a criminal action. You should understand that an intentional tort may also give rise to criminal prosecution because the same act may violate criminal law.

2. You should understand the rationale underlying a different standard of proof in tort cases than in criminal cases.

3. You should distinguish battery from assault.

4. You should understand the concept of consent, and how it may constitute a defense in some intentional tort cases.

5. You should understand that there are three broad categories of intentional torts: interference with personal rights, interference with property rights, and interference with economic relations.

6. You should know the difference between libel and slander, when proof of actual damages is required in each type of case, and the various defenses and privileges available to the defendant in a defamation suit.

7. You should know the four different types of invasion of privacy.

8. You should be familiar with each of the specific intentional torts, including interference with economic relations, discussed in the textbook.

Learning Hints

1. Sometimes an action can give rise to both a civil action and a criminal prosecution, as in the case of battery. However, in a civil case, the burden is on the plaintiff to prove each and every element by a preponderance of the evidence.

2. Because the standard of proof is different in a civil case and less stringent, a civil judgment holding a defendant liable for committing an intentional tort is generally not admissible in a subsequent criminal prosecution of the defendant for the same act.

3. Because the standard of proof is different in a criminal case, and more stringent than in a civil case, evidence that a defendant has been convicted of a crime is generally admissible in a civil case for damages arising form the same act.

4. Assault and battery differ in that assault does not require physical contact with the plaintiff or anything connected with the plaintiff, and battery does not require awareness or apprehension of a threat to physical safety. If A makes threatening gestures toward B, there may be an assault, but there is no battery. Likewise, if A sneaks up behind B and knocks B unconscious without B ever having been aware of the threat, there is battery, but there is no assault. In most battery cases, however, assault is also present.

5. In considering the confinement element of false imprisonment, keep in mind that confinement must involve a substantial restriction of the confined person's freedom of movement of which he is aware, and there must be no reasonable escape route available.

6. Problems sometimes arise in trying to decide whether a statement is libel or slander. Some have suggested that embodiment in some permanent form (not merely putting the statement in writing) should be the test for libel. Thus, some courts have found that pictures, signs, movies, and statues were libelous. While broadcast defamation is generally considered to be libel, in many states the status of radio and television broadcasts is still unclear.

7. The reason the plaintiff must prove actual damages in most slander cases but in relatively few libel cases is that the law perceives libel as being more damaging to reputation than slander. The actual damages that must be proved in most slander cases are fairly specific; e.g., lost business, lost job opportunities, lost profits.

8. In some intentional infliction of emotional distress cases problems arise because the plaintiff is extremely susceptible emotionally; i.e., the plaintiff is not a person "of ordinary sensibilities." Generally, these overly sensitive plaintiffs cannot recover--unless the defendant was aware of their heightened susceptibility.

9. The four types of invasion of privacy are four separate torts, not four elements of the tort of invasion of privacy. Therefore, the plaintiff need only prove one of the four to recover for invasion of privacy.

10. Truth is a complete defense in defamation cases, but is not a defense in invasion of privacy cases.

True-False

In the blank provided, put "**T**" if the statement is True or "**F**" if the statement is False.

_____ 1. Generally, merely threatening someone without any indication of intent to carry out the threat does not create liability for assault.

_____ 2. The same behavior may give rise to both criminal and tort liability.

_____ 3. A person who causes something to enter the property of another without permission commits trespass

_____ 4. The plaintiff's burden of proof in a tort case is proof beyond a reasonable doubt.

_____ 5. Torts are crimes against a person or their property.

_____ 6. There can be no liability for false imprisonment if the plaintiff had a reasonable escape route.

_____ 7. Basketball players who angrily charge into the stands to yell at fans may be liable for the tort of assault, even if the basketball players do not hit the fans.

_____ 8. A store owner must use his or her conditional privilege to detain a suspected shoplifter for a reasonable length of time or they may be liable to the person detained for false imprisonment.

_____ 9. Hannah finds a check in the curb that is payable to the order of Greta. Greta has indorsed the check. Hannah goes to her bank and cashes the check. Hannah may be liable to Greta for conversion.

_____ 10. Paul Politician wants to sue Global Magazine for libel and for comments it made about him in a recent edition of the magazine. Paul must prove that the magazine acted with actual malice in order to win the lawsuit.

Multiple Choice

Circle the best answer.

1. One difference between libel and slander is:
   a. Libel requires proof of publication but slander does not.
   b. Libel refers to written publications while slander applies to television and radio.
   c. Proof of actual damages is required in slander cases.
   d. A public figure cannot recover damages for slander but can recover damages for libel.

2. Which of the following would most likely not constitute battery?
   a. Intentionally blowing smoke into someone's face.
   b. Hitting a person with a snowball and causing injury.
   c. Pointing a gun at a person.
   d. Striking a person with a baseball bat.

3. A political billboard advertisement uses the picture of Tom, a well-known movie actor, without Tom's permission. Which of the following would be Tom's most likely recourse against the political party that produced this advertisement?
   a. Invasion of privacy
   b. Libel
   c. Slander
   d. Defamation

4. An action for appropriation of name or likeness:
   a. Requires proof of defamation.
   b. Protects a plaintiff's right to be secure in her person, place, or house.
   c. Compensates a plaintiff for the economic value of her celebrity.
   d. Requires proof of outrageous and wrongful conduct by defendant.

5. Which of the following statements is not true?
   a. A person must generally prove actual damages in order to recover for slander.
   b. Private statements made between spouses about someone are absolutely privileged and cannot be used for a successful defamation suit.
   c. Courts will allow recovery for mental injuries only if a battery has occurred.
   d. Defamation in a television news broadcast is considered to be libel.

6. In a brawl during a professional basketball game, several players charged into the stands to confront fans. Punches were thrown. Which of the following statements is true?
   a. Some players who threw punches at fans may be liable for the tort of battery.
   b. Some players who went into the stands may be liable to fans for the tort of assault, even if those players did not throw punches at fans.
   c. The fact that the game was televised nationally by ESPN and most all of the brawl was caught on tape would tend to be a preponderance of evidence for fans who want to prove a tort case.
   d. All the above.

7. In the case above concerning the brawl at a professional basketball game, which of the following statements is not true?
   a. It is possible that players could be found guilty and have to pay compensatory damages for injuries that they caused to some fans.
   b. It is possible that some players may be liable to fans for punitive damages in order to make an example of the players and reduce the chances that such behavior will happen again.
   c. Fans may bring either civil or criminal charges against the players, but not both.
   d. Fans who rushed the court and threw punches at players are potentially liable to the players for the torts of assault and battery.

8. Which of the following statements is not correct?
   a. Malicious prosecution provides remedies when criminal proceedings are wrongfully brought against a plaintiff.
   b. Wrongful use of civil proceedings can provide remedies when a wrongful civil suit is brought against a plaintiff.
   c. In order to win an abuse of process case, the plaintiff must show that the suit was brought without probable cause.
   d. No actual harm to property is necessary to successfully sue for trespass.

9. Crane contracted with Cool Carpets to install carpeting throughout her home. Crane is not happy with the quality of the work done by Cool Carpets. She goes on a crusade to tell everyone she can that the products and services sold by Cool Carpets is lousy. Which of the following may be the best resources for Cool Carpets against Crane?

    a. Sue Crane for libel

    b. Sue Crane for disparagement

    c. Sue Crane for Slander

    d. Sue Crane for infliction of mental distress

10. Williams hunts on Walker's land without permission. Williams kills two deer on Walker's land. Which of the following statements is not true?

    a. Williams may be liable to Walker for trespassing on his property.

    b. Since no actual harm occurred, Williams did not trespass on Walker's property.

    c. Williams may be liable to Walker for trespass to personal property since he killed deer that were on Walker's property.

    d. Williams may be liable to Walker for conversion and pay Walker for the reasonable value of the deer.

Short Essay

1. Rex forces Tom, a high school student, into his car. Rex drives Tom to an abandoned warehouse and sexually assaults him. After several hours, Rex releases Tom. Assuming Rex is arrested, what charges could be brought against him?

2. Store detains Wilma for suspected shoplifting. Assuming Wilma is innocent, what should the store do to avoid liability for false imprisonment?

3. The *Times* newspaper publishes a scathing article about Senator Smith. Many allegations of misbehavior are stated in the article. The resulting scandal causes Smith to lose her bid for re-election. Smith sues the *Times* for libel. What must Smith prove in order to win the lawsuit? What can Smith do if the statements made in the article are true?

4. Mr. Razhel is hypersensitive to smoke and lives next door to Mr. Monte Christo, a cigar aficionado. Their homes are 10 feet apart. Mr. Cristo smokes his cigar on his back deck, and some of the smoke wafts towards Mr. Razhel's property. Mr. Razhel claims that this smoke is causing him harm and that it is an intentional tort. What torts, if any, may be involved?

5. A and B had an oral agreement to merge their companies. Because the deal had not yet been completed in writing, C induces B to back out of the contract with A by making a higher offer. Has an intentional tort been committed?

6. Numerous celebrities and well-known public figures have been targeted by tabloid newspapers commonly sold at checkout counters in supermarkets. The headlines on the front of these newspapers have often made outrageous statements about the celebrities in order to induce purchases of the papers. What is the standard defense that newspapers use to avoid liability for interference with personal rights?

CHAPTER 7
NEGLIGENCE AND STRICT LIABILITY

Outline

I. Negligence: Unintentional breach of duty resulting in harm to another.

    A. Standard of reasonableness is flexible, but objective, standard.

    B. Plaintiff must prove that defendant had a duty not to injure plaintiff; that defendant breached that duty; that the defendant's breach was the actual and legal cause of the plaintiff's injuries.

    Example: <u>Diggs v. Arizona Cardiologists, Ltd.</u>: The Arizona Court of Appeals held that a consulting physician owes a duty of care to a patient.

    C. Negligence *per se* results when a defendant breaches a statutory duty, and the harm the statute was designed to prevent occurs to one the statute was designed to protect.

    Example: <u>Hernandez v. Flor</u>: A mobile home owner who violated a state statute requiring smoke alarms in mobile homes was found negligent *per se* in a tenant's death.

    D. Plaintiff must prove breach of duty, causation in fact, and proximate cause.

    Example: <u>In re: September 11 Litigation</u>: The court found that the crash of airplanes was a foreseeable hazard of negligently performed security screening.

    E. Rules of Causation:

        1. A defendant is not liable unless the breach of duty actually caused the plaintiff's injury. Courts consider whether an intervening force was foreseeable. If so, in general it will not excuse the defendant from liability.

        Example: <u>Jenson v. Eveleth Taconite Co.</u>, the court determined that the "Eggshell Skull" rule applies to emotional injuries as well as physical injuries.

        2. *Res Ipsa Loquitur* creates an inference of negligence.

II. Injury to Plaintiff: Negligent Infliction of Mental Distress

    A. Courts are increasingly permitting parties to recover for emotional distress resulting from witnessing harm to another.

    Example: <u>Izquierdo v. Ricitelli</u>: A man who sees his fiancé attacked by a dog is allowed to sue for infliction of emotional distress.

III. Defenses to Negligence:

    A. Contributory negligence (abolished in most states) in favor of Comparative negligence

    B. Assumption of the Risk: Requires proof that plaintiff voluntarily assumed a known risk.

    Example: <u>Powell v. Metropolitan Entertainment Co.</u>: Powell was found to voluntarily assume the risk of his hearing loss. He had experienced ringing in his ears from attending previous concerts and he knew that a Fogerty concert would be loud.

    C. Recklessness: A "conscious disregard for a known high degree of probable harm to another."

IV. Strict Liability

    A. Traditionally, strict liability imposed for abnormally dangerous or ultrahazardous activities.

    Example: <u>Klein v. Pyrodyne Corporation</u>, holding that conducting fireworks display is an abnormally dangerous activity for which a defendant may be held strictly liable (liability without fault.)

Learning Objectives

1.   You should know the elements of a negligence action.

2.   You should know the factors that must be considered when the "reasonable person" standard is used in a negligence case.

3.   You should understand the elements of the doctrines of negligence *per se* and *res ipsa loquitur* and when each doctrine is used.

4.   You should understand the problem for which the concept of "proximate cause" was developed, and the various definitions of proximate cause used by the courts.

5.   You should understand the operation of the defenses of contributory negligence and assumption of risk.

6.   You should know the two types of comparative negligence (pure and mixed) and how comparative negligence differs generally from contributory negligence.

7.   You should understand the difference between intentional infliction of emotional distress and negligent infliction of emotional distress.

8.   You should understand strict liability, when it is applied, and the effect it has upon the defenses of contributory negligence and assumption of risk.

9.   You should distinguish negligence from intentional torts, and distinguish the tests of causation used in each instance.

Learning Hints

1.   Negligence is a fact-sensitive determination requiring a judge or jury to balance considerations of what is a reasonable act under a particular circumstance. For example, a person may drive a reasonable speed on a bright clear sunny day, but driving that same speed may be unreasonable at night during a blinding snowstorm.

2.   Negligence is tested by an objective standard that examines the defendant's behavior--not by a subjective standard that examines the defendant's mental state. The behavior required for negligence is the failure to act as a reasonable person would have acted in the circumstances.

3.   The reasonable person standard is very flexible, and this flexibility is necessary because of the variety of situations to which negligence must be applied. Among the factors that are considered under the reasonable person standard are the reasonable foreseeability of the harm resulting from the defendant's behavior, the likely severity of this reasonably foreseeable harm, the social utility of the defendant's conduct, and the ease or difficulty of avoiding the risk of harm associated with the defendant's conduct. For example, negligence might not be present if the harm is too unforeseeable or too trivial, if the defendant's activity is extremely valuable to society, or if there was little that the defendant could have done to avoid the risk of harm.

4.   Negligence *per se* is an alternative way of establishing breach of duty. It requires proof of three things: violation of a statute; a plaintiff who suffers harm of a sort the statute was intended to prevent; and a plaintiff who is within the class of persons intended to be protected by the statute. Of course, it is sometimes difficult to ascertain the intent of the legislature with regard to the second and third elements of proof.

5.   Causation in a negligence case has two separate elements. One is causation in fact, in which the court asks if the injury to the plaintiff would have occurred without the defendant's breach of duty. If the answer is "yes," the test is not met and the defendant is not liable. Assuming that the answer is "no" and causation in fact exists, the next question is whether the injury to the plaintiff is too remote for the defendant to fairly be held liable. This is the problem of proximate causation. Most American courts use some test of reasonable foreseeability as the test for proximate cause.

6. The test of proximate cause, unlike the test of cause in fact, is a question of law for a judge. Consequently, a court may determine that an intervening cause (for example, an assault by a third party against the plaintiff) was not the proximate or legal cause of the injury to the plaintiff, even though it was the cause in fact of his injuries.

7. Like negligence, contributory negligence is also an objective standard of behavior, which asks roughly what the reasonably self-protective person would have done to prevent harm to himself in the situation.

8. Assumption of risk is the knowing and voluntary acceptance of a risk of harm to oneself. Unlike contributory negligence, it is tested by a subjective standard of what the plaintiff actually knew and intended.

9. Strict liability is "liability without fault" in the sense that it imposes liability on the defendant regardless of his intent, recklessness, or negligence. This does not mean, however, that strict liability is automatic liability, for there must be a determination that the innocent defendant should bear this risk of harm rather than the innocent plaintiff who has been injured.

10. In some states, contributory negligence or comparative negligence is not a defense to strict liability. However, assumption of the risk may be a defense in such cases, or may be treated as a factor in a comparative fault analysis.

True-False

In the blank provided, put "**T**" if the statement is True or "**F**" if the statement is False.

_____   1. Generally, a defendant is not liable to a plaintiff for negligence unless he breached a legal duty to the plaintiff.

_____   2. Failure to use reasonable care is a breach of legal duty to a plaintiff in most cases.

_____   3. The doctrine of *res ipsa loquitur* may be especially useful for plaintiffs in product liability cases.

_____   4. Breach of statutory duty can result in liability under the theory of "negligence per se."

_____   5. If a plaintiff is found even slightly at fault under comparative negligence, the plaintiff cannot recover any damages against a negligent defendant.

_____   6. Assumption of risk may be a good defense for a defendant in a strict liability lawsuit.

_____   7. Assumption of risk may be a good defense for defendants in a case involving recklessness on the part of the defendant.

_____   8. A foreseeable intervening force will not excuse the defendant from liability.

_____   9. An objective standard of conduct for people in our society is the reasonable person rule.

_____   10. A relationship between the parties can impose a duty of care on one of them not to injure the other.

Multiple Choice

Circle the best answer.

1. Which of the following relationships may impose a special duty on a defendant with regard to a plaintiff that might not otherwise exist?

    a. Landlord/tenant.

    b. Common carrier and passenger.

    c. Innkeeper and customer.

    d. All of the above.

2. Proximate cause:
   a. Holds defendants liable for foreseeable results of their negligence.
   b. Requires that the defendant be present when the harm occurs.
   c. Requires the defendant to be the actual cause of harm.
   d. Allows the plaintiff to recover even if the defendant is not the cause of the harm.

3. Ford is having problems with a defective braking system in the Focus. Before he can take his car in on a recall, Hal is seriously injured in a car accident when the brakes in his Focus failed. Hal was not wearing a seatbelt. Which of the following is the most correct statement?
   a. Ford is totally liable because the braking system was defective.
   b. Ford is not liable because Hal was not wearing a seatbelt.
   c. Ford would be liable under comparative fault.
   d. Hal would win the case if contributory negligence is used.

4. Assume in the case above that the state Hal is driving in at the time of the accident has a statute requiring drivers and passengers in vehicles to wear their seatbelts. Which of the following is the most correct statement?
   a. Hal may be negligent *per se*.
   b. The fact that Hal was violating the law absolves Ford of all liability.
   c. Hal can still recover under contributory negligence.
   d. Ford is not liable under comparative fault.

5. Recklessness occurs:
   a. When a defendant's behavior indicates a "conscious disregard for a known high degree of probable harm to another," and a plaintiff is injured as a result.
   b. Failure to use reasonable care in protecting oneself from injury.
   c. Voluntary assumption of a known risk.
   d. Intentionally causing another harm.

6. Years ago, several young women were killed in Indiana when their Ford Pinto exploded upon impact in an accident. It was later shown that the gas line in the Pinto was especially vulnerable to impact. The families of the women sued Ford. Which of the following statements is most correct?
   a. Ford is not liable because the girls assumed the risk in driving the Pinto.
   b. The families may be able to successfully sue for negligence by invoking the doctrine of *res ipsa loquitur*.
   c. Ford would not be liable under strict liability.
   d. The families could easily prove that Ford was reckless in designing the Pinto.

7. Peggy is doing yard work while her 3-year-old daughter Amanda is playing. Peggy goes into the house for just a couple of minutes. When she returns, she cannot find Amanda. After searching frantically for several minutes, Peggy discovers that Amanda had gone through an open gate in their neighbor's fence and had fallen into their swimming pool. Efforts to revive Amanda are not successful. Which of the following is not true?
   a. Peggy may be able to sue the neighbors for her emotional distress in witnessing the drowning of Amanda.
   b. Under comparative fault, both Peggy and the neighbors could share liability for Amanda's death.
   c. Peggy will win in a negligence lawsuit against the neighbors if contributory negligence is used.
   d. The neighbors are negligent for allowing the gate to be open.

8. Sam is using a Manly saw while doing some woodworking in his shop. As Sam is feeding a board into the saw, the saw hits a knot in the wood that causes Sam's hand to lunge forward. Sam loses two fingers in the accident. Sam sues Manly for his injuries. Which of the following is the most accurate statement?

   a. Sam will lose this case because he assumed the risk of using the saw.

   b. Manly is liable under strict liability because the saw was defective.

   c. Manly is liable under negligence.

   d. Manly is liable for recklessness for producing a dangerous product.

9. Janet's dog bites Mel the mailman as he is delivering mail to Janet's house. Which of the following is true?

   a. Janet may be liable to Mel under strict liability.

   b. Janet may be liable to Mel under negligence.

   c. A reasonable person would have had her dog restrained and unable to bite visitors.

   d. All of the above.

10. Paula is talking on her cell phone while driving down the street. She becomes preoccupied with her conversation, drifts across the median and strikes a van driven by Connie. Connie's husband Bob is a passenger in the van. Bob suffers from multiple sclerosis. Nobody appears to be seriously hurt in the accident. However, because Bob does suffer some bruises and a slight neck injury, he is taken to the hospital. While in the hospital, Bob contracts pneumonia and dies. Which of the following is true?

   a. Under the general causation rules, Paula may be liable for Bob's death.

   b. Paula is not liable for Bob's death because he died of pneumonia.

   c. Paula is not liable for Bob's death because the multiple sclerosis is what really caused his death.

   d. The hospital is liable for negligence in allowing Bob to die of pneumonia.

Short Essay

1. Alex, an amateur chemist, mixed two unknown chemicals together, which resulted in a massive explosion. The explosion knocked out power to the entire city. The power outage hit Betty, who lived a mile from Alex, and her freezer lost current. As a result, all of her frozen meat thawed and had to be thrown away. Betty sued Alex for $500 for the loss of the meat. Is Alex liable?

2. Bob stops by the car dealership in Phoenix where he works as a salesman. It is a hot July day. Bob thinks he is only going to be in the dealership for a few minutes, so he leaves his young grandson, Joey, in the car. Bob actually spends 45 minutes in the dealership. When he returns to his vehicle, he discovers that Joey is dead. Discuss Bob's potential liability in this case.

3. Brad and Jen have a party at their home. During the party, Matt drinks a great deal of alcoholic beverages. When Matt drives home later that night, he strikes Wally, a pedestrian, and kills him. Discuss the liability involved in this case.

4. What is the difference between the "cause in fact" and the "proximate cause" of an injury?

5. How does the doctrine of *res ipsa loquitur* apply to someone who wants to sue Chrysler for negligence?

6. Jim and Judy are having dinner in a nice restaurant. While Judy is eating her meal, she discovers a large, dead cricket on her plate. Is it likely that Judy could sue the restaurant for emotional distress in this case?

7. Steve is mowing his yard with his Lawn Guy mower on a crisp October morning. The ground is covered with dew. While mowing on a slope, Steve slips on the dew and his foot comes in contact with the blade. Is Lawn Guy responsible for Steve's injuries?

CHAPTER 8

THE NATURE AND ORIGINS OF CONTRACTS

Outline

I. What is a Contract? A contract is a legally enforceable promise.

   A. Elements: agreement supported by consideration, voluntarily entered into by parties with capacity, for a legal purpose

   B. Development of contract law: The law has evolved from a free-market theory to a developing concept of protecting consumers and workers

II. The Uniform Commercial Code (UCC) Article 2 governs contracts for the <u>sale of goods</u>. "Goods" must be distinguished from "services." The sale of goods (tangible personal property) falls under Article 2, while services do not fall under the UCC at all.

III. Creation of Practical Contract Rules

   A. UCC is more flexible than common law contracts.

   B. The UCC imposes a duty of good faith and fair dealing under Article 2.

     Example: <u>Race v. Fleetwood Retail Corp. of Washington</u>: Fleetwood is found liable for the bad faith breach of the covenant of good faith and fair dealing.

   C. Some sections of the Code impose a different and higher standard of behavior for "merchants."

IV. Contracts for the International Sale of Goods

   The U.N. Convention on the International Sale of Goods (CISG) is similar to the Uniform Commercial Code and applies to U.S. companies unless they choose not to have the law apply and give notice in their contracts that is law does not apply.

V. Types of Contracts

   A. Valid contract meets the legal requirements for a contract.

   B. Unenforceable contracts meet legal requirements but will not be enforced by a court.

   C. One or both parties may cancel a voidable contract, while void contracts lack one or more of the basic requirements for a contract.

   D. Unilateral contract is a contract with only one promise by one party (for example, an offer for a reward); a bilateral contract consists of promises by both parties.

   E. A contract may be executed (completely performed by all parties) or executory (not fully performed).

   F. A contract or contract term may be express or implied.

     Example: <u>Staley v. Taylor</u>: The parties' conduct in this case inferred a promise not to block Staley's ocean view.

VI. Equitable concepts important to contract law

   A. Quasi-contract: A contract implied in law to avoid unjust enrichment by one party at the expense of another.

     Example: In <u>Brewer v. New York</u>, the court found that a bankrupt company's bankruptcy trustee was allowed to recover payments mistakenly made to DOC after the filing date on a theory of quasi-contract (unjust enrichment)

B. Promissory Estoppel: a doctrine permitting a plaintiff to recover reliance damages from a defendant who makes a promise that he knows will induce reliance, in cases where the plaintiff actually and reasonably relies on the promise to his detriment.

Example: <u>Goff-Hamel v. Obstetricians & Gynecologists, P.C.</u>: The theory of promissory estoppel can be used to enforce a promise of employment at will where the plaintiff reasonably relies on a promise that the promisor could reasonably foresee would induce that reliance and where it would be unjust not to enforce the promise.

Learning Objectives

1. You should understand the evolution of contract theory from a laissez faire perspective to a consumer-protection perspective.

2. You should be able to identify the elements of a contract.

3. You must know the difference between bilateral and unilateral contracts.

4. You must know the difference between void and voidable contracts.

5. You must know the difference between express and implied contracts.

6. You must know the difference between executed and executory contracts.

7. You must be familiar with quasi-contract, and the difference between a contract implied in law and one implied in fact.

8. You must be familiar with promissory estoppel and, the fact that in some situations promissory estoppel can be substituted for some required element of a contract.

9. You should understand the significance of the Uniform Commercial Code and the circumstances in which it applies.

10. You should understand the practical differences between application of the U.C.C. and common law.

11. You should know that the CISG is a uniform code for international contracts.

12. You should have an awareness of cyber-contracts.

Learning Hints

1. Probably the most important social factor underlying the change from nineteenth century contract law to twenty-first century contract law was the rise of the large private group, mainly the corporation. This development produced countless disparities of bargaining power and resulting injustices when such groups contracted with individuals or smaller groups. The response to this was government intervention, often to set the terms of the contract in order to protect the weaker party to the contract.

2. One of the most significant changes in modern contract law has been the adoption of the Uniform Commercial Code, which is in effect in all states except Louisiana (the only civil law state). This Code changes the common law rules in some important respects, and it is generally more flexible and commerce-friendly than common law.

3. The Uniform Commercial Code (UCC) applies to any contract for the sale of goods. It is <u>not</u> limited to contracts where the parties are merchants.

4. An unenforceable contract cannot serve as the basis for a lawsuit by either party to the contract because it cannot be enforced. However, it is technically still a contract, even though unenforceable, and may be valid for other purposes. For example, the fact that a contract is unenforceable will not block a suit for intentional interference with contractual relations because technically a contract exists, though it is unenforceable, and can be interfered with.

5. Among the things that might happen when a contract is voidable are that the party with the power to avoid the contract (such as a party who has been defrauded) may choose to go ahead and perform the contract and bind the other party to the contract; the party with the power to avoid the contract may

refuse to perform the contract and assert a defense if sued by the other party to the contract; the party with the power to avoid the contract may choose to rescind if the contract is executed; i.e., has already been performed. Rescission is a remedy whereby the court effectively cancels the transaction and restores each party to his pre-contract position.

6. "Void contract" is a contradiction in terms because such an agreement is not a contract at all, since it lacks one or more requirements for a contract.

7. Perhaps the most important feature of an express contract is that the parties have stated its terms <u>in words</u>, either oral or written.

8. Note that technically a contract is executed only when all parties have fully performed.

9. Quasi-contract is a strange legal fiction that is applied in a variety of different situations. All of the situations involve the idea of <u>unjust enrichment</u>, because they all involve a benefit conferred on the defendant by the plaintiff (the enrichment), with the defendant's knowledge at the time the benefit was conferred, under circumstances where it would be unjust for the defendant not to pay the plaintiff for the benefit.

10. Under Article 2 of the Uniform Commercial Code, "goods" are moveable, tangible objects. In every contract problem, you must first ask yourself whether the contract is one for the sale of goods. If the contract does involve the sale of goods, the applicable UCC rule will apply. If the contract is not for the sale of goods, or it is for the sale of goods but no UCC rule covers the situation, common law contract rules will apply instead. As you will see in the later contracts chapters, common law contract rules and UCC rules are sometimes very different.

True-False

In the blank provided, put "**T**" if the statement is True or "**F**" if the statement is False.

_____ 1. Article 2 of the Uniform Commercial Code covers the sale of services, such as tax preparation services.

_____ 2. All United States companies must comply with the Convention on the International Sale of Goods (CISG).

_____ 3. The UCC does not apply in cases where both parties are merchants.

_____ 4. Even if both parties intend to create a contract, no enforceable contract exists unless expressly created under the U.C.C.

_____ 5. Marty Minor cancels his contract for the purchase of electronic equipment from Circuit City. This is an example of a voidable contract.

_____ 6. An express contract must be in writing.

_____ 7. Quasi-contract is a legal fiction created by a court to avoid injustice

_____ 8. Your car breaks down on a lonely road late at night. You call Tom's Tow on your cell phone and they send a tow truck to pick up you and your car. This is an example of an implied contract.

_____ 9. If a person voluntarily receives a benefit from another party where it would be unfair to keep the benefit without paying for it, this is a situation where the doctrine of promissory estoppel would apply.

_____ 10. Courts treat contracts as bilateral rather than unilateral whenever it is possible to do so.

Multiple Choice

Circle the best answer.

1. An executed contract is a contract is:
   a. A contract fully performed by all persons.
   b. Voidable by either party.
   c. A contract that only may be enforced by one party.
   d. A void contract.

2. Brown enters into an agreement on October 1 with Superior Siding to install vinyl siding on his home beginning on October 15. The job will take Superior three weeks to complete and Brown will pay the $15,000 cost of the siding when the job is complete. Which of the following is most true?
   a. This is an example of an implied contract.
   b. This is an example of an executory contract.
   c. This is an example of a quasi contract.
   d. This is an example of an executed contract.

3. Acme contracts to sell 1,000 widgets to Jones for $5,000. This is an example of:
   a. a bilateral contract.
   b. a sale of goods that is covered by Article 2 of the U.C.C.
   c. a valid contract.
   d. all of the above.

4. Don mistakenly planted two new flowering trees on Bob's property. Bob knew that Don was planting the trees, but didn't inform him.
   Under what theory is Bob obligated to pay Don for the value of the trees?
   a. Promissory estoppel.
   b. Express contract.
   c. Contract implied in fact.
   d. Quasi-contract.

5. Which of the following statements concerning the International Sale of Goods is not correct?
   a. The CISG only applies to contracts for the sale of goods.
   b. The CISG has been ratified by the United States in the 1986 convention.
   c. The CISG applies to U.S. companies unless they choose not to have the law apply and give notice of that fact within the contract.
   d. The CISG applies to every contract for the international sale of goods.

6. Tammy orally agrees to sell her house to Finch for $100,000. Which of the following is true?
   a. This is an unenforceable contract because a contract for the sale of real estate must be in writing to be enforceable.
   b. This is an implied contract.
   c. This is a quasi contract.
   d. This is a unilateral contract.

7. Harold tells Sally, "I will give you $25,000 if you can graduate from college with a GPA of 3.0 or better." Which of the following is most true?
   a. This is not a bilateral contract because only Harold is making a promise.
   b. Harold may be bound to pay Sally if she does as he asks under the doctrine of promissory estoppel.
   c. This is an example of a unilateral contract.
   d. All of the above.

8. Harvey promises to pay Hal $500 if he breaks Howard's legs because Howard failed to pay back a loan to Harvey. This is an example of a(n):
   a. void contract.
   b. voidable contract.
   c. implied contract.
   d. bilateral contract.

9. Beaver and Gilbert start mowing Frank's lawn without talking to Frank first. Frank is home and sees the boys mowing the lawn. The boys work hard and ask Frank for payment after completing the job. Which of the following is the best chance for Beaver and Gilbert to recover a fair price for mowing Frank's lawn?
   a. Frank and the boys had an implied contract.
   b. Frank and the boys had an express contract.
   c. The boys may be able to recover under quasi contract theory.
   d. The boys can recover because this is a bilateral contract.

10. Which of the following is true?
    a. Courts in the 19th century were more likely to interfere in private contracts than are courts today.
    b. Courts today are more likely to protect big businesses instead of consumers.
    c. Many contracts today are effected or controlled to some extent by legislation at both the state and federal level.
    d. The U.C.C. has brought complete uniformity to commercial transactions in all states.

Short Essay

1. Darla had her hair colored by a local beauty salon. Unfortunately, her hair turned green as a result. She wants to sue the salon for damages under a theory of breach of implied warranty under the U.C.C. May she do so? Why or why not.

2. Assume that rather than having her hair colored at a local salon in the above situation, Darla purchased hair color at a local drug store. After her hair turned green, Darla wants to sue the manufacturer of the hair-coloring product for breach of implied warranty under the U.C.C. May she do so? Why or why not?

3.   Tammy is a teacher. She sells her used car to Barb, a beautician. Does Article 2 of the U.C.C. apply to Tammy? Is Tammy a merchant?

4.   What is the important legal difference between a void contract and a voidable contract?

5.   Amy agrees to sell her used car to Kendra for $5,000. Amy delivers the car and the title to Kendra and Kendra pays Amy with a certified check. Discuss this situation using the terminology covered in the chapter.

6.   Paula tells Paul that she will pay him $2,000 if he will paint the outside of her house. A week later, Paul shows up at Paula's house and begins painting. After Paul has been painting Paula's house for two days, she tells him she is not going to pay him anything because they did not have a contract. Discuss the rights of the parties in this situation.

7.   Would Article 2 of the U.C.C. apply to the sale and installation of replacement windows in Johnson's house?

8.   Why are courts today more willing to interfere in contracts than they were a century ago?

CHAPTER 9
CREATING A CONTRACT: OFFERS

Outline

I.   An agreement, or "meeting of the minds" may be defined as an Offer + Acceptance.

II.   What is an Offer? An offer is the manifestation of a willingness to enter into a contract if the other party agrees to the terms.

   A. Requires a present intent to offer, which is definite, and is communicated to the offeree.

   Example: <u>Republican National Committee v. Taylor</u>: The appeals court reiterates the lower court's holding that the offer of the $1 million reward became a binding contract upon acceptance. Note that on appeal, the RNC does not challenge this finding. Instead, the crux of RNC's argument – and hence, the opinion – is that even if the ad were an offer to contract, the "challenge statement" was not false. The court found that the challenge statement was not ambiguous and did not falsely allege that the Republican plan would balance the budget. The court affirmed summary judgment in favor of the RNC.

   Example: <u>Key v. Corvell</u>: The terms of the education agreement were found by the court to be too indefinite to form a contract.

   Example: <u>ProCD, Inc. v. Zeidenberg</u>: Contract terms appearing inside a software box are enforceable.

III. Special Problems

   A. Advertisements: Are generally not treated as offers.

   Example: <u>Leonard v. Pepsico, Inc.</u>: The general rule is that an advertisement does not constitute an offer, rather they are mere requests to consider and examine and negotiate.

   B. Rewards: Offer for a reward is an offer for a unilateral contract.

   C. Auctions: Generally an auction is a request for bids

IV.   What terms are included?

   A. If the offeree read the terms or a reasonable person should have notice, the offeree is bound.

   Example: <u>Aronson v. University of Mississippi</u>: Many courts have held that a contractual relationship exists between a student and a university based on the terms of a student handbook, catalog, or other statement of university policy.

V.   Termination of the Offer.

   A. By its terms.

   B. Lapse of reasonable time, revocation prior to acceptance.

      1. Exception: Option contracts that require new consideration.

      2. Exception: Estoppel.

   C. Firm offers under the UCC.

      1. Must be in a signed writing by a merchant, which contains assurances that it will be held open.

      2. Outer limit of irrevocability is three months.

   D. Unilateral contract offers: Generally cannot be revoked if the offeree has begun performance.

   E. Revocation: Must be received to be effective.

F. Rejection by the Offeree terminates the Offer.

   Example: <u>Giovio v. McDonalds</u>: The court found that GEICO's offer worked as a counteroffer, and thus did not constitute an acceptance of Giovo's $18/day request. The appeals court held that the circuit court should have denied the McDonalds' motion for summary judgment on their settlement defense and should have granted Giovo's motion.

G. Death or Insanity of either party; destruction of subject matter; intervening illegality also terminate offers.

H. Destruction of subject matter.

I. Intervening illegality.

Learning Objectives

1. You should understand the meaning of an offer, offeror, and offeree, and the requirements for an effective offer: intent, definiteness, and communication to the offeree.

2. You should understand how courts use offer and acceptance to define an agreement and "meeting of the minds."

3. You should be aware of the two main factors courts use to judge whether a person intended to enter a contract: definiteness and communication.

4. You should know what factors the courts consider when deciding whether a given term was included in the offer (and therefore in the contract).

5. You should know how an offer is terminated.

6. You should know the exceptions to the general rule that the offeror can revoke his offer at any time before the offeree accepts it.

7. You should know the meaning of the term "estoppel" and how it relates to the resolution of problems concerning offers.

8. You should know the rules governing when the offeror may revoke an offer for a unilateral contract.

9. You should understand the difference between an acceptance and counter-offer.

10. You should have an awareness of cyber contracts and shrink wrap contracts.

Learning Hints

1. "Offer" and "acceptance" are words used by courts to describe a factual situation requiring proof of a statement indicating a present intent to enter into a contract.

2. In order to determine whether there is a legally effective offer, courts must determine the <u>intention</u> of the offeror. This intention, however, is determined by using an objective, rather than subjective, test. Thus, if a reasonable person would believe that an offeror had indicated a present willingness to enter into a bargain, the court may determine that an offer was made, even though the offeror denies any such intention.

3. Keep in mind that the words "offer" and "acceptance" used in contract law have special <u>technical, legal meanings</u> that may be different from the way these words are used in everyday speech. For example, advertisements often use the word "offer," but we have seen that advertisements are generally presumed <u>not</u> to be offers.

4. When you make an offer to another person, you give that person the power to legally bind you to a contract obligation merely by accepting your offer. For this reason, courts will not lightly assume an offer has been made.

5. There are three elements of an offer: an objective manifestation of a present intent to contract, the use of reasonably definite terms, and the communication of the offer to the offeree.

6. Advertisements are generally presumed <u>not</u> to be legally binding offers, even if the advertiser uses the word "offer." This means that the person who reads the advertisement cannot bind the advertiser merely by appearing and saying "I accept." The person who reads the ad is treated as the offeror, not as an offeree.

7. One of the exceptions to the general rule that the offeror can revoke any time before acceptance is the situation when parties have entered an option contract. An option contract is an agreement in which the offeree has paid the offeror something to keep the offer open for a certain period of time. During that period of time, the offeror cannot revoke. If the offeree decides to accept the offer during that period of time, the offeror must go through with the deal. However, the offeree has no obligation to accept during the duration of the option.

8. A request for bids is treated as a request for offers. Bids are generally treated as offers, which the other party may accept or reject. However, this rule may be changed by statute. For example, many states have statutes prescribing the manner and effect of bids made by governmental units.

True-False

In the blank provided, put "T" if the statement is True or "F" if the statement is False.

_____ 1. Courts rely on objective manifestation of intent in determining whether an offeree has made an offer.

_____ 2. If facts indicate that a term was left out because parties were unable to reach agreement, it would probably mean the intent to contract was absent and no contract was created.

_____ 3. An advertisement in a Cabela's catalog for a tent listed at a certain price is generally considered to be an invitation to make an offer and not an offer.

_____ 4. An ad for a $25 reward for the return of a lost dog is not considered to be an offer.

_____ 5. Only a merchant can make a firm offer under the UCC

_____ 6. John bids on an antique at an auction. John is making an offer. The auctioneer can accept or reject the offer.

_____ 7. A firm offer can normally be revoked any time prior to acceptance of the offer.

_____ 8. An option is a separate contract with the limited purpose of holding an offer open.

_____ 9. Tracy offers to sell her car to Greta for $5,000. Greta impliedly rejects this offer when she counteroffers a price of $4,000.

_____ 10. An advertisement of a reward is an example of an offer for a unilateral contract.

Multiple Choice

Circle the best answer.

1. A firm offer by a merchant:
   a. Must be made in a signed writing.
   b. Is effective for the period stated in the offer, even if the term exceeds three months.
   c. Only applies in cases where both parties are merchants.
   d. Requires a signature of both parties.

2. J.D. tells Ken, "I will trade you several baseball cards for your autographed picture of Michael Jordan." Which of the following is not true?
   a. J.D. has made an offer to Ken.
   b. J.D. has given Ken an invitation to make an offer.
   c. No offer was made because J.D.'s comment is not definite.
   d. J.D.'s comments do not constitute an offer because they do not indicate a present intent to contract.

3. At a local auction, Jim bid $5.00 for a painting valued at $500.00. No one else bid, so the auctioneer withdrew the painting before "hammering down" his acceptance. Jim argues that placing the item on the block was an offer, which he legally accepted. Is he correct?

   a. No, the auctioneer must deliver the painting to Jim before there is an acceptance.

   b. No, the auctioneer may withdraw the item before accepting it by "hammering down" the item.

   c. Yes, placing an item for auction is an offer.

   d. Yes, Jim is entitled to the item under the doctrine of promissory estoppel.

4. Which of the following is an offer?

   a. A newspaper advertisement for groceries

   b. "I will pay you $25 if you mow my lawn today."

   c. "I would like to buy your car."

   d. A sale item shown in a catalog

5. Winkler's Jewelers sends a letter to past customers advertising a special two-week sale on a particular bracelet at a certain price. The letter is signed by Jim Winkler, President. Which of the following statements is accurate?

   a. The letter is not an offer, but an invitation to negotiate.

   b. Winkler's could revoke this offer anytime before a customer accepts it.

   c. This is an irrevocable firm offer.

   d. This offer remains open indefinitely.

6. If the letter from Winkler's in the above question does not mention anything regarding the time that the offer is valid,

   a. Winkler's could revoke the offer anytime.

   b. The offer can never be revoked.

   c. The offer can be revoked after a reasonable time.

   d. The offer is automatically revoked after six months.

7. Mabel tells Frank she will pay him $2,000 if he paints her house. Frank buys some paint and equipment and begins painting Mabel's house. The day after Frank starts painting the house, Mabel tells him she has changed her mind and revokes her offer. Which of the following is true?

   a. Mabel owes Frank for the time and materials he has already invested in the project.

   b. Mabel can revoke her offer anytime, so Frank is out of luck.

   c. This is a firm offer so Mabel cannot revoke the offer.

   d. Mabel must permit Frank to finish the job once he starts it.

8. In the fall of 1981, Farmer Hicks wrote to City Slicker, a food wholesaler, and offered to sell Slicker his entire crop of persimmons for $500. Slicker did not reply, and Hicks did not contact him again. In the fall of 1982, however, persimmons were scarce, and Slicker wrote Hicks, "I hereby accept your offer."

   a. There is a contract because Hicks never said how long his offer would remain open and never revoked his offer before Slicker accepted it.

   b. There is a contract if Slicker subjectively intends to contract.

   c. There is no contract because Hicks' offer was terminated by the passage of a reasonable time before Slicker accepted it.

   d. There is no contract to sell Slicker the entire crop for $500, but Hicks must sell Slicker persimmons at the new market price.

9. Which of the following is not an effective way to terminate or revoke an offer?

    a. The death of the offeror before the offer was accepted.

    b. Jane is thinking of buying a car from Cindy. Before Jane can accept Cindy's offer, the car is destroyed in a tornado.

    c. The contract performance becomes illegal before the acceptance is made.

    d. The offeree accepts the offer before receiving a mailed revocation from the offeror.

10. Martha pays Howie $25 to not sell his car for three days so that Martha can decide if she wants to buy it. This is an example of:

    a. A counteroffer

    b. An option

    c. An acceptance of the offer

    d. Promissory estoppel

Short Essay

1. Iowa Furniture Mart runs television commercials advertising a special three-day Labor Day sale on recliners. Is this a firm offer?

2. Stevens Construction Co. is developing a bid to Fellowship Church for a new church building. Stevens asks for bids from subcontractors such as plumbers, electricians, and bricklayers. Who is making offers in this process?

3. John offered to sell his house to Mary, but before Mary could accept, John's house burned down. What is the legal status of John's offer? Why?

4. Sylvia attends an auction that is advertised as being "without reserve." Sylvia really likes an antique candle holder that is being auctioned. Apparently, nobody else has much of an interest, so Sylvia's opening bid is the highest bid on the candle holder. Can the auctioneer reject Sylvia's offer?

5.	Rick tells Mona, "I will give you $3,000 for your car." Mona says, "Great, you have a deal." What has taken place here?

6.	What kinds of things do the courts look at in determining whether the offeror has a present intent to contract? Judy hears Bill offer to sell his car to Stan for $7,000. Judy says, "I will take it." Is there an acceptance here?

CHAPTER 10
CREATING A CONTRACT: ACCEPTANCES

Outline

I.   What is an Acceptance? An acceptance is an expression of present willingness to enter into a bargain based on the terms of an offer.

    A. Requires present intent to contract and may be express or implied.

        Example: Workmon v. Publishers Clearing House: An offer must be construed as a whole, and an acceptance must meet all conditions of the offer.

    B. "The Battle of the Forms Provision:" The UCC adopts a rule that changes the common law rule that an acceptance must "mirror the terms" of the offer.

        Example: JOM, Inc. v. Adell Plastics, Inc: JOM proved that a term makes a material alteration if it would result in unreasonable surprise or hardship.

    C. Acceptance of Unilateral Contract Offers: The offeree must perform the requested act or make the requested promise.

    D. Accepting a bilateral contract: the offeree may expressly or impliedly accept the offer.

    E. In general, silence does not constitute acceptance; however, previous dealing by the parties or trade custom may change this rule.

    F. Who Can Accept the Offer? Generally, only the original offeree

    G. What if writing is anticipated: Whether or not an agreement exists prior to a written agreement is based on the intention of the parties

        Example: Sprout v. Bd. of Ed.: The court found that a preliminary agreement to settle an employee grievance is not a contract because both parties expected the agreement to be memorialized by a writing and approved by the board.

    H. Communication of Acceptance: The offeror may stipulate terms of acceptance. Example: Farago Advertising, Inc. v. Hollinger International, Inc.: An offeror can dictate the manner of acceptance. When Farago signed and returned the written document, it was the offer and stipulated how it must be accepted, which was that it must be signed by both parties to be effective.

    I. Authorized Means of Communication

        1. As a general rule, an acceptance is effective when dispatched if dispatched by authorized means. Under modern law, authorized means includes any reasonable means.

            Example: Aetna Life Insurance Co. v. Montgomery: A change of beneficiary form was found to be effective upon dispatch.

        2. Either promise to ship or shipment constitutes acceptance unless otherwise agreed.

Learning Objectives

1.   You should understand the significance of an effective acceptance in that an acceptance creates a contract and it is then too late for the offeror to revoke the offer.

2.   You should understand that under common law, an acceptance that changed a material term of the offer constituted a counter-offer, which is treated as a new offer.

3.   You should note that the UCC "battle of the forms" provision provides that a contract may be created, if the parties intend to contract, even though the terms of the acceptance do not mirror the terms of the offer.

4.   You should know the requirements of a valid acceptance.

5. You should know how offers for unilateral contracts are accepted.

6. You should know how offers for bilateral contracts are accepted.

7. You should be aware of the fact that sometimes acceptance is created by the offeree's <u>conduct</u> rather than by his words.

8. You should know that silence is not generally considered to be acceptance; you should also know the exceptions to this rule.

9. You should know the rules concerning acceptance when the parties anticipate creating a written contract.

10. You should know the general rules about when acceptances by different means are considered to be communicated and therefore effective.

11. You should have an awareness of cyber contracts and browse wrap contracts.

Learning Hints

1. The significance of an offer is that it creates the power of acceptance. A valid offer may be accepted by the words, "I accept," which has the effect of creating an agreement.

2. Once an offer has been accepted by an offeree, it is too late for the offeror to revoke his offer.

3. Once an offeree has accepted an offer, it is too late for the offeree to change his or her mind and reject the offer.

4. A counteroffer rejects the terms of the original offer, and thus terminates the power of acceptance. A counteroffer is a new offer, creating the power of acceptance in the other party.

5. An offeree must show a present intent to contract in order to make a valid acceptance. This means that the offeree must show that he is serious and ready to enter into a binding contract on the offeror's terms. Like intent to make an offer, intent to accept an offer is judged by an objective standard. This standard becomes important in certain acceptance situations, such as where the parties have an oral agreement, anticipate that they will later put their agreement in writing, but never do so. In such cases, the court's resolution of the question whether a contract exists without the writing will depend on what the court determines, using the objective standard, about the parties' intent. If the parties act as if they intend to make a contract at the time they reach their oral agreement, the court will enforce this oral agreement– even when one of the parties later changes his mind and refuses to sign a written version of the contract.

6. Even though a party's conduct, rather than his words, can constitute acceptance, failure to respond (usually in the form of silence) normally does not constitute acceptance. The general rule is that an offeror cannot unilaterally impose the duty to reply or be bound on an offeree. This means that a contract would <u>not</u> be created in a case where the offeror said, "I offer this to you at $5. If I don't hear from you in two days, we have a contract." There are several exceptions to this rule, however. Situations in which a party's silence or failure to act shows acceptance include a situation in which the offeree has expressly agrees that his silence will signal acceptance (for example most book and record clubs operate on this principle), or a situation in which the past dealings of the parties or the custom in their business is such that failure to object signals acceptance, or in a situation in which one person allows another to perform a service without objection, knowing that payment is expected for the service.

7. Remember that the offeror is the "master of the contract," meaning that he may propose whatever contract terms he desires, no matter how unreasonable. To create a valid acceptance, the offeree must accept all of the offeror's terms exactly as they are stated in the offer. In addition, the offeree must satisfy any stipulations the offeror has included in the offer concerning the method and time of acceptance (for example the offer must state "You must respond by registered letter," or "You must accept by noon on September 20").

8. There are three elements in a legally valid acceptance: intent to contract, communication of the acceptance, and agreement to the offeror's terms as set forth in the offer. The question of <u>when</u> an acceptance is communicated and therefore effective is really a separate, and subsequent, issue. You

must first show that the acceptance is characterized by the required intent, communication, and agreement to the offeror's terms. Only then do you ask when the acceptance was communicated to the offeror and therefore effective.

9. If the offeree has used a method of communication that was expressly or impliedly authorized by the offeror, the acceptance is communicated and effective when it is <u>sent</u> (in legal terms, "dispatched"), not when it is received by the offeror. An "authorized" means of communication is a method that is suggested by the offeror, used by the offeror in making the offer, or commonly used in the parties' trade or business. If the offeree uses a method of communication that was not authorized, the effectiveness of his acceptance will be delayed until it is actually <u>received</u> by the offeror.

10. You should be aware of the problems that sometimes arise when the parties deal at a distance or through any means of communication in which there is a time lag between dispatch of the acceptance by the offeree and receipt of the acceptance by the offeror. For instance, sometimes, an attempted revocation and an attempted acceptance cross in the mail. The offeror can protect himself or herself against the chance that he will be bound to a contract before he receives the acceptance by clearly stating in his offer that acceptance is only effective when he actually receives it. The offeror may also wish to require that the acceptance by received by him on or before a certain date to be effective.

True-False

In the blank provided, put "**T**" if the statement is True or "**F**" if the statement is False.

_____ 1. Under the UCC, the parties may enter in a binding contract even though the terms of the acceptance differ from the terms of the offer.

_____ 2. Under the Battle of the Forms, no contract is created when the offeree's acceptance includes additional or different terms than those proposed by the offeror.

_____ 3. An offeror cannot stipulate the manner of acceptance under the UCC.

_____ 4. The offeree's silence may constitute an acceptance based on the past course of dealing between the parties.

_____ 5. A counter-offer is a new offer.

_____ 6. As a general rule, acceptance is effective only when received by the offeror if the offeree has used an authorized means of communication.

_____ 7. Randy offers to sell some furniture to Marla for $1,000. Emily hears about this and offers Randy a check for $1,000. Emily has accepted Randy's offer and has created a contract.

_____ 8. No contract exists when the parties fail to sign a written agreement that was made after the parties had come to an agreement and concluded negotiations for the most part.

_____ 9. If the offeror does not stipulate a method for acceptance, the offeree can accept the offer within a reasonable time by any reasonable means of communication.

_____ 10. If the offeree has dispatched inconsistent responses to the offer by sending both a rejection and an acceptance, whichever response reaches the offeror first will determine whether a contract is created.

Multiple Choice

Circle the best answer.

1.   The UCC "Battle of the Forms" provision:

    a.   Adopts the common law "mirror image rule."

    b.   Changes the common law "mail box" rule.

    c.   Provides a contract can be formed even though terms of the acceptance differ from terms of the offer.

    d.   Makes it a crime to alter the terms of an offer.

2.   Carla places an advertisement in the local paper offering a reward of $100 for her lost poodle, Poochie. Which of the following is true?

    a.   A contract is created when Fred calls Carla and tells her that he accepts her offer.

    b.   A contract is created when Barb tells Carla, "I will find your precious Poochie."

    c.   An acceptance of the offer must be communicated to Carla.

    d.   Loren accepts the offer when he finds Poochie and takes her to Carla.

3.   John orally offered to sell Shirley his car for $350.00. He stipulated that the manner of acceptance must be in writing. Shirley may accept the offer:

    a.   Only in writing.

    b.   Only orally.

    c.   Only by payment of $350.

    d.   By any reasonable means.

4.   Marla offers to sell her car to Brad on June 1. She tells Brad that she must receive an acceptance from him within a couple of days or she will sell the car to someone else. Brad sends Marla a letter of acceptance and a check on June 3. Marla sells her car to John on June 4. On June 5, Marla receives Brad's acceptance. Which of the following is true?

    a.   Brad made a timely acceptance.

    b.   An acceptance in this case is valid with it is mailed, so Brad owns the car.

    c.   Since Marla did not actually receive the acceptance on time, she properly sold the car to John.

    d.   None of the above.

5.   Sam and Dave entered into an oral contract for the sale of goods; however, Sam said "I want to wait to see how this looks in writing before I sign off on it." Later, Sam refused to sign the written contract. Is there an enforceable contract between the parties?

    a.   There is no contract because the parties intended there would be no agreement unless reduced to writing.

    b.   There is no contract because a contract must be in writing to be enforceable.

    c.   There is no contract unless both parties are merchants. Under the UCC, an oral contract between merchants is enforceable regardless of whether the parties intended to reduce it to writing.

    d.   There is a contract.

6. Suppose the same facts in case number 4 above, except that Marla said nothing about actually receiving the acceptance from Brad. Which of the following is true?

    a. An acceptance is effective upon dispatch or in this case when Brad mailed his acceptance to Marla.

    b. John accepted the offer on Marla's car before Marla received Brad's acceptance, therefore John owns the car.

    c. Acceptance is valid only when it is received by the offeror.

    d. Brad must give acceptance by telephone or in person.

7. Which of the following would constitute an acceptance of an offer?

    a. Seller responds to buyer's offer to buy 1,000 widgets at $5 per widget by shipping the widgets to the buyer and notifying the buyer of the acceptance.

    b. Buyer responds to seller's offer by mail to sell widgets at a certain price by mailing an acceptance to the seller.

    c. Seller receives buyer's letter of acceptance. The seller has requested that the acceptance be by telegram.

    d. All of the above.

8. Brown offers by telegram to sell Black 1,000 widgets at $5 per widget. Brown's offer states that acceptance by mail is advisable. At 1:00 p.m. on October 10, Black sends Brown a letter stating his acceptance of Brown's offer. At noon on October 10, Brown sends Black a telegram revoking his offer. Black receives the telegram at 3:00 p.m. Which of the following is true?

    a. Brown revoked the offer before Black gave his acceptance, so there is no contract.

    b. Black followed the expressly authorized means of acceptance, so Brown's acceptance is effective upon dispatch.

    c. The acceptance should have been by telegram in the same manner the offer was communicated.

    d. The acceptance is by non-authorized means, so it is not effective until received.

9. Which of the following is not required for a valid acceptance to take place?

    a. Communication of the acceptance must be done by the means authorized by the offeror.

    b. Clear, objective intent by the offeree to make an acceptance.

    c. The offeree makes no material changes from the offer.

    d. Communication of the acceptance by the offeree may be done by unauthorized means.

10. Which of the following statements is not true?

    a. Under the "mirror image rule," an acceptance shall mirror the original offer made by the offeror.

    b. Under the "Battle of the Forms," a timely expression of acceptance creates a contract even if it includes some different terms from those in the original offer.

    c. If both parties are merchants, additional terms in the offeree's form are not included in the agreement if these terms materially alter the offer.

    d. Silence can never constitute an acceptance.

Short Essay

1. Tim offers to sell his baseball card collection to Tom. Ted hears this conversation and tells Tim he accepts his offer. Has an agreement for Ted to buy Tim's baseball card collection been made?

2. Sue Ellen offers to sell her car to Lucy. Sue Ellen tells Lucy, "If I do not hear from you in three days, we have a deal and you have yourself a wonderful car." Lucy does not respond to Sue Ellen in the three days. Is there a contract?

3. Harvey tells Helen, "I will give you $100 if you find my lost cat, Bootsie." Discuss how Helen can accept Harvey's offer.

4. When will an acceptance by the authorized means of communication not be effective on dispatch? What is the reason for this exception to the general rule?

5. Ryan tells Jim if he wants to buy Ryan's boat, Jim must call Ryan on his cell phone by no later than 2:00 p.m. on June 5. Could Jim accept Ryan's offer with a mailed acceptance?

6. Mary offers to sell Lou her big screen television. Lou mails an acceptance letter and check to Mary on April 3. On April 4, Ted offers Mary a lot more money for her big screen television. On April 5, Mary receives Lou's acceptance letter. Can Mary sell the television to Ted since he is offering to pay her more and because he made his offer before Lou's acceptance letter arrived?

7. Ted offers to sell 100 units of Blue Widgets to ABC Co for $10 a unit. Acceptance is by any reasonable commercial means. ABC Co. faxes an acceptance with the additional term that the widgets are guaranteed for 30 days. Ted ships the widgets, but disclaims any guarantees. Is there a contract?

CHAPTER 11
CONSIDERATION

Outline

I. Consideration in General

    A. Under common law, a promise is generally unenforceable unless it was a bargain–requiring that a person has given up something in exchange for the promise.

        Example: <u>Dela Zoppa v. Dela Zoppa</u>: A woman's palimony suit is successful because she lived with her partner before marriage and because their agreement encompassed more than a sexual relationship.

    B. Consideration is defined as something of <u>legal value</u>: Bargained for and given in exchange for a promise (or an act) to do something a person has no legal duty to do, or a promise to refrain from doing something one has a legal right to do constitutes legal value.

    C. Generally, courts to do not inquire into the adequacy of consideration, however, consideration that is so inadequate as to be a gift rather than a contract may fail as adequate consideration.

        Example: <u>McBee v. Nance</u>: A deed to a house was found to be adequate consideration for a promissory note in the amount of $15,000.

II. Rules of Consideration

    A. Preexisting Duty: As a rule, performing or agreeing to perform a preexisting duty is not consideration, because it cannot constitute legal value.

        A promise to perform a preexisting contractual duty cannot support an agreement to modify a contract under traditional common law rule; new consideration is required.

        Example: <u>M. Gold & Son, Inc. v. A.J. Eckert, Inc.</u>: Holding that a modification of a contract constitutes the making of a new contract and must be supported by new consideration.

    B. The Uniform Commercial Code changes the rule and makes a modification of an existing contract for the sale of good enforceable without new consideration. The modification must be <u>commercially reasonably</u> and <u>in good faith</u>.

    C. Promises to Discharge Debts for Part Payment

        1. A promise to discharge a <u>liquidated debt</u> for part payment is generally unenforceable.

        2. A promise to discharge an <u>unliquidated debt</u> constitutes an enforceable <u>accord and satisfaction.</u>

    D. Past consideration is not consideration. Forbearance to sue, however, constitutes consideration to support a new agreement, if the promisee in good faith releases a valid claim in exchange for another's promise.

        Example: <u>In re Lovekamp</u>: If a person who benefited makes a promise to pay for an act or forbearance, that promise is gratuitous and cannot be legally enforced.

        Example: <u>Duncan v. Duncan</u>: In order for a contract to be enforceable, it must be supported by consideration. Consideration exists if the promisee, in return for the promise, refrains from doing anything that he has a right to do.

    E. Mutuality of obligation is required and an illusory promise creates an unenforceable contract.

    F. Under the doctrine of <u>promissory estoppel</u>, a promise that is not supported by consideration may be enforceable under the equitable theory that the promise induced <u>reliance</u> by the promisee, and the reliance was reasonable.

    G. Firm offers, under the UCC, require no additional consideration.

H. Bankruptcy and the expiration of a statute of limitation normally discharge or void promises made before their occurrence.

Learning Objectives

1. You should understand the rationale for the common law's requirement of consideration.

2. You should recognize that the requirement of consideration has changed, and that statutory law such as the UCC or equitable principles like promissory estoppel may change or eliminate the requirement in certain cases.

3. You should know that an agreement not supported by consideration is generally unenforceable by either party.

4. You should be able to give a definition of consideration.

5. You should understand why promises to perform a pre-existing obligation are not consideration.

6. You should understand why past consideration and illusory promises are not consideration.

7. You should know when a promise to settle a debt is enforceable, and understand the difference between a liquidated and unliquidated debt.

8. You should understand how the doctrine of promissory estoppel is sometimes used as a substitute for consideration.

9. You should understand the potential effect of bankruptcy and the expiration of a statute of limitation enforceability of consideration.

Learning Hints

1. Consideration is defined as something of "legal value." This may be further defined as a promise to do something someone is not legally obligated to do, or to refrain from doing something one is legally entitled to do.

2. Under this definition, a promise to do something one is already obligated to do generally cannot constitute consideration.

3. Likewise, under this definition, a promise not to do something that one is not legally entitled to do cannot constitute consideration.

4. Even though one of the elements of consideration is that something with "legal value" must be given in exchange for the promise, consideration is not required to have economic or monetary value. For example, the making of a promise can be consideration, even though the promise itself has no monetary value.

5. It is very important to remember that promises can be consideration. Many students think that no consideration exists until the promised act is actually performed, but this is not true. When a promise serves as consideration, the consideration arises at the moment the promise is communicated to the promisee.

6. Promissory estoppel is based on the idea of protecting justifiable reliance. Therefore, a promise is sometimes enforced even if it is not supported by consideration if the promise has caused the promisee to act in reliance upon it, and it would be unfair to not enforce the promise.

True-False

In the blank provided, put "T" if the statement is True or "F" if the statement is False.

_____ 1. Consideration may be either an act or a promise.

_____ 2. Generally, a promise to do something one is already obligated to do cannot constitute consideration for a new promise.

_____ 3. Damages incurred because of reliance on a promise, even if the promise is not supported by consideration, may be recovered in some cases under the doctrine of promissory estoppel.

_____ 4. The courts generally do not concern themselves with adequacy of consideration.

_____ 5. Part payment of an unliquidated debt can result in an accord and satisfaction.

_____ 6. When a person agrees not to do something that he has a legal right to do in exchange for the promisor's promise, this is legal value.

_____ 7. Consideration is not required to have monetary or economic value, just legal value.

_____ 8. The promise to perform a pre-existing duty is consideration.

_____ 9. Agreements to modify contracts for the sale of goods must be supported by consideration.

_____ 10. A composition agreement between a debtor and his creditors for sixty cents on the dollar is binding.

Multiple Choice

1. Which of the following would not constitute consideration for a new promise?
   a. A promise to perform a service.
   b. A promise to pay money.
   c. A promise to refrain from doing something one is not entitled to do.
   d. A promise not to collect a debt which is due and owing.

2. Under the UCC, a modification of a contract:
   a. Requires new consideration to be enforceable.
   b. Only requires new consideration if the parties are merchants.
   c. Does not require new consideration even if the parties are not acting in good faith.
   d. Does not require new consideration but is subject to the UCC requirement of good faith.

3. A person who relies on another's promise may be entitled to enforce that promise, even though the promise is unsupported by consideration, under which of the following theories?
   a. Contract implied in fact.
   b. Promissory estoppel.
   c. Quasi-contract.
   d. Gratuitous promise.

4. Mark agrees to build a house for Martha for $180,000. When digging for the foundation, Mark encounters more hard rock in the ground than he anticipated. Which of the following statements is true?
   a. Mark can demand more money from Martha because of the unforeseen problems with rock.
   b. Mark has a pre-existing duty to build the house for $180,000.
   c. Mark could successfully modify the contract to collect more money from Martha if he also provides more consideration, such as a fancier trim or more concrete for sidewalks.
   d. Both b and c.

5. Bart owes Marge $1,000. Bart sends Marge a check for $750 marked "paid in full." Which of the following statements is true?
   a. Marge and Bart entered into a binding accord and satisfaction, so the debt is paid in full.
   b. This is an unliquidated debt, so the payment of $750. satisfies the full debt.
   c. This is a liquidated debt. Bart still owes Marge $250.
   d. This is a composition, so the $750 payment is effective to satisfy the full debt.

6. Art agrees to supply Bill's IGA grocery store with tomatoes for one year at $1.25 per pound. The hurricane season in Florida has damaged the tomato crop. Retail prices are now over $3 per pound. Art asks Bill's IGA for a higher price for the tomatoes. Which of the following statements is most accurate?

   a. Art has a pre-existing duty to provide the tomatoes at $1.25 per pound, so Bill's IGA has no obligation to agree to a higher price.

   b. Art is seeking to modify a contract for the sale of goods, so Art must provide consideration for the modification to be binding.

   c. Art and Bill's IGA have agreed to a novation.

   d. The court would likely rule that unforeseeable difficulties have made it impossible or at least impractical for Art to perform under the terms of the contract.

7. Which of the following would be classified as consideration in a contract?

   a. Forbearance to sue

   b. Promise to perform a pre-existing contractual duty

   c. Promise not to commit a crime

   d. An illusory promise

8. Which of the following would not be classified as consideration to form a binding contract?

   a. A promise of a sizeable gift to a charity. The charity relies on this promise.

   b. Telling a farmer, "I will buy all the apples I want from you."

   c. Agreeing to pay your creditors 80 cents on the dollar.

   d. Agreeing with a debtor to settle on a disputed debt for less than the full amount.

9. Rubber-Maiden agrees to sell plastic trash barrels to Wal-Mart at a certain price for a year. Due to the rising price of plastic, Rubber-Maiden tells Wal-Mart it must increase its price on the trash barrels by 20%. Which of the following is not true?

   a. A sales contract cannot be modified without consideration. Rubber-Maiden must provide Wal-Mart with additional consideration in return for the higher price on the trash barrels.

   b. Wal-Mart could agree to modify the contract and pay a higher price for the trash barrels.

   c. The court could rule that the rising price of plastic is an unforeseeable circumstance that makes it difficult for Rubber-Maiden to perform under the original terms of the contract.

   d. A sales contract can be modified without additional consideration.

10. Which of the following statements regarding consideration is not true?

    a. Generally, the courts will not concern themselves with adequacy of consideration.

    b. A promise to give someone $1,000 for graduating from college two years ago is binding.

    c. Courts would generally not enforce a contract if the inadequacy of consideration is apparent on the face of the agreement.

    d. Nominal consideration is usually not recognized by the courts.

Short Essay

1. Ray owed David $500. David agreed to release Ray from the debt if Ray would paint David's apartment. Is this agreement supported by consideration? Explain.

2. Bert promises to pay Ernie $10,000 because Ernie lost a lot of weight a year ago on the Adkins Diet. Is this promise binding on Bert?

3. Mark agrees to build a house for Jane for $200,000. Mark encounters a lot of hard rock in the building lot and seeks another $10,000 from Jane. Jane and Mark agree to terminate their old contract and enter into a new contract for $210,000. All of the other terms in the contract are virtually the same as the old contract. What is this new agreement called? How would the courts view the new agreement?

4. Hank promises to provide Rhoda with widgets at $1 per widget for the next year. Suddenly supply and demand forces cause widget prices to skyrocket. What could Hank argue in trying to sell widgets to Rhoda at a higher price than they agreed on in their contract?

5. Anderson promises to give State University $3 million to build a new football complex. Is this promise binding upon Anderson?

6. Ann owes money to Julie. The parties cannot even agree on the amount owed. Julie insists Ann owes her $5,000. Ann believes she owes Julie $3,500. If Julie agrees to accept $3,750 from Ann as full payment, what is this called and is it binding upon both parties?

CHAPTER 12
CAPACITY TO CONTRACT

Outline

I. Minors' Contracts: The minor is given the right to disaffirm (cancel) his/her contracts.

    A. Rationale: The contract is only voidable by the minor, that is, only the minor has the right to disaffirm. Adults who contract with minors are bound by the contracts. The rationale is to protect the·minor.

    Example: <u>NYC Mgmt. Group Inc. v. Brown-Miller</u>: A minor was allowed to disaffirm a modeling contract even though her mother also signed the contract.

    B. The Minor may disaffirm during minority or within a reasonable time afterward.

    C. Ratification: A minor who does not disaffirm within a reasonable time after attaining majority loses the right to disaffirm. Any action or words showing a desire to be found by the contract after the minor reaches majority, acts as ratification.

    Example: <u>In re Score Board, Inc.</u>: An attempted disaffirmance of a contract is invalid because the minor, Kobe Bryant, continued to perform contractual duties after attaining majority.

    D. Consequences of disaffirmance: Under modern trend, minors are entitled to the return of their property and must put the seller in *status quo*.

    E. Barriers to Disaffirmance: Many courts today require the minor to place the adult in *status quo* in some circumstances in order to ameliorate the harsh effects of the rule that minors lack capacity to contract.

    Example: In <u>Sheller v. Frank's Nursery and Crafts, Inc.</u>, a minor could not use her minority to avoid an arbitration clause in her employment contract.

    Example: <u>Mitchell v. State Farm Automobile Insurance Co.</u>: A person under 18 lacks capacity to contract and can avoid contracts made during that time.

    F. Necessaries are those things essential to a minor's welfare. Minors are generally required to pay the <u>reasonable value</u> of necessaries rather than the contract price.

    Example: <u>Schmidt v. Prince George's Hospital</u>: Medical expenses are necessaries for which a minor can be held liable.

II. Contracts of mentally impaired and intoxicated persons

    A. Test of incapacity is whether the party, at the time of contracting, could understand the nature and effect of the contract.

    Example: <u>Saret-Cook v. Gilbert, Kelly, Crowley, and Jennett</u>: An employee who signed a release of all claims against her employer was not allowed to avoid the release because of the benefits she received in exchange for signing the release.

Learning Objectives

1. You should understand the difference between a void and voidable contract.

2. You should understand the right of a minor or one lacking capacity due to mental impairment to disaffirm a contract.

3. You should understand the concept of ratification.

4. You should know why contracts made by minors are voidable, and why these contracts are voidable at the election of the minor, but not at the election of the adult party to the contract.

5. You should understand the time period during which a minor is allowed to disaffirm.

6. You should know the different approaches taken in cases involving the return of consideration by the disaffirming minor where the consideration has been lost, stolen, destroyed, or dissipated.

7. You should know the various ways in which ratification may be accomplished.

8. You should know what "necessaries" are, the rules governing the minor's liability for them, and the reason that contracts for necessaries are not voidable.

9. You should know the test of incapacity usually applied when a party to a contract is alleged to be mentally impaired or intoxicated.

10. You should know when the contracts of the mentally impaired are treated as void rather than voidable.

Learning Hints

1. A contract made by a minor is voidable by the minor but not by the adult. This means that the minor may elect to disaffirm or to ratify the contract.

2. In general, an adult contracts with a minor at his own risk. Generally, a minor is not required to place the adult in *status quo* (that is, in the same position he would have been had the contract not been executed); this rule, however, has been changed in some states.

3. Except for contracts that affect title to real estate, a minor can disaffirm a contract at any time from the making of the contract until a reasonable time after reaching the age of majority.

4. Cases in which the consideration received by the minor has been lost, stolen, destroyed, or dissipated have caused much disagreement concerning the minor's ability to disaffirm. A few states allow the minor to rescind in such cases, but require him to pay the adult party to the contract the reasonable value of the consideration he received.

5. Keep in mind that failure to disaffirm within a reasonable time after reaching the age of majority extinguishes the right to disaffirm, and also constitutes ratification.

6. In order to understand the rule making infants (minors) liable in quasi-contract for necessaries, suppose that a grocery store sells a minor a loaf of bread for $100. The minor will not be able to avoid paying for the bread, but he will only be liable for its reasonable value. This rule encourages adults to provide necessaries to minors, but prevents them from imposing unconscionable bargains on these minors.

7. The bargains of the mentally impaired are void only when a court has previously determined the person to be mentally incompetent. This ruling is very different from the ruling an ordinary court makes in a case where it is alleged that a contract is voidable on the grounds of mental impairment.

8. The rule that contracts of the mentally impaired or intoxicated can be ratified only after the person has regained mental capacity or sobriety reflects the same policy as the rule allowing minors to ratify their contracts only after attaining the age of majority. In each case, the capacity to contract is a precondition to ratification, for surely the person who lacks capacity to contract also lacks the capacity to ratify.

9. A minor who contracts for necessaries is able to disaffirm when he is furnished necessaries by a parent or guardian. In this situation, disaffirmance is permitted because there is no need to ensure that adults will have an incentive to provide necessaries to the minor.

10. While a contract entered into by an intoxicated party may be voidable if the party failed to understand the nature of the agreement, courts generally do not favor releasing a party from an obligation because he was voluntarily intoxicated. Thus, a court may find that the party has ratified the contract if he does not act promptly in notifying the other party of his election to rescind as a result of intoxication.

True-False

In the blank provided, put "**T**" if the statement is True or "**F**" if the statement is False.

_____ 1. Only a minor may only rescind a contract by a minor.

_____ 2. A minor may disaffirm a contract even after attaining majority.

_____ 3. Any contract by a person who lacks the mental capacity to contract is void, regardless of whether that person has been adjudicated mentally incompetent.

_____ 4. Today, minors who disaffirm a contract are often required to place the other contracting party in *status quo*.

_____ 5. A minor can generally only ratify a contract after attaining majority.

_____ 6. A minor who misrepresents his age to an adult will be estopped from disaffirming his contract with the adult in some states.

_____ 7. Emancipation gives the minor the capacity to contract.

_____ 8. Minors are normally liable for the reasonable value of necessaries provided to them.

_____ 9. Agreements made by persons who have been adjudicated insane are generally voidable.

_____ 10. Like minors, people lacking mental capacity can disaffirm their contracts, and on disaffirmance, must return any of the consideration that they still have.

Multiple Choice

Circle the best answer.

1. Which of the following is an example of a void contract?
   a. A contract between a minor and another minor.
   b. A contract between a minor and an adult who does not know the first party is a minor.
   c. A contract between a minor and an adult who knows the first party is a minor.
   d. A contract between a person who has been adjudicated mentally incompetent and another party.

2. Jan, who was being treated for manic-depression, a serious mental illness, (but had not been adjudicated incompetent), rented an apartment for herself and her child. Assuming that the apartment is a "necessary:"
   a. Jan must pay the contract price for the apartment.
   b. Jan must pay the reasonable value of the apartment rental.
   c. Jan is not obligated to pay for the apartment unless she chooses to do so.
   d. The contract is void.

3. Nan has had a history of mental problems. Nan enters into a contract to buy a series of books advertised on television. Which of the following statements is most accurate?
   a. If the court finds that Nan lacked the mental capacity at the time the transaction was made, the contract is probably voidable.
   b. The contract is void.
   c. If Nan disaffirms the contract, she does not need to return any books she received.
   d. The books would likely be classified as necessaries.

4. Billy, a minor, buys a small house. Which of the following statements is true?

    a. A minor cannot disaffirm a real estate contract.

    b. Billy can ratify this contract before attaining majority.

    c. Billy must attain majority before disaffirming a real estate contract.

    d. Billy may disaffirm the contract at any time during minority.

5. Generally, a contract entered into by an intoxicated person:

    a. Is void.

    b. Is voidable under all circumstances.

    c. Is voidable only if the intoxicated person lacked mental capacity to contract at the time of entry into the contract.

    d. Is illegal.

6. Marty, a minor, trades his Toyota in for a used Honda at Honest Hank's Used Cars. Hank later sells the Toyota to Millie. After experiencing some difficulties with the Honda, Marty disaffirms the contract. Under the UCC, which of the following statements is not true?

    a. Marty can get his Toyota back from Millie.

    b. Marty can recover money from Hank, but he cannot recover his Toyota from Millie.

    c. Millie must give the car back to Marty and recover her purchase price from Hank.

    d. Hank must give Marty reasonable value for the Toyota.

7. Which of the following is true regarding minority?

    a. A minor can normally disaffirm a contract during minority and for a reasonable time after attaining majority.

    b. An adult can disaffirm a contract with a minor.

    c. A minor may ratify a contract while still a minor.

    d. Under common law, a minor who disaffirms a contract and who no longer has the consideration given by the adult party does not have a duty to place the adult in *status quo*.

8. Mona Minor misrepresents her age to Johnson so that Johnson will sell furniture to Mona. Which of the following statements is true?

    a. Mona may be estopped from raising the defense of minority.

    b. Mona may be allowed to disaffirm the contract, but to place Johnson in *status quo*.

    c. Mona may be able to disaffirm, but she may be liable to Johnson for the tort of deceit.

    d. All of the above.

9. Which of the following statements is not true?

    a. Emancipation does not normally give the minor the capacity to contract.

    b. Minors are generally liable under quasi-contract theory for the reasonable value of necessaries provided to them.

    c. Minors are liable for the value of necessaries they have purchased under a contract, but have not received at the time they disaffirm.

    d. Some courts today hold that a disaffirming minor must return the adult to *status quo*.

10. Mike has been adjudicated insane. Which of the following is not true?

   a. Contracts made by Mike after the adjudication are void.

   b. Contracts made by Mike after the adjudication are voidable.

   c. Mike may be liable for the reasonable value of necessaries.

   d. Mike's personal representative may be able to ratify contracts made by Mike.

Short Essay

1. Sally, a minor, buys a car from Bally Motors. After Sally reaches the age of majority, can she still disaffirm the contract?

2. What is the reason for requiring minors to pay on a quasi-contract basis for necessaries furnished to them before they disaffirmed the contract for the necessaries?

3. While Sally is still a minor, she wrecks the car she purchased from Bally. Can she still disaffirm the contract? Must she return Bally to *status quo*?

4. Rita, a minor, signs a one year lease at Alpine Manor Apartments for $500 per month in rent. Rita lives at Alpine for two months before she disaffirms her lease. Must Rita pay Alpine for the rent? Is this a necessary?

5. Bud is an older person who seems to drift in and out of mental sharpness. Bud contracts to buy a car from Roberts Motors. Discuss Bud's ability to enter into a contract and whether he would have the ability to void the contract.

6. Sue is a mature looking 17-year-old. She tells Acme she is 18 so that Acme will sell a television to her. Since Sue is a minor who misrepresented her age, can she still disaffirm her contract with Acme?

CHAPTER 13
VOLUNTARY CONSENT

Outline

I.   An agreement must be entered into voluntarily.

A. Contracts entered into as a result of misrepresentation, fraud, duress, undue influence, or mistake are voidable. The contract may be rescinded (cancelled) or if no performance has taken place, it may be disaffirmed.

B. A person may ratify an agreement if he waits an unreasonable time after discovery to rescind the contract.

II. Misrepresentation

A. Misrepresentation as a legal action is not just identifying an untrue assertion. It is a material fact justifiably relied on to the detriment of the person relying on the assertion, and it is a basis for contract rescission. Fraud is a misrepresentation made knowingly and with intent to deceive.

1. Fraud must include the intent to deceive (*scienter*).

2. Fraud can be the result of silence if the party to the contract has a duty to disclose.

3. Fraud in the execution involves misstatements regarding the content or legal effect of a contract.

B. Misrepresentation of Fact v. Opinion

This is a question of fact.

Example: Morehouse v. Behlman Pontiac-GMC Truck Service, Inc.: The court found that a used car salesman's representation about the condition of a minivan constituted material misrepresentations of fact.

C. Justifiable reliance. As a general rule, people must act reasonably to protect themselves.

Example: Griesi v. Atlantic General Hospital: It is not unreasonable to rely on information provided by a CEO in making a career decision about which corporation could best meet a job candidate's needs and plans.

D. Is failure to disclose to the other party all the material facts misrepresentation? Today, many courts have relaxed the doctrine of *caveat emptor* and placed an affirmative duty to disclose on sellers if the facts were not discoverable by the buyer.

Example: In Hord v. Environmental Research Institute of Michigan, use of an old financial statement as a reflection of the current financial status of the company was an element of fraud.

Example: Columbia/HCA Healthcare Corp., et al v. Cottey: The court finds that the hospital's failure to disclose its discretion to rescind the Top Hat Plan is sufficient to find that the hospital misrepresented the contract by silence.

III. Duress and undue influence

A. Duress is wrongful coercion. Question: When does "hard bargaining" constitute economic duress? Ask whether the act left the other person with no reasonable alternative but to enter the contract.

Example: In Crosstalk Productions, Inc. v. Jacobson, plaintiff's claims were sufficient to allow them to proceed under a theory of economic duress.

B. Undue influence is wrongful persuasion. In most cases, it involves a special relationship of trust or confidence between the parties.

IV.   Mistake

   A.   Mistake prevents the "meeting of the minds," and requires proof of an untrue belief about a material fact.

   B.   Mistake can be mutual or unilateral. It is generally easier to rescind a contract for mutual mistake.
         Example: Lehrer v. State of Washington: The court found that a psychiatrist who agreed to resign from a hospital in return for the removal of personal conduct records from his files is not allowed to use the doctrine of mistake when the disciplinary board continued to pursue complaints levied against him.

Learning Objectives

1.   You should understand the difference between a contract that is voidable and one that is void.

2.   You should be able to define misrepresentation and explain the difference between innocent, negligent, and fraudulent misrepresentation.

3.   You should be able to distinguish undue influence from duress.

4.   You should understand the difference between the traditional definition of duress and the modern approach permitting rescission in cases involving economic duress.

5.   You should understand the difference between unilateral and mutual mistake, and to explain why it is generally easier to rescind in cases involving mutual mistake of fact.

6.   You must know the remedies available to the injured party (or parties) when a contract is voidable.

7.   You must know the elements of misrepresentation, and the two additional elements of fraud.

8.   You should understand the different remedies the plaintiff may get in a fraud case which are not available in a misrepresentation case.

9.   You should be familiar with the typical situations where undue influence occurs.

10.   You should understand the concept of "justifiable reliance" in misrepresentation and mistake cases.

Learning Hints

1.   Misrepresentation, mistake, duress, and undue influence are legal theories supporting a finding that a contracting party did not, in reality, consent to the terms of an agreement. Generally, if a contracting party can establish the elements of one of these theories, he/she may rescind the contract. However, he is not required to do so, and may choose not to rescind.

2.   Generally, courts today are more willing to permit rescission under these theories than in the past, when the doctrine of caveat emptor was a central theme in contract law.

3.   Materiality is tested by an objective standard. Material facts are generally those that would induce a reasonable contracting party to enter into the contract. Materiality is determined on a case-by-case basis, and the standard varies with the needs, interests, and expertise of the contracting party.

4.   The requirement that there be a causal connection between the misrepresentation and a party's entry into the contract in fraud and misrepresentation cases is not the same thing as the requirement of materiality. The causal connection requirement is concerned with whether the party actually relied on the statement, not with whether a reasonable person would have thought the information was important to his or her decision. Often, people entering a contract actually rely on nonmaterial misrepresentations, or fail to rely on clearly material misrepresentations. For fraud or misrepresentation to exist, both materiality of and actual reliance on the misstatement must be present. If one or the other requirement cannot be proved, fraud or misrepresentation does not exist.

5.   The "justifiable reliance" element that is required in fraud and misrepresentation cases is not as big a bar to relief as it used to be. Very stringent duties of investigation were once imposed on the relying party, whereas today this is often not the case. Also, the standard varies with the relative expertise of the

parties. For example, "justifiable reliance" does not mean the same thing in the sale of a used car to an auto mechanic as it would in the sale of a used car to a novice driver.

6. A newly emerging form of duress is <u>economic duress</u> (sometimes called "business compulsion"). This concept refers to the various forms of economic pressure, such as threats of economic harm, which can be applied in the business context. Generally, the threatened harm must be such that a serious economic loss would occur if the threat were carried out. Courts usually make a distinction between situations in which the party applying duress takes advantage of the other party's difficult financial condition and situations in which the party applying duress actually created the other party's bad financial situation and then took advantage of it. Despite the fact that the conduct sounds unacceptable in both situations, most courts would find economic duress only in the second case.

7. You should notice that fraud and misrepresentation share several elements in common, with fraud including the two additional elements of knowledge and intent to deceive. The distinction between fraud and misrepresentation is important because the victim of fraud has more remedies available to him.

8. Keep in mind that lack of capacity to contract, which was the subject of the previous chapter, is not the same thing as undue influence. Victims of undue influence usually have legal capacity to contract, but the stronger party to the transaction, with whom they are in a confidential relationship, overwhelm their powers of judgment and common sense.

True-False

In the blank provided, put "**T**" if the statement is True or "**F**" if the statement is False.

_____ 1. In order to rescind a contract for misrepresentation, the plaintiff must prove fraud (that is, intent to deceive).

_____ 2. A person may not be entitled to rescind a contract for misrepresentation if he waits too long to do so after discovering the misrepresentation.

_____ 3. A person can recover damages for undue influence as well as rescind the contract.

_____ 4. "This is the best computer on the market" is an example of misrepresentation.

_____ 5. Some courts today may determine that a seller of real estate committed fraud by not disclosing certain facts about the home to the buyer.

_____ 6. If the injured party to a voidable contract rescinds the contract, he returns what he has received and recovers what he has given under the contract.

_____ 7. Modern courts hold that a threat of physical injury must exist before they find duress.

_____ 8. A key element in undue influence cases is that a dominant person in a confidential relationship took advantage of the other party.

_____ 9. A mutual mistake is a basis for rescinding the contract.

_____ 10. Fraud in the execution allows a party who has been misled about the content of a contract or its legal effect to rescind the contract.

Multiple Choice

Circle the best answer.

1. Which of the following is not a required element of misrepresentation?

    a. Scienter

    b. Justifiable reliance

    c. A material fact is involved

    d. Other party can show detriment

2. Chick sold Alison a television set he knew no longer worked. However, in order to make the sale, he told her it was in good condition. Under these circumstances:

   a. Either party may rescind the contract.

   b. Only Alison may rescind the contract.

   c. Alison cannot rescind the contract, but she is entitled to damages for fraud.

   d. Alison can rescind the contract, and she also may be entitled to additional damages for fraud.

3. Which of the following is a required element of fraud?

   a. Scienter

   b. Misrepresentation was knowingly made

   c. A material fact was involved

   d. All of the above

4. In order to rescind a contract for undue influence:

   a. The plaintiff must prove the other party intentionally deceived him.

   b. The plaintiff must prove he lacked the capacity to contract.

   c. The plaintiff must prove the other party took unfair advantage of him in persuading him to enter into the contract.

   d. The plaintiff must prove he was mistaken about an important fact in entering into the contract.

5. Gail goes to Friendly Finance Co. for a loan. Fred, the loan officer, tells Gail the interest rate is 16%. Fred prepares the loan papers and tells Gail, "The note just repeats everything we talked about." Fred persuades Gail to sign the note. Gail was not aware that Fred had changed the interest rate in the note to 30%. Which of the following is most true?

   a. Gail should have read the note. She is stuck with the 30% rate.

   b. Friendly is liable for misrepresentation.

   c. Friendly is liable for fraud in the execution.

   d. Scienter was not present in this situation.

6. Nathan is a 12-year-old baseball card collector. While browsing at JD's Collectibles, Nathan spots a Jackie Robinson baseball card that is marked with a $5 price. Nathan knows that the card is worth much more than that. Nathan buys the card for $5. Later, JD's Collectibles demands that Nathan return the card because a JD employee had mistakenly priced the card at $5 instead of $500. Which of the following statements is most true?

   a. This is a mutual mistake, so the contract should be rescinded.

   b. This is fraud because Nathan is guilty of scienter.

   c. The court may grant rescission even though this is a unilateral mistake because Nathan knew of the mistake.

   d. Rescission will not be granted because this is a unilateral mistake.

7. Which is a true statement about mistake?

   a. Mistakes about one's ability to perform under a contract are not the type of mistake that will enable one to avoid contractual liability.

   b. Mutual mistake makes a contract void, while unilateral mistake makes a contract voidable.

   c. Mistake includes situations where both parties erroneously believe that some future event will occur and contract on that basis.

   d. Today, mistake of law is never a basis for avoiding contractual liability.

8. Groucho is old, feeble and wealthy. Though Groucho has three children, he spends the last ten years of his life with his companion, Liz. During this time, Groucho gives some of his property to Liz because of how well she is treating him. Groucho's children protest because they want this property. Which of the following statements is most accurate?

   a. Liz may be liable for duress.
   b. Liz may be liable for undue influence
   c. Liz has committed fraud.
   d. Liz may be liable for the tort of deceit.

9. Val-Mart tells Put a Sock in It sock company that it will no longer carry its socks if it increases its prices. Which of the following is most true?

   a. Val-Mart may be liable for duress if the sock company can show that Val-Mart's threat is wrongful because it involves economic harm.
   b. This is not duress because Val-Mart did not threaten the sock company with physical harm.
   c. Val-Mart is liable to the sock company for undue influence.
   d. Val-Mart is liable to the sock company for fraud.

10. Which of the following is not true?

    a. Bob wants to buy Jean's house. If Jean does not tell Bob about serious problems with the foundation, Jean could be liable for fraud.
    b. If Bob buys Jean's house and later learns of problems with the foundation, Bob may be able to rescind the contract.
    c. If Bob buys Jean's house and later learns of the foundation problems, Bob may be able to affirm the contract and sue Jean for the tort of deceit.
    d. Because of *caveat emptor*, Jean is not liable to Bob for fraud.

Short Essay

1. Marty bought a used car from Rodney. Marty asked Rodney whether the car had ever been in an accident and Rodney assured him it had not been. Unknown to either party, the car had been "totalled" in an accident before Rodney purchased it. Marty has discovered this fact and seeks to rescind the contract. Discuss two theories under which Marty may be entitled to rescind the contract.

2. Jan goes to Better Buy to purchase a computer. The salesperson tells Jan that, "you cannot go wrong with this Pell model." If Jan buys the Pell computer and then finds that it is not right for her, can she successfully hold Better Buy liable for misrepresentation?

3.   What kinds of things could the Better Buy salesperson say that could be considered misrepresentation?

4.   Distinguish between misrepresentation and fraud.

5.   Taylor tells Bob of Friendly Bob's Motors that he wants to buy "that beautiful Mustang on your lot." Bob thinks Taylor is referring to the red Mustang convertible, but Taylor is actually referring to the yellow Mustang parked next to it. Discuss this situation.

6.   Shelly wants to buy Irma's car. Irma knows that there are some serious problems with the car, but she does not say anything to Shelly. Shelly buys the car and later has some major repairs because of the problems that Irma failed to disclose. Can Shelly rescind the contract?

CHAPTER 14
ILLEGALITY

Outline

I.   The Effect of Illegality

    A. Courts generally will not enforce illegal agreements but leaves the parties as it finds them. Illegality is behavior that violates a statute or a rule of common law.

       Example: <u>Nieman v. Provident Life and Accident Insurance Co.</u>: An unlicensed attorney who was illegally practicing law is unable to claim disability benefits from an insurance company due to his inability to practice law.

    B. Sometimes a court will permit recovery if the parties are ignorant of the facts

    C. Parties protected by regulatory statutes may be entitled to enforce the agreement if public policy is served

II. Contracts to commit illegal acts

    A. Contracts illegal by statute

    B. Licensing statutes: Agreements in violation of regulatory licensing statutes are generally unenforceable; however, agreements in violation of a revenue-raising statute are often enforceable.

       Example: In <u>Birbrower, Montalbano, Condon & Frank, P.C. v. Superior Court</u>, a firm forfeited its fees because the attorneys were not licensed to practice in California.

III. Contracts Which Violate Public Policy

    A. Public policy is determined by a court and reflects acceptable social or economic behavior

       Example: <u>A.Z. v. B.Z.</u>: A contract that would allow a former wife to implant pre-embryos from her former husband was contrary to public policy and was not be enforced.

    B. Exculpatory Clauses

       Example: <u>Johnson v. New River Scenic Whitewater Tours, Inc.</u>: New River is unable to enforce an exculpatory clause against a child who was killed on a whitewater rafting trip.

    C. Contracts in restraint of trade ("non-compete clauses.)

       Example: In <u>Advanced Marine Enterprises, Inc. v. PRC Inc.</u>, a noncompetition agreement was enforceable because it was not unreasonably broad or oppressive.

    D. Unconscionability: Under this doctrine, a court may refuse to enforce a contract or contract clause it finds to be "unconscionable."

       1. Generally requires finding that parties lacked equal bargaining power and contract contains substantively unfair provision.

          Example: <u>Alexander v. Anthony, Int'l., L.P.</u>: The court found a contract to be unconscionable and unenforceable where one party, the employer, with far greater bargaining power, persuaded the employee to sign a decidedly one-sided agreement.

       2. UCC 2-302 is the UCC provision on unconscionability; the Restatement has adopted a similar approach.

Learning Objectives

1.   You should understand the concept of public policy, which may be determined by a court.

2.	You should understand that a court will generally refuse to enforce an agreement it finds to violate public policy; further, the general rule is "hands off" illegal contracts, so that the court will leave the parties as it finds them.

3.	You should know when "ignorance of the facts" making a contract illegal will enable a party to recover damages or consideration.

4.	You should know the situations in which a party is permitted to rescind an illegal contract and obtain relief.

5.	You should know when a court will enforce the legal portions of a contract that also contains an illegal term.

6.	You should know and understand the difference between an illegal wager and a legal risk-shifting contract or speculative bargain.

7.	You should know and understand the difference between licensing statutes that are intended to raise revenue and those which are intended to protect the public, and you should know the significance of this distinction in situations where the party violating the licensing statute is seeking relief under a contract.

8.	You should understand that the concept of unconscionability is a powerful concept because courts may use this concept to invalidate agreements.

Learning Hints

1.	Generally speaking, the courts will not enforce illegal bargains at all, and will leave the parties to such an agreement in the position in which it finds them. This is what is meant by the phrase "hands off illegal agreements" in the textbook. The courts will usually deny even a quasi-contract recovery in the case of an illegal bargain. The reason for this "hands off" policy is to reinforce the public policies making such agreements illegal in the first place, mainly by deterring parties from entering into such agreements.

2.	In some situations, however, a party to an illegal agreement is given some relief when this can be done without seriously undermining the public policies making the agreement illegal. In other situations, parties are felt to be deserving of relief despite these public policies.

3.	It is not a simple matter to determine public policy, because this concept reflects current social, economic, and political realities. For example, some courts have invalidated "surrogate motherhood" contracts on the theory that such contracts violate general public policy, and also violate public policy that underlies adoption statutes.

4.	In addition to being illegal, exculpatory clauses can often be attacked on the grounds that they were not the product of voluntary consent, or that they are unconscionable.

5.	The materials you have already studied concerning duress, undue influence, and capacity are relevant to the general issue of shockingly unequal bargains.

6.	Today most unconscionability problems arise in the context of contracts for the sale of goods so are usually treated under the Uniform Commercial Code. However, unconscionability also exists as a common law concept and is often applied in the context of contracts that do not involve the sale of goods.

7.	Unconscionability is a concept that cannot be defined very specifically. Courts give this concept content by injecting their notions of fairness and sound public policy into the decisions in which unconscionability is an issue. The courts often distinguish between substantive unconscionability, which involves unfairness in the terms of the contract itself, and procedural unconscionability, which involves the way in which the agreement was reached, including things like terms in fine print, contract language which is not understandable by the ordinary person, high-pressure sales tactics, and one party's ignorance, limited education, or lack of fluency in the language. Some courts hold that both procedural and substantive unconscionability must be present for a contract to be illegal on the grounds of unconscionability.

8. "Covenants not to compete" are agreements in restraint of trade. In other words, a party to an employment contract may agree that he/she will not compete with the other party in the event the employment relationship is terminated. Such agreements are enforceable only if reasonable both to geographic location and to time.

True-False

In the blank provided, put "**T**" if the statement is True or "**F**" if the statement is False.

_____ 1. Illegal contracts are generally unenforceable.

_____ 2. A person who makes a bad deal with a car dealer for the purchase of a new car could probably argue that the contract is unconscionable.

_____ 3. An agreement in violation of a revenue-raising licensing statute is almost always unenforceable.

_____ 4. June forgets to renew her city license for her business. Until she renews her license, all sales made by June's business are illegal.

_____ 5. Exculpatory clauses that seek to avoid liability for willful misconduct are unenforceable.

_____ 6. When a contract is illegal, courts usually will not allow even a quasi-contractual recovery.

_____ 7. In some cases, a party who rescinds a contract before any illegal act has been performed will be allowed to recover the consideration he has given to the other party pursuant to the contract.

_____ 8. Employee agreements not to compete are usually judged by a stricter standard than agreements for the sale of a business.

_____ 9. The legal parts of a divisible contract are enforceable.

_____ 10. Despite the "hands off" rule, in cases where a person whom a statute seeks to protect enters into an agreement in violation of the statute, the protected person is permitted to enforce the agreement.

Multiple Choice

Circle the best answer.

1. Which of the following situations is not an illegal contract?
   a. An agreement between Toni and Al for Al to rough up one of Toni's skating competitors.
   b. An agreement between Friendly Finance and Bill, a collector, for Bill to run a past due debtor of Friendly's off the road in order to repossess a car.
   c. Friendly Finance charges Sue 38% interest on an unsecured loan. The maximum interest rate in that state is 36%.
   d. Tina buys property insurance on her new car.

2. A standardized form contract where the parties lack equal bargaining power is called:
   a. An adhesion contract.
   b. Unconscionable per se.
   c. A licensing statute.
   d. A Restatement contract.

3. The concept of "unconscionability":
   a. Only applies in contracts for the sale of goods under the UCC.
   b. Only applies in contracts under common law.
   c. Looks to factors like unequal bargaining power and the party with superior bargaining power imposing unfair terms on the other party.
   d. Is clearly defined by the UCC.

4. Which of the following situations would most likely be enforceable?
   a. All businesses in Genoa City are required by city ordinance to pay an annual fee and obtain a license. Hallie buys some goods at Handy Hardware. Handy forgot to renew its license.
   b. April buys a life insurance policy from Primer Co. Pete, the agent who sells April her policy is not actually licensed to sell insurance.
   c. Doug hires Cathy to represent him in a large civil lawsuit. Cathy has never passed the bar exam.
   d. Iowa requires plumbers to be professionally licensed. Steve contracts to provide plumbing services to Howard. Steve has never obtained a plumbing license.

5. Which of the following would the courts most likely not consider to be illegal?
   a. An unfair contract between Carl Consumer and Big Corporation.
   b. Big Corp., in Denver hires Debbie, an attorney. The employment contract states that if Debbie leaves Big, she cannot practice as an attorney for a year within 1,000 miles of Denver.
   c. Kramer moves his grocery store to a new, bigger building. Kramer sells his old building to Hamilton. The contract states that Hamilton or any other owner of the building cannot open a grocery store there for five years.
   d. Hair Dye Co. sells hair dye to retail stores and beauty salons. The labels on the containers of hair dye state that if anyone is injured by the product, the damages will be a refund of the purchase price of the hair dye. Sally is severely burned on her scalp by a Hair Dye product.

6. A fiduciary:
   a. Is a person in a position of trust or confidence.
   b. Is a person who entered into an illegal agreement.
   c. Is an employee who signed a covenant not to compete.
   d. Is a person who is entitled to enforce an illegal contract.

7. Which of the following is not true?
   a. A parking garage states on its receipts that it is not liable for its own negligence. The garage will not be liable for damages to customers' cars resulting from negligence by the garage.
   b. Commodity transactions are an example of legal speculative bargains.
   c. Blue Laws may limit or prohibit the sale of some goods on Sunday.
   d. Abe represents Indian Tribe A as a lobbyist in its efforts to keep its casino open. Indian Tribe B also hires Abe to represent them and to lobby to keep the casino operated by Tribe A closed. The agreement between Tribe B and Abe may be illegal.

8. Which of the following is an enforceable agreement?
   a. A contract with someone who does not have a license as required by a revenue raising statute.
   b. A contract with someone who does not have a license as required by a regulatory statute.
   c. An agreement in violation of a state gambling statute.
   d. An indivisible contract that contains an illegal clause.

9. Cleaver decides to move his successful clothing store in Mayfield to a newer, bigger building. Cleaver does not want the buyer of the building to operate a clothing store there. Jim Bob wants to purchase the Cleaver building and open a strip club that serves meals and liquor. Which of the following is true?

   a. Cleaver's agreement not to compete is illegal because it is in restraint of trade.

   b. Cleaver's agreement not to compete would also apply to a strip club.

   c. City ordinance may prevent the sale of the building to someone intending to open a strip club because such a sale may be opposed to public policy.

   d. Jim Bob will not be able to open the club because regulatory statutes would require him to have a professional license to own such a club.

10. Rona opens a bank account with Windy City Bank. The fine print in the contract stipulates large monthly service fees, and large fees for overdrafts and stop payment orders. The bank did not disclose this information to Rona at the time she opened her account. Which of the following is most accurate?

    a. The court may find this contract to be unconscionable.

    b. The court may look unfavorably upon the bank since this appears to be a contract of adhesion.

    c. Federal laws may require the bank to disclose important contract terms to customers.

    d. All of the above.

Short Essay

1. Many states that at one time enforced Blue Laws have in recent years changed their laws to allow sales on Sunday, including the sale of liquor. Discuss the reasoning for Blue Laws and the reasoning for rescinding these laws.

2. Mary Ann is interested in buying stocks from her broker, Gilligan. Are there regulatory statutes requiring investment brokers to be licensed? Why?

3. Are restrictive covenants in restraint of trade ever enforceable? If so, under what circumstances?

4.   Are exculpatory clauses in contracts enforceable?

5.   Vanna has been a sports anchor at WWOW in Boston for 10 years. Vanna is popular with the viewers. Her contract with WWOW has a non-compete clause. If she leaves the station, she cannot take a job with another station within 50 miles for one year. Station WHEW in Boston makes Vanna an offer she cannot refuse, so she leaves WWOW in May when her contract terminates. Is the restrictive clause in Vanna's contract with WWOW enforceable?

6.   There is a growing scandal in the financial community that is generally called "predatory lending." This basically involves taking advantage of poorer people's economic position by offering them disguised loans at usurious rates through related transactions. One such practice is found in the "rent-to-own" industry. After the rental period is over, the sale of the goods is made at top rates. Is this possibly usurious?

7.   Herman is offered a job with Big Shot law firm in New York. The contract is fair and reasonable except for a restrictive clause that would forbid Herman from practicing law anywhere in the State of New York for 10 years if he would ever leave Big Shot. How might the courts view this contract?

CHAPTER 15
THE FORM AND MEANING OF CONTRACTS

Outline

I. Statutes of Frauds: All states have statutes requiring certain kinds of contracts to be evidenced by a writing.

    A. Contracts which fall "under the Statute of Frauds" include these: executors of estates to be personally liable, collateral contracts, transfers of interest in real property, and contracts incapable of being performed within one year.

    B. If a contract falls under the Statute of Frauds, the effect is to make oral contracts <u>unenforceable</u>, not void or voidable.

    C. In some states, the doctrine of <u>promissory estoppel</u> will permit a plaintiff to recover damages even though oral contract would otherwise be unenforceable.

II. Particular Contracts Covered by the Statute of Frauds

    A. Contracts to Answer for the Debt of Another (Collateral contracts)

    Exception: The "leading object" doctrine is an exception to this rule. Under this doctrine, if a person promising to secure the debt of another, is motivated by personal benefit, the oral promise is enforceable.

    Example: <u>Nakamura v. Fujii</u>: A promise to pay Nakamura later, upon demand, if he paid the Fujii's daughters' tuition was not a guarantee to pay the debt of another, but rather an independent contract between Nakamura and Fujii. Therefore, it is enforceable as an oral contract.

    B. Contracts transferring interest in land

    Exception: "Part performance" of a contract for sale of land. This requires that the buyer has taken some affirmative act of ownership toward the property and paid part of the purchase price.

    C. Bilateral Contracts that cannot be performed within one year. Courts narrowly construe this test. Thus, if there is any way the oral agreement could be performed within one year, it is not unenforceable under this test.

    Example: <u>Popajz v. Peregrine Corp.</u>: Reliance solely on an oral promise of continued employment is not sufficient to avoid the statute of frauds.

    D. Judicial Admission

    Example: <u>Wehry v. Daniels</u>: The court finds that an exception to the statute of frauds exists in the sale of a racing helmet when the purchaser of the helmet admits to the existence of the contract.

III. What kind of writing is required?

    A. Generally, most states required only a memorandum of the agreement, signed by the party to be charged.

    Example: <u>Connor v. Lavaca Hospital Dist.</u>: A promise that is not enforceable within a year is within the statute of frauds.

IV. The Code's Statute of Frauds Provision: Adds the sale of goods for more than $500 to the list of contract types covered by the Statute of Frauds.

V.   Interpreting Contracts:

   A.   Rules of construction: Courts try to determine the "principal objective" of the parties.

   Example: <u>Evergreen Nat'l. Indemnity Co. v. Tan It All, Inc.</u>: The court found that an insurance term clearly and specifically covered equipment loss for a 100 square foot area outside of Suite C-5 and refused to expand coverage beyond that area.

   B.   Parol Evidence Rule: If a written contract is the "final and complete expression of agreement" between the parties, evidence of additional or different terms is not admissible.

      1.   Exceptions arise; for example, if the parties lacked consent or the contract is ambiguous or incomplete, the rule does not apply.

   Example: <u>Burke v. Manfroni</u>: The court found that a written lease agreement that covers all terms cannot be varied by oral agreement.

   Example: <u>MCC-Marble Ceramic Center v. Ceramica Nuova D'Agostino, S.P.A.</u>: A court can consider parol evidence in a contract dispute governed by the U. N. Convention for the International Sale of Goods.

Learning Objectives

1.   You should understand that many oral contracts are enforceable. Only those contracts prohibited by the statute of frauds are unenforceable.

2.   You should understand the difference between an unenforceable and a void or voidable contract. An oral contract that is fully executed (fully performed) cannot be rescinded because it was not in writing.

3.   You should understand the "parol evidence rule," which prohibits introduction of evidence that contradicts the terms of a written agreement.

4.   You must know the types of contracts that are required by the statute of frauds to be evidenced by a writing.

5.   You must know the legal status of a contract that falls within the requirements of the statute of frauds but fails to comply with those requirements.

6.   You should be aware of the role that promissory estoppel sometimes plays in making enforceable oral contracts which would otherwise be unenforceable under the statute of frauds.

7.   You should know the difference between an original contract and a collateral or guaranty contract, and the practical significance of this distinction under the statute of frauds.

8.   You should know when part performance of an oral contract for the sale of an interest in land exists, and the effect this has under the statute of frauds.

9.   You should know the rules governing what matters must be included in the written memorandum required by the statute of frauds.

10.   You should know the general rules the courts use in interpreting written contracts.

11.   You should have an understanding of The Electronic Signatures in Global and National Commerce Act and the Uniform Electronic Transactions Act.

Learning Hints

1.   The statute of frauds lists several different kinds of contracts that must be in writing to be enforceable. These include contracts in contemplation of <u>marriage</u>, contracts that cannot be performed within one <u>year</u>, contracts for the sale of <u>land</u>, contracts by <u>executors</u>, <u>guarantor</u>/ee (collateral) contracts, and, under the UCC, contracts for the <u>sale</u> of goods for $500 or more. A good way to remember these categories is to remember "MYLEGS."

2.   Not all oral contracts are unenforceable. In fact most oral contracts are completely enforceable. Only those required to be in writing by the statute of frauds must be in writing to be enforceable.

3. The "writing" required by the Statute of Frauds is something less than a formally written contract signed by all parties. Generally, to satisfy the statute of frauds, there must be a written memorandum, containing all material terms of the agreement, signed by the party to be charged (that is, the party relying on the statute of frauds as a defense).

4. Three features of seventeenth century English law caused the original statute of frauds to be enacted: oral contracts were enforceable, the parties to the contract could not testify at trial, and there were few legal devices for correcting unfair jury verdicts. Therefore, it often occurred that parties "proved" the existence of an oral contract through paid, perjured testimony. As a result, Parliament required those contracts in which the potential for fraud was great, or the consequences of fraud were especially serious, to be evidenced by a writing to be enforceable.

5. An oral contract that would be considered unenforceable under the statute of frauds is still valid if it has already been performed or if neither party objects to its enforcement.

6. Technically, one of the types of contracts covered by the statute of frauds—a contract in which an executor or administrator promises to be personally responsible for the decedent's debts—is also a collateral or guaranty contract.

7. Be sure you notice that the situations in which part performance of an oral contract for the sale of land takes the contract outside the statute of frauds are very similar to the situations in which promissory estoppel takes a contract outside the statute of frauds.

8. Remember that the statute of frauds rule covering contracts that cannot be performed within one year after their formation applies only to executory bilateral contracts. This means that if the contract has been completely executed (performed), the statute does not apply to it.

9. The "party to be bound" or the "party to be charged" whose signature must appear on the writing is the party who is trying to use the statute to escape the contract. This is typically a party who refuses to perform, who is sued as a result, and who argues that the contract is unenforceable under the statute of frauds. The other party's signature need not appear in order for the reluctant party to be bound.

10. As the textbook makes clear, the "exceptions" to the parol evidence rule are not really exceptions at all, because they all involve situations in which a party is not trying to contradict the terms of the writing, but is trying to challenge the underlying validity or explain the meaning of the writing.

True-False

In the blank provided, put "**T**" if the statement is True or "**F**" if the statement is False.

_____ 1. Contracts that cannot be performed within one year must be in writing to be enforceable.

_____ 2. Carol co-signs on a note for Ben at First State Bank. The agreement must be in writing in order to be enforceable.

_____ 3. The "part performance" exception arises in cases where a person seeks to enforce an oral promise for the sale of land.

_____ 4. A party is allowed to introduce oral testimony to show that she entered into the contract represented by the writing based on fraud.

_____ 5. If a person orally misrepresents the condition of real property, that misrepresentation will be inadmissible in court under the parol evidence rule.

_____ 6. An oral contract that has been fully performed by both parties need not be evidenced by a writing.

_____ 7. Promissory estoppel will sometimes make enforceable an oral promise that would otherwise be unenforceable because of the statute of frauds.

_____ 8. Courts will interpret a contract based on the principal objective of the parties.

_____ 9. The UCC's requirement for a writing involving the sale of goods for $500 or more also requires that the quantity of goods be stated in the writing and that the writing be signed by the party to be charged.

_____ 10. The statute of frauds mandates that the entire contract be in writing.

Multiple Choice

Circle the best answer.

1. The statute of frauds requires, at a minimum:

   a. A writing signed by both parties.

   b. An unsigned memorandum.

   c. A memorandum signed by the "party to be charged."

   d. A formal written contract that fully integrates all the terms of the agreement.

2. Which of the following agreements does not require a writing to be enforceable?

   a. Todd agrees to sell his house to Callie.

   b. Edna sells $450 of widgets to Loren.

   c. Fran agrees to pay Bank if Pete does not pay his loan with them.

   d. Wally signs a three-year contract to play baseball for the New York Yankees.

3. The part performance exception in contracts for the sale of land requires that the person seeking to enforce an oral contract establish:

   a. Payment of purchase price.

   b. Payment of part of the purchase price.

   c. Some action indicating ownership of the property.

   d. Both payment of some consideration and some action indicated ownership of the property.

4. An oral employment contract to hire a person "for life:"

   a. Is enforceable under the statute of frauds.

   b. Is unenforceable because of the part performance exception.

   c. Is unenforceable under the main purpose exception.

   d. Is unenforceable because it cannot be performed within one year.

5. Which of the following situations would defeat the statute of frauds requirement of a writing for a sale of goods of $500 or more?

   a. Wilt, a very large man, orally agrees to purchase from Obers Clothing five custom-made suits for $4,500. Obers makes a substantial start on the suits and then learns that Wilt wants to back out of the contract.

   b. Hank orally agrees to sell 1,000 widgets at $3 per widget to Patty. Hank delivers the widgets to Patty and she accepts them.

   c. Tom orally agrees to buy 500 widgets at $3 per widget from Irma. Tom pays Irma $1,500.

   d. All of the above.

6. Which of the following is not an exception to the parol evidence rule?

   a. Bernie wants to introduce oral terms consistent with the written agreement he has with Sara to fill in the gaps that exist in the written contract.

   b. Carla claims she and Ben orally agreed to some terms before they signed their written contract.

   c. Vera wants to introduce oral testimony to show when her contract with Stan was to begin.

   d. Ray wants to introduce oral testimony to help clear up ambiguous terms in his contract with Kendra.

7. Which of the following is not true regarding the statute of frauds?

   a. Bill orally agrees to buy Rita's house. Bill moves into the house and makes some improvements to it. Bill's part performance probably makes the oral agreement enforceable.

   b. Tammy frequently uses her bank's online banking service. Tammy deposits and withdraws money online. She must enter her account at the bank's Web site by providing a password. The password could serve as the necessary signature under the statute of frauds.

   c. The signatures of both parties to a contract are required under the statute of frauds.

   d. A memorandum satisfies the writing requirement of the statute of frauds.

8. Which of the following would require a writing to be enforceable?

   a. Rick, executor of his aunt Joan's estate, promises Irene, one of Joan's creditors, that he will be personally liable for making sure she is paid in full.

   b. Sue co-signs on her son's loan at the bank.

   c. Pat, a supplier for Sally's Signs, signs on a note of Sally's at the bank to insure that Sally stays in business.

   d. Vern agrees to a one semester contract to teach at State U.

9. Which of the following statements is not true?

   a. Ambiguities in an insurance contract will be resolved against the insurance company that drafted the contract.

   b. A party to a contract cannot introduce proof of an oral agreement that was made subsequent to the written contract.

   c. Written terms control printed terms in the event of a conflict in a contract.

   d. Contracts made in certain professions may contain words with particular meaning in that profession.

10. If a contract does not comply with the statute of frauds, it is:

    a. void.

    b. fully enforceable by either party.

    c. voidable.

    d. unenforceable.

Short Essay

1. Barb agrees to sell widgets at $3 per widget to Tina and a written contract is executed. The contract specifically mentions the quantity of widgets, the delivery date, and other relevant information. However, price is not mentioned in the contract. Can Barb give oral testimony to show that the parties intended for the price to be $3 per widget?

2. Bob orally agrees to sell Kay 500 widgets at $3 per widget. Could Kay argue that the contract is unenforceable?

3. In the case above, suppose Bob ships the widgets and Kay accepts them. Can Kay later argue that the contract is unenforceable because it is not in writing?

4. In the case above, suppose Bob delivers 200 widgets and Kay pays for them. Can Kay later argue that the contract is unenforceable because it is not in writing?

5. The Nolans have agreed to purchase vinyl siding from ABC Siding for $15,000. ABC prepares a form contract that describes the main points of the contract, including the price of the siding, all the work that will be done by ABC, and the time for performance. The Nolans sign the contract. Does this contract satisfy the statute of frauds? Is there anything else that the Nolans may want to ask for in this case?

6. Discuss the part performance exception in contracts for the sale of land and requirements of the person seeking to enforce an oral contract. What must that person establish?

CHAPTER 16
THIRD PARTIES' CONTRACT RIGHTS

Outline

I. Assignment and delegation in general

    A. A contract consists of rights and duties. A transfer of rights is called an <u>assignment</u>; a transfer of duties is <u>delegation</u>.

    B. Most, but not all, contracts are assignable. If the assignment would materially alter the duties of the promisor, the assignment contract is unenforceable.

       Example: <u>Claremont Acquisition Corp. v. General Motors Corp.</u>: A bankruptcy trustee can assign a contract so long as the assignee gives adequate assurance of future performance. This was not the case here, thus this contract's assignment failed.

II. Consequences of assignment

    A. An original promisor may assert defenses against the assignee that he could assert against the assignor (that is, the original contracting party.)

    B. An assignee can assert the original rights of the assignor against the promisor.

    C. Assignor should notify the promisor of the assignment.

    D. Assignors who are paid for making an assignment are held to make certain implied guaranties about the assignment.

III. Consequences of delegation

    A. Like assignment, not all duties are delegable.

       Example: <u>Riegleman v. Krieg</u>: A patient was found to have delegated his duty to pay his law firm.

    B. Generally, an assignment of rights includes a delegation of duty under both the UCC and Restatement.

       Example: <u>Rosenberg v. Son, Inc.</u>: An assignment of rights and duties is not a novation and the original party to the contract remains liable for its breach along with the assignees.

IV. Third-Party Beneficiary Contracts

    A. There are two types of third-party beneficiaries under a contract: Intended and Incidental.

       1. An Intended beneficiary is either a <u>donee</u> or <u>creditor</u> beneficiary, and acquires rights to enforce the original contract depending on which category of beneficiary he/she is.

          Example: <u>Caba v. Barker</u>: Residual beneficiaries of a will are held to be donee beneficiaries of the contract between the testator and her attorney to make the will invulnerable to contest.

       2. An Incidental beneficiary acquires no contract rights.

          Example: <u>Mortise v. United States</u>: After being accidentally assaulted during a National Guard field training exercise, the Mortises tried to sue the Federal Government. They could not so they tried to make themselves beneficiaries of an insurance agreement between the Federal government and the county government. The court ruled that unintended beneficiaries could not benefit from the insurance agreement.

    B. A Donee Beneficiary is a beneficiary of a contract where the promisee's primary purpose was to make a gift to the third party. A donee beneficiary can enforce the contract against the original promisor, but not promisee.

Example: <u>Cherry v. Crow</u>: The estate of a prisoner who died under the care of a prison hospital sued for breach of contract; and, although a third party beneficiary does not ordinarily benefit, in this case the third party donee beneficiary was an intended beneficiary and can sue.

C. Creditor Beneficiaries: If the promisor's performance will satisfy a legal duty that the promisee owes a third party, the third party is a creditor beneficiary and may enforce the contract against both the promisee and promisor.

Learning Objectives

1. You should be able to compare contract rights and duties with assignment and delegation of rights and duties.

2. You should understand the difference between contract rights and duties which are assignable or delegable and those which are not.

3. You should understand the difference between creditor and donee beneficiaries, and incidental beneficiaries.

4. You should understand who the assignor, assignee, and promisor are in the context of an assignment, and what the rights and duties of each are after the assignment occurs.

5. You should understand exactly what a delegation of duties involves and what the rights and duties of the parties are after the delegation occurs.

6. You should know why the assignee should give notice of the assignment to the promisor.

7. You should know what implied warranties an assignor who is paid for the assignment to the assignee gives.

Learning Hints

1. In every bilateral contract situation there is a promisor and promisee, and each party has corresponding rights and duties. Thus either party (or both) may generally assign rights and transfer duties to a third party, who then acquires certain rights and duties under the contract.

2. A delegate of a duty under a contract must consent to that delegation and assume the duty under the contract in order to be obligated to the promisee.

3. An assignment of rights generally includes a delegation of duty under the UCC and the Restatement.

4. Public policy favors assignment, and anti-assignment clauses are strictly construed and may be unenforceable in some cases for public policy reasons.

5. A third-party beneficiary will only acquire contract rights if he/she is an intended beneficiary. An example of an intended beneficiary is the beneficiary under an insurance contract.

6. Remember that an assignment does not require formalities, a writing, or consideration to be valid.

7. Assignments are not permitted in situations where the assignment would materially change the promisor's duty or the promisor's risk. This means that an assignment of an insurance contract by the party who is both the insured and the beneficiary to another who becomes both insured and beneficiary would be invalid.

8. An example of a situation in which a delegation of duties would be invalid because it is a delegation of duties which depend on personal skill, character, or judgment would be a situation in which B, who is an artist, assigns his contract to paint A's portrait to C, who is not an artist.

9. Remember that the assignee must give notice of the assignment to the promisor or the promisor is not bound to render performance to the assignee. This means that if the promisor renders performance to the assignor because he has not been notified of the assignment, the promisor is discharged and the assignee would be forced to sue the assignor to obtain the assigned benefit.

10. If a duty is properly delegated but the assignee fails to render performance to the promisor, the assignor is still liable to the promisor, and will therefore be legally required to render performance himself. Then the assignor would be forced to sue the assignee to obtain reimbursement for his performance of the delegated duties.

True-False

In the blank provided, put "**T**" if the statement is True or "**F**" if the statement is False.

_____ 1. Delegation of contract duties generally extinguishes the contract obligations of the delegating party.

_____ 2. Assignment of rights generally includes delegation of duty.

_____ 3. A transfer of rights under a contract is called a delegation.

_____ 4. An assignment of rights for consideration generally includes an implied warranty that the claim is valid.

_____ 5. An incidental beneficiary generally does not acquire contract rights.

_____ 6. Employment contracts are generally nonassignable.

_____ 7. Life insurance contracts are a form of creditor beneficiary contracts.

_____ 8. If the promisor was a minor at the time the contract was made and it is later assigned, he will have the same defense of lack of capacity against the assignee as he would have had against the assignor.

_____ 9. A new, separate agreement that releases the promisor and substitutes another party to assume the promisor's duties is called a novation.

_____ 10. Phil has an agreement to mow Doris's lawn each week for $25. Phil asks Colby to mow Doris's lawn this week. If Colby does a poor job of mowing the lawn, Phil is still liable to Doris.

Multiple Choice

Circle the best answer.

1. Which of the following third parties cannot enforce the original contract?
   a. Donee beneficiary.
   b. Assignee.
   c. Creditor beneficiary.
   d. Incidental beneficiary.

2. City negotiates with Developer to build a really nice shopping area. Liz owns land a short distance from the proposed development. Which of the following statements is true concerning Liz?
   a. Liz is an incidental beneficiary and she has no rights under the proposed contract.
   b. Liz is a creditor beneficiary and she has rights in the event that the proposed contract falls through.
   c. Liz is a donee beneficiary and she has rights in the event that the proposed contract falls through.
   d. It is likely that City and Developer intended to benefit Liz with the development.

3. Generally, an assignor for value does not impliedly warrant:
   a. That the obligor has the capacity to contract.
   b. That the assignor has not assigned the claim to any one else.
   c. That the claim is valid.
   d. That the obligor has the money to pay the claim.

4. A Novation is:

   a. An agreement between two promisees to shift the risk of the contract to a third party.

   b. An agreement between the promisor and promisee in which the promissee agrees not to default.

   c. An agreement between the promisor and promisee to release the promisor from liability after the assignment.

   d. An agreement between the promisee and another party that needs to be enforced.

5. Crank borrows money from 1st Bank to buy a home and he gives 1st Bank a mortgage on the house. 1st Bank sells the mortgage to United Bank. Which of the following is not true?

   a. 1st Bank gives an implied guarantee to United Bank that the mortgage contract is legal.

   b. United Bank should give Crank notice of the assignment.

   c. 1st Bank cannot assign Crank's contract to United Bank because such an assignment is contrary to public policy.

   d. 1st Bank gives an implied guarantee to United Bank that it has good title to the rights assigned to United Bank.

6. Farmer has a contract to supply Barb's IGA grocery story with all of the Red Delicious apples it needs. Barb's IGA assigns its contract rights to Albertson's, a much larger grocery store. Which of the following statements is true?

   a. Farmer's duties will be materially altered under this assignment.

   b. Barb's IGA cannot assign its contract rights in a requirements contract to Albertson's.

   c. With an assignment of its rights to receive the apples, it is assumed that Barb's IGA would also delegate its duty to pay Farmer to Albertson's as well.

   d. All of the above.

7. Stan has a contract to supply widgets to Brad for one year. Stan has difficulty coming up with the necessary widgets, so he asks Brad if Rob can substitute for him and supply widgets to Brad. Brad and Rob agree and execute a new contract for the sale of widgets. This is an example of:

   a. An assignment.

   b. A novation.

   c. A delegation of duties.

   d. A third-party beneficiary.

8. Jackson buys furniture from Iowa Furniture Mart on credit. Jackson sells the furniture to Smith and Smith agrees to complete the payments to Iowa Furniture Mart. Iowa Furniture Mart is:

   a. A creditor beneficiary.

   b. A donee beneficiary.

   c. An incidental beneficiary.

   d. An assignor.

9. Grant buys a life insurance policy for $100,000 and names his wife, Gail, as beneficiary. Grant dies and the insurance company pays Gail the $100,000 proceeds of the policy. Gail is:

   a. An incidental beneficiary.

   b. A creditor beneficiary.

   c. A donee beneficiary.

   d. An assignor.

10. Which of the following statements is not true?
    a. Contracts can expressly forbid assignments.
    b. Contracts involving personal skill, such as an artist contracting to do a painting, are generally nonassignable.
    c. Many states may limit or outlaw wage garnishments.
    d. Contracts not to compete with a buyer of a business are generally nonassignable with the sale of the business.

Short Essay

1. Mike was employed as a store clerk for a local toy store. The store was sold to new owners, and Mike now argues that sale of the store terminated his employment contract because the contract was not assignable. Is this employment contract assignable? Why or why not?

2. Dealer lied about the quality of a car to Simpson to induce Simpson to buy the car. Simpson bought the car and finances it through the dealer. Dealer sold the note to Bank. Can Simpson use his defense of fraud (lying about the car) that he has against the dealer against Bank?

3. When Dealer sells the note to Bank in the above case, what guarantees does the Dealer make to Bank?

4. Art contracts with Johnson to do home repairs for Johnson. Art is really busy, so he assigns the job to Ralph. Discuss this situation.

5. Edy hears that the city and an Indian tribe are negotiating to build a huge casino on a certain tract of land. Edy immediately buys some land nearby so that she can put an ice cream store next to the casino. Negotiations between the tribe and the city break down and the project is abandoned. Can Edy sue the city?

6. Archie buys a life insurance policy on his life and names his wife, Edith, as beneficiary. Archie dies. The life insurance company refused to pay Edith on the policy because they claim Archie lied about his age when he applied for the policy. Can Edith sue the life insurance company?

7. Fast Eddie is a con artist. One of his favorite scams is to take a legitimate IOU note and resell it multiple times to various buyers. Last Tuesday, he sold the $10,000 note discounted to $9,000 to 10 different buyers—one per hour starting at 10 AM and ending at 7 PM. He took all the money and now is working on his tanning program on the beaches in Rio. Assuming we cannot locate Freddy, who can collect on the note?

CHAPTER 17
PERFORMANCE AND REMEDIES

Outline

I. Duty to Perform under a Contract
    A. May be qualified by a condition
        1. Types of conditions include precedent, subsequent, and concurrent
    B. Standards of Performance
        1. Substantial performance: Standard that falls short of complete performance but does not constitute material breach

            Example: Johnson v. Schmitz: A graduate student is allowed to sue the University for breaching its promise to safeguard students from academic misconduct, to investigate and deal with charges of academic misconduct, and to address charges of academic misconduct in accordance with its own procedures.

            Example: M.J. Oldenstedt Plumbing Co., Inc. v. K-Mart Corp.: By agreeing to the project's timetable and falling substantially behind schedule twice, Oldenstedt Plumbing did not substantially perform the contract.
        2. Anticipatory repudiation occurs when a promisor, prior to time for performance, indicates an intent not to perform his or her duties under the contract
    C. Special Problems
        1. A "personal satisfaction" clause arises when the promisor agrees to perform to the promisee's personal satisfaction.
        2. "Time is of the essence" creates a "strict performance" standard so that failure to perform as required by the contract results in a material breach.

II. Excuses for Non-Performance
    A. Impossibility (includes "commercial impracticability or commercial frustration.")
    B. Examples include death of promisor, intervening illegality, destruction of subject matter.

III. Discharge
    A. Release of contractual obligations occurs through performance, agreement, waiver, or intentional alteration of the instrument.
    B. All states also discharge obligation through statutes of limitations.

IV. Remedies (Damages or remedies for Breach of Contract.)
    A. Damages must be proved with reasonable certainty.

        Example: Dupont Flooring Svs. v. Discovery Zone, Inc.: The court found that the Discovery Zone could not recover lost profits because it could not prove its loss with certainty.
    B. Kinds of damages recoverable include compensatory, consequential, nominal, liquidated, and punitive.

        Example: Deli v. University of Minnesota: Emotional distress damages cannot be recovered on a contract's breach except in extraordinary cases where a tort accompanies the breach.

        Example: Guillano v. Cleo Inc.: Liquidated damages are a stipulated sum agreed on by the parties at the time they enter into their contract.

C. Plaintiffs have a duty to mitigate (avoid or minimize) damages.

> Example: <u>Manuma v. Blue Hawaii Adventures, Inc.</u>: Dinner cruise entertainer did not fail to mitigate his damages by refusing employer's offer of alternative employment because the alternative work of manual labor or light maintenance was not "substantially similar" to his lost position as an entertainer.

D. Equitable remedies may be ordered when damages at law (money damages) are inadequate. The most common equitable remedies are specific performance and injunction.

> Example: <u>ILan Systems, Inc. v. NetScout Service Level Corp.</u>: Specific performance is allowed when items are unique or not replaceable le as a practical matter. ILan could purchase comparable software on the open market; therefore, ILan is not entitled to specific performance.

Learning Objectives

1. You should understand that performance and remedies are really separate topics.

2. You should understand that performance issues arise in determining whether there has, in fact, been a breach. These issues include the question of whether performance was due (or whether there are conditions to performance), the standard of performance, and excuses for performance.

3. You should note that a court will always award damages at law (money damages) rather than impose equitable remedies (such as an injunction or specific performance) in a breach of contract case, so long as the non-breaching party can be adequately compensated by money damages.

4. You must understand what a condition is, what conditions precedent, subsequent, and concurrent are, and how each type of condition affects the duty to perform under a contract.

5. You must know the difference between complete performance, substantial performance, and material breach, and the effects of each on the rights and duties of the parties to the contract.

6. You should know the rules governing contracts to perform to personal satisfaction.

7. You should know the rules concerning the time for performance.

8. You should know all of the different ways in which the doctrine of impossibility can excuse the duty to perform.

9. You must know all of the different ways in which a party can be discharged from the duty to perform.

10. You must know what compensatory, consequential, nominal, liquidated, and punitive damages are and when each type is available in a contract case.

Learning Hints

1. Performance conditions may be express, implied in fact, or implied by law. An example of a condition implied by law is the condition that performance obligations should occur simultaneously. This means that a person must be ready, willing, and able to tender his performance in order to successfully sue the other party for breach if the other party fails to perform as promised.

2. There are two standards of performance: complete performance and substantial performance. Courts generally adopt a substantial performance standard in contract cases where it is very difficult to perform perfectly. For example, construction contracts generally impose a substantial performance standard on the parties.

3. Just because a court imposes a substantial performance standard does not mean that a party may not sue the other party for breach. However, in the event the breach is non-material, the non-breaching party will still be obligated to perform (for example, to pay the contract price for construction), but he may be entitled to subtract from that contract price the loss caused by the breach.

4. Keep in mind that conditions precedent and subsequent have the same practical result: both make the duty to perform conditional upon the occurrence of some future event.

5. In contracts to perform to the personal satisfaction of the other party, the standard of performance is a subjective one (whether the other party is honestly dissatisfied) when the contract involves matters of personal taste, comfort, or judgment, and objective (whether the other party's dissatisfaction is reasonable) when the contract involves matters of mechanical fitness, utility, or marketability. An example of a contract involving matters of personal taste, comfort, or judgment would be a contract for the painting of a portrait, and an example of a contract involving matters of mechanical fitness, utility, or marketability would be a contract for the installation of a furnace.

6. In order for impossibility to excuse the duty to perform, the contract must be for a personal service and the promisor must die or fall victim to an incapacitating illness. If the promisor's duty to perform could be carried out by someone else, performance will not be excused.

7. If the contract is executory, compensatory damages can be computed by subtracting the plaintiff's cost of performance from the value of the promised performance. If A is to sell B a bike for $100, B's recovery (if any) when A breaches would be the reasonable value of the promised bike minus $100. If the contract is executed and the performance is defective, compensatory damages are computed by subtracting the value of the defective performance from the value of the promised performance. In the above example, if A sells B a defective bike, B could recover the reasonable value of the bike as promised minus the actual value of the defective bike he received.

8. It is hard to give a general definition of consequential damages, but examples of consequential damages are easy to name. They include personal injury, damage to property that is not the subject of the contract, lost profits, and lost business good will.

9. The general test of whether an equitable remedy is appropriate is whether there is an adequate legal remedy available to the plaintiff. This usually means that the types of money damages discussed in the textbook are inadequate.

10. Keep two things in mind about liquidated damages provisions: the reasonableness of the stipulated figure is determined from what the parties knew or should have known at the time the contract was entered, not from the plaintiff's actual damages; and once the two tests for the enforcement of a liquidated damages provision are met, the court will enforce the provision even if the plaintiff's actual damages are higher or lower than that figure.

True-False

In the blank provided, put "**T**" if the statement is True or "**F**" if the statement is False.

_____ 1. If the subject matter of a contract is destroyed through no fault of a party, a contracting party may be excused from performance.

_____ 2. A strict (or complete) performance standard violates public policy and therefore is not applied in breach of contract actions.

_____ 3. Mary promises to pay Herb $1,000 if he graduates from college with honors. This is a condition subsequent.

_____ 4. A "Time is of the essence" clause in a breach can lead to material breach if performance is not timely.

_____5.   A condition precedent is a condition that must occur before a party is obligated to perform a contract.

_____6.   A contractor who substantially performs is normally entitled to the contract price less any damages for less than complete performance.

_____7.   Joe tells Siding Co. he will not be able to pay for the vinyl siding that the company had contracted with Joe to install on Joe's home next month. Siding Co. can anticipate Joe's repudiation of the contract and sue him for breach of contract.

_____8.   The object of compensatory contract damages is to put the plaintiff in the position he would have been in had the contract been performed as promised.

_____9.   Jones was to sell a large quantity of oranges to Smith. Several hurricanes have severely damaged the orange crop. Jones may be able to argue commercial impracticability as an excuse for non-performance.

_____10. Punitive damages are normally recoverable in breach of contract lawsuits.

Multiple Choice

Circle the best answer.

1.   Under the doctrine of anticipatory repudiation:

    a.   A contracting party may sue for breach in cases where a party repudiates the contract before performance is due.

    b.   A contracting party may be excused from performance in cases where performance is impossible or impracticable.

    c.   A contracting party may recover his expectation interest for breach of contract, including incidental and consequential damages in some cases.

    d.   A contract party can limit his remedies for breach by agreement.

2.   Which of the following statements is not true regarding liquidated damages?

    a.   An agreed upon amount of damages that is too large may be seen as a penalty and therefore be rejected.

    b.   Liquidated damages are enforced even if the actual amount of damages can easily be determined.

    c.   An amount that is too small may be rejected as being unconscionable.

    d.   The parties agree in the contract what the damages will be if either party breaches.

3.   Which of the following standards of performance is usually applied in an action for breach of a construction contract?

    a.   "Time is of the essence."

    b.   Strict or complete performance standard.

    c.   Substantial performance standard.

    d.   Liquidated damage clause.

4.   Donna breaches her contract to sell widgets to Dan at $5 per widget. As a result, Dan is unable to fill an order for his customer, Bernie. Bernie goes elsewhere to buy widgets. The fact that Donna's breach of contract caused Dan to lose a sale is an example of:

    a.   Consequential damages.

    b.   Punitive damages.

    c.   Compensatory damages.

    d.   Nominal damages.

5. Sam lost a finger in an accident when the blade from his lawnmower flew off. His injuries for pain and suffering and the medical expenses that he incurred as a result of the defective blade are best described as:

    a. Expectation damages.

    b. Liquidated damages.

    c. Incidental damages.

    d. Consequential damages.

6. Carl breaches his contract to sell a rare Babe Ruth autographed baseball to Rod. Carl offers to pay Rod damages. Rod refuses. Which of the following is most accurate?

    a. Carl only owes Rod nominal damages.

    b. Rod may be entitled to specific performance.

    c. Rod is entitled to punitive damages.

    d. Rod is only entitled to damages if he and Carl had a liquidation of damages clause in their contract.

7. Which of the following is not an example of discharge of a party's duty to perform a contract?

    a. The party waives his right to complete performance by accepting slightly defective goods.

    b. Jane cannot sue Terri for breach of a contract that happened 15 years ago.

    c. Paula pays Ted for goods with a bad check.

    d. Frank delivers conforming goods to Tina, who pays Frank in full, in cash.

8. Which of the following is not true?

    a. Crank, a fisherman, contracts with Orange Lobster restaurant to deliver lobsters within 12 hours of the catch. Time is of the essence.

    b. Johnson informs Smith that she will not be able to deliver the contracted goods next week as called for in the contract. Smith can anticipate Johnson's breach and buy the goods from someone else.

    c. A person may reject a portrait done by an artist based on the fact that the artist does not perform to the personal satisfaction of the subject.

    d. Substantial performance is considered to be complete performance.

9. Siding Co. contracts to install $15,000 of vinyl siding on Fern's house. Fern signs the contract. Work is to begin in three weeks. The job will take three weeks for Siding Co. to complete. The contract calls for full payment when the job is completed. Which of the following statements is true?

    a. This is an example of concurrent conditions.

    b. This is an example of express conditions.

    c. This is an example of condition subsequent.

    d. Both a and b.

10. Which of the following is not true?

    a. The court could grant equitable relief if legal remedies are not adequate.

    b. An injured party has a duty to mitigate damages.

    c. Specific performance is generally available in breach of contract suits involving the sale of new furniture.

    d. Nominal damages may be awarded where there is a breach of contract, but which caused no actual damages.

Short Essay

1. Irene agrees to sell her television to Judy. If nothing is said about when performance will take place, what will the law infer?

2. Discuss equitable remedies and the types of equitable remedies available to the courts.

3. A contracted to install irrigation ditches on Y's farm. Shortly after A and Y entered the contract, a flash flood devastated Y's land, making A's job much more difficult and expensive, though not impossible. What is the traditional attitude of the common law to A's claim that he should be excused from performance due to impossibility? What relatively new doctrine might A use to get himself excused from performance?

4. Oscar owns a manufacturing company that makes widgets. Oscar has a contract with Dolan to sell widgets for the next year at $3 per widget. Without warning, the employees at Oscar's plant go on strike. An unsuccessful attempt is made to hire replacement workers. What could Oscar argue as an excuse for non-performance?

5. Paige offers to sell her car to Michelle for $5,000. Michelle agrees to pick up the car on December 10, but a week before the delivery date, Michelle tells Paige that she is not going to buy the car after all. What could Paige do at this point? If Paige sells her car to Donny for $5,500, can she still sue Michelle for breach of contract?

6. ABC Shippers agreed to ship a load of grain from New York to Iran by way of the Suez Canal. The shipping price was $40,000. Because of conflicts in the area, the canal was closed, and ABC will have to go around Africa to deliver the grain at a cost of $80,000. The shipper now seeks enforcement of the contract per the original terms, and ABC claims a defense of commercial impracticality and/or commercial frustration. Who wins?

7. Ace Accounting is hired by Handyman Construction Co. to provide accounting and tax services. Handyman's books from its first two years of existence are a mess. Ace is hired not only to do current accounting work, but to clean up the past records for Handyman. Ace does its best to bring the books up to date and to provide updated financial statements. However, it is clear that some of the necessary information is incomplete or missing. Is Ace entitled to its full fee despite the fact that the job is probably not fully complete? Why?

CHAPTER 18
FORMATION AND TERMS OF SALES CONTRACTS

Outline

I. Application of the Uniform Commercial Code

    A. Article 2 applies to all contracts <u>for the sale of goods</u>.

    B. Some contracts are "mixed" (include both sale of goods and provision of services. Article 2A applies here). In this case, the test is "which predominates."

    Example: <u>Heart of Texas Dodge, Inc. v. Star Coach L.L.C.</u>: The customization of a truck was found to be a sale of services rather than a sale of goods because the predominant feature was the furnishing of services and labor.

    C. A lease of goods does not constitute ownership, but in most states, Article 2 and Article 9 of the UCC are applied by analogy.

    D. UCC Article 2 differs from traditional contract law because it is more <u>flexible</u> and based on concepts of <u>reasonableness</u> and <u>good faith</u>.

        1. Some UCC sections apply a different standard to contracts between merchants.

II. Formation of sales contracts.

    A. Parties may enter into a contract under the UCC by their behavior or conduct.

    B. The UCC contains "gap filler" provisions to fill in terms of contracts where the parties omitted such terms or stated them indefinitely. (quantity terms, delivery terms and time terms)

III. The Code also contains some specific rules governing title of goods.

    A. For example, title passes when the seller has completed delivery. If delivery is made without moving the goods, title passes at the time and place of contracting.

    Example: <u>Butler v. Beer Across America</u>: Under the UCC, a sale consists in the passing of title from seller to buyer. Title to goods passes at the time and place of shipment when the contract does not require the seller to make delivery at the destination.

    Example: <u>Sutton v. Snider</u>: The owner of a motorcycle who consigned it to a dealer was unable to recover the motorcycle from a buyer who bought the motorcycle from the dealer in the ordinary course of business.

    B. Title and third parties.

        1. A seller who has voidable title can pass good title to a good faith purchaser for value.

        Example: <u>Alsafi Oriental Rugs v. American Loan Co.</u>: Where person obtained goods through a consignment, that person had voidable title and was empowered to pass title to oriental rugs to third party.

        2. A buyer in the ordinary course of business takes goods free of any security interest in the goods that their seller may have given a third party.

    C. Risk of loss: The Code rejects the rule that risk of loss is based on title, and adopts specific rules governing risk of loss.

        1. Certain kinds of contracts are shipment contracts; under shipment contracts, risk passes to the buyer when goods are delivered to the carrier.

        2. Destination contracts require the seller to guarantee delivery to a specific destination; seller bears the risk of loss until delivery to that destination.

        3. If goods are to be delivered without being moved, risk passes to the buyer when buyer has power to take possession of the goods.

Example: <u>Harmon v. Dunn</u>: The death of a horse during the process of its sale raised the question of whether the seller or buyer bore the risk of loss when the horse died. Risk passed when the bailee recognized the buyer's regret to possess the horse.

D. Under the UCC, risk of loss and title may differ in "Sales on Trial.

   1. In a Sale or Return contract, title and risk of loss rest with the buyer.

   2. In a Sale on Approval, risk of loss and title remain with the seller.

   3. In a sale on consignment, consignor has title to and risk of loss of goods

     Example: <u>In Re Corvette Collection of Boston, Inc.</u>: Goods delivered to a dealer on consignment are subject to the consignee's creditors unless the consignor complies with the requirements set forth in Article 9, posts a sign informing creditors of the consignee that the goods belong to the consignor, or unless people in the area generally know the consignee sells goods for other people.

Learning Objectives

1. You should understand that common law rules regarding contracts for the sale of goods have been changed because all states but Louisiana have adopted the Uniform Commercial Code.

2. You should know what the Uniform Commercial Code (UCC) is, and to what kinds of contracts it applies.

3. You should know how the UCC defines "merchant" and what provisions treat merchants differently from non-merchants.

4. You should know how the UCC rules about creation of contracts differ from contract law rules about creation of contracts.

5. You should know how the UCC "fills gaps" when a contract does not specify price, time, delivery, or quantity.

6. You should know the UCC rules about when title passes from seller to buyer.

7. You should know the three situations in which the UCC protects a purchaser's title in goods against the rights of third parties.

8. You should understand the rules for determining who bears the risk of loss under a sales contract.

9. You should know terms that create a shipment or destination contract under the UCC.

10. You should know the difference between a sale or return contract, sale on approval contract, and consignment, as well as the rules governing title and risk of loss for each.

Learning Hints

1. Article 2 of the UCC applies to contracts for the sale of goods. The Code does not apply to other kinds of contracts, like service contracts and employment contracts. Article 2A applies to contracts for the sale of goods. However, other statutes may apply in special cases. For example, many states have contracts regulating the provision of insurance.

2. It is not always easy to tell whether a contract is governed by the UCC. Some contracts are "mixed" because they provide both for the sale of goods and provision of services. In such cases, courts look to see "which predominates."

3. The UCC changes the common law rules in certain instances. However, if a specific code provision does not address an issue, the courts apply common law rules. Examples of common law rules that apply in sales cases are the rules governing rescission for lack of capacity and lack of reality of consent (e.g., misrepresentation, fraud, and duress).

4. Generally, the UCC adopts a more flexible approach to contract law, and contracts may be formed by the conduct of the parties. It is still necessary, however, to find that parties intended to contract in order to find an enforceable contract under the UCC.

5. Sometimes the UCC has special, tougher rules for "merchants." A merchant is a person who is in the business of selling goods of the particular type involved in the case. For example, J.C. Penney is a merchant of clothing. But if you sell your used coat to your roommate, you are not a merchant. However, don't think that the UCC only applies to merchants. The UCC applies to all sales of goods. It will be helpful to go back through the chapter and make a list of the rules that apply only to merchants.

6. Under contract law, the offeror was the "master of the contract" in all regards. If the offeree wanted to accept an offer, he had to accept it totally and not add anything new to it. That rule has been modified under the UCC Under the Code, a court would look at how the parties acted and what they said to determine if there was an agreement between them. It doesn't matter if the offeree has added some new terms in his acceptance, so long as the acceptance was timely and definite. If, however, an offeree said something to the effect that "I am only accepting if you agree to my new terms," that would not be a valid acceptance, even under the UCC.

7. You will learn that the UCC permits parties to have a contract even though they have left some terms open. To provide a means of resolving disputes that arise over open terms, the U.C.C "gap-filling" provisions supply presumptions that are to be applied when the parties have failed to agree upon one or more terms. Notice that these presumptions draw upon prevailing practices in the particular market or industry involved (for example, if a price term is left open, the UCC presumes that the price is to be a "reasonable price" at the time and place for delivery).

8. "Title" means ownership, "risk of loss" means financial responsibility for the consequences of any disastrous occurrence (such as theft or destruction) that may befall goods, and "insurable interest" means the right to take out insurance on the goods.

9. There are a lot of rules to remember about title and risk of loss. You will probably find it helpful to make up a chart showing the point at which title and risk of loss pass to the buyer. Think of the process of selling goods as a continuum in time, beginning with the moment the contract is created and ending with the delivery of goods to the buyer. In between these two points there is a lot of variation. In some contracts, shipment of the goods across great distances is required; in others, the buyer must pick the goods up from a warehouse or at the seller's place of business. You can draw these possibilities along a "time line" and mark the point at which title and risk of loss would pass. Notice that title will generally pass when the seller has completed his obligations concerning physical delivery of the goods. Notice that risk of loss generally passes at the point at which the buyer has the right to control the goods (and is likely to have insurance to cover their loss).

10. In some sales, there is the express possibility that the buyer may send the goods back to the seller (as in the case in sale or return, sale on approval, and consignment sales). There are special rules about title, risk of loss, and creditors' interests for these situations that you should add to your chart.

True-False

In the blank provided, put "**T**" if the statement is True or "**F**" if the statement is False.

_____ 1. When a contract calls for sales of both services and goods, Article 2 of the UCC will apply if the sale of goods is the incidental part of the contract.

_____ 2. Risk of loss is always determined by who has title to the goods under the UCC.

_____ 3. Requirements contracts are invalid since the exact quantity of merchandise to be purchased is unknown.

_____ 4. Buyers generally obtain an insurable interest in goods when the goods have been identified to the contract.

_____ 5. Under the UCC, a valid contract may exist even if the parties have not expressly agreed upon the price of the goods to be sold.

_____ 6. In a sale or return, the return of the goods is at the buyer's risk.

_____ 7. If goods are shipped FOB, the seller bears the risk of loss until they are received by the buyer.

_____ 8. In a "sale on approval," the risk of loss passes to the buyer as soon as he receives the goods in the mail.

_____ 9. Title and risk of loss always pass to the buyer at the same time.

_____ 10. It is possible for one who buys goods from a seller with voidable title to obtain good title to the goods.

Multiple Choice

Circle the best answer.

1. Couch owned two-dozen tires, warehoused in XYZ Warehouse on a negotiable warehouse receipt. Couch sold the tires to Smith. Under these facts:

    a. Risk of loss passes to Smith when Couch negotiates the warehouse receipt to him.

    b. Risk of loss passes to Smith when Warehouse acknowledges in writing it is holding the tires for Couch.

    c. Risk of loss passes to Smith passes to Smith when Warehouse delivers the tires to him.

    d. Risk of loss passes to Smith upon entering the contract of sale with Couch.

2. Which of the following is not a "shipment" contract?

    a. FOB shipping point

    b. FAS

    c. No arrival, no sale

    d. CIF

3. Wally stole a diamond ring from Shirley and sold it to Marty, who knew the ring was "hot." Under these facts:

    a. Marty has good title to the ring.

    b. Marty has better title to the ring than Shirley.

    c. Marty is a good faith purchaser for value.

    d. Shirley retains title to the ring.

4. Wally stole a diamond ring from Shirley and sold it to Marty, who did not know the ring was "hot." Under these facts:

    a. Marty has good title to the ring.

    b. Marty has better title to the ring than Shirley.

    c. Wally is a good faith purchaser for value.

    d. Shirley retains title to the ring.

5. Gail bought a television at Best Buy and wrote a bad check. Shortly after taking the television home, Gail sold the television to Russ for value. Russ had no idea Gail had purchased the television with a bad check. Under these circumstances:

   a. Best Buy can recover the television from Russ.

   b. Russ can keep the television because Gail had voidable title.

   c. Russ cannot keep the set because Gail is a thief.

   d. Russ can keep the television because this is an example of an entrustment.

6. Ted places some goods in Bill's store to sell for him. Bill will earn a commission on the sale. Before the goods are sold, Bill's creditors take action against him for unpaid debts. Under these circumstances:

   a. The creditors can never take the goods that really belong to Ted.

   b. The creditors can take possession of all of the goods in Bill's store.

   c. Ted can protect his interest in the goods by posting a sign in Bill's store indicating that Ted is the owner of those goods.

   d. Bill has title and risk of loss for the goods Ted placed in his store.

7. Jane sold some patio furniture in a garage sale to Sue. Sue told Jane that she would stop by the next day with a truck to pick up the furniture. That night, through no fault of Jane's the furniture was destroyed in a strong storm. Under these circumstances:

   a. Jane bears the risk of loss because Sue had not picked up the furniture yet.

   b. Jane bears the risk of loss because she is a merchant and had not yet delivered the goods.

   c. Sue bears the risk of loss because Jane is a non-merchant who had tendered delivery.

   d. Risk of loss always passes upon delivery of the goods, so Jane bears the risk of loss.

8. The local PTA sold candy for a fundraiser. The candy was purchased from Acme Candy Company. PTA could return any unsold candy for a full refund. PTA sent 200 bags of candy back to Acme. Unfortunately, the candy melted during shipment and was ruined. Between Acme and PTA, who is responsible for loss?

   a. Acme because this is a sale on approval and risk of loss never passed to PTA.

   b. PTA because this is a sale or return and the risk remains with the buyer until the goods are returned.

   c. Acme because this is an example of FOB destination.

   d. PTA because this is a sale on consignment.

9. Jones sold Smith 1,000 widgets. The contract called for Jones "to ship" the widgets with UPS on June 14th. Somehow, the widgets were lost during shipment. Between Jones and Smith, who is responsible for the loss of the widgets?

   a. Smith, because this is a shipping point contract, so title passed when the goods were turned over to UPS.

   b. Jones, because this is a destination contract and title does not pass to Smith until Smith receives the goods.

   c. Jones, because this is a sale on approval and Jones did not yet approve the goods.

   d. Smith, because this is a consignment sale and he had not yet received the goods.

10. Johnson Co. contracted to sell all of their widget production to Davis Company. During the first three years of the contract, Johnson sold Davis 5,000, 5,500, and 5,200 widgets respectively. In the fourth year of the contract, Davis demanded that Johnson sell them 15,000 widgets. Since Johnson was unable to produce that many widgets, Davis sued Johnson for breach of contract. Given these facts:

   a. Davis would win because Johnson was unable to perform according to the contract.

   b. Johnson would win because the contract did not specify a quantity of merchandise so the contract is unenforceable.

   c. This is an example of a requirements contract.

   d. Johnson would win because under an output contract, both parties must act in good faith. The amount of quantity demanded by Davis does not constitute good faith.

Short Essay

1. Tammy buys a car from Honest Hal's Motors. Hal has a loan from First State Bank secured by the cars in his inventory. If Hal defaults on his loan with First State Bank, can the bank recover the car from Tammy? Why or why not?

2. H.G. Gloom, Inc. agreed to sell widgets to Bill Bonnie. No special provision as to when the price was to be paid was included in the contract, and there is no established industry custom. Is there an enforceable contract between the parties? Why or why not?

3. Earl has 1,000 bottles of whiskey stored at Ajax Warehouse. Earl sells all of the whiskey to Pearl, who has no intention of moving the whiskey at this time. Describe when title to the whiskey will pass from Earl to Pearl.

4. Sally took her diamond ring to Brown's Jewelry Store for repairs. Somehow, a clerk at Brown's sold the ring to Jim by mistake. Sally demands that Jim return the ring to her. Jim refuses. Who is entitled to the ring? Why?

5. Tracy bought a big screen television at Iowa Furniture Mart (IFM) by writing a check for the full amount. After Tracy took the television home, he sold it to Mary for value. The check to IFM bounced and IFM takes action against Mary. Can IFM recover the television set from Mary?

6. When does title to goods pass when they are shipped using a bill of lading?

CHAPTER 19
WARRANTIES AND PRODUCT LIABILITY

Outline

I. Warranty theory.

Product liability is based the following legal theories: warranty: contract, negligence, and strict liability.

A. Express warranties

1. Express warranties arise when a seller makes a statement of fact or a promise concerning the goods that becomes a part of the bargain between the parties.

2. Example: <u>Bobholz v. Banaszak</u>: Statements made by the seller of a boat that the boat was in perfect and excellent condition, and that it had been properly maintained and winterized were held to be part of the basis of the bargain because the statements induced the buyer to purchase the boat.

B. Implied warranties are imposed under the UCC The implied warranty of merchantability and the implied warranty of fitness for a particular purpose.

1. The implied warranty of merchantability requires that goods be fit for their ordinary purpose.

Example: In <u>Denny v. Ford Motor Co.</u>, a Ford Bronco II that had a propensity to roll over on paved roads was not fit for use as an on-road vehicle and breached its implied warranty.

Example: <u>Mexicali Rose v. Superior Court</u>: A chicken bone in a chicken enchilada did not constitute breach of implied warranty of merchantability under the "foreign-natural" test of merchantability of food.

2. The implied warranty of fitness for a particular purpose arises when the sellers knows the particular purpose for which buyer is purchasing the goods and knows that the buyer is relying on the seller in making the purchase.

Example: <u>Klein v. Sears & Co.</u>: the seller was found liable for breach of warranty of fitness in sale of riding lawnmower.

3. The implied warranty of title protects the buyer's ownership of goods purchased from seller.

II. Exclusion of Modification of Warranties

A. The UCC code provision 2-316 permits exclusion of limitation of warranties. It is difficult, if not impossible, to make an express warranty and limit or disclaim it at the same time.

Example: In <u>Thacker v. Menard</u>, a written estimate with a clear disclaimer did not constitute a contract offer.

B. Disclaimer of Implied Warranties

1. The UCC permits a seller to exclude the implied warranty of merchantability. The seller must mention the word <u>merchantability</u> and the disclaimer must be <u>conspicuous</u>.

2. The implied warranty of fitness for a particular purpose must be disclaimed in writing. It must be conspicuous.

3. A disclaimer that meets these requirements may be unenforceable because it is <u>unconscionable</u> under the UCC.

4. A seller may also limit its liability for breach of warranty. If a limitation of liability is unconscionable or fails of its essential purpose, it is unenforceable.

C. Beneficiaries of contract warranties

    1. Under the UCC (2-318), a person who is not in privity with the seller (that is, who did not purchase the goods directly from the seller) may be unable to recover damages under a warranty theory. However, the consumer may still recover damages under a negligence or strict liability theory.

    Example: <u>In Re Air Crash Disaster at Sioux City Iowa on July 19, 1989 Banks v. United Airlines, Inc.</u>: The court held in an air disaster case, the family of a victim could not sue the hydraulic system manufacturer because there was no privity between plaintiff and defendant.

    Example: <u>Bryant v. Hoffman-LaRoche, Inc.</u>: A patient receiving free samples of medicine from her doctor, who had received the samples from a manufacturer, was not entitled to the benefits of the implied warranties of merchantability or fitness because no privity existed between the patient and the manufacturer of the pharmaceuticals.

    2. Under the Magnuson-Moss Warranty Act of 1975, if a seller of a consumer product that costs more than $5 gives the consumer a written warranty, certain requirements apply, and there are different provisions for a full or limited warranty.

III. Negligence: Breach of a duty of care by a seller resulting in a foreseeable injury to the purchaser may constitute negligence.

A. Examples include inadequate inspection, negligent manufacturing processes, misrepresentation of fitness for a purpose, negligent product design, and negligent failure to warn.

    Example: <u>Weigl v. Quincy Specialties Company</u>: A manufacturer of lab coats is liable for damages for defective design, negligent testing, failure to warn, and breach of warranty when a person was severely burned while wearing a lab coat.

IV. Strict liability. Under the Restatement 402A, a plaintiff may recover under this theory if the following elements are proven:

A. Elements: Product sold by a <u>merchant-like seller</u> in a <u>defective condition</u> <u>unreasonably dangerous</u> to the <u>ultimate user or consumer</u> who sustains <u>physical harm or property damage</u> as a result of the defect.

    Example: <u>Uniroyal Goodrich Tire Co. v. Martinez:</u> To establish a design defect under section 402A of the Restatement (Third) of torts, a claimant must establish that the defendant could have provided a safer alternative design. The design must be reasonable—it must be able to be implemented without destroying the utility of the product.

B. Issues arise in determining whether a product is <u>unreasonably dangerous</u> or <u>defectively designed</u>. Courts generally look to the "state of the art" at the time of manufacture.

C. Defenses include misuse of the product alteration of the product after manufacture, and assumption of the risk.

D. "Industry-wide" liability is an outgrowth of strict product liability. Under this theory, a large number of people who were injured by defective products (for example, asbestos), may sue multiple manufacturers engaged in making that product. Liability is determined on a basis of market-share.

E. Statutes of Repose may limit the ability of an injured party to bring a tort-based suit to 10 years after the product was sold to the user. These statutes may be modified in the case of harms that are not discovered until years later, like DES.

Learning Objectives

1. You should note that "products liability" includes several different legal theories used by persons injured by defective products.

2. Each theory, whether negligence, warranty, or strict liability, has different requirements and, in some cases, different defenses.

3. The evolution of product liability law has not been smooth. Instead, it has evolved piecemeal as court recognized different theories and permitted expansions of doctrine and exceptions.

4. You should understand that a plaintiff may maintain an action based on several different theories, but will not be entitled to recover multiple damages if the seller/manufacturer is found liable under more than one theory.

5. You should know what an express warranty is and how an express warranty may be created.

6. You should know what the implied warranty of merchantability guarantees, as well as when that warranty arises.

7. You should know what the implied warranty of fitness for a particular purpose guarantees, as well as when that warranty arises.

8. You should know what the implied warranty of title is, as well as how it differs from the other warranties discussed in Chapter 18.

9. You should know how the seller may disclaim or exclude various warranties.

10. You should become familiar with the kinds of circumstances in which attempted disclaimers of warranties may be found unconscionable, and should know the standards provided by the Uniform Commercial Code for determining whether a limitation of warranty liability should be enforced.

11. You should know the persons, in addition to the purchaser of the product, who may be allowed to benefit from a warranty.

12. You should become familiar with the major provisions of the Magnuson-Moss Warranty Act.

13. You should know the kinds of circumstances in which a seller may be held liable in a negligence-based product liability action.

14. You should know the basic elements of strict liability, as well as how strict liability is different from liability for negligence and liability for breach of warranty.

15. You should know the defenses available in a strict liability action.

16. You should know what the industry-wide liability doctrine is and how it applies.

Learning Hints

1. Breach of warranty actions are most like contract actions, and the remedies generally include contract-like damages. For example, a person who proves breach of express or implied warranty against the seller should be able to recover "expectation damages" or "basis of the bargain damages," which generally is the difference between the value of the product, as warranted, and its actual value as a result of the defect.

2. In breach of warranty cases, however, the consumer may also recover other contract damages. These may include "consequential damages," which are damages that are foreseeable as a result of the breach. In some cases, a consumer who is injured by a defective product may recover damages for personal injury in the form of "consequential" damages under a breach of warranty theory.

3. Most consumers who suffer physical injury as a result of a defective product will sue under a "strict liability" or "negligence" theory. Under this theory, the consumer does not have to establish privity of contract (which may be required in some states under a warranty theory). Disclaimers of liability by sellers are unenforceable under this theory.

4. A strict liability theory dispenses with the requirement that the consumer prove the seller was negligent in manufacturing, designing, packaging or distributing the product. All the purchaser must prove is that the product was "defective" and "unreasonably dangerous," and that this resulted in physical injury or property damage to the purchaser.

5. Product misuse, alteration and assumption of the risk are defenses to an action under strict liability; these defenses, as well as contributory or comparative negligence, are also permitted in negligence actions. However, product misuse that is foreseeable may not relieve a seller of liability.

6. No formal language or written guarantee is necessary for a seller to make an express warranty. If the seller describes the goods, makes a statement of purported fact or a promise concerning the goods, or displays a sample or model of the goods to the buyer, an express warranty may be created. Where an express warranty is created, the goods must measure up to the description, statement of purported fact, promise, sample, or model. If the goods do not measure up, there is a breach of warranty. Be aware, however, that a seller's mere commendation of the goods or a seller's generalized opinion concerning value of the goods does not ordinarily rise to the level of an express warranty. Instead, such statements are considered to be only "sales talk" or "puffing."

7. Remember that even if a statement or other act by the seller appears at first glance to be an express warranty, there is actually no express warranty (and hence no liability for breach of express warranty) unless the seller's statement or other act became part of the bargain. This generally means that what the seller said or did must at least have been a contributing factor in the buyer's decision to purchase the goods. Obviously, the part of the bargain test cannot be satisfied in a situation in which the buyer did not know about the seller's statement until after the buyer had purchased the goods.

8. Express warranties may be made through the seller's advertising material.

9. It is exceedingly difficult, if not virtually impossible, for a seller to make a fully effective disclaimer of liability for an express warranty once the seller has made an express warranty. A Seller can, however, limit his liability for breach of express warranty by putting a clause in the contract that provides for an exclusive or limited remedy in the event of a breach of warranty. For example, such a clause could provide that the remedy for breach of warranty is limited to repair or replacement of the defective goods. Courts uphold these clauses unless they are unconscionable.

10. The implied warranty of merchantability is an automatic guarantee of reasonable quality in sales of goods made by merchants, unless, of course, the merchant has disclaimed the warranty properly. A merchant is one who is in the business of selling a particular type of goods. Do not forget that the implied warranty of merchantability arises only if the seller is a merchant when selling the particular goods being sold. For example, the implied warranty of merchantability is not created when a seller who is in the business of selling automobiles sells his neighbor a refrigerator from the seller's basement.

11. The implied warranty of fitness for a particular purpose is based on the seller's knowing or having reason to know: (a) the special, individual, or particular purpose for which the buyer wants the goods; and (b) that the buyer is relying on the seller to select goods suitable for fulfillment of that purpose. Note that if the basic elements of an implied warranty of fitness for a particular purpose are present, even a seller who is not a merchant may be found to have made this implied warranty. As with the implied warranty of merchantability, however, the seller may disclaim liability for breach of the implied warranty of fitness for a particular purpose.

12. Remember that the implied warranty of merchantability guarantees that the goods will be fit for the ordinary purposes to which such goods customarily are put, and that the implied warranty of fitness guarantees that the goods will be fit for the particular, individual purpose of the buyer. This means that in some cases, goods that are adequate enough to pass the merchantability test may fail the fitness for particular purpose test. In other cases, however, the goods may be such that both the implied warranty of merchantability and the implied warranty of fitness for a particular purpose are breached.

13. The implied warranties of merchantability and fitness for a particular purpose are fairly easy for sellers to exclude or disclaim, provided that the seller follows the disclaimer rules set out in the UCC Look closely at the disclaimer rules set out in your text and note that the rules differ somewhat, depending upon which implied warranty the seller is attempting to exclude.

14. Negligence law focuses on whether the seller failed to use reasonable care in connection with the designing, manufacturing, or marketing of its product. In other words, negligence is a fault-based legal theory that focuses on the conduct of the seller. Strict liability, on the other hand, is a legal theory that focuses on the condition of the product itself, rather than on the conduct of the seller. Strict liability is liability imposed without regard for whether the seller was somehow at fault in its conduct. This means that under strict liability, it is possible that a seller could be found liable for injuries caused by a defective, unreasonably dangerous product, even if the seller used all due care to prevent injuries. In a negligence suit, the seller would not be held liable if the seller exercised reasonable care, even though injuries nevertheless resulted.

15. Strict liability requires that the product must be in a defective condition that makes the product unreasonably dangerous. This is really two requirements in one. First, the product must be defective. Second, the product must be unreasonably dangerous because of its defective condition. It is not enough that the product is merely defective. For example, a dishwasher that does not run properly is defective, but it is not unreasonably dangerous. However, if a defect in the dishwasher causes the machine not only to fail to run properly but also to explode violently, the dishwasher is both defective and unreasonably dangerous.

True-False

In the blank provided, put "**T**" if the statement is True or "**F**" if the statement is False.

1. Today's product liability rules are much more favorable to plaintiffs than during the 19th century.

2. Tom buys clothing from the Crooks Brothers Website based on descriptions and pictures shown there. Crooks Brothers has expressly warranted that the clothes sold to Tom will match the description shown on the Web site.

3. Norma sells her used furniture to her friend Diane. Norma is making an implied warranty that the furniture is merchantable.

4. It is easy for sellers to disclaim express warranties.

5. Dork offers a warranty on its air conditioners that will cover replacement of parts, but it does not include any labor costs incurred in repairing the air conditioner. This is an example of a limited warranty.

6. If the plaintiff brings her product liability suit on a strict liability theory but she was not in privity with the defendant, she will lose her suit on that basis.

7. If a seller is not a merchant with respect to the goods of the kind being sold, that seller cannot be held, under the Uniform Commercial Code, to have made or breached the implied warranty of fitness for a particular purpose.

8. As a general rule, a seller of goods is held to have impliedly warranted that he had the right to sell the goods and that the goods are free of any claims or liens about which the buyer has not been made aware before the sale.

9. Albertson's grocery stores has an obligation to inspect all products before placing them on the shelves.

_____ 10. The Magnuson-Moss Warranty Act does not require sellers of consumer products to make written warranties.

Multiple Choice

Circle the best answer.

1. An action against a manufacturer for failing to use reasonable care in manufacturing his product is best described as a suit in:
   a. Strict liability.
   b. Breach of implied warranty of fitness.
   C Breach of express warranty.
   d. Negligence.

2. A written warranty disclaimer is least likely to be effective to disclaim:
   a. The implied warranty of merchantability.
   b. The implied warranty of fitness.
   c. Liability for injury caused by a defective product under strict liability.
   d. A written warranty disclaimer is effective to disclaim all implied and express warranties, as well as liability for defective products under strict liability.

3. Jill accidentally cut off her ring finger on her left hand while using an electric knife to carve her Thanksgiving turkey. The accident occurred when she placed her left hand on the turkey to steady it. Jill sued the manufacturer of the knife, alleging she is entitled to recover damages under a strict liability theory. In her action under a strict liability theory, which of the following is Jill not required to prove?
   a. That the manufacturer was regularly engaged in the business of selling electric knives.
   b. That the knife was defective and unreasonably dangerous.
   c. That the manufacturer was negligent either in designing the knife or failing to properly inspect the knife for defects before sale.
   d. That Jill suffered physical injury or property damage as a result of using the product.

4. Howard decides to mow a vacant lot with his lawnmower. The lot is covered with tall, thick weeds and rocks. While mowing the vacant lot, Howard is injured when the mower throws out a rock that hits him in the head. Howard sues the lawnmower manufacturer. What is the most likely outcome of his lawsuit?
   a. Howard will win if he sues the manufacturer for negligence in designing the lawnmower.
   b. Howard will win on a breach of express warranty case.
   c. Howard will lose the case because of product misuse.
   d. Howard will win based on breach of implied warranty of merchantability.

5. Which of the following is a key factor in strict liability cases?
   a. The manufacturer of the product did not use reasonable care.
   b. The buyer relied upon the seller's expertise when buying the product.
   c. The product is fit for normal use.
   d. The product is unreasonably dangerous.

6. Helmetco manufactures football helmets. Tommy is seriously injured during a football game when his helmet is jammed into the ground. Tommy sues Helmetco. Which is most likely true?

    a. Tommy will lose the case because there was no privity between him and Helmetco.

    b. Helmetco may be able to successfully argue that the helmet was state of the art.

    c. Tommy will win under strict liability because the helmet was unreasonably dangerous.

    d. Tommy will win under implied warranty of merchantability because the helmet was not fit for normal use.

7. Sarah buys a chicken salad at Chicken D'Lite restaurant. While Sarah is eating her meal, she discovers the remains of a rat in the salad. Sarah becomes quite ill and has serious psychological problems for some time. Sarah sues the restaurant. What is likely Sarah's best argument?

    a. Implied warranty of merchantability because it was unreasonable for Sarah to expect to find rat remains in her salad.

    b. Implied warranty of fitness for a particular purpose.

    c. Strict liability.

    d. Implied warranty of title.

8. Todd sells his car to Bob. Bob is not aware that Todd owes money on the car to Last Chance Bank. The bank brings an action against Bob to get the car back. Which of the following is Bob's best chance to win against the bank?

    a. Implied warranty of merchantability.

    b. Express warranty.

    c. Implied warranty of title.

    d. Strict liability.

9. Susan sells computers for Best Buy. Allen is shopping for a computer. Allen finds a computer he likes and Susan tells him that "this is our most popular computer." She also tells him that "this computer is just right for you." Allen buys the computer and has nothing but problems with it. Allen brings a suit against Best Buy. Which of the following is most likely true?

    a. Best Buy is liable for breach of express warranty.

    b. Best Buy is liable for breach of implied warranty of fitness for a particular purpose.

    c. Best Buy is not liable for breach of express warranty because Susan was just engaged in sales talk.

    d. Best Buy is liable under strict liability.

10. Which of the following is a valid disclaimer for the implied warranty of merchantability?

    a. A written disclaimer in fine print on the back of the receipt.

    b. "All warranties are disclaimed."

    c. Buyer takes the product "as is."

    d. A written disclaimer that is conspicuous and mentions the word "merchantability."

Short Essay

1. Jane wanted to purchase a new "EZ" brand vacuum cleaner but the particular vacuum cleaner she wanted was not in stock. The seller showed Jane pictures of several different vacuum cleaners in a catalog and she selected a green vacuum cleaner. The seller ordered the vacuum cleaner but when it arrived, the vacuum cleaner was blue instead of green. Which, if any, warranties did the seller breach under these circumstances?

2. Gail sells some of her old furniture to Stan. What implied warranty or warranties would Gail make to Stan? Would the implied warranty of merchantability apply to Gail? Why or why not?

3. In the question above, assume that Stan is seriously injured when a hidden defect in the furniture causes him to fall. Can Stan sue Gail under strict liability?

4. Orville Dull, an accountant, took a break for lunch and went to the Griese Grill, a fast food restaurant. Remembering a recent Griese advertisement that stated "our pork tenderloins are made from nothing but the highest grade of pork available," Dull ordered pork tenderloin as part of his lunch. After popping the first bite of it into his mouth, Dull began to choke and gasp for air. An alert Griese employee rushed Dull to the local hospital's emergency room, where a physician extracted from Dull's throat a large rubber band that had two paper clips fastened to it. Still attached to and partially covering the rubber band and paper clips was some of the crunchy coating used by Griese on its tenderloins. Dull, who was hospitalized for three days, experienced significant pain and suffering while his throat was healing. On what warranty-based legal theories would Dull have an excellent chance of prevailing in a suit against Griese? State the reasons for your answer.

5. Elmer is seriously injured while using a table saw that he had purchased 14 years ago. The saw malfunctioned while Elmer was doing some woodworking. Elmer is suing the manufacturer of the saw based on strict liability. Given that Elmer lives in a state with a statute of repose, will he be successful in suing the manufacturer for damages?

6. In the question above, assume that the saw manufacturer did not have a warning with the product when it was sold. Would Elmer be able to successfully sue because no warning label was placed on the product?

7. Querck Pharmaceuticals pulled the arthritis drug Bioxx off the market when evidence was shown that the drug could cause heart problems. Discuss the kind of potential liability for Querck in selling Bioxx.

8. Wimpie loves hamburgers. In fact, Wimpie loves hamburgers so much that for twenty-five years, Wimpie would eat hamburgers almost every day at McDonald's. Wimpie has a severe heart attack. He sues McDonald's. What would be Wimpie's best basis for a successful lawsuit? What would McDonald's likely argue in defense?

9.   Don started smoking cigarettes in the 1920's. In 1932, Don was stricken with lung cancer. What would have been the likely outcome of a lawsuit against a tobacco company at that time?

CHAPTER 20
PERFORMANCE OF SALES CONTRACTS

Outline

I.   Article II of the Uniform Commercial Code governs performance of sales contracts.

    A.   General UCC provisions apply, such as the requirement of "good faith", and the fact that courts may interpret sales contracts by relying on past course of dealing and customs and practices of the trade, unless there is a conflict between them and the express terms of the contract.

    Example: Weisz Graphics Division of the Fred B. Johnson Co., Inc. v. Peck Industries, Inc.: The court held that a time limitation of 12 months on releases was standard in the industry and became part of the parties' agreement.

    B.   Under the UCC, a party may waive the right to cancel a contract if he or she fails to object to breach; there is also a presumption favoring assignment and delegation of duties under the UCC unless the contract expressly forbids them or there is a good reason for the original party's performance.

II.   Basic obligations as to delivery

    A.   The basic duty of the seller is to deliver the goods, and the buyer is to accept and pay for the goods. Unless the parties agree otherwise, the place of delivery is the seller's place of business. (UCC 2-308).

    B.   If the seller is required to ship the goods, the seller must make a reasonable contract with a carrier and notify the buyer that the goods are shipped.

    C.   The buyer has the right to inspect the goods; but under the terms of cash on delivery (COD) the buyer must pay for the goods before inspection unless marked "inspection allowed".

III. Acceptance, revocation and rejection

    A.   Acceptance occurs if a buyer fails to reject the goods within a reasonable time. To reject, the buyer must notify the seller and specify the defect. Acceptance of part of a commercial unit is usually acceptance of the whole.

    Example: Weil v. Murray: Goods that a buyer has in its possession necessarily are accepted or rejected by the time a reasonable time for inspecting those passes.

    B.   If the seller has reason to believe the buyer will accept nonconforming goods, the seller can take a reasonable time to reship conforming goods, even though original time for delivery has expired.

    C.   A buyer may revoke acceptance of nonconforming goods where the nonconformity substantially impairs the value of the goods and (2) the buyer accepted them without knowledge of the nonconformity or because of assurances by the seller that the nonconformity would be cured. Revocation must be invoked prior to substantial change in the goods.

    Example: North River Homes, Inc. v. Bosarge: The court held that the purchasers effectively revoked acceptance of a mobile home.

    D.   The seller has the right to cure breach by reshipping conforming goods, so long as performance can be completed within time for original performance.

    E.   After rejection, buyer's duties depend on whether the buyer is a merchant or non-merchant:

        1.   A non-merchant, must hold the goods with reasonable care, but is not obligated to ship them back to the seller.

        2.   A merchant must follow reasonable instructions of the seller, and, absent other instructions, must try to resell the goods if they are perishable.

IV.   Assurance, repudiation, and excuse

A. A party may demand assurance if there is a reasonable basis for believing the other party may not be able to perform.

Example: <u>LNS Investment Co., Inc. v. Phillips 66 Co.</u>: Where the purchasers of a large quantity of plastic bottles had reasonable grounds for insecurity concerning the performance of the seller, the purchaser was justified in requesting assurances that the seller would perform its obligations under the contract and also justified in suspending its performance of the contract when adequate assurances were not forthcoming.

B. The UCC recognizes the doctrine of <u>anticipatory repudiation</u> and the doctrine of <u>commercial impracticability</u>, which excuses performance for unforeseen events making it difficult or impossible to perform.

Learning Objectives

1. You should understand the importance of the doctrine of "good faith" under the UCC, which imposes on every contract for the sale of goods a duty of good faith in its performance. The concept of "good faith" is defined as "honesty in fact," and cannot be disclaimed by the parties. Thus a court may consider "good faith" in determining whether a breach of contract has occurred, and if so, an appropriate remedy.

2. In interpreting sales contracts, you should note that the UCC places great importance on past dealings between contracting parties and on custom and trade practice. Absent express contract language to the contrary, a court will consider these factors in determining breach and appropriate remedies.

3. You should know the basic obligations of the seller regarding delivery.

4. You should be able to describe the buyer's right of inspection and know how the buyer's right of inspection differs in a C.O.D. sale.

5. You should know the legal effect of acceptance of goods and be able to identify conduct on the part of the buyer-indicating acceptance.

6. You should be able to describe the buyer's rights upon improper delivery and should know what is necessary for a valid rejection.

7. You should be able to recognize actions a seller can take when the buyer rejects the goods. You should also be able to describe the buyer's duties concerning rejected goods.

8. You should know the meaning of the term "revocation of acceptance" and what is necessary to make a valid revocation.

9. You should know what a party's rights are when he has justifiable concern about the other party's ability to perform the contract.

10. You should know when a party to a contract is excused from performing his obligations.

Learning Hints

1. The UCC applies to contracts for the sale of goods. In sales contracts, the Code adopts a "strict performance" standard. This standard, however, is softened by Code provisions giving a seller an "opportunity to cure" non-conformity, and a provision requiring prompt rejection and notice by the purchaser.

2. The UCC permits a buyer to "revoke his/her acceptance" under certain circumstances. This provision has been used by consumers in "lemon car" cases and in similar cases to reject goods which are non-conforming, but which the seller continues, unsuccessfully, to attempt to fix in order to "cure" the defects.

3.   Buyers normally have the right to inspect <u>before</u> they pay. However, in a C.O.D. (cash on delivery) sale, the buyer must pay before inspection unless there is some glaring defect in the goods that the buyer can perceive without an inspection. The fact that C.O.D. buyers must pay before inspection does <u>not</u> mean that they lose their right to reject, revoke, or bring suit for breach of contract. It simply means that the buyer must take some legal action to reclaim his money.

4.   Don't get the terms "acceptance," "rejection," and "revocation" as used in this chapter mixed up with the same terms as they are used in the chapters dealing with <u>creation</u> of contracts. In this chapter, we're talking about a buyer's acceptance or rejection or revocation of acceptance of the seller's performance of his contractual obligation to deliver goods, whereas in the earlier chapters we were talking about acceptance, rejection, or revocation of offers to determine whether a contract was ever created in the first place.

5.   When goods are delivered to the buyer, he has a reasonable time to inspect them. If the buyer wants to reject the goods, he must act quickly. He must give the seller notice of rejection in which he describes the defects in the goods. He must be careful not to do anything that would contradict the seller's ownership of the goods (such as continuing to use them after a reasonable period for inspection has elapsed), or he will be considered to have accepted the goods.

6.   Note that when there has been a rejection of goods, the seller has a certain amount of time in which he has the right to cure the defect or deliver conforming goods. Therefore, even if the buyer wants out of the contract once he has received defective goods, the seller still has another chance to get it right.

7.   A buyer accepts the seller's performance when he indicates that the goods are satisfactory, or when he treats the goods in a way that shows ownership of them (such as using them after a defect is discovered or taking them on vacation with him), or when he merely fails to make a proper rejection. In other words, if the buyer fails to do any of the things required for a valid rejection, he is considered to have accepted. For example, if goods were delivered to you in a defective condition that made them totally worthless and you put them in your basement and did not use them but delayed notifying the seller for a period of time that would be considered unreasonable, you are considered to have accepted the goods.

8.   Once the buyer has accepted the goods, he's normally stuck with them. He may still have remedies against the seller for breach of contract, but he no longer has the right to send the goods back unless the circumstances are such that he can revoke his acceptance of the goods.

9.   Once the buyer has accepted the seller's performance, he must have a very good reason for revoking or undoing his acceptance of the goods. For one thing, he must be able to show that the defect was serious enough to constitute a substantial impairment of the value of the goods. Second, he must be able to show that he had a good reason for not rejecting the goods in the first place, such as the fact that the defect was difficult to discover earlier or the seller gave assurances that the defect would be cured. Third, the buyer must go through the same steps to make a valid revocation that were necessary for a valid rejection; i.e., notice within a reasonable time. Finally, the condition of the goods must be such that there has not been a substantial change in their condition.

10. Remember: rejection is done <u>instead</u> of acceptance. Revocation is done <u>after</u> acceptance.

11. A buyer's responsibilities toward goods rightfully rejected depends on whether the buyer is a merchant or not. Generally, a non-merchant buyer only has the duty to exercise reasonable care toward the goods and is not required to ship them back to the seller. A merchant buyer, however, must follow the seller's reasonable instructions regarding the goods, and must, in the case of perishable goods, attempt to sell them for the seller absent contrary instructions.

True-False

In the blank provided, put "T" if the statement is True or "F" if the statement is False.

_____ 1. In all contracts of sale of goods, the buyer and seller must act in good faith.

_____ 2. Trade practices will always prevail over the express terms in a sales contract.

_____ 3. A buyer of goods may accept or reject partial commercial units.

_____ 4. If no agreement is made, goods are to be delivered at the buyer's place of business.

_____ 5. Under the UCC, the buyer is responsible for making a reasonable contract with a carrier for delivery of the goods if the contract is silent as to delivery.

_____ 6. A buyer who accepts nonconforming goods does not necessarily forfeit his remedies against the seller.

_____ 7. To make a proper rejection of goods, the buyer should notify the seller within a reasonable time and state the reasons for the rejection.

_____ 8. A non-merchant buyer who rejects goods must follow any reasonable instructions the seller gives concerning what to do with the goods.

_____ 9. Normally, the buyer has the right to inspect the goods before he accepts or pays for them.

_____ 10. If the delivery date has expired, the seller is never entitled to the right to cure delivery.

Multiple Choice

Circle the best answer.

1. Smith made a contract with Jones to buy ten tons of coal per month for one year. Jones delivered the coal ten days late for six months and Smith did not object. On the seventh month, Smith sought to cancel the contract because of late deliveries. Under these circumstances:

   a. Smith can cancel the contract.

   b. Jones can cancel the contract.

   c. Smith has waived his right to cancel by not objecting to late deliveries.

   d. The UCC would require any waiver to be in writing in order to be effective.

2. Which of the following statements is not true?

   a. A buyer usually must pay for goods in a C.O.D. sale before inspecting them.

   b. Delivery is assumed to take place at the seller's place of business unless otherwise stated.

   c. Clearly expressed contract terms will prevail over course of dealing.

   d. The duties of the buyer can never be delegated.

3. If the parties do not otherwise agree:

   a. A buyer must pay for goods upon contracting.

   b. A buyer must pay for goods upon identification of the goods to the contract.

   c. A buyer must pay for goods upon delivery.

   d. A buyer may pay for goods on credit.

4. Once a buyer has accepted goods:

   a. He cannot later reject them.

   b. He can later reject them for nonconformity even if that nonconformity does not affect the value of the goods.

   c. He can reject them even if He doesn't give the seller timely notice that the goods are nonconforming.

   d. He does not forfeit or waive remedies against the seller for any nonconforming goods.

5. Which of the following is not true of a seller's duties and rights/
   a. The seller cannot demand to be paid in cash.
   b. The seller must tender delivery to the buyer.
   c. The seller must make a reasonable contract with a carrier for shipping the goods.
   d. The seller may have the right to cure beyond the delivery date of the contract if the seller has reason to believe that the buyer would accept nonconforming goods.

6. Carol bought a new car from Motown Motors. Carol soon discovered that the engine has serious problems. She has taken the car to Motown several times during the last month and each time the seller has assured her that the problems would be fixed, but the problems remain. Carol wants the dealer to take the car and return her money. Under these circumstances, Carol:
   a. Can reject the car, stating her reasons.
   b. Can revoke her acceptance, since there is a substantial nonconformity that Carol did not know about at the time she bought the car.
   c. Must keep the car since she already accepted it.
   d. None of the above.

7. Scalina Brothers sells produce to Bob's General Store. On a recent shipment, much of the lettuce was not in good condition. What would be the most reasonable action for Bob's to take in this situation?
   a. Send the lettuce back to Scalina.
   b. Throw the lettuce away and take a loss.
   c. Hold the lettuce with reasonable care and wait for the seller to take it.
   d. Follow the reasonable instructions of the seller.

8. XYZ Manufacturing enters into a contract with Sanders Corp. to sell Sanders 10,000 widgets by July 10th. In late May, the workers at Sanders go on a prolonged strike. XYZ is concerned about Sanders' ability to perform the contract. What could XYZ do?
   a. Demand assurance.
   b. If assurance is not given, treat the contract as repudiated.
   c. Cancel the contract based upon commercial impracticability.
   d. All of the above.

9. Associated Grocers orders 20 train carloads of apples from Simpson. Simpson sends the apples to Associated. Upon inspection, Associated determines that a number of apples in 4 of the train cars do not meet normal standards. Which of the following is not a possible action for Associated?
   a. Accept all 20 carloads of apples.
   b. Reject the 4 carloads with spoiled apples and accept the other 16 carloads.
   c. Reject the spoiled apples in the 4 train cars, accept the rest in those cars and the remaining 16 cars.
   d. Accept the 20 carloads of apples, and get a discount for the damaged goods.

10. Which of the following is true?
   a. A buyer may reject a C.O.D. shipment if the goods obviously do not conform to the contract.
   b. A seller of goods cannot demand to be paid in cash.
   c. If the contract is silent as to delivery, delivery may be made in installments.
   d. If the contract is silent as to the place of delivery, delivery is assumed to be made at the buyer's place of business.

Short Essay

1. The Sports Nut has ordered baseball caps from Caps R Us for years. Sometimes Caps R Us has delivered caps of all different colors and Sports Nut has always accepted them. Sports Nut ordered 200 navy blue baseball caps to be delivered on April 20th. On April 18th, Caps R Us delivered 200 royal blue baseball caps. Is Caps R Us entitled to cure the tender of delivery? How would your answer change if the nonconforming caps were delivered on April 20th?

2. Florida Furniture Mart (FFM) orders a large quantity of furniture from Hickory Co. When the furniture is delivered, FFM discovers that some of the furniture is damaged. What are some of the options available to FFM?

3. In the question above, how would your answer change if Cal Consumer bought the merchandise from Hickory?

4. Ginger sells a large shipment of dresses to Mary Ann. The dresses are to be delivered on August 15th. On August 1st, Mary Ann notifies Ginger that she will not be able to pay for the goods. What should Ginger do?

5. From the question above, suppose Mary Ann changes her mind and on August 12th she notifies Ginger that she wants the dresses after all. Can Mary Ann still purchase the dresses?

6. Byron is very unhappy. He took delivery of a new computer from Gizmo's last week, and it has given him nothing but grief. As an expression of his anger, he takes the defective computer back to Gizmo's place of business late at night, and because the store is closed for the night, he leaves the computer at the front door with a note expressing his revocation of his earlier acceptance. During the night, the computer is stolen. Who is responsible for the loss?

CHAPTER 21
REMEDIES FOR BREACH OF SALES CONTRACTS

Outline

I. Remedies in general.

    A. The object of a remedy is to put the injured party in the same position he/she would have been had the contract been performed. The parties may provide their own remedies by contract.

    B. Liquidated damages are damages the parties agreed on in the contract as the amount that will be paid in the event of breach.

    C. Consequential damages are damages, such as injury to a person or his property, that were foreseeable as a result of breach.

        1. Consequential damages may be excluded or limited in commercial (not consumer) contracts, so long as that exclusion or limitation is not unconscionable.

        Example: Moore v. Coachmen Industries, Inc.: A limited warranty expressly limiting consequential damages was effective in the case of an RV destroyed by an electrical fault.

    D. The UCC statute of limitations provides that an action for breach of sales contracts must be filed within four years after the breach.

        Example: Poli v. DaimlerChrysler Corp.: The cause of action for a purchaser of an automobile began when the car developed serious, persistent problems, not when the car was purchased. Therefore, the purchaser timely filed the lawsuit for breach of warranty.

II. Seller's remedies.

    A. In general, a seller has number of remedies against a breaching buyer under the UCC.

        1. The seller may cancel the contract. If in the process of manufacturing, the seller should choose an alternative under 2-704(2) that will minimize or mitigate loss.

        Example: Madsen v. Murrey & Sons Co., Inc.: The courts held that the seller should have mitigated damages after breach of contract by the buyer. The seller should have finished completing construction of the pool tables and not dismantled the tables, using materials for salvage and firewood.

    B. The seller may resell the goods and recover damages, including incidental damages.

    C. In some cases, the seller is entitled to the purchase price. If, for example, goods are specially manufactured goods and not suitable for resale, the seller may be entitled to the purchase price.

    D. If the buyer wrongfully rejects or repudiates the goods, the seller is entitled to the difference between the contract price and the market price of the goods, and lost profit (UCC 2-708).

    E. If the buyer is insolvent, the seller may withhold delivery, and has the right to require the return of any goods obtained within the previous 10 days.

III. Buyer's remedies.

    A. A buyer has a number of remedies under the UCC. Upon rightful rejection or revocation of acceptance, the buyer may cancel, recover the purchase price paid to the seller, and recover damages.

        Example: Jewish Federation of Greater Des Moines v. Cedar Forrest Products, Inc.: When the buyer cancelled a contract to manufacture a customized building, the seller was entitled to recover the profit it would have made from full performance of the contract even though it also had been able to resell some of the items it had acquired in anticipation of the contract for the same price as called for in the contract.

B. The Buyer can <u>cover</u>, which means he can purchase substitute goods. If so, he is entitled to recover <u>incidental</u> and <u>consequential</u> damages.

Example: <u>KGM Harvesting Co. v. Fresh Network</u>: The court held that an aggrieved buyer can choose to seek damages from a defaulting seller based on the cost of cover.

C. Consequential damages, such as the buyer's lost profits and personal injuries caused by breach, can be recovered in some circumstances.

D. Damages for defective goods are determined by the difference between the value of goods received and their value had they been as warranted.

Example: <u>Jetpac Group, Ltd. v. Bostek, Inc.</u>: Breach of contract resulted in damages for breach of warranty, consequential damages or lost profit, and incidental expenses.

E. If the goods are <u>unique</u>, the buyer may have equitable remedies, such as <u>specific performance</u>.

Learning Objectives

1. You should understand that the UCC provides several remedies to sellers and buyers in breach of sales contract cases. The damaged party must generally select among the remedies.

2. You should note that upon a seller's breach, a buyer is entitled to <u>cover</u> (that is, to purchase other goods to minimize damages) but it is not required to do so under the UCC.

3. Likewise, a seller may resell goods in the event of breach by the buyer, but is not required to do so.

4. You should understand that the seller or buyer, in statements (2) and (3) above must, however, mitigate damages in order to recover <u>incidental</u> or <u>consequential</u> damages for breach of sales contract.

5. Underlying the notion of freedom of contract is the notion that parties should be able to break contracts (and pay damages) as well as make contracts. Consequently, courts are reluctant to award <u>punitive</u> damages for breach of sales contracts, especially in the case of commercial contracts.

6. You must recognize liquidated damages provisions and know the tests for their enforceability.

7. You must recognize consequential damages identify the various types of consequential damages, and know when they are recoverable.

8. You must know what the UCC statute of limitations is and the way operates.

9. You should be able to list the five general remedies available to the seller when the buyer breaches a sales contract.

10. You should know the conditions under which the seller can resell the goods after the buyer's breach, and the damages the seller can recover after he resells.

11. You should know the two possible measures of the recovery available to the seller when the buyer fails to accept the goods or repudiates the contract and the seller elects not to resell.

12. You should be able to list the four general remedies available to the buyer when the seller breaches a contract for the sale of goods.

13. You should know the general test for determining the buyer's recovery when the seller fails to deliver the goods.

14. You should know the general test for determining the buyer's recovery when the seller delivers defective goods.

15. You should know the general test for determining the buyer's recovery when the seller fails to deliver and the buyer covers.

Learning Hints

1. The UCC adopts a "strict performance" standard, which means that a material breach of contract occurs when there is a failure to deliver conforming goods under a contract. In the event of a seller's breach, however, the buyer is required to give notice to the seller of the breach, and the seller will have an opportunity to cure the breach.

2. If the seller breaches the contract, the buyer is entitled to certain remedies. In general, the buyer is <u>not</u> required to "cover" (that is, to obtain the goods elsewhere), but her failure to do so will limit the buyer's ability to recover <u>consequential</u> damages, such as lost profits, as a result of the breach.

3. In some cases, the buyer may be entitled to <u>specific performance</u>, which means that the buyer may enforce the contract and obtain the goods. This remedy is limited to cases where the goods are unique, and thus damages <u>at law</u> (money damages for breach) are inadequate.

4. The UCC provides that a seller who has already begun manufacturing the goods, upon breach of contract by the buyer, must minimize damages by acting in a commercially reasonable manner. In some cases, this requires the seller to complete manufacture and attempt to resell the goods to another buyer.

5. You will notice that, after some introductory material, the chapter is organized around the different seller and buyer remedies the UCC makes available. In studying the chapter, keep this organization in mind. You might want to outline the chapter, treating each remedy individually under these general headings.

6. Remember that the term "consequential damages" is a broad one. It includes personal injury damages, property damage (meaning damage to property other than the goods sold), lost profits, lost business opportunities, and the like.

7. In product liability cases, where consumers sue for defective goods, some courts use the tort statute of limitations even in cases brought under the UCC This statute of limitations usually begins to run when the plaintiff actually suffered injury or discovered or should have discovered a defect in the goods. The point of using the tort statute of limitations in these cases is to give additional protection to the buyer.

8. As the text tells you, the seller is entitled to the purchase price of goods lost or damaged after the buyer assumed the risk of their loss.

9. Section 2-702(2) of the UCC, which gives the seller the right to reclaim goods received on credit by the buyer while insolvent, is basically the UCC's version of the common law remedy of rescission for fraud. The "fraud" here is the buyer's receipt of the goods in a situation where it is unlikely that he will be able to pay for them. The seller must demand the return of the goods within ten days of their receipt, and must actually know about the buyer's insolvency. However, this ten-day requirement does not apply when the buyer has made a written misrepresentation of solvency within three months before delivery.

10. Section 2-715(2)(b) of the UCC says that the buyer can recover for personal injury or property damage resulting from a defect in goods sold when these damages are "proximate" results of the defect. Just what "proximate" means in this context is unclear, but the intent of the Code's drafters was to limit the seller's liability for certain unforeseeable losses.

True-False

In the blank provided, put "**T**" if the statement is True or "**F**" if the statement is False.

_____ 1. A woman is burned when using a bottle of hair dye. A limitation of liability clause on the bottle's label restricts any damages from the use of the product to a refund of the purchase price. This clause will be enforceable.

_____ 2. S sells goods to B and ships the goods on June 2nd. On June 3rd, S learns that B is insolvent. S can recover the goods that are now in B's possession.

_____ 3. Liability for consequential damages cannot be limited or excluded by agreement, even if the limitation is not unconscionable and the exclusion does not apply to personal injuries.

_____ 4. The UCC statute of limitations provides that a lawsuit for breach of contract must be filed within 10 years after the breach occurs.

_____ 5. Heinz enters into a contract to sell a large quantity of ketchup to Price Chopper. Price Chopper then wrongfully breaches the contract. Heinz can probably recover the purchase price of the ketchup from Price Chopper.

_____ 6. Specific performance is a remedy that is used by buyers in most breach of sales contract cases.

_____ 7. Under the UCC, a plaintiff must always sue within four years of the time the defect is discovered regardless of when the harm is discovered.

_____ 8. Incidental damages include storage charges, and sales commissions paid when the goods were resold.

_____ 9. Breach of sales contract suits must be filed within 4 years of the date the goods were sold.

_____ 10. If the seller breaches the contract and the buyer elects not to cover, the buyer can still recover the difference between the contract price and the market price at the time the buyer learns of the seller's breach.

Multiple Choice

Circle the best answer.

1. In the event a buyer breaches a contract, which of the following is <u>not</u> a seller's remedy under the code?
   a. Cancel the contract.
   b. Withhold delivery of undelivered goods.
   c. Sue the buyer for punitive damages.
   d. Recover the purchase price of goods delivered to or accepted by the buyer.

2. Which of the following statements concerning mitigation of damages under the UCC is not correct?
   a. A seller has no duty to mitigate damages in a case where the buyer willfully breaches a contract.
   b. A seller is only required to follow a reasonable course of action to mitigate damages.
   c. A seller's decision to stop manufacture of goods may not be commercially reasonable in some breach of contract cases.
   d. A seller must choose an alternative (to complete manufacture or sell uncompleted goods) that will minimize the loss.

3. Taylor enters into a contract with Player, a 7-foot, 300 pound professional basketball player, to make 10 custom-made suits. After Taylor is 15% of the way through making the suits, Player tells him that he does not want the suits. Which of the following is probably the most reasonable course of action for Taylor?
   a. Sue Player for the full purchase price of the suits.
   b. Sue Player for lost profits.
   c. Stop making the suits and seek damages for time and materials up to that point.
   d. Finish the suits and resell them.

4. Shelly sells 5,000 widgets to Billy for $10,000. Billy breaches the contract. Shelly then sells the 5,000 widgets to Millie for $8,000. Shelly also incurred an additional $500 in extra freight costs to ship the goods to Millie. Shelly sues Billy for breach of contract. Which of the following is most correct?
   a. Shelly has no case against Billy since she was able to sell the widgets to Millie.
   b. Shelly is entitled to $2,500 from Billy.
   c. Shelly can recover the purchase price of $10,000 from Billy.
   d. Shelly can recover $2,000 from Billy.

5. When a buyer accepts goods from the seller that are somewhat defective, the buyer may still recover:

   a. The difference between the value of the goods received and the value the goods would have had if they had been as warranted.

   b. Incidental damages.

   c. Consequential damages.

   d. All of the above.

6. Which of the following is <u>not</u> one of the remedies available to the seller when the buyer breaches a contract for the sale of goods?

   a. Cancellation of the contract.

   b. Cover.

   c. An action for the price of the goods.

   d. Recovery of the seller's lost profit on the deal.

7. A buyer orders a one-of-a-kind Rolls Royce. The dealer breaches the contract. The buyer sues for breach of contract. What would be the most likely remedy?

   a. Difference between contract price and market price of the car.

   b. Covering.

   c. Specific performance.

   d. Canceling the contract and recovering damages.

8. The objective of remedies for breach of contract is to:

   a. Put the injured party in a better position than if the contract had been performed.

   b. Punish the breaching party.

   c. Put the injured party in the same position as if the contract had been performed.

   d. None of the above.

9. Herman sells goods to Lilly and ships the goods. Herman later learns that Lilly is insolvent. What recourse is available to Herman?

   a. Herman can stop delivery of the goods.

   b. Herman can recover goods from Lilly within 10 days of delivery.

   c. Herman can recover the goods from Lilly any time if Lilly gave Herman written misrepresentation of her solvency within the last 3 months.

   d. All of the above.

10. Ward agreed to sell Wally 1,000 ordinary light bulbs. Ward later breaches the contract. Which of the following would not be a reasonable remedy for Wally?

    a. Sue for specific performance.

    b. Cover and find the light bulbs elsewhere.

    c. Recover the difference between the contract and market prices of the light bulbs.

    d. Cancel the contract and recover damages.

Short Essay

1.   A orders ball bearings from B for his manufacturing operation, telling B that he needs them for machinery used to fulfill a contract with another party, and that if B does not perform A will not have time to obtain substitute goods. The reasonable value of ball bearings of this sort is $10,000. B ships A some defective ball bearings worth $2,000. As a result, A cannot fulfill his other contract and loses $25,000 in the process. A also incurs $300 in costs for storing the defective bearings. A sues B. What damages can A recover?

2.   Describe under what circumstances courts will allow liquidated damages clauses.

3.   A agrees to sell his used car to B for $5000, but then B repudiates the contract. After being forced to wait one month and spending $50 in storage costs for the car, A sells it to C for $4500. What is A required to do before he can recover from B damages based on the resale? Assuming A does this, what amount can he recover from B?

4.   The Hendersons ordered the best quality Andersen Windows from Home Depot for their new home. Home Depot delivered a lower quality of Andersen Windows. Discuss the remedies available to the Hendersons.

5.   Rodney purchased a weed-whacker from a local hardware store. He intended to use the weed-whacker to clear a field for Farmer Brown on Saturday. Two days after he purchased the weed-whacker, Rodney discovered it was defective and could not be repaired. Rodney paid $50.00 for the weed-whacker and lost $20.00 in profits from his contract with Farmer Brown. In addition, Rodney injured his ring finger when the weed-whacker malfunctioned. Discuss the kinds of damages Rodney may recover for breach of contract in this case and explain each.

6.   Tommy has a baseball card collection. Tommy goes to JD's Cards and is told that they can sell him a 2001 Barry Bonds card for $20. Due to a mistake by a JD's clerk, the store is unable to come up with the card. What would be the reasonable thing for Tommy to do?

7.   Tammy has the baseball that Barry Bonds his for his 700th homerun. She agrees to sell it to Mike for $500,000. However, before delivering the ball to Mike, Pedro offers her $750,000 for it. She sells the baseball to Pedro. What remedy would probably be available to Mike?

8.   Larry sells 1,000 widgets to Mary. The widgets are shipped on June 3rd and are delivered to Mary on June 5th. On June 6th, Larry learns that Mary is insolvent and on the brink of filing for bankruptcy. What actions can Larry take at this point?

9.   In the above case, how would your answer change if Larry had received a statement from Mary a month before delivery stating that Mary's business was doing well financially?

CHAPTER 22
THE AGENCY RELATIONSHIP--CREATION, DUTIES, AND TERMINATION

Outline

I.   Agency relationships arise when one person (the agent) acts for the benefit of and under the direction of another (the principal).

   A. Agency relationships may arise from agreement or may be implied from the circumstances.

   Example: Iragorri v. United Technologies: The court ruled that Otis Elevator Company was not responsible for the negligence of Columbian Companies that installed and maintained an elevator which did not function properly and caused Iragorri's death. The Columbian Companies were not acting for the benefit or the control of Otis.

   Example: Kakides v. King Davis Agency: The court dismissed the sexual harassment claim of a real estate agent against the agency she worked for because she was an independent contractor and not an employee, therefore Title VII did not apply to her.

   B. Generally, the capacity of the principal determines the agent capacity to contract on behalf of the principal.

II. An agent owes certain duties to the principal.

   A. An agent is a fiduciary and owes a duty of loyalty to the principal.

   Example: Cameco v. Gedicke: Agents should avoid the possibility of violating the duty of loyalty to their principals.

   B. Usually, a dual agency is a breach of duty of loyalty; however, an exception arises when the dual agent is merely a middleman (as in real estate contracts).

   C. An agent breaches the duty of loyalty if he disclosed confidential information obtained in the agency relationship.

   Example: Pacific Aerospace and Electronics v. Taylor: The court ruled that former employees of a company were violating their duties of confidentiality and loyalty when they compiled a list of customers and their characteristics for a new and competing business they were forming.

   D. An agent must obey instructions, exercise care and skill, and communicate information to principal.

   Example: Ikola v. Schoene: The court found that a jury should determine whether a real estate agent violated her duty of reasonable care and skill when she failed to give the seller's disclosure statement to Ikola and when she also misrepresented that Ikola had no right to an inspection .report.

   E. An agent has a duty to account for funds and property, and to keep funds separate from her own.

III. Types of Agents

   A. Commercial agents take orders on behalf of their principal and are usually compensated by payment of a commission. Agents usually possess the authority to contract on behalf of their principals and they usually do not bear financial risk of nonpayment by the purchaser.

   B. Employees are dependent agents who are under the control of their employer as to both the objective of their work and the means used to achieve it.

   C. Independent contractors are under the control of their principals as to the result of their work, but not the means to achieve it.

IV. Duties of principals to agents.

    A. A principal must compensate the agent. Under the <u>procuring cause</u> rule, if an agent was the primary factor in a purchase or sale, he may be entitled to the commission regardless of who eventually completes the sale.

        Example: <u>Christensen Sales Agency v. General Time Corporation</u>: An agent has a right to a commission even after the termination of the agency if he was a substantial factor in the sale.

    B. Special Rules:

        1. Duration of agency will be a reasonable one (absent express agreement);

        2. A real estate broker is generally entitled to a commission when she procures a "ready, willing, and able" buyer.

        3. It is customary for a company to pay an insurance agent a commission on all premiums paid on the insurance contract sold.

V. Termination of agent's powers.

    A. By agreement.

    B. Either party may terminate an agency based on mutual consent at any time.

        1. An agency coupled with an interest arises when the power of agency is given as security; such an agency is irrevocable without the consent of the agent.

        2. Termination of an agency may be prohibited under federal and state law (as, for example, in cases of illegal discrimination based on race, color, sex, etc.).

        3. Termination by operation of law, including death or insanity or bankruptcy of either party.

    C. An agent may still be liable to <u>third persons</u> after termination of the agency unless the principal gives <u>actual notice</u> or the third party has <u>constructive notice</u> of the termination.

        Example: <u>Johnson v. Nationwide Insurance Company</u>: Under the doctrine of apparent authority, Nationwide was liable to Johnson when a former agent sold her an investment he no longer had the actual authority to sell.

Learning Objectives

1. You should understand that an agency is a relationship that may arise through express agreement, or may be implied from circumstances.

2. Generally, an implied agency only arises when the principal acts in such a way as to imply that an agency exists.

3. You should know what a principal is and what an agent is, and should understand how the agency relationship may facilitate business transactions.

4. You should recognize the numerous ways in which the agent's duty of loyalty can arise, and should be aware of the potential problems that accompany any self-dealing by the agent.

5. You should be aware of the agent's general duty to obey instructions, but be able to recognize the special circumstances in which the agent will be excused for violating instructions.

6. You should become familiar with the agent's general duty to exercise care and skill, as well as the agent's duty to communicate, to the principal, agency-related information that comes to the attention of the agent.

7. You should be aware of the risks an agent faces when she commingles personal property with agency property, or when she uses the principal's money or property for her (the agent's) own personal purposes.

8. You should be aware of the general nature of the duties the law will impute to the principal in the absence of contractual provisions to the contrary.

9. You should understand the general rights of the agent to compensation, including the rights an agent may have to receive contingent compensation, such as commissions, upon termination of the agency.

10. You should recognize the general situations in which the principal has a duty to reimburse or indemnify the agent.

11. You should be able to distinguish among commercial agents, employees, and independent contractors.

Learning Hints

1. An agency relationship is an important legal concept because it facilitates commercial enterprise. Utilizing an agency relationship, a principal may do business with many individuals from corporate entities.

2. An agency relationship may arise as a result of an express agreement. Certain kinds of agency agreements, for example real estate agency agreements between a principal and agent, must be in writing in order to be enforceable in many states.

3. There are many kinds of agency relationships. One of the most common is the employee/employer relationship.

4. An agency relationship may also arise as a result of circumstances. In some cases, for example, a court may find that a principal has created the implied authority for an agent to act on his/her behalf. This relationship may even arise in cases where the parties do not believe such an agency to exist.

5. The agent's duty of loyalty lies at the very heart of the agent's responsibilities to the principal and governs all of the agent's activities. Any time an agent engages in self-dealing or appears to be engaging in an improper act, the agent is in violation of this duty unless the principal approves of the activity. Accordingly, the agent must fully and openly disclose all conflicts and potential conflicts to the principal.

6. If an agent's activities could lead to any appearance of impropriety, the agent must make a full disclosure to the principal. Therefore, an agent's purchases from the principal or an agent's sales to the principal fall into the category of activities that must be disclosed to the principal, in order that the principal is not taken advantage of by the agent. Further, if the agent is serving two principals (making the agent a dual agent), the agent possesses dual loyalties and must disclose the situation to both principals.

7. Because the agent is acting on behalf of the principal, it follows that the agent has a duty to follow the principal's instructions. However, in certain situations, the agent may have implied authority to deviate from the principal's instructions. These situations usually occur when the principal cannot be reached immediately and some emergency threatens to damage or destroy agency property. As the agent has been hired to further some goal in connection with the principal's property, it would not be in the best interests of either the agent or the principal if the property were damaged. Accordingly, the agent may possess special authority to supersede the principal's instructions.

8. Because the agent is considered to be one with the principal, the principal is entitled to any gifts the agent receives from third parties in connection with the agency. This follows from the agent's duty of loyalty. Any of these gifts might encourage an agent to pursue self-interest over the interests of the principal. Therefore, the gifts will belong to the principal unless the principal consents to the agent's keeping them, after a full and open disclosure by the agent.

9. The agent's duty of loyalty clearly is violated if the agent discloses the principal's confidential information to others without the principal's consent, or uses the confidential information to benefit him or herself. The agent's duty not to make such uses of the principal's confidential information continues even after the agency has terminated. After termination of the agency, the former agent may use the general knowledge and skills he gained while working for the principal, however. Therefore, it is important that a distinction be made between general knowledge and skills on the one hand, and confidential information or trade secrets on the other. In order for information to be considered a trade

secret, the principal must have taken significant steps to keep the information substantially secret, and must generally have allowed only a limited number of persons to have access to it, on strictly a confidential basis.

10. If an agent uses agency property for personal purposes or commingles agency and personal property, the agent may be subjected to liability. Being inconsistent with the best interests of the principal, these practices smack of a conflict of interest. In order to discourage these practices, the principal may, where the agent has engaged in such a practice, choose to take the benefit of any contract the agent enters into-- because the agent in theory was to have been acting for the principal. Alternatively, where the agent has engaged in such a practice, the principal may choose to disavow any responsibility for transactions that were not profitable and/or sue the agent for conversion.

11. The agent's ability to recover from the principal for expenses incurred is of the same general nature as a quasi-contract remedy. It would be unduly harsh not to require the principal to pay for the benefits that an agent in good faith has bestowed upon the principal. Similarly, fairness demands that the principal indemnify the agent for loss experienced by the agent while acting on behalf of the principal. Of course, the principal is not held liable to the agent for the amounts of the agent's expenses if the expenses were unauthorized. For similar reasons, the principal has no obligation to indemnify the agent for a loss experienced by the agent if the loss resulted from some fault on the part of the agent.

12. The agent's entitlement to commissions–even after termination of the agency–is based on reasoning akin to what is set forth in #7, above. The agent should recover the commission when his or her activities were the procuring cause of a completed transaction. Otherwise, the principal or a subsequent agent will be receiving a windfall at the expense of the original agent.

13. Commercial agents have the ability to contract on behalf of their principals; they generally do not bear financial risk of nonpayment by purchasers; they take orders on behalf of their principals and generally are paid commissions for their work. Employees are under the control of their employers both as to the objective of their work and the means used to achieve it. Independent contractors are usually only under the control of their principal as to the result of their work.

True-False

In the blank provided, put "**T**" if the statement is True or "**F**" if the statement is False.

_____ 1. When an agency is terminated, actual notice to everyone who dealt or might deal with the agent is necessary.

_____ 2. An agent may represent both parties to a contract if each principal is fully informed of this situation and consents to it.

_____ 3. An agent is always liable to the principal for not following the principal's instructions.

_____ 4. One aspect of the agent's duty of loyalty is that an agent cannot ever compete with his principal, even after the agency has ended.

_____ 5. Under the duty of loyalty, an agent must avoid even the appearance of impropriety.

_____ 6. An insurance agent terminates his employment with the insurance company. The agent decides to keep the computer that was furnished for him by the company. The agent is liable for conversion.

_____ 7. Under the procuring cause rule, an agent is not entitled to receive commissions on sales that occur after the agency relationship is terminated.

_____ 8. Marriage does not automatically make each spouse the agent of the other.

_____ 9. An exception to the rule that either party to an agency relationship has the power to terminate the agency at any time is agency coupled with an interest.

_____ 10. Agency at will generally empowers either an agent or principal to terminate the agency relationship at any time, even if the agency agreement states that the agency will continue for a certain length of time.

Multiple Choice

Circle the best answer.

1. Which of the following statements is not true concerning termination of an agency relationship?
   a. Bill and Barbara Bailey place an advertisement in the local newspaper disclaiming any future liability for debts incurred by their son, Bronco. This is an example of constructive notice.
   b. First Bank can pay on checks drawn against Fred's account even for a short time after Fred's death.
   c. Donna pledges stock to a credit union as collateral on a loan. Donna can revoke the credit union's power to sell the stock.
   d. Ken sells life insurance for Bet Your Life Insurance Company. Ken can generally terminate this relationship anytime.

2. In an agency relationship where the agency is coupled with an interest:
   a. Only the principal may terminate the agency.
   b. The agent must consent in order for the principal to terminate the agency.
   c. Neither party may terminate the agency.
   d. None of the above is correct.

3. Which of the following is true concerning agency?
   a. A minor cannot serve as an agent.
   b. All agents must be compensated.
   c. The agency relationship must be in writing.
   d. A minor who enters into a contract made by his agent may still be able to avoid the contract.

4. A "fiduciary relationship" means:
   a. That the principal owes a duty of loyalty to the agent.
   b. That the agent owes a duty of loyalty to the principal.
   c. That both parties owe a duty of loyalty to each other.
   d. That neither party owes a duty of loyalty to the other.

5. Jane prepares tax returns each year for Barb. Which of the following is a duty Jane owes to Barb?
   a. Jane owes Barb the duty of loyalty. Jane must keep Barb's tax information confidential.
   b. Jane owes Barb the duty to exercise care and skill. As a paid tax professional, Jane should be able to prepare Barb's return in a competent fashion.
   c. Barb is attempting to take deductions that are marginal at best. Jane has a duty to make Barb aware of this situation.
   d. All of the above.

6. Jenny sells life insurance for several life insurance companies, including Atlantic Life. Which of the following statements is not true concerning Atlantic's duties to Jenny?

   a. Jenny may be entitled to commissions from Atlantic for years after she leaves the company.

   b. Atlantic must reimburse Jenny for amounts she spends for lunches with clients.

   c. Atlantic must make accurate records of Jenny's commissions available to her.

   d. Atlantic may have a duty to reimburse Jenny for advertisements she paid for in the local paper that only mentioned Atlantic Life policies.

7. Which of the following statements is true concerning agency?

   a. The procuring cause rule may allow an agent to earn a commission even after termination of the agency relationship.

   b. Carl prepared Acme's corporate tax return and filed it late due to no fault on the part of Acme. As a result of the late filing, Acme owes a penalty to the state. Acme cannot deduct the penalty from Carl's fees.

   c. Fran has Ed work on her car. Ed cannot keep the car until Fran pays him for the repairs.

   d. Dane works as a commissioned salesman for Rich. The employment contract calls for Rich to pay Dane a draw. The contract does not address the possibility of the draws exceeding Dane's commissions. Rich will generally be able to recover overpayments to Dane.

8. As an employee at Woody's Grocery Store, Earl learned from Woody how to recognize truly fresh produce when farmers brought their produce to the store. After he ceased being Woody's employee, Earl opened his own grocery store and put his knowledge about recognizing fresh produce to good use. Earl's store became well known for its fine produce. Soon, Woody's former customers began buying their produce and other groceries at Earl's store instead of at Woody's. Woody then sued Earl for the damages allegedly resulting to him because of the loss of customers. Woody will

   a. Win the suit because Earl, in operating a business that competed with Woody's, used confidential information belonging to Woody.

   b. Lose the suit, because Earl was merely making permissible use of general knowledge he had gained while working for Woody.

   c. Win the suit, because an agent's duty of loyalty always prohibits him from going into competition with the principal even after the agency relationship has ended.

   d. Lose the suit even though Earl used confidential information, because nothing in the facts indicates that Earl had agreed in writing not to use such information.

9. Janet sells cosmetics on a part-time basis for Avalon. Which of the following statements concerning this agency relationship are not true?

   a. Janet is not obligated to keep sales revenue received from customers separate from her own funds.

   b. Janet has a duty to Avalon to accurately report income she receives from customers.

   c. Janet has a duty to account for samples of products and inventory to Avalon.

   d. Janet may be guilty of embezzlement if she pockets income received from customers.

10. Which of the following statements concerning agency is true?

   a. A gratuitous agent owes a higher degree of skill to her principal than does a compensated agent.

   b. A middleman in a contract is a dual agent and therefore liable for breach of loyalty.

   c. Agents, after terminating the agency relationship, can use the general knowledge and skills learned while working for the principal, even in competition with the former principal.

   d. The agent's duty of loyalty does not include just the appearance of impropriety.

Short Answer:

1.   Bart agrees to put Sam's Super Bowl championship autographed football in his sports store to sell for $1,500. Sam agrees to pay Bart a 15% commission for selling the ball. If Joe comes in the sports store and offers Bart $1,200 for the ball, can Bart accept this offer?

2.   What kind of notice should a principal who no longer wants to be bound by the acts of his former agent give in order to prevent the agent from continuing to make contract in the principal's name.

3.   Hardy is a CPA who prepares Hunter's tax return for a fee. Hardy prepares Hunter's return at the end of the filing season when he is really rushed for time and he misses several deductions that cost Hunter hundreds of dollars in tax liability. What responsibility does Hardy owe to Hunter?

4.   In the question above, assume Hardy is just Hunter's neighbor who knows something about taxes and he does Hunter's return gratuitously. What is Hardy's responsibility to Hunter in this situation?

5. Mr. Donnie Dim worked as a research assistant for a law firm while he was attending State U School of Law. He found a way to hack into proprietary legal research databases and do his research at little or no cost to his firm. His performance was so good that the law firm offered him a full time job on graduation from law school. The hacked databases find out about Danny's scam and sue the law firm for damages. The law firm claims it did not know of Donny's actions and would not have condoned it. Was Danny acting as the firm's agent?

6. John's wife Jane has made numerous purchases from 3 different stores on John's charge account. If John no longer wishes to be liable for Jane's purchases, what action should he take?

7. Tanya accepts a sales position with a life insurance company. After spending 6 months on the job, Tanya notifies the company that she will no longer be representing them. What kind of agency relationship is this?

CHAPTER 23

LIABILITY OF PRINCIPALS AND AGENTS TO THIRD PARTIES

Outline

I. Agent's authority to bind the principal.

    A. The agent's authority is either <u>actual</u> or <u>apparent</u>. It may also arise as a result of <u>ratification</u> of the agent's actions by the principal.

        Example: <u>Shurgard Storage Centers v. Safeguard Self-Storage</u>: Unless otherwise agreed, the authority of an agent terminates if, without knowledge of the principal, he acquires adverse interests or if he is otherwise guilty of a serious breach of loyalty to the principal.

    B. Actual authority is either express or implied.

        1. Express authority arises from express language in an agency agreement—for example, a power of attorney is an express agency agreement.

        2. Implied authority arises because an agent possesses the implied authority to do whatever is reasonably necessary to accomplish the objectives of the agency. The test is the "justifiable belief of the agent."

    C. Apparent authority is based on conduct by the principal that causes a third person to reasonably believe an agency exists. The test is the "justifiable belief of the third party."

        Example: <u>Houck v. The Feller Living Trust</u>: The sole trustee for the Feller trust gave a power of attorney to Kelly. He then borrowed money from Houck, pledging trust property as security. When Kelly defaulted on the loans, Houck attempted to take possession of the trust property. The court found that the trust was not liable because Kelly had neither actual nor apparent authority. There was no apparent authority because Houck could not reasonably believe that Kelly had authority to bind the trust on his personal loans.

    D. Ratification occurs when a principal authorizes an act of an agent after the act was done. Test is the "intention of the principal."

        Example: <u>North American Specialty Insurance v. Employer's Reinsurance</u>: NAS accepted and retained payment of the premiums on bonds that it knew were unauthorized when they were issued. When 12 of the bonds resulted in defaults, NAS argued that it was not responsible to pay the claims on them because they were unauthorized. The court disagreed, saying that NAS impliedly ratified the unauthorized issuance when it accepted the premiums.

        1. Requires proof that the agent acted on behalf of the principal and principal had capacity to act.

II. Related liability Issues: Liability of principal.

    A. Principal is generally bound by agent's representations if the agent had express, implied, or apparent authority to make such statements. The principal is generally liable for misrepresentations made by the agent under these theories.

        1. A principal may give notice of lack of agent's authority through an <u>exculpatory clause</u>. However, many courts permit a third party to rescind a contract for misrepresentation even though the contract contains such a clause.

    B. Payments to the agent discharge debt to the principal; the principal is not bound if the agent colludes with the third party to withhold such payments from the principal.

    C. Principal's liability for acts of subagents: A subagent is an agent of the agent. Both the principal and agent may be bound by the authorized acts of the subagent.

III. Contract liability of the agent.

A. Generally, the agent is not liable for the contracts made on behalf of the principal. Exceptions include: unauthorized actions by the agent, nonexistent or incompetent principals, and agreements by the agent to assume liability, undisclosed or partially disclosed principal.

Example: River Colony Estates v. Bayview Financial Trading Group: Dix, the agent of River Colony, took out loans at a higher rate of interest than River Colony expected. When River Colony sued the lender, the lender argued that, under agency law, River Colony had constructive knowledge of the loan rates because Dix was its agent. The court refused to dismiss River Colony's claim. It reasoned that the agent's knowledge is not imputed to the principal when the agent and the third party collude to withhold information from the principal.

B. Liability is imposed on an agent who has exceeded his authority based on an implied warranty of authority.

C. If the principal is not in existence or is incompetent, the agent is liable. In addition, an agent may become a party to a contract along with the principal, thus assuming liability.

D. If the principal is disclosed, the contract is between the principal and third party.

Example: Hirsch v. Columbia University: Hirsch left a tenured position to join the faculty at Columbia. To induce her to take the position, Columbia's Dean of Medicine wrote a letter promising she would be recommended for tenure. When she was denied tenure, in part because she had not been hired in the standard manner, she sued the Dean, claiming that he had assured her that her hiring was following Columbia's standard hiring procedure. The court held that the Dean was not liable because he signed the letter as an agent on behalf of a disclosed principal.

E. If the principal is undisclosed, the agent is liable (but the agent may be entitled to indemnification from the principal).

Example: H.A. Smith Lumber and Hardware v. Decina: When Decina contracted to purchase materials from H.A. Smith lumber, he failed to disclose that he was acting on behalf of his corporation when he filled out the credit application. The court found that Decina was personally liable on the contract because his principal, the corporation, was undisclosed.

F. A principal is partially disclosed when the third person knows he is dealing with an agent but does not know the identity of the principal. The agent is liable on contracts on behalf of a partially disclosed principal.

IV. Liability for torts.

A. Principals are liable for the torts of their agents under three theories:

1. Direct liability (Principal was directly liable, for example, in negligently hiring or supervising the agent.)

2. *Respondeat superior*: Principals (generally employers of tort-feasing employees) may be liable to third persons injured by the torts of their agents under this theory of imputed liability.

Example: White v. Revco Discount Drug Centers: Even proof that an employee violated specific instructions of the employer in committing the tort generally will not relieve the principal from liability.

Example: TGM Ashley Lakes v. Jennings: Jennings was murdered in an apartment by a man employed by her landlord. If the landlord had checked out the man's criminal history, it would have discovered that he had spent much of his adult life in prison for felony convictions, including rape. The man had keys to Jennings's apartment, despite the fact that the apartment complex had had numerous unforced entries and burglaries during the six months before the murder. The court found the landlord liable for Jennings's murder under a theory of direct liability. This is because it was negligent in its hiring and supervision of the murderer.

3. Liability for negligence of agents is common, but courts are less likely to impose liability on principals for their agents' intentional torts.

4. Agent generally cannot avoid liability for his own torts.

5. It was once difficult to convict the employer for a crime committed by an employee; newly revised criminal codes are more likely to impose such liability.

B. Criminal Liability

1. Foreign Corrupt Practices Act
   a. Payments made by any U.S. individual or firm to foreign officials for the purpose of obtaining business are illegal.
   b. Payments to secure routine governmental action are legal.
   c. Companies may be liable for the actions of their foreign agents.

Learning Objectives

1. You should understand the difference between duties and liabilities of an agent regarding a principal, and that of an agent and principal to third parties.

2. You should understand the different legal implications of an express, implied, and apparent agency.

3. You should understand the concept of *respondeat superior* and the difference between and employee and independent contractor.

4. You should understand the circumstances under which a principal may be directly liable for the torts of his agent.

5. You should know how apparent authority may arise, and should recognize that where the agent possessed apparent authority, the principal's liability to third persons is the same as if there had been actual authority.

6. You should understand how ratification of an unauthorized act may occur, and what the effect of ratification is.

7. You should be able to distinguish among agencies involving disclosed, undisclosed, and partially disclosed principals. It is also important that you be familiar with the liability the principal and the agent may face in each of these three agency situations.

8. You should understand the liability of the agent to third persons when the agent has committed unauthorized acts, and should know why the agent is obligated to indemnify the principal when the principal is held liable to the third party in cases involving apparent authority.

9. You should become familiar with the rules governing when a principal is held accountable for the representations of an agent. You should also understand how a properly constructed exculpatory clause may minimize, for principals, problems of this nature.

10. You should know how to determine whether information given to an agent is considered notice to the principal.

11. You should understand the main points of the Foreign Corrupt Practices Act.

Learning Hints

1. Whether a principal will be bound to a third party on contracts made by an agent depends on the agent's authority to act for the principal. That authority may be express, implied, or apparent.

2. A principal may also be bound on contracts if he/she ratifies the acts of the agent.

3. Generally, a principal will be liable for representations made by the agent, if those representations were made with authority.

4. Whether an agent is personally bound on contracts made on behalf of a principal depends on whether the principal was disclosed to the third party.

5. A principal may be liable for the torts of his/her agent under the theory of direct liability, or respondeat superior.

6. Remember that an agent may have authority to bind the principal even though the principal has not specifically authorized the agent to do the particular act done by the agent. The doctrines of implied authority and apparent authority, if made applicable by the facts of a given case, may lead to the kind of result described in the preceding sentence.

7. The legal effect of the agent's authorized actions is, in most circumstances, that the principal is bound to the same degree the principal would have been bound if the principal had done the act personally.

8. The principal is the source of actual authority and apparent authority. Both actual authority (which may be express or implied) and apparent authority depend upon some action or inaction by the principal.

9. It will be easier for you to distinguish between implied authority (which is a form of actual authority) and apparent authority if you learn the respective tests for each. The test for implied authority is the justifiable belief of the agent, whereas the test for apparent authority is the justifiable belief of the third person with whom the supposed agent dealt. In either situation, however, the justifiable belief must stem from something the principal has said or done, or has failed to say or do. It is in that sense that the principal is the source of all authority.

10. The agent assumes certain risks when she is part of an undisclosed or partially disclosed agency. The foremost risk is that the agent may be held liable if the principal fails to perform. There is some consolation for the agent in that if the agent acted with authority, the agent has a right to be indemnified by the principal in the event that the agent is held liable to the third person. This will be small consolation, however, if the principal's reason for failing to perform the principal's obligation to the third person was the principal's weak financial position or, worse yet, the principal's bankruptcy. In those situations, the agent's right to be indemnified by the principal may become virtually meaningless.

11. When an agent performs unauthorized acts or makes unauthorized representations, the agent, rather than the principal, is the party who is liable to the third person with whom the agent dealt. The principal cannot be held liable to the third person where the principal has done nothing to create actual authority or provide the basis for apparent authority. If the agent had no actual authority but did possess apparent authority, the principal will be liable to the third person, but the agent, in turn, will have an obligation to indemnify the principal.

12. When the agent "represents" a nonexistent or incompetent principal, the agent clearly is the party who will be liable to the third person with whom the agent dealt. In such an instance, there is no principal with legal capacity to be bound by any contract.

13. Be certain to remember that notice given to an agent is considered as notice to the principal only if the information relates to the business of the agency. Therefore, in determining whether a third person's giving of notice to an agent constitutes notice to the principal, one ordinarily must do more than merely inquire as to whether the party receiving the notice was an agent of the principal. It is usually necessary to make a further inquiry concerning whether the information given to the agent by the third person pertained to the business of that particular agent's relationship with the principal.

14. It is logical that a principal is not bound by an agent's action where the agent was involved in a conflict of interest situation of which the third person was aware. The agent has a conflict of interest when he is acting to serve his own interests or those of the third party, rather than those of the principal. As you have already learned, an agent is to subordinate his own interests to those of the principal. If the third person with whom the agent dealt is aware of the conflict or is an active participant in it, the agent's action cannot be said to have been taken with apparent authority, because the third person could not have had a justifiable belief that the agent was authorized to take such an action.

15. The difference between direct liability and liability under respondeat superior is that with direct liability, the principal really is being held accountable for her own tort or wrongdoing, not necessarily for that of the agent. Perhaps the agent did commit a tort (for which the agent himself will be liable), but the principal may have committed a separate tort by being negligent in supervising the agent or by being involved in the agent's wrongdoing--such as by directing the agent to commit the tortious act. Imposing direct liability on the principal would be appropriate in such instances. Of course, the agent would also be liable for his tort. Holding a principal liable on the basis of respondeat superior is something different. Under respondeat superior, the principal is held liable for the torts of her employees if the torts were committed in the scope of employment. No active fault or wrongdoing on the part of the principal is required. Respondeat superior is grounded on the public policy of giving injured third persons another, presumably, financially responsible party to look to besides the employee for payment of the injured parties' damages. Once again, even if the principal is held liable under respondeat superior, the employee who actually committed the tort is held liable in his own right.

True-False

In the blank provided, put "**T**" if the statement is True or "**F**" if the statement is False.

_____ 1. It was once difficult to convict the employer for a crime committed by an employee; however, newly revised criminal codes are more likely to impose such liability.

_____ 2. Art signs a contract as a real estate agent to sell Deb's house. This is an example of express authority.

_____ 3. An agent has the implied authority to do whatever is reasonably necessary to accomplish the purposes of the agency.

_____ 4. Apparent authority protects the agent from liability for unauthorized acts of a principal.

_____ 5. Ministerial acts may be delegated by an agent to her employees.

_____ 6. A bar owner may be liable for one of his employees assaulting a patron under the doctrine of _respondeat superior_.

_____ 7. If an agent represents an unincorporated association, the agent will be personally liable to the third person with whom the agent dealt in the event that the association fails to perform.

_____ 8. It is possible that one may be liable for the acts of someone posing as her agent, even though no actual authority had been given to the person who posed as the agent.

_____ 9. The rights and duties of the parties when the principal is partially disclosed are essentially the same as when the principal is disclosed.

_____ 10. A principal must fully understand the legal significance of all material facts before ratifying the acts of an agent.

Multiple Choice

Circle the best answer.

1. Jane was hired as a janitor for a local cleaning service. While cleaning a client's home, she negligently left a bucket of water in front of the front door. When the client came home from work, she slipped and fell over the bucket. Who may the client sue, if any?

   a. Only the agent (Jane) is liable for her own torts.

   b. Only the principal (the cleaning service) is liable for the negligent acts of its agents.

   c. Both Jane and the cleaning service may be liable.

   d. Neither is liable, because a principal and agent are only liable for intentional, not negligent torts.

2. Pam asks Olivia to sell her house for her while Pam is in Australia for one year. The agreement is in writing. Which of the following statements is not true concerning this arrangement?

   a. Olivia possesses express authority to sell Pam's house.

   b. Olivia possesses apparent authority to sell Pam's house.

   c. Olivia is probably an attorney-in-fact for Pam.

   d. Olivia possesses Pam's power of attorney.

3. In the above case, suppose Pam asked Olivia to sell her house for as close to $150,000 as she could. Which of the following statements is not true?

   a. The agreement between Pam and Olivia makes Olivia a general agent for Pam and capable of conducting a variety of transactions for Pam other than selling her house.

   b. Olivia would likely possess implied authority to sell the house for slightly less than $150,000 if she has reason to believe that Pam would accept the lower offer.

   c. Olivia may possess inherent power to contact Pam's insurance agent if a hail storm damaged several windows in Pam's house.

   d. Olivia is likely considered to be a special agent who has the authority to sell Pam's house.

4. Kay is a real estate agent who contracts to sell Dean's house. In order for Kay to bind Dean to a real estate contract, Kay must:

   a. Be an independent contractor.

   b. Be a general agent.

   c. Possess either actual or apparent authority.

   d. Be a special agent.

5. Which of the following is not a requirement of ratification?

   a. The principal must have had the capacity to do the act both when it was done in the principal's name by the agent and at the time of ratification.

   b. Ratification must be done before cancellation by the third person.

   c. Only the entire act of the agent can be ratified.

   d. The principal must express her intent for ratification.

6. Andrea signs a promissory note at Third Bank as president of Pip Co. Which of the following would be the best way for Andrea to sign the note so that she can avoid personal liability on it?

   a. Andrea

   b. Andrea, Agent

   c. Pip Co. by Andrea, President

   d. Andrea, Disclosed Agent

7. Which of the following statements is true?

   a. An agent is personally liable to third parties on contracts made on behalf of undisclosed principals.

   b. An undisclosed principal cannot sue to enforce a contract made on her behalf.

   c. An agent generally has liability on contracts made for a disclosed principal.

   d. An agent has the right of indemnification against an undisclosed principal even when the principal is insolvent.

8. An agent may become personally liable to third parties under which these circumstances:
   a. Unauthorized actions by the agent.
   b. Incompetent principals.
   c. Undisclosed principals.
   d. All of the above.
9. Which of the following statements is not true?
   a. An agent who commits a criminal act under instructions of his principal is guilty of the crime.
   b. The FCPA considers payments a company makes to government officials to secure routine governmental action to be illegal.
   c. U.S. companies that retain foreign agents to solicit business abroad should establish an FCPA compliance program.
   d. Companies using foreign agents should conduct regular audits of their agents' expenditures.
10. A principal's ratification:
   a. Cannot be of an act of someone who had not been appointed as an agent at all.
   b. May be of an act of an agent who has exceeded the authority given to him.
   c. May be of the beneficial parts of an agent's unauthorized act, without an assumption of the burdensome parts thereof.
   d. Cannot be found to have taken place unless the principal expressly states that she wishes to ratify the unauthorized act.

Short Essay

1. Fred is an electrician. John is a builder who builds a large number of houses each year. John hires Fred to do the wiring of all of his houses. Fred has no time to work for anyone else but John. Is Fred an employee or an independent contractor?

2. If Fred is driving from one of John's houses to another one to do some wiring and he runs over a small child, would John be liable for Fred's actions?

3.   Phillip hired Ace to collect a debt from Scott. He told Ace, "I'll leave the methods to you, but make sure you get the money." As it turns out, Ace is a violent person with a history of serious fights. Phillip could have discovered this but failed to check on Ace's background. When trying to collect the debt, Ace beat up Scott and injured him. Scott sued <u>Phillip</u> for damages. What result is likely and why?

4.   Sally is an attorney negotiating to purchase a large tract of land for V-Mart. V-Mart is an undisclosed principal in this case. If the seller of the land breaches the contract, can Sally sue them?

5.   Margaux and Sabrina were the best of personal friends and met for drinks at the local pub after work. Margaux is a CPA and partner in the M and M CPA firm, and Sabrina works there as a receptionist and is not a CPA. While at the pub, they met Spenser, and Sabrina told Spenser that she could prepare his taxes as a CPA. Margaux winks in acknowledgement of the conversation. Subsequently, Sabrina poorly prepares Spenser's taxes. Spenser now wants to sue M and M CPAs for malpractice. Who is liable?

6.   Marvin sells siding for Basler's. Marvin tells a prospective customer that the insulated siding should save the homeowner 20% on home utility costs. If Marvin does not have express authority from Basler's to make this guaranty, who will be liable to the customer if the siding does not produce a utility savings?

7.   Slick is a life insurance agent who misrepresents some facts about policies to a prospective customer. The policy contains an exculpatory clause. If a customer purchases a policy when relying on Slick's misrepresentations, can she later rescind the contract?

CHAPTER 24
EMPLOYMENT LAWS

Outline

I. Health and safety legislation.

   A. Workers' compensation.

      1. In the 19th century, an employee injured on the job was often barred from recovering damages under the defenses of <u>contributory negligence</u> and <u>assumption of the risk</u>. Under the <u>fellow-servant rule</u>, an employer avoided liability if the negligence of another worker caused the harm.

      2. Most states today have adopted workers' compensation laws. These <u>eliminate fault</u> as a basis of liability; in return, the amount the employer must pay is limited.

      3. An employee can only recover if within the class of employees covered by the law; further, the injury must be <u>work-related</u>.

   B. OSHA (Occupational Safety and Health Act of 1970) applies to all businesses that affect interstate commerce.

      1. Imposes duty on employers to prevent workplace hazards and authorizes labor department to issue health and safety standards.

      2. The Family and Medical Leave Act, passed in 1993, provides job security, as well as reasonable leave periods to employees with serious health conditions.

      Example: <u>Caldwell v. Holland</u>: The Family and Medical Leave Act allows working men and women to balance the conflicting demands of work and personal life.

II. Wages and pensions.

   A. Fair Labor Standards Act mandates a minimum hourly wage and overtime wage, and prohibits oppressive child labor.

   B. Most states have laws protecting workers by limiting the amount of wages that can be garnished.

   C. Employment Retirement Income Security Act (ERISA) adopted in 1974, regulates the management and vesting of established retirement plans.

III. Collective bargaining and union activities.

   A. The Norris-LaGuardia Act was the first act prohibiting the enforcement of yellow-dog contracts.

   B. The National Labor Relations Act recognizes the right of workers to organize and bargain collectively.

   C. The Labor-Management Relations Act was passed in 1947 to limit what was seen to be excessive power of unions. This act declares certain union and employer practices to be unfair labor practices.

      Example: <u>Local 14 United Paperworkers Int'l Union, AFL-CIO v. NLRB</u>: The court held that the employer did not unfairly discriminate against striking employees.

   D. The Labor-Management Reporting and Disclosure Act further checks unions by promoting honesty and democracy in running the union's internal affairs.

IV. Employment discrimination.

    A. The Equal Pay Act of 1963 prohibits sex discrimination in pay.

        Example: <u>Hoban v. Texas Tech. Univ.</u>: A female first responder who was being paid less for comparable work than a male colleague has a viable claim under the Equal Pay Act.

    B. Title VII of the Civil Rights Act of 1964 prohibits discrimination on the basis of race, color, religion, sex, or national origin and applies to employers in interstate commerce with at least 15 employees.

        1. Discrimination includes not only intentional discrimination but also acts that have a discriminatory impact. It encompasses sexual harassment as a form of discrimination.

            Example: <u>Faragher v. Boca Raton</u>: An employer is responsible for the sexually hostile environment created by a supervisor with authority over an employee.

            Example: <u>EEOC v. Waffle House Inc.</u>: Congress gave the EEOC the same enforcement powers under the ADA that it gave under Title VII.

        2. Discrimination is permitted if a characteristic is a bona fide occupational qualification, but not BFOQ exception is permitted with respect to discrimination based on race or color.

    C. The Civil Rights Act of 1991 overturned several Supreme Court decisions in discrimination cases and will likely increase successful discrimination suits in the future.

    D. ADEA (Age Discrimination in Employment Act) prohibits employers of 20 or more from discriminating against employees based on age.

        Example: <u>General Dynamics Land Systems, Inc. v. Cline</u>: The Supreme Court found that the Age Discrimination in Employment Act of 1967 did not prevent discrimination of younger employees in favor of older employees.

    E. The Americans with Disability Act (ADA) protects qualified individuals with a disability from discrimination. A qualified individual is one who can perform the essential functions of a job with or without reasonable accommodation of the disability.

        Example: <u>Raytheon v. Hernandez</u>: The Supreme Court finds that a jury must decide if Hughes applied a neutral, generally applicable no-rehire policy in rejecting Hernandez's application or if the decision was motivated by Hernandez's disability.

V. Employment at will.

    A. This doctrine permits employers to fire an employee who was hired "at-will" (without a specific term).

    B. Court-created exceptions include cases striking down the at-will doctrine on grounds of (1) public policy (2) implied terms of the employment contract and (3) the implied covenant of good faith.

    C. Employees who report employer wrongdoing to the appropriate agencies are protected under the theory of wrongful discharge in violation of public policy.

        Example: <u>Akers v. Kindred Nursing Ctrs. Ltd. P'ship d/b/a Southwood Health</u>: A LPN who refused to violate state and federal patient care laws is allowed to bring a suit for wrongful discharge in violation of public policy.

VI. Employee privacy.

    A. The Employee Polygraph Protection Act prohibits private employers from using such tests to screen applicants and in other instances.

    B. Some courts have held that drug tests violate the employee's right to privacy, but there are exceptions.

        Example: <u>Bennett v. Massachusetts Bay Transportation Authority</u>: MBTA had a right to test Bennett for drug use because of the compelling interest in public safety regarding transit drivers.

Learning Objectives

1. You should understand how the changes in society have affected the court's and legislature's attitude toward common law employment doctrines, such as the at-will doctrine, as well as, how contemporary realities of the workplace have led to increased legislation with worker-protection as a goal.

2. You should note that anti-discrimination laws are a continuous source of litigation and that the opinions of the courts clearly shape and define the boundaries of protections under these laws.

3. You should understand the application of the Occupational Safety and Health Act (OSHA). You should know not only the general reach of the Act, but also the procedures that must be followed in the enforcement of its provisions.

4. It is important to be aware of the impact that the workers' compensation laws have had on the legal treatment of injuries in the employment setting. This requires an understanding of how the statutory scheme has transformed the traditional tort recoveries in the workplace.

5. You should understand the Fair Labor Standards Act (FLSA) and its exemptions.

6. You should be able to identify and distinguish the various labor laws that grew out of the Depression. Understand how each supplements the others, and be able to recognize their general theme of providing a balance between labor and management.

7. In the context of the various labor laws, understand what constitutes unfair labor practices for labor and management. Know why each practice is considered unfair.

8. Recognize the types of discrimination prohibited by the Civil Rights Act. You should understand the BFOQ exception. You should also understand how the Act is administered.

9. Compare and contrast the Equal Pay Act with the Civil Rights Act. You should also understand the Age Discrimination Act and be able to see how these three acts complement each other.

10. You should be familiar with the Employment Retirement and Income Security Act, and understand its general purpose. Be aware of the standards that ERISA imposes on new and existing pension plans.

11. You should be familiar with the employment-at-will doctrine, the judicially created exceptions to the doctrine, and the reasons these exceptions have been created.

12. You should be familiar with recent legislation, such as the Americans with Disabilities Act, protecting disabled workers, and with legislation, such as the Age Discrimination in Employment Act protecting workers from age discrimination.

Learning Hints

1. Common law doctrine, like the employment-at-will doctrine, may be limited by court decision or by legislative action. For example, some courts have prohibited firing an employee-at-will for "whistle blowing," because permitting such firing violates public policy.

2. Most states today have adopted workers' compensation laws protecting workers injured on the job. The structure of these laws is generally to establish an administrative framework within which determination of injury and payment is made. While abolishing contributory negligence and other employer defenses to protect workers, the legislatures also have limited, in some cases substantially, the awards available to injured workers.

3. Note how OSHA differs in its approach from the approach that underlies tort law. In tort law, the courts generally allow private employers great discretion in how the workplace is maintained. However, if injuries occur, the employer will usually be liable to the injured party. OSHA, on the other hand, represents a more centralized approach to job safety. Under its coverage, health and safety standards take on the force of law.

4. Under OSHA the states are able to enforce their own health and safety programs as long as they are as stringent as the federal program. Labor leaders have complained that the states are not enforcing the law and that the Reagan Administration does not decertify the states that fail to live up to federal standards.

5. Workers' compensation is a continuation of recent trends in tort laws, which are making property owners more and more responsible for injuries which occur on their property and which they may be in the best position to avoid or minimize. Without access to the common law tort defenses, the employer will almost always have to pay for job related injuries, notwithstanding the negligence of the injured employee. The recoveries under workers' compensation, however, are generally quite low. This influences plaintiffs with strong cases to sue in tort for which jury awards can be quite large. However, in such a tort action, the defendant will have available to him the traditional defenses of contributory negligence and strict liability.

6. You might notice that most of the laws discussed in this chapter only affect businesses that are engaged in interstate commerce. This is because these laws are federal laws that draw their authority from the Commerce Clause. However, the courts have construed the concept of "interstate commerce" quite broadly, allowing laws enacted pursuant to the Commerce Clause to reach almost all commercial behavior.

7. Note that the labor laws are premised on the notion that competition will not function in the labor market. They assume that workers will almost always be unable to individually bargain with employers. Therefore, these laws give labor a limited exemption from the antitrust laws to the extent that the union is bargaining for legitimate benefits. The labor laws represent the government replacing its bias toward a market approach with a notion of countervailing power as a means of protecting private interests.

8. The other laws in this chapter represent other methods of protecting private interests. Rather than pursuing the market or countervailing power (as in labor relations), they illustrate the third approach to restraining private power--strict government regulation.

9. The anti-discrimination laws raise a number of problems. The debate ranges from the legality of reverse discrimination to the definition of substantially equal work. Throughout this debate, one common question arises: Is the purpose of the anti-discrimination laws to achieve equal opportunity or equal results?

10. Recent legislative acts have protected workers from discrimination based on age or disability. The scope and effect of these recent laws, such as the ADA and ADEA, will likely continue to be defined by court decisions well into the future.

True-False

In the blank provided, put "**T**" if the statement is True or "**F**" if the statement is False.

_____ 1. The Employee Retirement Income Security Act (ERISA) requires employers to establish and fund pension benefit plans.

_____ 2. All employees are covered by worker's compensation.

_____ 3. The Equal Pay Act forbids racial discrimination regarding pay.

_____ 4. The Age Discrimination in Employment Act protects employees over 40 years of age against age discrimination.

_____ 5. The Fourth Amendment prevents private employers from unreasonably searching their employee's desks, files, etc

_____ 6. Most states have statutes limiting the amount of a debtor's wages that can be garnished.

_____ 7. ERISA requires that employers establish pension plans.

_____ 8. A business can never discriminate based on religion, sex, or national origin.

_____ 9. While a BFOQ exception exists for race discrimination, it is not available for religious discrimination.

_____ 10. Discrimination has been interpreted over the years to include not only intentional discrimination, but also acts that have discriminatory impact.

Multiple Choice

Circle the best answer.

1. Which of the following laws is not administered by the EEOC?
   a. Americans with Disabilities Act
   b. Age Discrimination in Employment Act
   c. Equal Pay Act
   d. National Labor Relations Act

2. Which of the following does not forbid sex discrimination in employment?
   a. Section 1981.
   b. The Equal Pay Act.
   c. Title VII.
   d. Executive Order 11246.

3. Which of the following federal laws prohibits oppressive child labor?
   a. OSHA
   b. Workman's compensation laws
   c. Fair Labor Standards Act
   d. None of the above

4. Natalie is a teacher. She pays into a state retirement fund through her school. She will be considered vested after 10 years of membership in the pension plan. Which of the following laws regulate pensions and vesting?
   a. Employment Retirement Income Security Act
   b. Fair Labor Standards Act
   c. Family and Medical Leave Act
   d. OSHA

5. Inga works on the assembly line for a small manufacturing firm. Inga has had some credit problems. Her creditors want to garnish her wages. Which of the following would generally regulate wage garnishment?

   a. Fair Labor Standards Act

   b. State wage statutes

   c. National Labor Relations Act

   d. Labor-Management Relations Act

6. Which of the following is not true of the Civil Rights Act?

   a. Sexual Harassment is covered under this act.

   b. Affirmative action has been used in enforcing the act.

   c. Bona fide occupational qualifications exceptions are allowed with respect to discrimination based on race.

   d. The EEOC feels that mandatory arbitration agreements deny employee rights to bring independent discrimination claims.

7. Which of the following statements is true?

   a. The employment at will doctrine enables either the employer or employee to terminate the employment relationship at any time.

   b. Whistle-blowing is a valid reason for an employer to fire an employee.

   c. Companies can fire employees any time even if there is a contract implied through company policy handbooks, manuals, etc.

   d. Companies can terminate an employee at any time even if the company does so in bad faith.

8. Exemptions from the workers' compensation statutes frequently include:

   a. Employers with three or fewer employees.

   b. Farmers.

   c. Household services employees.

   d. All of the above

9. Which of the following statements regarding the Americans with Disabilities Act is not true?

   a. A person is considered disabled if she has a physical or mental impairment that substantially limits one or more of her major life activities.

   b. A qualified person can do the functions of the job with reasonable accommodation.

   c. What is a reasonable accommodation may depend upon the size of the employer and the employer's income.

   d. A disabled person who is discriminated against may sue for damages, but he is not entitled to punitive damages.

10. Which of the following laws pertains to possible union corruption?

   a. Labor-Management Relations Act

   b. National Labor Relations Act

   c. Labor-Management Reporting and Disclosure Act

   d. Norris-LaGuardia Act

Short Essay

1. Briefly discuss three recent exceptions to the employment at will doctrine developed by the courts.

2. Roy is a 69-year-old who plans on retiring to Arizona in one more year. Roy decides to buy a house in Arizona. He chooses a home and then goes to Desert Bank for a loan. The loan officer tells Roy that his bank cannot offer him a 30-year mortgage because Roy will not be around to pay it off. What law protects Roy in this situation?

3. Prior to passage of worker's compensation laws by the states, what were some defenses that employers would use to avoid liability for injuries to employees?

4. Vicki teaches accounting courses at a community college. The college administration suspects that at least a few employees are improperly using their computers. Hidden cameras are installed around campus, including in faculty offices. Ted, a faculty member, is caught using the internet for purposes other than those dealing with his teaching. The college fires Ted. Discuss the privacy issues in this case.

5. Bob teaches at a college. Bob is diagnosed with multiple sclerosis. Bob's muscular functions decline over the years. What would be some reasonable accommodations for the college to make for Bob to allow him to continue teaching as long as possible?

6. Marlo is employed as an accountant for a large company. Marlo's father is seriously ill and Marlo wants to take time off to take care of him. What are Marlo's rights under the Family and Medical Leave Act?

7. Joe Shoehorn works in the shoe department of a large department store. He is paid on commission and gets 10 percent of every sale he makes. These commissions are applied against the minimum wage that is required by both federal and local laws. The store has instituted a practice where Joe loses his commission if he fails to mark the bottom of each sold shoe with a transaction number (the number is used to track refunds, etc.). A number of customers object to having their shoes marked up in this manner, and Joe loses commissions on those sales. Joe files a complaint under the Fair Labor Standards Act. Who wins?

CHAPTER 25
WHICH FORM OF BUSINESS ORGANIZATION?

Outline

I. Different types of business organizations.

    A. Sole proprietorship (business operated by person as his own personal property).

    B. Partnerships (voluntary associations designed to carry on business for profit).

        1. In a general partnership, each partner shares in the profits and losses of the business.

        2. In a limited partnership, limited partners may share in the profits without becoming personally liable on the debts of the business.

    C. A corporation is a separate legal entity. Shareholders of a corporation are not personally liable for its debts.

        Example: LaMontagne Builders v. Bowman Brooks Purchase Group: The court found, based on Brooks's pattern of false statements on financial statements, that he was using the corporate entity to promote injustice and fraud. The court pierced the corporate veil and made Brooks, a corporate officer, personally liable for the corporate debt.

    D. Other forms include the business trust and real estate investment trust, and joint-stock association.

II. Factors in choosing a form of business organization.

    A. Limited liability.

        1. Liability of limited partners and shareholders in a corporation is limited to their investment; general partners and sole proprietors have the risk of unlimited personal liabilities.

    B. Taxation: Different advantages accrue to partnerships and corporations.

        1. An S Corporation is taxed like a partnership.

        2. There are different advantages of corporate taxation and of sole proprietorship and partnership taxation.

    C. Formalities

        1. Formalities required for creation of a corporation or a limited partnership, such as filing with government officials, are not required for individual proprietorships or general partnerships.

        2. A minority shareholder may be "frozen out" by the majority.

        Example: Brooks V. Hill: Minority stockholder oppression is not the same as misrepresentation and cannot be used as such.

    D. There are also Financing and Management advantages and disadvantages relating to different business organizations.

    E. Legally, a corporation continues after the death or insolvency of a shareholder, but a partnership is dissolved upon the death of a partner.

    F. It is easier to sell one's investment in a publicly held corporation. A partner is generally not entitled to force the partnership business to be liquidated.

    G. Limited liability companies: LLCs are similar to corporations and are separate and distinct from their members. Members share in the management of the entity in proportion to their capital contributions.

        Example: Estate of Countryman v. Farmers Cooperative: A limited liability company supplied the propane that caused an explosion in a home. A lawsuit was filed against Keota, a partner that owned 95 percent of the LLC. The court ruled that the limited liability structure of the LLC would not protect Keota from liability because the state's limited liability statute imposes liability on partners who engage in tortuous conduct. Thus, if the trial court finds that Keota was negligent, it will be personally liable for the loss.

Example: In Re Garrison-Ashburn, LLC: One equal owner (Comer) of an LLC attempted to sell land owned by the LLC after the other principal (Chapman) filed for personal bankruptcy. Chapman attempted to block the sale because the operating agreement required consent of two officers before land could be sold. The court permitted the sale to proceed because state law provides that a member is dissociated from an LLC upon the filing of bankruptcy. Comer then had the right to remove Chapman as an officer and elect himself to a second LLC office.

III. Franchising.

A. Terms of the franchise are important: Franchising is a contractual relationship, and typically the franchisor is a corporation and the franchisee forms a corporation to operate the franchised business.

Some complaints associated with franchising include the fact that the contracts are typically "contracts of adhesion" with terms favoring the franchisor.

B. As a result of franchising problems, both the federal and state governments now generally regulate the franchise relationship.

Example: Zeidler v. A&W Restaurants: Zeidler's failure to obtain insurance for the restaurant constituted a clear violation of the license agreement and was a valid reason for termination of the license.

Learning Objectives

1. You should be able to identify different factors one should consider in determining which business organization would best achieve an organizer's goals.

2. You should be able to explain the difference between a partnership, sole proprietorship, and corporation.

3. You should be able to identify tax implications of various forms of business organization.

4. You should be able to identify management and formation differences between the various forms of business organizations.

5. You should know which business organizations are entities separate from their owners, as well as the purposes for which they are considered to be separate from their owners.

6. You should know the basic differences between general and limited partnerships.

7. You should understand the limited liability advantage of the corporation.

8. You should be able to recognize the different types of corporations.

9. You should know what a franchise is and why businesspersons choose to buy franchises, as well as the major legal problems that may accompany the use of franchises.

10. You should be able to identify federal and state legislation that may impact upon the franchise agreement.

Learning Hints

1. One significant advantage of a corporation is that it limits liability of the shareholders to their investment in the corporation. However, in smaller Subchapter S corporations, most lending institutions will require personal as well as corporate liability as a condition to lending money to the business.

2. One significant advantage of a corporation is the fact that it continues on after the death of its stockholder(s). In the case of a partnership, the partnership will terminate by law upon the death of a general partner.

3. A determination of the appropriate organization form for a business must be made on a case-by-case basis. The owners of each business have objectives that may make one business form superior to another in the context of their respective situations. That one business organization form works well for one particular business does not necessarily mean that the same form will work well for a different business.

4. A sole proprietorship is the easiest business organization to create. A person merely establishes a business, and the sole proprietorship is created automatically.

5. The sole proprietor has unlimited liability for the obligations of the business operated as a sole proprietorship. Unlimited liability means that creditors of the business can attach the sole proprietor's individual assets (her house, her car, etc.) if the assets of the business are insufficient to pay the creditors' claim against the business.

6. It is extremely easy to create a partnership. Persons who do not know they are creating a partnership create many partnerships. Even though persons may say they are not partners, they may actually have created a partnership if they share profits and otherwise act as if they are partners.

7. Note that the shared ownership requirement in the definition of a partnership refers to shared ownership of the <u>business</u>, not necessarily shared ownership of the assets. The two most important factors tending to indicate shared ownership of the business are the sharing of profits and the sharing of the management of the business. Remember that two persons may perform different management functions and still be partners. For example, one partner might solely be in charge of hiring employees and the other partner might solely be in charge of purchasing inventory. In addition, it is important to remember that the shared ownership need not be an equal sharing of ownership. Different partners may contribute different amounts of capital to the partnership and still be partners. Certain partners may receive a larger share of the profits than other partners do. There is still a partnership in such situations.

8. Limited partners are not held personally liable for partnership debts beyond the limited partner's investment in the partnership. Do not forget, however, that a limited partner is entitled to such a limit on his personal liability only if he refrains from participating in the management of the partnership. If one who started out as a limited partner becomes involved in management of the partnership, he thereby becomes a general partner and, in the process, loses the benefit of the restrictions on liability otherwise extended to limited partners.

9. Unlike the sole proprietorship or the partnership, a corporation is an entity separate from its owners in all respects. In fact, managers of the corporation need not be shareholders in the corporation.

10. The corporate form of business may not be used improperly; however, if it is used in such a manner, the court may "pierce the corporate veil." When this occurs, shareholders may be held personally liable. Although courts do not routinely pierce the corporate veil, they will do so where those who formed the corporation provided it with a grossly inadequate amount of capital. In such situations, a fraud on creditors is likely, and the corporate entity must be disregarded and access to shareholder assets must be allowed in order to enable legitimate claims of creditors to be satisfied. Similarly, courts

will pierce the corporate veil and subject shareholders to personal liability where it is proved that shareholders merely treat the corporation as an extension of themselves, such as by having the corporation pay their personal expenses. In instances of this sort, the corporation is merely the alter ego of the shareholders and not really a separate entity anyway. Shareholders must deal with the corporation at arms' length, just as unrelated persons would do in a business setting. The subject of piercing the corporate veil is dealt with in more depth in Chapter 27 of your text.

11.   A franchise is not really a form of business organization. Instead, it is a form of business opportunity. A franchise may be operated as a sole proprietorship, partnership, or corporation, or in any other form of business organization.

12.   The chief legal problems in franchising result from an inherent aspect of franchising: the franchisor's desire to control the quality of the franchisees' products and services. Contracts of adhesion, unreasonable franchise terminations, and antitrust violations may result from the franchisor's intent to dominate the franchisor-franchisee relation and thereby maintain quality control.

True-False

In the blank provided, put "**T**" if the statement is True or "**F**" if the statement is False.

_____   1.   If shares of one corporation are exchanged with another, the transaction is tax-free.

_____   2.   A major advantage of corporations is that the shareholders have limited liabilities.

_____   3.   In order to create a general partnership, the partners must execute an express agreement.

_____   4.   A partnership is a taxable entity.

_____   5.   General partners have apparent authority to bind the partnership.

_____   6.   A partner's liability for partnership debts is not limited to the amount of her contribution of capital to the partnership.

_____   7.   A major disadvantage of the partnership form of business is that partnerships are entities on which income tax is imposed.

_____   8.   The law does not treat a close corporation as an entity separate from its owners.

_____   9.   A limited liability company can have unlimited owners who can share in the management of the company.

_____   10.   If a franchisor exercises substantial control over a franchisee's operations, the franchisee may not be considered an independent contractor and the franchisor may be liable for torts committed by the franchisee's employees.

Multiple Choice

Circle the best answer.

1.   In which of the following ways have state and federal governments regulated franchises?

   a.   The Federal Trade Commission requires by rule that franchisors disclose certain information to prospective franchisees.

   b.   All states have enacted uniform franchising laws designed to protect franchisees.

   c.   Many states prevent deceptive advertising of franchise opportunities through their deceptive trade practices or consumer protection legislation.

   d.   Both (a) and (c) are correct.

2.   A "close corporation":

   a.   Is a limited partnership.

   b.   Is a publicly held corporation selling shares to investors.

   c.   Is a corporation in which family members hold stock.

   d.   None of the above is correct.

3.   Bob, Joe, and John want to start a sporting goods store. Bob has worked in the sporting goods industry. The plan is for Bob to manage the store. Joe and John will invest money in the business, but neither of them will be involved in managing the store. Which of the following statements is most true?

   a.   This business is a general partnership.

   b.   John and Joe are limited partners.

   c.   This business is a sole proprietorship.

   d.   This business is a franchise.

4.   Which of the following statements regarding business structure is not true?

   a.   A general partner has unlimited liability.

   b.   Corporations pay income tax.

   c.   LLCs pay income tax.

   d.   A sole proprietor pays income tax on income generated by her business.

5.   Which of the following types of businesses would generally not be required to file articles of organization with the secretary of state?

   a.   Sole proprietorship

   b.   Corporation

   c.   Limited liability company

   d.   Limited partnership

6.   Which of the following statements is not true concerning S Corporations?

   a.   S Corporations can have no more than 75 shareholders.

   b.   Shareholders in an S Corporation must be individuals or estates.

   c.   S Corporations pay income tax.

   d.   Shareholders in an S Corporation must consent in writing to having the corporation taxes as a partnership.

7.   Which of the following is not an advantage to ownership in a publicly traded corporation?

   a.   Continuity

   b.   Limited liability

   c.   Double taxation

   d.   Liquidity of investment

8. Jane's lifelong dream has been to start her own business. She has decided to open a women's clothing store. She comes to you for advice as to what type of ownership structure to choose for her business. Jane stresses to you that she does not want to be personally liable for her store's losses and liabilities and she does not want double taxation. Which one of the following types of business structures would you recommend to Jane?

    a.   Sole proprietorship

    b.   Limited liability company

    c.   General partnership

    d.   Corporation

9. Earl Overbearing is in charge of nearly all of the management duties for a real estate sales business. Which of the following is an accurate statement about the relationship between Overbearing and the business?

    a.   If the business is operated as a limited partnership, Overbearing cannot be a limited partner.

    b.   If the business is operated as a close corporation, Overbearing must be a shareholder.

    c.   If the business is operated as a corporation (close or otherwise), Overbearing will be personally liable for the debts of the corporation.

    d.   None of the above.

10. Tom is a franchisee for a Highway 99 service station. Which of the following is a potential disadvantage to Tom as a franchisee?

    a.   Highway 99 may provide financing for Tom's business.

    b.   Highway 99 will help Tom advertise his business.

    c.   Highway 99 has the right to terminate Tom's franchise each year.

    d.   Highway 99 may help train Tom's employees.

Short Essay

1. Shelly wants to open a restaurant. After studying the various types of business ownership structures, Shelly decides she wants her business to be a sole proprietorship. What are some reasons that Shelly may have picked this type of business?

2. Earl and Pearl are partners in a travel agency. Earl dies. Is the partnership dissolved? Can Pearl still operate the business?

3. Arthur King is the chief executive officer of Camelot, Inc., a close corporation. He is also the majority shareholder in the corporation. King knows that two lawsuits are about to be filed against Camelot. One pertains to an alleged breach of a contract to which Camelot was a party. King had been actively involved in the negotiation of the terms of the contract. The other lawsuit that will be filed against Camelot pertains to an automobile accident allegedly caused by the negligence of Lance Allot, a Camelot employee. Allot was acting within the scope of his employment when the accident occurred. King is concerned that he could face personal liability for damages that may be awarded in these suits, if Camelot's assets prove insufficient to satisfy the damage awards. Should he be concerned? Why or why not?

4. Tinker was a limited partner in Evers & Chance Limited Partnership. Evers and Chance were the firm's general partners. Tinker had invested $50,000 in the limited partnership. Evers and Chance had each invested $10,000. Originally, Evers and Chance had done all of the managing of the partnership business. As time went on, however, Tinker became involved, along with Evers and Chance, in management of the firm's business activities. After this change in responsibility for management had taken place, Evers (while in the course of partnership business) negligently caused crippling physical injury to Cobb. Assume that Cobb's tort claim is a valid one worth at least $500,000, an amount easily in excess of not only the initial contributions to the partnership but also the value of all partnership property and assets. What is the extent of liability (if any) that Tinker, Evers, and Chance, respectively, may have to Cobb?

5. Legal Eagles law firm was founded as a general partnership. What would be some advantages for Legal Eagles to switch to a limited liability partnership?

6.   Kim and Jan formed a limited liability company called K and J Tax Services. Gene is unhappy with his tax return that was prepared by K and J. Gene claims that K and J did a poor job of preparing his tax return and that the IRS is auditing him as a result. Gene sues Kim and Jan for malpractice. Are Kim and Jan personally liable for the return prepared for Gene?

7.   How are LLCs and S Corporations similar to each other? How do they differ?

8.   Terry and Paul are partners in a business that engages in the installation and servicing of telecommunications equipment. Because of a defective installation of some equipment by Terry, one of its customers lost a substantial number of phone orders and is now suing the partnership. Assuming Paul was not involved with any services to this particular customer, can be held personally liable for the harm done by his partner, Terry?

CHAPTER 26
PARTNERSHIPS

Outline

I. Creation of a partnership.

    A. No express agreement is necessary, and one who receives a share of profits from a business may be treated as a partner.

        1. A partnership is an association of two or more persons carrying on a business for profit as co-owners.

        2. An individual, partnership, or corporation may qualify as a legal person who can form a partnership.

        3. One who shares in the management of the business as well as in the profits is more likely to be considered a partner.

        Example: <u>Chen v. Wang</u>: There was no partnership because when there is no written agreement sufficiently establishing a partnership, the intent of the parties is considered as well as the facts and circumstances surrounding the alleged formation of the entity. There must be a meeting of the minds to create a partnership.

    B. A partnership can also arise through <u>estoppel</u>. A person may hold another liable as a partner if she proves that she relied on the holding out of the partnership or consent of the partner. This is a device to protect creditors who rely on a party's purported status as a partner.

II. Nature of the partnership.

    A. The partnership is a separate entity from the partners for some purposes, and an aggregate of the individual partners in other instances.

    B. It is highly desirable to have written articles of partnership even though this is not absolutely necessary.

III. Management and authority of partners.

    A. Each partner normally has an equal voice in managing the business.

    B. Authority to act for a partnership may be express, implied, or apparent.

    C. Even if a partner lacked authority to contract for the partnership, ratification by the other partners makes the contract enforceable against the partnership.

    Example: <u>QAD Investors v. Kelly</u>: Kelly was personally liable on a note signed by his partner. The court found the existence of apparent authority because Kelly's conduct was such that it would lead a reasonable third party to believe that his partner was acting as an agent of the partnership when he signed the note.

IV. What is Partnership Property?

    A. All property originally contributed to the partnership as well as that purchased later is partnership property.

    B. Any partner with authority to do so may convey real property. The partners as tenants in partnership hold the property.

V. Other issues.

    A. Compensation of partners.

        1. Compensation is presumed to be the partner's share of profits. Absent agreement, profits are shared equally.

B. Duties of partners.

   1. The duties of partners are substantially the same as those of agents to principals.

      Example: <u>Silverberg v. Colantuno</u>: Partners owe each other a fiduciary duty; and, in this case, Silverberg did not breach that duty by hiding or misrepresenting material fact.

C. Enforcement of partnership rights and liabilities.

   1. Partners become jointly liable on debts of the partnership; and, under the doctrine of *respondeat superior*, a partner is liable for torts committed by other partners.

D. Dissolution of the partnership occurs when a partner ceases to be associated in the carrying on of the business. A person who wrongfully dissolves a partnership loses the right to demand a winding up and liquidation and forfeits the right to participate.

E. Winding up: The purpose of winding up is to liquidate assets and bring affairs of partnership to an end.

   Example: <u>Long v. Lopez</u>: The court found that the partner who negotiated the settlement agreement during the winding up was acting reasonably since he saved the partnership a substantial amount of money. Partners therefore were liable on the settlement agreement.

   Example: <u>Vargo v. Clark</u>: Barron & Cohn did not lose what they believed in good faith to be limited liability for their investment in a railroad, even though Illinois law prohibit limited partnerships in railroads.

F. Continuation: Many partnership agreements provide there is no dissolution upon death or withdrawal of a partner; Some contain buyout agreements.

G. The non-continuing partner becomes a creditor of a continuing partnership.

H. A dissociation of the partnership can take place without a dissolution and a winding up.

   Example: <u>Warnick v. Warnick</u>: The appellate court held that the trial court did not properly determine Randall's share of the partnership distribution. Applying RUPA's default provision, the appellate court found that the advances by the other two partners were loans to the partnership. This made them partnership creditors who must be paid before assets can be distributed to the partners.

VI. Limited Partnerships

   A. Purpose is to permit some partnership investors to limit liability.

   B. Statutory formalities must be complied with; a limited partner who takes control of the business is liable to partnership creditors like a general partner.

      Example: <u>Gregg v. S.R. Investors, Ltd.</u>: Under Illinois law, a person who makes a contribution to a business enterprise and erroneously but in good faith believes that he or she has become a limited partner is not a general partner and is not bound by its obligations.

Learning Objectives

1. You should understand how a partnership is created.

2. You should understand the implications of agency law for partners within a partnership.

3. You should be able to articulate the duties that a partner owes other partners.

4. You should distinguish between a partner's express, implied, and apparent authority to act on behalf of the partnership.

5. You should know the kinds of provisions customarily contained in articles of partnership.

6. You should understand how the concept of estoppel may be used to hold someone liable as if he were a partner, even though he may not actually have been a partner.

7. You should know when an individual partner can bind the partnership, when a majority vote of partners is required, and when unanimous agreement of the partners is necessary.

8. You should understand limited partnerships and limited liability limited partnerships.

9. You should be able to distinguish partnership property from a partner's individual property, and should know the rights of partners in partnership property.

10. You should understand charging orders and assignments of partnership interests.

11. You should become familiar with the purposes for which a partnership is regarded as an entity separate from the partners comprising it.

12. You should know the duties a partner owes to the partnership and the other partners, as well as the rights a partner possesses in a partnership.

13. You should understand the differences between dissociation and dissolution.

Learning Hints

1. Parties may form a partnership without express agreement. In fact, a partnership may arise even though the parties did not actually intend to create a partnership.

2. A partnership creates certain rights and duties in the partners. One right is the right to share equally in the profits of the partnership even if the partners have not contributed equally to the partnership.

3. A partnership may arise when creditors allege the existence of a partnership. In some cases creditors argue partnership by estoppel based on their reasonable reliance of a partnership.

4. A partner may have express, implied, or apparent authority to act for the partnership. These concepts are similar to the agency concept of authority.

5. At common law, any partner is liable for the entire debt of the partnership if the other partners are judgment proof.

6. The partnership agreement (often called the Articles of Partnership) is the basic governing document of the partnership. It usually defines the most basic rights and obligations of the partners. Remember, however, that a valid partnership may exist even though the parties do not have a written partnership agreement.

7. When partnership by estoppel applies, the persons represented to be partners are treated as partners only for the purpose of holding them liable to a creditor, and not for any other purpose. Hence, the persons held liable under this doctrine do not acquire any of the rights associated with being partners.

8. The best way to understand the distinction between trading and nontrading partnerships is to understand that trading partnerships require substantial working capital. In other words, business needs to borrow money. For example, manufacturing firms are trading partnerships because they need to borrow significant amounts of money to finance their purchases of raw materials. They need to borrow money because a substantial period of time elapses between their purchase of raw materials and their sale of the finished product. If one understands this, it is easy to see why a partner in a trading partnership has implied authority or apparent authority to borrow money in the partnership's name.

9. Remember that unless the partners have agreed otherwise, the partners will share the profits equally among themselves. This is true even though initial contributions of capital by the various partners may not have been equal. It is quite common, however, for partnership agreements to provide that certain partners will receive a greater share of the profits than other partners will receive.

10. Similarly, unless the partnership agreement states otherwise, partners share partnership losses in the same manner in which they share profits, regardless of the respective amounts the individual partners contributed as capital. Of course, the various partners are free to agree that certain partners will bear a greater share of losses than will other partners.

11.   The <u>business judgment rule</u> protects a partner from liability to the partnership for "judgment calls" that turn out to be unfortunate decisions. If the partner undertakes a reasonable investigation before making a business decision and acts honestly when making the business decision, a court will not hold the partner liable for the negative consequences the partnership experienced as a result of the incorrect decision. The rationale for the rule is that a court is not equipped to make business judgments.

12.   The agency law principles regarding tort and criminal liability also exist in partnership law. You should review the discussion of those concepts in the agency law materials if you find them confusing in terms of law.

True-False

In the blank provided, put "**T**" if the statement is True or "**F**" if the statement is False.

_____   1.   Absent express agreement, any partner may sell or mortgage partnership property.

_____   2.   An explicit restriction on a partner's express or implied authority may prevent the partner from having apparent authority.

_____   3.   Larry, Moe, and Curly are partners in an accounting firm. Curly wants to withdraw from the partnership. Curly is entitled to receive the value of his partnership interest only if the partnership can pay its other creditors first.

_____   4.   The Uniform Partnership Act has been adopted by a majority of states in the United States.

_____   5.   Ben and Joyce prepare tax returns on a part-time basis. The check each other's work and share their fees. This business may be considered a partnership even though Ben and Joyce never formally agreed to form a partnership.

_____   6.   Mark and Jack pool their resources and buy a large tract of land. They plan on developing the land for residential and commercial use. Mark and Jack do not plan on doing business together after this project is finished. This is an example of a joint venture.

_____   7.   Jean, Jane, and Joan form a partnership to operate a women's clothing store. Jean invests more time and money in the business than do the other two partners. Jean will receive more of the profits from the business even if the partners do not have an agreement for how profits and losses are to be shared.

_____   8.   Although the partnership will face liability for a tort committed by a partner while acting within the scope of partnership business, the other partners who did not commit the tort cannot be held liable.

_____   9.   Roz decides to sue the law firm of Crane, Crane, and Moon for improperly handling a legal case for her. Under her state's common name statute, Roz must get personal service on each of the three partners.

_____   10.   Partners are prohibited from selling to or buying from the partnership.

Multiple Choice

Circle the best answer.

1. B, P, and T formed a partnership. They made no express agreement as to how profits were to be divided. Of the $50,000 initial capital of the firm, B and P each contributed$20,000; T contributed $10,000. The partnership had a profit of $30,000 during the first year of business. What is P's share of the profit?

   a. $10,000.

   b. $12,000.

   c. $15,000.

   d. $17,500.

2. Tom, Chris, and John are partners in a liquor store. The partnership agreement states that only Chris has the authority to buy liquor from suppliers. Tom orders a large quantity of beer from a beer distributorship. Which of the following statements is true?

   a. Since Tom does not have express authority to buy beer, the partnership is not bound to this contract.

   b. Tom can bind the partnership to this contract because he has apparent authority.

   c. Tom cannot bind the partnership to this contract because he does not have implied authority.

   d. Chris and John must ratify Tom's unauthorized actions in order for the partnership to be bound to the contract.

3. Tom, Taylor, and Rhonda are partners in a sporting goods store. Which of the following statements is not true concerning their partnership?

   a. If the partners do not have an agreement that spells out sharing of profits, the profits should be shared equally among the three partners.

   b. Losses will be shared in the same way as profits unless an agreement states otherwise.

   c. If Tom invests more time and money into the business, the partners can make an agreement that gives Tom a bigger share of the profits.

   d. All of the above are correct.

4. Which of the following statements is not true concerning a partnership?

   a. A partner has a duty not to compete against the partnership.

   b. Partners are liable for honest errors of judgment in transacting business for the partnership.

   c. If an outsider gives some information to one partner, all partners are normally assumed to be informed.

   d. Partners have a right to be reimbursed for expenses they incur on behalf of the partnership.

5. M is a partner in a retail toy store business. The partnership frequently must borrow money to purchase inventory and satisfy other requirements. Needing money to pay personal debts, M borrowed $10,000 from Local Bank, and signed the name of the partnership on all loan documents. Although she told the Bank the money was for the partnership, she used it for herself. M cannot now repay, and the Bank has sued the partnership. Is the partnership liable?

   a. No, because M acted outside the scope of her authority;

   b. No, because M committed fraud.

   c. Yes, because borrowing is in the ordinary course of business and M had apparent and implied authority to borrow money for the partnership.

   d. Yes, because the intentional tort of the partner M is imputed to all members of the partnership.

6.   Which of the following statements regarding limited partnerships is true?

a.   Limited partners must be listed on a certificate filed with the Secretary of State when the limited partnership is formed.

b.   Limited partners are liable for the debts of the partnership.

c.   The death of a limited partner dissolves the partnership.

d.   A limited partner who acts like a general partner is not liable to the creditors of the partnership.

7.   Rob, Buddy, and Sally are partners in a business that books entertainment acts in clubs across the country. The partners share profits and losses equally. If the partners decide to dissolve the partnership, which of the following statements is true?

a.   Debts the partnership owes to Sally must be paid first.

b.   Buddy, who contributed no assets to the partnership, will still receive an equivalent return of capital even though the partnership agreement is silent on this matter.

c.   Amounts loaned by Rob to the partnership are actually treated as capital investment.

d.   Debts owed to Third Bank must be paid first.

8.   Jerry, George, and Elaine are partners in a restaurant. George decides that he is tired of the restaurant business and wants to sell his partnership interest to Kramer. Which of the following statements is not true?

a.   The partnership agreement may declare that there is no dissolution in the event that a new partner replaces an existing partner.

b.   The partners may have a buy-out agreement that allows George to sell his partnership interest to Kramer.

c.   When Kramer joins the partnership, he becomes liable for all previous obligations of the partnership.

d.   The continuing partners could join in a novation with First Bank, a creditor of the partnership, to relieve George of his liability as a partner for the debt.

9.   Lucy, Fred, and Ethel are partners in a coffee shop. Which of the following statements concerning dissolution is not true?

a.   Fred's untimely death will dissolve the partnership.

b.   The three partners decide to dissolve the partnership. Lucy does all of the work in winding up the partnership, so she is entitled to compensation.

c.   If Fred wrongfully dissolves the partnership, he cannot participate in the winding up process.

d.   Lucy feels that Fred and Ethel have consistently breached their partnership duties. The partnership is losing money. Lucy may be able to obtain a court order to dissolve the partnership.

10. Kyle, Tara, and Maggie formed a partnership to operate an obedience school for dogs. Kyle and Tara each contributed capital of $20,000. Maggie contributed $10,000. The three partners agreed that Kyle and Tara would each assume 45 percent of any losses of the business, and that Maggie would assume the remaining 10 percent of the losses. Their agreement contained no express provision concerning how profits were to be divided. During the first year of operation, the business made $60,000 in profits. What is Maggie's share of the profits?

a. $12,000.

b. $6,000.

c. $20,000.

d. $10,000.

Short Essay

1. Walton, Sr., the sole owner of a small retailing business, was attempting to purchase some goods on credit from a manufacturer with whom he had not done business previously. In talking in person with the manufacturer's representative, Walton pointed to his daughter, Waltona (a nationally known retailer who was also visiting for a few days). Walton then stated that: "my partners and I have always paid our bills on time." Waltona heard and saw what her father had said and done, but she made no comment in the presence of the manufacturer's representative. The manufacturer's representative knew, however, that Waltona was neither her father's partner nor otherwise involved in business with him. The manufacturer thereafter sold Mr. Walton goods on credit, and Walton failed to pay for them when payment was due. If the partnership has no assets, and the manufacturer sues Waltona and Walton under these facts, against whom (if anyone) will it be successful?

2. Barry, Victor, and Greg form a partnership that sells diet supplements to athletes. Greg spends far more time working in the business than do the other two partners. How could the partners arrange to pay Greg a salary?

3. John, Al, and Michelle are partners in a pizza restaurant. John owes Shark Finance Co. a great deal of money. Can Shark attach to any partnership property? How could John arrange to pay off Shark from his partnership profits? What could Shark do to try to seek repayment through John's interest in the business?

4. Ally is a partner in an accounting firm. Can Ally accept after-hours tax and accounting clients as a sideline business?

5. Bob, Caryl, Ted, and Alice formed a partnership to operate a restaurant called "Our Town." They each contributed funds and/or equipment for use in the restaurant, and Ted contributed a used van he already owned. Several months later, Ted "borrowed" the van to take it on vacation. He claims he has the right to use partnership property so long as it benefits at least one party. Is he correct?

6. You seek legal representation from the firm of Winkem, Blinkem, and Nod. You believe that Nod charged you for work that he did not do. What is y our recourse in this instance?

7. Sallie and Susan were old college friends who both graduated with degrees in horticulture. Sallie established a nursery business in 1970. In 1979, Susan joined her. At first, Sallie paid Susan a salary, but beginning in 1980, Susan was paid 40 percent of the net income from the business. Sallie continued to own all the equipment, hire all employees, and was listed as "owner" on the business tax return. Susan was listed as "associate." In 2002, Sallie retired and seeks to sell the business in her own name. Susan claims that a partnership existed since 1980 and seeks an accounting. Who wins?

8. Jenna, Bobby, and Pam are partners in a retail clothing business. The business is unsuccessful and is insolvent. Describe a marshalling of assets.

9. Briefly describe why RUPA now uses the term dissociation in defining a change in the partnership relationship instead of dissolution as was defined in the UPA.

10. Briefly describe a limited liability limited partnership (LLLP).

CHAPTER 27

FORMATION AND TERMINATION OF CORPORATIONS

Outline

I. Nature of a corporation.

    A. A corporation is a separate legal entity.

    B. The three principal types of corporations are governmental/municipal corporations, nonprofit corporations, and for-profit corporations.

    C. The for-profit corporation is either a close corporation or publicly held corporation.

II. The pre-incorporation process.

    A. Promoters bring the corporation into being and owe a fiduciary duty to the corporation.

        1. Under agency law, promoters are liable on contracts they make on behalf of corporations. If the promoter, corporation, and third parties agree to substitute the corporation for the promoter, this is a <u>novation</u> and releases the promoter from liability.

    B. Liability of corporation: The corporation may pay promoters for their services. If the board acts to adopt the contract after incorporation, or accepts the benefits of the contract, the corporation is liable (except in Massachusetts).

    Example: <u>Crye-Leike Realtors v. WDM, Inc.</u>: A corporation may become liable on a pre-incorporation contract executed by its promoter if the corporation subsequently ratifies or adopts the contract.

    C. A corporation must prepare articles of incorporation complying with state's incorporation statute. Many corporations "shop around" for the state that offers most benefits to the enterprise.

    D. There are mandatory and optional contents of the articles of incorporation.

    E. The corporate by-laws establish rules for the conduct of the internal affairs of the corporation.

    F. Under the *ultra vires* doctrine, a transaction beyond the corporation's power may be unenforceable, but courts have taken different positions on this issue.

    G. Problems of defective incorporation: Under the revised MBCA, the filing of the articles of incorporation is conclusive proof of incorporation. Historically, in a *de jure* corporation, the promoters had substantially complied with all mandatory provisions. The *de facto* corporation exists when there is an honest attempt to comply with the mandatory provisions of the statutes.

    Example: <u>Hildreth v. Tidewater Equipment Co.</u>: The court found that Hildreth's business is a *de jure* corporation, despite his failure to fully comply with state rules governing a foreign corporation doing business in the state. Thus, he was not personally liable on its debts. Since his contracting partner believed he was a corporation, there was no reason to not treat him as one.

    H. Piercing the corporate veil.

        1. In some cases a shareholder may be held personally liable on a corporate debt. Under capitalization, or cases where a corporation is the alter ego of the shareholder may create such a situation.

    Example: <u>Crane v. Green & Freedman Baking Company</u>: Courts should consider the respect parol by shareholders themselves to the separate corporate identity, fraudulent intent of defendant, and the degree of injustice visited on litigants in determining to pierce the corporate veil.

III.   Close corporations.

    A.   Characteristics include few shareholders who are active in the business and live in same area. There is no established market for the stock.

    B.   Most states have enacted laws recognizing close corporations and addressing special problems.

       Example: <u>F.B.I. v. Moore</u>: The court upheld transfer restrictions, concluding that they are attempts to maintain the family-nature of the corporation. The buyer clearly had notice of them though they were not noted conspicuously on the stock certificates.

    C.   Courts have begun to recognize a fiduciary duty in officers and majority shareholders to treat minority shareholders fairly.

       Example: <u>Sennerikuppam v. Datel Engineering</u>: Datel did not breach his fiduciary duty as a majority shareholder by selling stock at a price unavailable to Senneerikuppam and thus oppressing him as a minority stockholder.

IV. Termination of corporation.

    A.   A corporation may terminate by agreement, or be dissolved by judgment of a court.

       Example: <u>Balsamides v. Perle</u>: Perle should be required to sell his stock to Balsamides because of the vendetta Perle created against Balsamides

Learning Objectives

1.   You should understand the obligations and liabilities of a corporate promoter.

2.   You should understand the problems of a defectively formed corporation.

3.   You should understand the formalities required to incorporate and circumstances under which a court will "pierce the corporate veil."

4.   You should be able to recognize and distinguish the main characteristics of the various types of corporations.

5.   You should know the legal principles governing the promoter's and the corporation's liability on pre-incorporation contracts, including what must be done to relieve a promoter of liability on a preincorporation contract and what must take place before the corporation itself is held liable on such a contract.

6.   You should understand the respective functions of the articles of incorporation and the by-laws.

7.   You should understand how the term <u>doing business</u> may mean different things, depending upon whether the issue to be resolved pertains to jurisdiction over a foreign corporation, or to taxation of a corporation, or to the need for a foreign corporation to qualify to do business in another state.

8.   You should know how a corporation may be dissolved, and should understand that it is more difficult to dissolve a corporation than it is to dissolve a partnership.

Learning Hints

1.   A corporation is a separate legal entity. One of the principal advantages of incorporation is that the liability of shareholders is limited to the value of the shares in the corporation. An exception arises, however, in cases where courts have permitted a creditor to "pierce the corporate veil" in order to hold shareholders personally liable for the debts of the corporation.

2.   Legal issues may arise as a result of the preincorporation process. Generally, promoters are personally liable for contracts they make on behalf of the corporation; however, a corporation generally ratifies the contracts of the promoters so that it becomes liable for such contracts.

3. In order to incorporate, incorporators file articles of incorporation in a state where it desires to be incorporated. This may be any state, if the corporation is engaged in the interstate commerce.

4. A corporation is largely a creature of statute. It is not possible to create a corporation "accidentally." To incorporate a business, a person must at least substantially comply with the formalities required by the applicable state incorporation law.

5. Note that a corporation is an entity separate and distinct from its shareholders and managers for all purposes, including, domicile, liability, existence, and taxation.

6. The promoter performs an important economic function in our society by bringing together people who have business ideas but lack money, and people who have money but lack new business ideas. For performing this function, the promoter generally is compensated. However, the usual rule is that the corporation is not <u>required</u> to compensate the promoter for that work. The reason for this rule is that the services are performed before the corporation exists. Therefore, technically speaking, nothing was done <u>for</u> the corporation. Remember, however, that promoters have fiduciary duties to the corporation despite its non-existence at the time of the promotional activities.

7. Do not confuse the terms <u>articles of incorporation</u> and <u>certificate of incorporation</u>. The articles are the basic governing document of the corporation. They state many of the rights and responsibilities of shareholders and managers of the corporation. The certificate of incorporation is a document issued by the secretary of state to certify that a particular corporation exists in the eyes of the law.

8. As stated above, the articles of incorporation serve as the basic governing document of the corporation. In that sense, the articles are analogous to a constitution. The by-laws of the corporation are analogous to statutes. Just as statutes cannot be inconsistent with the governing constitution, by-laws cannot be inconsistent with the governing articles of incorporation. The by-laws contain important matters, but not matters as fundamental as those in the articles. This distinction in the importance of the respective provisions in the articles and the by-laws helps explain why ordinarily the articles may be amended only by a vote of the shareholders, whereas the by-laws may be amended by a vote of the board of directors. Note, however, that the articles of incorporation and the by-laws cannot contain anything contrary to the state incorporation statute.

9. Another variation on the piercing the corporate veil theme is the accepted doctrine that courts will hold a parent corporation liable for the obligations of its subsidiary corporation if the parent dominates the subsidiary and the domination results in some improper purpose. These cases may involve a parent corporation that creates a subsidiary corporation, gives it very few assets, and then directs most of the subsidiary's actions and uses the subsidiary, as its instrument for incurring debt the parent otherwise would incur. In such situations, there is a great potential for creditors to be defrauded, because the subsidiary would not have the financial ability to pay its debts. Allowing the creditor to hold the parent liable for the debts prevents misuse of the corporate form.

10. Note that when a foreign corporation does business in another state, it need not incorporate in that state. It must merely qualify to do business there.

11. Close corporations differ from publicly traded corporations in that no established market for the stock exists and there are only a few shareholders, who are probably active in the company. The potential for conflict among shareholders is particularly true for close corporations.

True-False

In the blank provided, put "**T**" if the statement is True or "**F**" if the statement is False.

_____ 1. A nonprofit corporation is formed and operated by private persons. It does not seek to make a profit.

_____ 2. The public at large generally holds the stock of a close corporation.

_____ 3. Shareholders of a close corporation are personally liable for corporate debts.

_____ 4. Promoters are agents of the corporation prior to its incorporation.

_____ 5. A corporation cannot exist if it is not permitted to make a profit.

_____ 6. A court will pierce the corporate veil and impose liability on a shareholder for a corporate debt whenever that person is the corporation's majority shareholder.

_____ 7. Corporations are generally required to compensate promoters for the services that they render during the pre-incorporation period.

_____ 8. If a foreign corporation sends a delivery truck driven by an employee into a state and the employee's negligence while operating the truck there causes an accident in which another party is injured, the corporation will be subject to a suit by the injured party in that state's courts.

_____ 9. The MBCA mandates that the articles of incorporation include the number of shares of capital stock the company is authorized to issue.

_____ 10. The *ultra vires* doctrine holds that acts done by a corporation that is beyond the authority granted it by either the state of incorporation or its articles are void.

Multiple Choice

1. Which of the following would most likely be contained in a corporation's bylaws rather than in its articles of incorporation?
   a. Time and place of shareholder meetings.
   b. The address of the initial registered office of the corporation and the name of its registered agent.
   c. The number of shares of capital stock that the corporation is authorized to issue.
   d. The name of the corporation including "Inc." or "Co." or some other indication of corporate status.

2. Which of the following under the MBCA is not mandatory to include in the articles of incorporation?
   a. The name and address of each incorporator.
   b. The name of the corporation.
   c. The par value of the shares of corporate stock.
   d. The name of the corporation's registered agent.

3. In determining which state within which to incorporate, a corporation engaged in interstate commerce:
   a. Must incorporate in the state of its principal place of business.
   b. Must incorporate in the state where its principal stockholders reside.
   c. May incorporate in any state that offers the most benefits to the business.
   d. May incorporate in as many states as it chooses.

4. Ed is the primary shareholder of Mister Ed Co. Ed invested very little money in his corporation and he pays for some personal assets and expenses from corporate funds. This situation is probably an example of:
   a. A de *facto* corporation
   b. A *de jure* corporation.
   c. Corporation by estoppel.
   d. Piercing the corporate veil.

5. In order for a creditor to "pierce the corporate veil":
   a. There must be domination of the corporation by one or more of its shareholders.
   b. A shareholder must dominate the corporation for an improper purpose.
   c. The corporation must agree to indemnify shareholders in the event of their personal liability.
   d. Both (a) and (b) are correct.

6. Which of the following is not true concerning defective incorporation?

   a. Under the old MBCA, all persons who assume to act as a corporation before the certificate of incorporation has been issued are jointly and severally liable.

   b. The revised MBCA holds liable only those promoters, managers, and shareholders who both participated in policy decisions and who knew of the defective incorporation.

   c. A promoter pretending to represent a corporation when no attempt to incorporate has been made can avoid contracts made with businesses on behalf of the corporation.

   d. A *de jure* corporation is treated as a corporation except in instances involving a *quo warranto* proceeding.

7. Art is a promoter who is forming Zits Co. Which of the following statements is true?

   a. Art enters into a lease contract with Jameson in the name of and based on the credit of Zits. Jameson knows that Zits does not exist yet. If Zits Co. is never actually formed, Art will likely be held personally liable on the contract.

   b. The MBCA does not allow Zits to issue shares of stock to Art in return for his pre-incorporation services.

   c. When Zits is formed, it is automatically liable on contracts made by Art.

   d. Art can be released from liability on contracts formed before incorporation if he, Zits, and the other contracting party agree to a novation.

8. Which of the following constitute(s) "doing business," for purposes of whether a foreign corporation must qualify to do business in a state?

   a. Taking orders and filling them from outside the state.

   b. Taking orders and filling them from outside the state, if the salesperson resides within the state.

   c. Maintaining, within a state, a stock of goods from which to fill orders.

   d. Both b and c.

9. A, B, C, and D are shareholders in a close corporation. The four shareholders cannot seem to agree on anything concerning the business. Which of the following statements is not true?

   a. Courts cannot intervene without statutory authority even if the close corporation cannot operate profitably because of deadlock between majority and minority shareholders.

   b. Under a right of first refusal, if B wants to sell her shares to F, the corporation or the other shareholders are first given the right to purchase the shares.

   c. Under a buy and sell agreement, B is required to sell her shares to the corporation at an agreed-upon price.

   d. Under a consent restraint, the other shareholders must agree to B's sale of shares to F.

10. Which of the following statements is true?

    a. X and Y corporations merge and form Z corporation. Both X and Y corporations are dissolved.

    b. M's failure to file the corporation's annual report could result in dissolution of the corporation.

    c. Directors of a corporation could propose dissolution and a majority of shareholders who are entitled to vote could vote to dissolve the corporation.

    d. All of the above.

Short Essay

1. Sharon, Sandy, and Linda want to form a corporation for the floral shop that they are planning to open. They are confused about the differences between the articles of incorporation and the bylaws. Briefly distinguish between articles and bylaws. Which of these would control more of the day-to-day operations of the corporation?

2. Tammy is a promoter for Acme Co. Briefly describe Tammy's duties as a promoter. Also describe Tammy's liability to the corporation and to third parties. Is the corporation required to pay Tammy for her services as a promoter?

3. Under what circumstances may the court decide to pierce the corporate veil?

4. Harold, Hillary, and Heidi form a close corporation for their cleaning business, Happy Cleaners. What are some of the primary characteristics of a close corporation?

5. Johnny Walker wants to start up a pet walking service in New York City. He intended to incorporate the business, but because his business was so successful, he never got around to dealing with all the paperwork. Under the proposed incorporation, he was to be the sole shareholder of the corporation. Last week, one of Johnny's client's dogs broke loose from the pack and knocked over Peter Pedestrian, causing severe injury. What are the consequences to Johnny?

6.   The Railway R. Us Corporation is involved in operating a railroad in the Southwestern portion of the US. Sallie Shareholder is a part owner of the company through her ownership of 10 percent of the outstanding shares in the company. Last week, the management team of the corporation entered into a new labor contract with the Railway Workers Union employees of the company. Sallie objects to the content because she thinks it is too favorable to the union and now sues the corporation alleging that it entered into an *ultra vires* act. Who wins?

7.   Assume that Heidi in question # 4 above decides she wants out of the corporation because she cannot agree with Harold and Hillary about anything. Heidi wants to sell her shares to Howie. Discuss the different types of transfer restrictions that may hinder Heidi's ability to sell her shares to Howie.

CHAPTER 28
MANAGEMENT OF THE CORPORATE BUSINESS

Outline

I. The board of directors.

A. Directors have authority to manage the business of the corporation. In large corporations, directors tend to ratify management decisions by officers

B. General powers of the board include declaring a dividend, setting the price of stock, electing officers and filling vacancies on the board.

C. Some actions require <u>board initiative</u>, such as amendment of the articles of incorporation, merger or sale of corporate assets, or voluntary dissolution, with stockholder approval.

D. State statutes generally establish requirements for number of directors and their qualifications. Directors are elected by shareholders and normally hold office until the next annual meeting.

Example: <u>MM Companies v. Liquid Audio</u>: The court invalidated Liquid Audio's increase in the size of its board of directors. The increase was an attempt to prevent MM from taking control of the board. The court held that the business judgment rule was not appropriate when a board acts for the primary purpose of impeding a shareholder vote.

E. Procedure to fill Vacancies, Removal of Directors and Frequency of meetings may be determined by state statute, articles of incorporation, or the bylaws.

II. Duties of directors and officers.

A. The power of officers to bind the corporation is the same as that of any agent.

B. The officers and directors owe the corporation a fiduciary duty.

1. The "prudent person standard" and "business judgment rule" applies in cases where directors and officers are charged with failing to act with due care and diligence in corporate affairs.

Example: <u>In re the Walt Disney Co. Derivative Litigation</u>: The court refused to dismiss a derivative lawsuit challenging the compensation package for Disney's departing president. It believed that the plaintiffs had a cognizable claim that the board acted with an intentional lack of due care.

Example: <u>McMullin v. Beran</u>: It is a presumption that in making a business decision, the directors of a corporation acted on an informed basis, in good faith, and in the honest belief that the action taken was in the best interests of the corporation, i.e., the business judgment rule.

Example: <u>Omnicare v. NCS Healthcare</u>: The court found that the directors violated their fiduciary duty to the corporation by erecting a defensive device to protect a merger agreement. This deal protection device was held to be coercive.

2. Some states have enacted legislation designed to limit directors' liability for breach of the duty of care.

C. Directors and officers are not prohibited from entering into transactions with the corporation so long as they make full disclosure; they may not usurp corporate opportunity.

Example: <u>Telxon Corporation v. Meyerson</u>: The court refused to dismiss the corporate opportunity-based challenge to Meyerson's sale to the corporation. While the corporation's CEO may have signed off on the development of pen-based computers that is not sufficient. The board itself must have passed on the opportunity and that decision must have been an informed one.

D. Minority shareholders may file "freeze out" or "bad faith" suits where the acts of directors have abused their discretion.

E. Federal securities laws prohibit insiders from buyer or selling its stock.

III. Liability for torts and crimes.

    A. The corporation is liable for all torts committed by its employees within the scope of their employment under the agency concept of *respondeat superior*. Courts today may also impose criminal liability on the corporation for the acts of its directors, officers, or managers.

    Example: <u>Southern Management Corporation v. Taha</u>: After a jury exonerated SMC employees of malicious prosecution, they convicted the corporation of that same intentional tort. This could not be done since a corporation acts through its employees. The court ruled that a corporation could not be liable for a tort if none of its employees were liable for the tort.

    B. Officers and directors have been held personally liable or criminally liable for the illegal behavior of a subordinate if she knew or should have known of the illegal conduct and failed to take reasonable measures to prevent it. Corporations often indemnify officers and directors for the costs of defending and/or settling such suits.

    C. The Sarbanes-Oxley Act requires CEOs and CFOs of publicly traded corporations to certify that to their knowledge all financial information in quarterly and annual reports is not false or misleading.

    Example: <u>Southern Management Corporation v. Taha</u>: The court ruled that the restructuring payments were not extraordinary payments under the Sarbanes-Oxley Act. As such, the payments to the departing CEO and COO did not need to be placed in an escrow account pending the course of the securities law action against them.

Learning Objectives

1. You should understand the responsibilities to the corporation of directors and officers.

2. You should understand the circumstances under which a director or officer may be liable for torts and crimes committed by the corporation.

3. You should understand the circumstances under which the corporation itself may be subject to criminal prosecution as a result of the acts or breach of duty of its employees, directors, or officers.

4. You should understand the roles of the shareholders and the board of directors in the corporation.

5. You should know the rights and powers of the board of directors and the rights and powers of individual directors.

6. You should know how vacancies in the board of directors may be filled, as well as the bases upon which a director may be removed from the board.

7. You should understand how boards of directors use subcommittees.

8. You should know the inherent powers possessed by the officers of a corporation.

9. You should master the business judgment rule and its application, and should be aware of recent legislative responses to increased director liability.

10. You should know under which circumstances a corporation must or may indemnify an officer or director.

Learning Hints

1. The shareholders do not make management decisions; their power to influence management is to replace directors who then will replace the officers.

2. A board of directors manages the business of a corporation. However, in large corporations, the directors tend to ratify management decisions of top executives.

3. The board has some general powers; other actions, such as amending the articles of incorporation, require approval of the shareholders following board initiative.

4. Directors are not agents for the corporation. However, agency law principles apply in questions involving the power of an officer to bind the corporation.

5. No director by himself has any inherent power to act for the corporation, although the board of directors might grant him such power.

6. The business judgment rule is one of the most important legal rules in all of corporation law. The rule states that, absent bad faith, fraud, or breach of a fiduciary duty, the judgment of the board of directors is conclusive. The rule means that if the board acts honestly without any personal interest in the business decision and makes a reasonable investigation before making the business decision, the board will have no liability to the corporation, even though the decision ends up having a harmful effect on the corporation. The reason for the rule is that business managers, not courts, are best able to make business decisions. Therefore, a court will not substitute its judgment for that of the board, unless the board members failed to make a reasonable investigation, acted dishonestly, intended to defraud the corporation, or personally profited from the business decision.

7. Some examples may assist you in determining whether the business judgment rule would apply to a particular decision. The business judgment rule would not apply to a decision of the board to buy land if all the directors owned the land that the corporation buys because the directors personally profited from the transaction. Similarly, the rule would not apply to a decision of the directors to issue common stock to themselves. The rule would apply, however, to a board decision to open a new manufacturing plant, if the board made a reasonable investigation prior to making the decision.

8. The basis for making usurpation of a corporate opportunity improper is that the officer or director is stealing something (an opportunity) that belongs to the corporation.

9. As an employer, a corporation is liable for the torts of its employees, when the torts are committed within the scope of employment. This is the case because of the doctrine of respondeat superior, which you studied earlier in connection with agency law.

10. A corporation is not generally liable for the crimes of an employee, because most crimes require criminal intent. Because the corporation is not a natural person, it has no mental capacity and cannot form any intent to commit a wrong. However, if a high-level manager with discretionary authority has criminal intent while acting for the corporation, the manager's criminal intent will be imputed to the corporation, making the corporation guilty of the crime.

True-False

In the blank provided, put "**T**" if the statement is True or "**F**" if the statement is False.

_____ 1. Corporate directors may cause corporate funds to be contributed to charity only if the shareholders approve such a contribution.

_____ 2. A plan for XYZ Co. to merge with ABC Co. can be taken only through board initiative.

_____ 3. A freeze out plan that does not meet the fairness test may subject the directors to liability for breach of fiduciary duty to minority shareholders.

_____ 4. A director is an agent for the corporation.

_____ 5. Smiley, Inc. can adopt specific amendments to its articles of incorporation that remove breach of duty as a cause of action for monetary damages against directors under a self-executing statute.

_____ 6. <u>Board initiative</u> means that the power to conduct the day-to-day operations of the corporation initiates with the board of directors.

_____ 7. J.R. is president and a director of Ewing Oil. Marilee Stone approaches J.R. about a great deal on a refinery. J.R. would be usurping a corporate opportunity if he were to purchase the refinery for himself.

_____ 8. A director must refuse to vote for a proposed corporate course of action in order to not be held liable, if the board's actions constitute a failure to meet its duties to the corporation.

_____ 9. Shareholders elect the directors of a corporation.

_____ 10. Under the MBCA, the remaining members of the board of directors may fill vacancies on the board.

Multiple Choice

Circle the best answer.

1. Which of the following statements is true concerning directors or officers of a corporation?
   a. Indemnification of a director or officer is mandatory if the director or officer prevails on the merits of the suit against her.
   b. A director who is found liable to the corporation can be indemnified by the corporation.
   c. A director who is found guilty may not be indemnified under voluntary indemnification.
   d. A director who violates federal securities law may be indemnified by the corporation.

2. Which of the following statements is not true concerning the officers of a corporation?
   a. A vice-president may have implied authority to bind the corporation on contracts.
   b. The treasurer of a corporation generally has the authority to borrow money for the corporation.
   c. A corporate secretary would generally not have the authority to bind the corporation on contracts.
   d. The MBCA does not allow the same person to serve as president and secretary of a corporation.

3. Which of the following is a fiduciary duty of a director to his corporation?
   a. The duty to act within the authority of his position in the corporation.
   b. The duty to act diligently and with due care in conducting business for the corporation.
   c. The duty to act with loyalty and good faith for the benefit of the corporation.
   d. All of the above.

4. If a corporate officer exceeds his/her authority under the articles or bylaws:
   a. The officer is liable if the corporation is damaged by an act exceeding her authority under the by-laws.
   b. The officer is not liable in damages unless she knew that the act was outside the scope of her authority.
   c. If the transaction is *ultra vires*, and the director justifiably believed it to be within the scope of the corporation's business, she is not liable.
   d. Both (a) and (c) are correct.

5. Julie was a director of the Coca-Cola Company when it was decided to switch to the New Coke. The decision was universally ridiculed and the company decided to go back to the original Coke. Which of the following statements is not true concerning Julie and the other directors?

    a. The directors are not liable if they relied on information that was gathered by a management team that they trusted.

    b. Courts can generally substitute their business judgment for that of corporate managers, board members, or officers.

    c. The directors are not liable if they were not negligent in making the decision to switch to the New Coke.

    d. Julie could be liable if it was discovered that she was being paid by PepsiCo, Inc.

6. Monique, a director of Marginal Corp., owns real estate that Marginal wishes to purchase for expansion purposes. Monique paid $140,000 for the property ten years ago. She agreed to sell the land to Marginal for $230,000--the property's fair market value--after informing the other four directors what her cost was. The other four directors gave their approval. When a Marginal shareholder discovered Monique's profit, he sued her on behalf of Marginal to recover the profit she made through self-dealing. Is Monique liable?

    a. Yes, because directors are barred from doing business with the corporations for which they serve as directors.

    b. No, unless selling the property to Marginal was Monique's idea originally.

    c. Yes, unless the shareholders other than the one who brought suit all approved of the transaction.

    d. No, because she disclosed the profit she would make, a disinterested board approved, and the transaction called for a fair price.

7. Which of the following statements is not true concerning corporations?

    a. Directors can use the business judgment rule as a defense when they oppose a takeover if the directors can show that a reasonable person in their position would believe that the takeover presented dangers to the corporation.

    b. Directors must show that the defensive measures they used in opposing a takeover were reasonable given the threat to the corporate interest.

    c. To demonstrate good faith, a director must personally investigate all of the details of a business decision.

    d. A director can avoid liability if she can show that she acted in good faith, as a prudent person would do in similar circumstances, and if she can show she acted in the best interest of the corporation.

8. Which of the following statements is true concerning corporations?

    a. The MBCA requires that directors can only take action in an actual meeting.

    b. The MBCA does not allow directors to set their own compensation.

    c. Because directors are not employees of the corporation, they are not considered "insiders" for purposes of the legal rules governing insider trading of securities.

    d. Directors are generally liable for torts committed by officers they have appointed.

9. While at his office, Merle, the vice president of acquisitions for Normal, Inc., was called by a Solid Corp. attorney, who asked whether Normal would be interested in purchasing approximately 25 percent of the outstanding shares of Solid. Various things about Solid may have made the tentative proposal an attractive, not to mention financially feasible, prospect for Normal. Merle responded by telling the attorney what he (Merle) genuinely believed to be true. He (Merle) did not think that Normal would be interested. Merle (who is independently wealthy) said that he was willing to buy the shares personally, however. He purchased the shares for $10,000,000. A year later, he sold the shares to some private investors for $17,000,000. When the Normal directors discovered Merle's purchase and subsequent sale of the Solid shares, they sued him on behalf of the corporation. In view of the facts just stated, which of the following is accurate?

   a. Merle is not liable to Normal because he had no intent to defraud.

   b. Merle is liable to Normal for usurping a corporate opportunity.

   c. Merle exceeded his authority to act for Normal.

   d. Merle engaged in impermissible self-dealing with Solid.

10. Which of the following statements is true concerning corporate directors?

   a. Directors are agents of the corporation.

   b. The MBCA requires corporations to have a minimum of one director.

   c. Directors cannot legally communicate official corporate business through e-mail.

   d. The MBCA does not allow corporate boards to set the price of corporate stock.

Short Essay

1. Bernie is a director of BALCO Co. Bernie has missed the last two director's meetings. Can the shareholders remove Bernie if the corporate bylaws give the power of removal to the other directors?

2. Flushes R Us, Inc. (FRU) is a corporation whose principal business is the manufacturing and sale of toilets. Gert is the manager in charge of the employees in FRU's product delivery division. Eddie is one of the employees in that division. One day, while Eddie was en route to a retail customer's place of business (where he was to make a delivery of a large quantity of FRU toilets), Eddie negligently operated the truck he was driving and caused injury to a pedestrian. In doing so, Eddie was violating a specific corporate directive that employees were not to be negligent. The injured pedestrian filed suit against Eddie, Gert, and FRU in an effort to obtain money damages for her injuries. Who is liable? Why?

3.   Ellen is president of Ajax Co. Briefly describe Ellen's duties to Ajax.

4.   Dana is treasurer of Smith Co. In her capacity as treasurer, Dana borrows a large sum of money from National Bank. Was Dana authorized to do this in her capacity as Smith Co. treasurer? What can the corporation do in this situation?

5.   Ace Motors, an automobile manufacturer, has been experiencing problems with a particular model. Several people have been killed in accidents resulting from poor design and location of the fuel line in the car. Could officers and directors of the corporation be held liable for these damages and deaths?

6.   XYZ Corporation is headed by I. M. Bluster, a very dominant type of CEO, who is used to getting his way in all matters regarding XYZ. The board regularly capitulates to his demands. I.M. Bluster demanded that XYZ provide him with the exclusive use of an $18 million penthouse when he visits New York City. The corporation is headquartered in the Cayman Islands for tax purposes, but much of its business is conducted in New York City. The penthouse is booked as a corporate asset and is not part of I. M. Bluster's salary even though no other officials are allowed to use it. Does XYZ have a problem?

CHAPTER 29

FINANCING THE CORPORATION AND THE ROLE OF THE SHAREHOLDERS

Outline

I. Financing the corporation.

    A. Equity securities arise from the sale of ownership interests in the business; debt securities, and is typified by bonds and other obligations.

    B. Common stock:

        1. If the corporation only has one class of stock, it is common stock. If there is more than one class, the common shareholders usually bear the major risks and benefits of the business.

        Example: <u>Levco Alternative Fund Ltd. v. The Reader's Digest Association</u>: The court issued a preliminary injunction against the corporation's recapitalization plan. The special committee created to review the fairness of the proposal never considered whether the measure was fair to the Class A shareholders.

        2. Preferred stock gives shareholders a preference as to dividends and distribution of assets. Rights of preferred shareholders may vary.

    C. The stockholders must provide consideration for their shares (money, property, or services already performed).

    D. Shares may be assigned a value, called <u>par</u> value, in the articles of incorporation or a stated value at the time of issuance.

    E. Capital surplus arises when shares sell for more than their par or stated value.

        1. Directors may issue options to purchase shares of the corporation; options represented by certificates are known as warrants.

II. Debt securities.

    Corporations may borrow money by issuing debt securities. These include notes, debentures, and bonds.

III. The shareholder.

    A. Shareholders have few functions--their principal function is the election of the directors.

    B. A shareholder usually acquires stock by purchase.

    Example: <u>Elliott Associates L.P. v. Avatek Corporation</u>: A proposed merger required the consent of two thirds of the preferred stockholders.

    C. Annual Shareholder's meetings are required in all states but Delaware. The main purpose of the meeting is the election of directors. Notice is required before the meeting, but shareholders may waive notice.

    D. The MBCA requires a written document appoint a proxy as an agent to vote for a shareholder, and the SEC (Securities and Exchange Commission) regulates proxy statements.

    E. The bylaws govern procedures of the meetings.

    F. Shareholders have the right to ask questions and to propose resolutions at shareholders' meetings.

    G. Right of inspection and preemptive right:

    Example: <u>Dyer v. Indium Corporation of America</u>: The court found that Dyer had a right to inspect the corporation's records. He had a proper purpose for seeking access (valuation of his stock in order to evaluate the purchase offer). The corporation could not meet its burden of demonstrating that he was acting in bad faith.

H. Dividends: Declaration of dividends is subject to the business judgment of the board of directors.

    1. Types of dividends include cash and stock dividends. A preferred shareholder usually has preference in dividends.

    Example: <u>Lohnes v. Level 3 Communications</u>: Level 3 was not contractually bound to provide Lohnes with individualized notice of its stock split.

IV. Other shareholder rights in extraordinary transactions.

    A. Shareholders must approve amendment of the articles of incorporation; merger or consolidation also requires approval. Most states deny the right of appraisal if the shares are traded on a securities exchange.

    Example: <u>Cede & Company v. Cinerama</u>: The appraisal of Technicolor shares must include the value added by the merger plan.

    B. Lawsuits by Shareholders may be based on breach of contract; in some cases a class action may be brought. A shareholder may bring a derivative action on behalf of the corporation in unusual cases.

    Example: <u>In re Oracle Corporation Derivative Litigation</u>: Shareholders brought a derivative lawsuit against four corporate directors accused of engaging in insider trading. Specifically, they challenged the independence of the special litigation committee the corporation formed to investigate the derivative action. The court concluded that the corporation failed to demonstrate that the members of the committee were independent in light of the fact that they were charged with investigating a fellow professor and two large benefactors of their university.

    C. A shareholder is liable to the corporation in very limited circumstances, as when he purchases "watered stock."

    D. A shareholder has a right to sell or give away her shares unless there is a valid restriction.

Learning Objectives

1. You should understand the considerations in a court decision to uphold the board's defensive tactics.

2. You should understand the difference between common and preferred stock.

3. You should understand the rights and obligations of the holders of various types of stock.

4. You should know what types of consideration a corporation may receive in exchange for its shares.

5. You should know when a corporation may redeem its shares and when it may purchase its shares on the open market.

6. You should be able to recognize the many debt instruments a corporation may issue.

7. You should understand the role of the shareholders in a corporation's governance.

8. You should know how shareholder meetings (particularly special meetings) are called, what the notice requirements are for shareholder meetings, and what sorts of actions are taken at shareholder meetings.

9. You should understand what a proxy is.

10. You should know what cumulative voting is and how it enables minority shareholders to elect directors.

11. You should understand what preemptive rights are and what the right of appraisal is.

Learning Hints

1. There are two major sources of corporate financing: equity securities, which arise through the sale of ownership interests in the business, and debt securities, typified by bonds and other obligations of the business.

2. Common stock shareholders usually bear the major risks of the business and benefit most from its success.

3. Preferred stock gives the owner a preference as to dividends and distribution of assets.

4. The par value of shares may be established in the articles of incorporation; par value and stated value reflect the minimum amount of consideration for which the shares can be issued. In many cases, the shares are worth more than par or stated value and the directors have a duty to receive the fair value of the stock.

5. If the directors issue shares to such purchasers for less than the par or stated value of the shares, such a situation presents a "watered stock" problem. Watered stock is an easy problem to detect. For example, corporate directors issue one-dollar par shares for 75 cents per share. The "water" is 25 cents per share. (The term derives from the practice of dishonest cattlemen who took their cattle to the river to drink water before taking them to the stockyards. By doing so, the cattlemen caused their cattle to weigh more. The added weight was misleading, however, because it was attributable to water rather than beef.)

6. Proxies serve as a useful tool for management to control a corporation without management necessarily owning many shares itself. Most shareholders tend to sign and return proxies submitted to them by management, leading to the typical situation that what management wants to happen at a shareholders' meeting generally will happen. Of course, groups of shareholders may also seek the proxies of other shareholders, but such groups rarely have the success management ordinarily has in soliciting proxies.

7. Where cumulative voting is required by statute, as in a number of states, or is allowed by the corporation even though state law does not require it, a group of minority shareholders has an enhanced opportunity to elect a director of that group's choice. Your text sets forth the formula used, under cumulative voting, to determine the number of shares necessary to elect one director. As an illustration of how the formula works, assume that 1000 shares are being voted at the shareholders' meeting, and that four directors are to be elected. Applying the formula, one would divide 1000 (the number of shares being voted) by five (the number of directors to be elected, plus one). The resulting figure of 200 is then increased by one, meaning that 201 shares are needed to elect one director.

8. Some corporate transactions fundamentally change the character of the shareholders' investment. For this reason, the law requires shareholder approval before the fundamental change may occur. For example, a merger significantly increases the assets and liabilities of the corporation the shareholder owns and increases the number of shareholders who own the corporation. Also, an amendment of the articles of incorporation changes the basic governing document of the corporation. Hence, a shareholder vote must approve these transactions. By contrast, the sale of inventory in the ordinary course of business is a minor matter that does not require shareholder approval.

9. Note that before a corporation may pay any dividend to common shareholders, it must pay the preferred shareholders' dividend preference. If there is an arrearage on cumulative preferred shares, the entire arrearage must be paid before any dividend may be paid to common shareholders.

10. The existence of the right of appraisal recognizes that a shareholder needs a remedy when she votes against a merger, consolidation, or sale of substantially all the assets of the corporation that the shareholders as a whole approve. In such transactions, the shareholder's investment is being substantially changed against her will. The right of appraisal allows the shareholder to receive the value of her shares as of the moment before the transaction was effected. Hence, if the shareholder believes the transaction reduced the value of her investment, she may obtain the value of the investment prior to the transaction by enforcing her right of appraisal.

True-False

In the blank provided, put "**T**" if the statement is True or "**F**" if the statement is False.

_____ 1. A corporation can issue a class of stock that carries with it no right to vote for corporate directors.

_____ 2. Even if a shareholder is consistently dissatisfied with day-to-day operation decisions of the corporate management, the shareholder cannot on that basis enforce the right of appraisal.

_____ 3. Cumulative voting allows minority shareholders the opportunity to have representation on a corporate board.

_____ 4. Hardy owns stock in General Motors. Since Hardy is unable to attend the annual shareholder meeting, he can vote by proxy.

_____ 5. The decision by the board of directors to pursue litigation is not an ordinary business decision protected by the business judgment rule.

_____ 6. Trish owns debenture in SBA Co. Vern owns bonds in SBA. If SBA liquidates, Trish will likely be repaid more of her investment than will Vern.

_____ 7. Treasury shares must be resold for more than par value.

_____ 8. Although a corporation must issue common stock, it need not issue preferred stock.

_____ 9. Although preferred shareholders usually have a dividend preference over common shareholders, preferred shareholders often do not have the same rights to vote that common shareholders possess.

_____ 10. Carmen owns 1 percent of the stock of GC Co. If GC issues new shares of stock, Carmen has a preemptive right to purchase a proportionate number of the new shares so that she can maintain her 1 percent ownership in GC.

Multiple Choice

Circle the best answer.

1. Shirley owns preferred stock in BMI Corporation. Which of the following statements is not true concerning Shirley's investment?

   a. Shirley receives dividends on her stock before common shareholders in BMI receive their dividends.

   b. If BMI is dissolved, Shirley will be paid her share from the distribution of the assets before common shareholders are paid.

   c. Preferred shareholders, such as Shirley, always have voting rights.

   d. Shirley's preferred stock may be convertible into BMI common stock.

2. Sharon owns cumulative preferred stock in XYZ Co. For three years, the company struggled a great deal and no dividends were paid to either preferred or common shareholders. The company was profitable in the fourth year and is ready to pay dividends. Which of the following statements is true concerning Sharon's investment in XYZ preferred stock?

   a. Sharon will never receive dividends for those years the company could not afford to pay them.

   b. Sharon is entitled to receive all dividends from past years and the current year before common shareholders receive their dividends.

   c. Sharon will never receive more than her "normal" dividend each year even if her stock is participating.

   d. Sharon must be paid dividends every year since she owns cumulative preferred stock.

3. Which of the following statements concerning stocks is not true?

   a. Stock splits may be used to lower the price of stock so that more investors may buy it.

   b. Stock dividends increase a shareholder's stake in the corporation.

   c. The board of directors decides whether to declare dividends.

   d. An owner of participating preferred stock may share in profits with common shareholders over and above her "normal" dividend.

4. Dissolution of the corporation:
   a. Occurs when all corporate assets have been liquidated and distributed to creditors and shareholders.
   b. May be decreed by a court if the majority shareholder sells her shares.
   c. May occur as a result of vote by majority of the corporation's initial directors.
   d. May be decreed by a court against the will of the corporation's directors and at the request of creditors under appropriate circumstances.

5. Which of the following statements about shareholder rights is not true?
   a. Shareholders may sue the corporation for breach of the shareholder contract.
   b. A class action suit could be brought against the corporation by the shareholders of the same class of stock.
   c. A shareholder may bring a derivative action against the corporation if the board of directors refuses to do so.
   d. Damages in a successful derivative action are awarded to the shareholder who brings the action.

6. Cargo Corporation issues 100,000 shares of its $1 par value common shares for a total consideration of $50,000 cash, the fair market value of the shares. Is there anything wrong with this issuance?
   a. No, because they were issued for fair market value.
   b. No, because cash is a proper type of consideration for shares.
   c. Yes, because the fair market value must have been more than $50,000.
   d. Yes, because the shares were issued for less than their par value.

7. Which of the following statements regarding stock is true?
   a. Shareholders who knowingly receive dividends that were paid illegally must pay the amount back to the corporation.
   b. A shareholder can endorse the assignment form printed on the back of the stock certificate to transfer ownership of the stock.
   c. Shareholders in a close corporation may have an agreement that gives the other shareholders first right of purchase when another shareholder wants to sell her stock.
   d. All of the above.

8. Bing Co., a corporation listed on the New York Stock Exchange, is proposing a merger with Geller, another NYSE listed company. Green, a common stockholder in Bing Co., votes against the merger. Green now demands a right of appraisal. Which of the following statements is most accurate?
   a. Green cannot initiate the right of appraisal because she voted against the merger.
   b. Green cannot initiate the right of appraisal because she does not have the right to vote.
   c. Green does not need to inform the corporation of her intent to exercise the right of appraisal before the vote takes place.
   d. Green cannot bring a right of appraisal because Bing Co. is traded on a recognized securities exchange.

9. On September 15, 1990, Whitman signed a preincorporation subscription to buy 1,000 common shares of Slim Corp., a proposed corporation that was to be incorporated in a state that has adopted the Model Business Corporation Act. Slim was incorporated in Oct. 1, 1990 in such a state. Before Slim's board of directors took action to accept Whitman's preincorporation subscription, Whitman informed the board (on Oct. 2, 1990) that he was revoking the subscription. Shortly thereafter, the board voted to accept Whitman's subscription. When Slim attempted to force Whitman to buy the shares, he refused. Slim then sued Whitman. Is Whitman bound by his subscription?

    a. No, because he revoked it before the board accepted it.

    b. Yes, because less than six months elapsed between Whitman's signing of the subscription and the board's acceptance of it.

    c. No, because the corporation was not in existence at the time Whitman signed the subscription.

    d. Yes, because ordinary principles of contract law indicate that an offer cannot be revoked before it has been accepted.

10. Which of the following statements is true?

    a. The MBCA requires corporations to send its latest financial statements to a shareholder on request.

    b. The MBCA allows corporations to pay dividends, even if the payment would make the corporation insolvent.

    c. The MBCA give shareholders an absolute right to inspect the shareholder list.

    d. The MBCA allows shareholders to examine a corporation's books, but only if the shareholder has a proper purpose.

Short Essay

1. Wal-Mart has had several stock splits. Its stock price is hovering around $50 per share. Berkshire Hathaway, led by Warren Buffet, does not split its stock. Its price has been near $100,000 per share. What are some reasons why Wal-Mart would split its stock and Berkshire Hathaway chooses not to do so?

2. Roland Astute, a shareholder of Steamroller Corporation, uncovered evidence that, in his opinion, showed that the corporation's treasurer was embezzling corporate funds. Uncertain of whether the corporation's board of directors would agree with his assessment of what the evidence showed, Astute did not discuss the matter with the board or with other shareholders. After conferring with his attorney, Astute filed a derivative suit against the treasurer, in an attempt to recover for the losses the treasurer's actions had caused the corporation to experience. Under the circumstances, is Astute's derivative suit properly before the court? Explain.

3. Describe the ways that a person can become a shareholder of a company.

4. Nancy owns shares in ExxonMobil. Describe the MBCA requirements of notice concerning shareholder meetings.

5. Why do you think that Delaware's corporation laws now permit remote communication? What are the requirements for a remote participation meeting?

6. What is the significance of par value and stated value?

7. Sonia entered a stock subscription purchase plan with the newly formed Tort Corporation of America (TCA). TCA was formed in order to start a franchise chain of dog training schools. The terms of Sonia's subscription were for her to provide real estate having a $10,000 fair market value in return for ten shares of TCA common stock, valued at $1,000 each. After the purchase of the stock was completed, TCA found the land to be valued at $1,000 because of environmental problems. Can TCA sue Sonia for the $9,000 difference in value?

CHAPTER 30
SECURITIES REGULATION

Outline

I. Federal legislation.

    A. There are several federal acts regulating securities. These include the Securities Act of 1933, The Securities Exchange Act of 1934 and creation of the SEC (Securities and Exchange Commission) in 1934.

    B. The Securities Act of 1933 contains registration and anti-fraud provisions and restricts the issuer's ability to communicate with prospective purchasers of securities. The 1934 act contains mandatory disclosure provisions.

    C. The Securities and Exchange Commission (SEC) was created by the 1934 and administers the 1933 and 1934 Acts and other securities statutes.

    D. Investment contracts are specifically included in the definition of a security.

    Example: <u>SEC v. Charles Edwards</u>: The Supreme Court held that the sale-and-leaseback arrangement could be considered investment contracts that required registration under the federal securities laws. It concluded that the fact that the scheme offered a fixed, rather than a variable, return did not disqualify it from being treated as an investment contract governed by the securities law.

    II. The Securities Act of 1933.

    A. The 1933 Act has two principal components:

        1. Registration provisions

        2. Anti-fraud provisions

    B. Most of the information in the registration statement must be included in the prospectus.

    C. EDGAR is an electronic filing system now used by the SEC.

    D. There are some exemptions to the 1933 Act: Two types of exemptions are government issued or guaranteed securities, and short-term notes and drafts.

    E. There are also certain transaction exemptions. The most important are those available for issuers for private offerings, intrastate offerings and small offerings.

    F. Anti-fraud Provisions: A number of such provisions impose liability for improper offers and sales, for defective registration statements, and for other acts or omissions. Violation may result in both criminal and civil penalties.

    Example: <u>Gustafson v. Alloyd Company</u>: A contract of sale is not a prospectus that creates Section 12(2) liability.

III. Securities Exchange Act of 1934: This act is primarily concerned with disclosing material information to investors. It requires periodic disclosure by issuers of publicly held equity securities.

    A. Two types of securities must be registered under the 1934 Act.

    B. The Act requires that insiders individually file a statement disclosing their holdings. A regulation of short-swing profits is designed to stop speculative insider trading.

    Example: <u>Gallagher v. Abbott Laboratories</u>: Abbot did not have a duty to disclose all information relating to the FDA investigation as soon as it was available to the corporation. Firms are only required to reveal information when they issue securities.

    C. The Act also regulates proxy solicitations.

IV. Liability provisions of the 1934 Act.

    A. Liability Provisions provide remedies to victims of fraudulent, deceptive, or manipulative practices. These include:

        1. Manipulation of a security's price;

        2. Liability for False Statements in filed documents;

        3. Rule 10b prohibits the use of any manipulative or deceptive device.

    B. Rule 10b-5 imposes liability on persons who misstate material facts:

        Example: <u>SEC v. Zandford</u>: A securities broker stole money repeatedly from the investment account of one of his clients. The Supreme Court held that this conduct was within the parameters of Section 10(b) and Rule 10b-5 because the securities broker engaged in a scheme to defraud his client. It concluded that the securities sales and the broker's fraudulent practices were not independent events.

    C. Elements of a misstated or omitted fact include (1) materiality, (2) scienter, and (3) plaintiff must be actual purchaser or seller of securities, (4) reliance, and (5) action was brought within applicable statute of limitations.

        Example: <u>SEC v. Rubera</u>: The court held that Rubera did not violate Section 10(b) and Rule 10b-5 because he lacked scienter as to the false and misleading statements his agents made to investors. It concluded that he was unsophisticated and probably did not understand the company's poor financial condition.

    D. Conduct covered by Rule 10b-5 includes continuous disclosure obligations and trading on inside information.

        Example: <u>United States v. O'Hagan</u>: Philip Morris did not omit a material fact, thereby violating Rule 10b-5, when it failed to disclose a change in pricing strategy.

    E. Safe Harbor legislation discourages the filing of lawsuits, and protects companies that make optimistic forecasts about future earnings or new products.

V. Tender offer regulation.

    A. The Williams Act in 1968 amended the 1934 Act to provide investors with more information to make tender offer decisions. Most states have also enacted statutes regulating tender offers.

    B. Most states have enacted statutes regulating tender offers.

VI. State securities legislation.

    A. Frequently called "blue-sky laws," most regulate professional sellers of securities.

    B. The new Uniform Securities Act was The National Conference of Commissioners on Uniform State laws adopted the new Uniform Securities Act in August 1985.

Learning Objectives

1. You should be able to define a security.

2. You should understand the liabilities that federal securities laws impose on those who deal in securities.

3. You should know what insider trading is, and the limits placed on those with inside information.

4. You should become familiar with the registration requirements imposed by the Securities Act of 1933.

5. You should know the securities and transactions in securities that are exempt from the registration requirements of the 1933 Act.

6. You should understand the provision in Section 11 of the 1933 Act concerning liability for misleading or false information in a registration statement, and should understand, with regard to a Section 11 case, the defendant's burden of proving due diligence if he wishes to escape liability.

7. You should become familiar with the 1933 Act's other antifraud provisions besides Section 11.

8. You should understand the periodic disclosure requirements imposed by the Securities Exchange Act of 1934.

9. You should know how and why the SEC regulates solicitations of proxies.

10. You should be familiar with Rule 10b-5's broad prohibition of misstatements and omissions of material fact in connection with the sale or purchase of securities, as well as with the basic elements of a Rule 10b-5 claim by a purchaser or seller of securities.

11. You should understand how Rule 10b-5 applies to a purchaser's or seller's failure to make continuing disclosures of material facts, and should understand how Rule 10b-5 operates to prohibit insider trading on the basis of material information not generally available to the investing public.

12. You should be familiar with the SEC's regulation of tender offers, and with why such regulatory action is required by law.

Learning Hints

1. The federal and state securities laws define the term "securities" very broadly.

2. There are different securities acts that regulate securities. The Securities Act of 1933 is concerned primarily with public distributions of securities and is chiefly a one-time disclosure statute. The Securities Act of 1934 requires periodic disclosures from issuers of securities. The 1934 Act also created the Securities and Exchange Commission, which has authority to issue rules and regulations and bring enforcement actions against violators.

3. Transactions in securities are subjected to extensive regulation because of their inherent nature: they are intangible assets whose values are not apparent merely from an examination of a security certificate. Instead, an investor needs to be given information about the business issuing the security in order to make an informed investment decision. Because historically too little information has been voluntarily disclosed by issuers of securities, the securities laws require that issuers disclose the information an investor needs to make an informed investment decision.

4. A security is defined to include investment contracts. When one is investing in another person's business, one is not familiar with the business. One needs to be given information to determine whether to invest in the business.

5. With regard to the registration requirement imposed by the Securities Act of 1933, you should always remain mindful of the rule that every transaction in securities must be registered or be exempt from registration. Where registration of a securities offering is required, the prospective issuer must be very careful not to allow impermissible publicity concerning the proposed offering during the prefiling and waiting periods, and must also refrain from engaging in prohibited transactions during those periods.

6. When an exemption removes the need to register an offering with the SEC, the exemption may be either a securities exemption or a transaction exemption. The basic exemptions are explained well in your text. Do not forget, however, that a transaction exemption offers more narrow relief from the registration requirements than does a securities exemption. The transaction exemption is narrower, because it applies only to a particular sale of a certain security, not to subsequent sales of the same security. Even if a transaction exemption applies to a particular sale, subsequent sales would be subject to the registration requirement, unless, of course, another transaction exemption would apply.

7. Section 11 of the 1933 Act is an important liability provision dealing with errors in and omissions from registration statements. It is an unusual provision, in that purchasers need not show they relied on the error of omission or that they purchased the securities from the defendant. Neither must the plaintiff prove negligence or an intentional misstatement or omission on the part of the defendant. Instead, the defendant must prove due diligence if he wishes to escape liability.

8. In order to be entitled to the protection of the due diligence defense, the defendant in a Section 11 case must prove that he was not negligent in ascertaining the truthfulness of the registration statement. That is, the defendant must prove that he acted as a reasonable person would have acted under the same circumstances. This requires that most defendants make a reasonable investigation into the accuracy of the registration statement. It also shifts the burden of establishing the mental culpability of the defendant from the plaintiff to the defendant.

9. Provisions in the Securities Exchange Act of 1934, dealing with short-swing trading by insiders, rest on the logical presumption that a knowledgeable purchaser would not be buying and selling shares within such a short period if time if he were not using insider information. Remember, however, that the issuer of securities may recover profits made by a statutory on prohibited short-swing trading, without having to prove that the insider actually was relying on improper information in when he bought and sold the shares.

10. The SEC was given regulatory control over proxy solicitations and shareholder proposals because of the abuses that had arisen in large, public corporations. Because of widely dispersed bodies of small shareholders, self-perpetuating boards of directors who could ignore the demands of shareholders managed these corporations. The SEC proxy rules make it easier for shareholder democracy to be realized.

11. SEC Rule 10b-5, promulgated pursuant to the Securities Exchange Act of 1934, is an exceedingly important liability provision that prohibits a broad range of false statements, as well as failures to state material facts, in connection with the sale or purchase of securities. A considerable amount of litigation has stemmed from conduct that either the SEC or a private plaintiff claims was in violation of Rule 10b-5's broad proscription. Be certain to remember that in a Rule 10b-5 case, the plaintiff must prove that the defendant acted with scienter (an intent to deceive or defraud) and that the plaintiff, in purchasing or selling the securities, relied upon the defendant's false statement of a material fact. In a case involving an omission to state a material fact, reliance is not necessarily required.

12. Insider trading is swept within the Rule 10b-5 umbrella. The essential concept to be remembered concerning insider trading is that one who has inside information concerning certain securities and matters that may affect their value must either disclose the information or refrain from trading. It is a violation of Rule 10b-5 to buy or sell either on an exchange or in a direct transaction when one is privy to material information that is not generally available to the investing public. Remember, too, that the rule just stated applies to virtually anyone who obtains "inside" information, regardless of whether that person is an officer or director or other typical insider. A defendant who has violated Rule 10b-5 may experience potentially disastrous financial consequences.

True-False

In the blank provided, put "**T**" if the statement is True or "**F**" if the statement is False.

_____ 1. The Securities Act of 1933 requires issuers of securities to make periodic disclosures concerning the securities.

_____ 2. An investment contract not evidenced by a certificate is not a security for purposes of securities laws.

_____ 3. During the prefiling period, an issuer may publish a notice about a prospective offering.

_____ 4. EDGAR is an enforcement wing of the Securities and Exchange Commission.

5. Under the 1933 Securities Act, the SEC reviews registrations for completeness and for per se fraudulent statements.

6. Fraud claims under Section 10(b) and Rule 10b-5 must begin within three years of the time that the violation occurred and within one year after discovery of the violation.

7. Sales of limited partnership interests may be considered sales of securities, for purposes of the federal securities laws.

8. A company that makes optimistic forecasts about its future earnings cannot escape potential liability by warning the public about events that could undermine those forecasts.

9. A bidder making a tender offer may revoke the offer at any time.

10. During the waiting period following the filing of a registration statement with the SEC, the issuer of the security may neither offer nor sell the security.

Multiple Choice

Circle the best answer.

1. Which of the following statements is not correct?
   a. Once the SEC has declared a registration statement effective, the issuer is free to sell the securities if it provides the purchaser with either the preliminary prospectus or the final prospectus.
   b. Under SEC rules, shareholder sometimes may be able to compel the corporation to include shareholder proposals in the corporation's proxy statement.
   c. The Securities and Exchange Commission administers both the 1933 and 1934 Securities Acts.
   d. The 1934 Act contains mandatory disclosure provisions requiring periodic disclosures from issuers of securities.

2. The SEC's proxy rules:
   a. Contain requirements about proxy content so that the shareholder will know how the proxy will be voted.
   b. Must be complied with by corporate management but not by shareholders' groups that wish to solicit proxies.
   c. Require corporate management to include in its proxy statement, any proposals shareholders wish to have included therein.
   d. Apply regardless of whether the shareholders whose proxies are being solicited are holders of securities registered under the Securities Exchange Act of 1934.

3. X Co. makes a tender offer to by Y Co.'s stock. Y Co.'s management is fighting this action by X Co. Which of the following statements is not true?
   a. The Williams Act covers tender offers.
   b. Most states do not have statutes covering tender offers.
   c. Y Co. is making a hostile tender offer.
   d. Y Co. must keep the tender offer open for at least 20 days.

4. Which of the following statements concerning securities is not true?
   a. States have blue-sky laws that cover securities.
   b. Z Co. has a safe harbor for making optimistic forecasts about its future earnings potential as long as it also describes events that could undermine those forecasts.
   c. A person with inside information must either not trade in the stock or disclose the information before trading.
   d. The statute of limitations for insider trading is three years after the violations occur.

5. Which of the following is an exempt transaction from the antifraud provisions under the 1933 Securities Act?

   a. Sale of securities by an average investor
   b. Private offering
   c. Intrastate offering
   d. None of the above

6. Which of the following statements is true concerning the 1933 Securities Act?

   a. The purchaser of securities must prove reliance in order to recover under Section 11 of the Act.
   b. An investor must show she relied on misstatements or omissions of material fact in order to recover under Section 12(2) of the Act.
   c. Privity is required for a purchaser of securities to recover under Section 11 of the Act.
   d. The purchaser of securities must prove that the defendant acted negligently in order to recover under Section 11 of the Act.

7. Which of the following is required for Z Corporation to comply with the Securities Exchange Act of 1934?

   a. 10-K annual report that includes audited financial statements for the fiscal year.
   b. 10-Q quarterly report with unaudited financial statements.
   c. 8-K monthly report filed within 15 days of the end of the month.
   d. All of the above.

8. Which of the following statements is true concerning Section 10(b) and Rule 10b-5?

   a. Reliance is not required for cases involving omission of material facts.
   b. A purchaser of securities need only show that the issuer of securities acted with negligence.
   c. A person who refrained from investing in the securities because of false statements may recover lost profits.
   d. A broker need only disclose some of the facts about a security.

9. Which of the following actions by a corporate director would violate SEC Rule 10b-5?

   a. Usurping a corporate opportunity.
   b. Buying or selling corporate shares in reliance on inside information.
   c. Using corporate funds for personal purposes.
   d. All of the above.

10. Marty is good friends with the CEO of a major corporation. At a cocktail party, the CEO tells Marty of some major deals that the corporation is about to make. Marty buys a large block of the company's stock and makes a profit of $100,000 in a short period of time. Which of the following statements is not true?

    a. Marty is in violation of Rule 10b-5 for insider trading.
    b. Marty is not in violation of Rule 10b-5 because he traded the stock on an exchange and never met the buyer of the shares.
    c. Marty could be liable for treble damages of $300,000.
    d. Marty could be punished with a fine and a prison term.

Short Essay

1.   Give five examples of securities that are exempted from the registration provisions of the 1933 Act.

2.   Donna invests in Slick Co. stock. Donna seeks to recover damages when it is discovered that Slick's registration statement contains false information. What is necessary for Donna to recover for the false statements made by Slick?

3.   In the above case involving Donna, what is necessary for her to prove a Section 12(2) case involving misstatement of material facts in a prospectus?

4.   Irv, a custodian at Gargantuan Corp., was dusting a corporate executive's desk one evening when he discovered and read an interesting document containing information that was not available to the investing public. The information was such that if it were available to the investing public, the price and value of Gargantuan stock would soar. Irv informed his friend, Simone, of what he had read in the document. Simone then purchased 100 shares of Gargantuan stock from Cletus, without telling Cletus the information given to her by Irv. When this information finally was made available to the investing public, the value of Gargantuan stock indeed soared. Simone resold, at a substantial profit, the 100 shares she had purchased from Cletus. Cletus thereafter sued Simone in an attempt to recover the profit Simone had made. Simone denied any liability to Cletus, claiming that because she was not an officer, director, or employee of Gargantuan, she had done nothing wrong. Is Simone liable to Cletus? Why or why not?

5. Bill's broker strongly advised Bill to buy Glutton Co. stock. The broker does not tell Bill that his brokerage firm has taken a huge stake in the stock. Discuss Bill's case against the brokerage firm under Rule 10b-5 under the Securities Act of 1934.

6. T. Boone makes a hostile tender offer for stock of Petro Co. What process must Boone follow in making this offer?

7. Joe is a rich expert in stocks. Joe wants to buy and sell large quantities of Mertz Co. stock in order to cause the price of the stock to increase. Can Joe legally do this?

CHAPTER 31
LEGAL LIABILITY OF ACCOUNTANTS

Outline

I. Common law liability to the client.

    A. Contractual liability. Ordinarily, an accountant may not delegate her responsibilities without the consent of the client.

    B. Tort liability. Failure to comply with reasonable standards of care may result in liability under a <u>negligence</u> theory.

    Example: <u>Oregon Steel Mills v. Coopers and Lybrand</u>: Oregon Steel Mills was forced to delay a public offering because Coopers & Lybrand negligently provided incorrect accounting advice to the company. The court found that Coopers had no duty to protect Oregon Steel Mills against market fluctuations in the corporation's stock price. Therefore, Coopers did not have to pay the corporation the difference between what it received for the stock and what it would have received if the stock offering had not been delayed.

II. Common law liability to third persons.

    A. Historically, third parties not in privity (direct contractual relationship) with the accountant were unable to recover damages under a contract theory (except in third party beneficiary cases).

    B. Today, many courts refuse to apply the privity doctrine.

    C. The ultramares approach (No liability absent privity).

    D. The "Near Privity Approach" holds accountants liable in some cases. The restatement holds accountant is liable to those third parties who are "specifically foreseeable."

    Example: <u>Nycal Corporation v. KPMG Peat Marwick</u>: Nycal invested in Gulf, whose accountant was Peat Marwick, just before Gulf went bankrupt, and the court denied Nycal's attempt to make Peat Marwick liable to Nycal.

    E. Other approaches are the "reasonably foreseeable users" approach and the "Balancing Approach."

    Example: <u>Ernst & Young, L.L.P. v. Pacific Mutual Life Insurance Co.</u>: Pacific did not prove fraud against the accounting firm under a "reason to expect standard."

III. Statutory liability of accountants.

    A. Civil actions under the 1933 Act include liability for misstatements or omissions of material facts in the registration statements required by the Act.

    Example: <u>Endo v. Arthur Anderson & Co.</u>: Anderson was not liable to investors for a misleading omission under Section 11(a).

    B. Under the 1934 Act, liability is imposed for misstatement or omission of a material fact in connection with the purchase or sale of any security.

    C. In 1994 the Supreme Court stripped the SEC of authority to pursue accountants who aided and abetted corporate fraud. In 1995 Congress restored this power to the SEC.

    D. Both Acts have criminal provisions that may apply against accountants.

    E. State licensing boards also regulate ethical conduct of accountants. Limitation of accountant's advertising may be unenforceable if overbroad.

    F. Liability may differ depending on whether there is a qualified opinion, unqualified opinion, or enforceable disclaimer.

IV. Protection of accountants' papers.

    A. Working papers belong to the accountant.

    B. Communications between lawyers and clients are privileged; however, a privilege of confidentiality between accountant and client has not in the past been recognized in federal tax cases.

Example: <u>United States v. BDO Seidman</u>: Arthur Andersen was not held liable under Section 11(A) of the 1933 Act. The court found that Andersen's consent to republication of its 1985 statements without a warning footnote was not a misleading omission.

Learning Objectives

1. You should understand the difference between an action by a client and a third party for damages against an accountant.

2. You should understand the difference between an action in contract or tort against an accountant.

3. You should consider the ethical implications of accountants who voluntarily disclose improprieties of their clients to government officials.

4. You should understand the nature and extent of the accountant-client privilege.

5. You should understand the role of GAAP and GAAS in determining the liability of accountants.

6. You should understand the historical and present role of privity in the principles governing the legal liability of accountants.

7. You should know and understand the bases of an accountant's civil liability to a client for fraud, as well as liability based on the securities laws.

8. You should be able to recognize whether a specific act of an accountant creates potential liability and to whom the accountant may be liable.

9. You should know the sources of an accountant's criminal liability, including federal and state securities laws and tax laws.

10. You should know what protection is accorded to the work papers of an accountant, as well as who owns the work papers and who hold rights in them. You should know whether communications between an accountant and his clients are privileged, and if so, the extent of protection given to such communications.

Learning Hints

1. The law may apply different rules in an accountant liability case depending on whether the plaintiff suing the accountant is a client or a third party. Generally, a plaintiff who is a client may recover under contract or tort theory. Historically, however, third parties were often unable to recover under these theories because they were not in privity contractual relationship with the accountant.

2. Many courts today have refused to apply the privity doctrine to third party negligence suits against accountants, and there are many approaches to handling such suits.

3. Federal and state securities laws also give injured persons a right to sue in negligence or fraud; and both bodies of law contain criminal penalties.

4. The working papers of the accountant belong to the accountant, but the accountant generally must get the client's permission to transfer them to another accountant. Communications between accountants and their clients may be protected under state confidentiality statutes, but these are not always enforceable in federal courts.

5. As is the case with most professionals, the law nearly always permits accountants to set the standard by which they are judged. If an accountant has acted as the reasonably prudent accountant would have acted under same circumstances, the law will rarely impose liability upon the accountant. This explains why compliance with GAAP and GAAS will generally protect the accountant from liability. The only instance in which compliance with GAAP and GAAS may not relieve the accountant of liability is when the accountant has provided a misleading financial picture. Note that the standard is objective, rather than subjective. It is not enough that the accountant do her best. She must do what the reasonably prudent accountant would have done.

6. Note the varying levels of importance given to privity when you are studying the different bases of accountants' liability. For example, privity is required for most contract claims and often, but not always, required for negligence claims against accountants. Privity is not required, however, for fraud claims, Securities Act Section 11(a) claims, or Securities Exchange Act Rule 10b-5 claims.

7. Remember, as was pointed out in Chapter 31, that the purpose of the federal securities acts is to provide investors with information adequate to enable them to make informed investment decisions. Truth in securities transactions is valued highly, so it should not be surprising that the federal securities acts are structured in such a manner that accountants are subject to their provisions. Note the difference between Section 11(a) liability and Rule 10b-5 liability. Section 11(a) has a negligence standard, but Rule 10b-5 has a *scienter* standard. Under Section 11(a) the defendant must disprove his negligence. Under Rule 10b-5 the plaintiff must prove the defendant acted with *scienter*. Section 11(a) applies only to misstatements or omissions in registration statements under the Securities Act while Rule 10b-5 has a broader sweep, prohibiting misstatements or omissions of material fact in connection with any securities transaction in interstate commerce.

8. Note that an accountant may have criminal liability for actions for which he also has civil liability. In other words, the same action by an accountant may have both civil and criminal consequences. Criminal proceedings against an accountant do not bar civil proceedings based on the same wrongful activity, and vice versa.

True-False

In the blank provided, put "**T**" if the statement is True or "**F**" if the statement is False.

_____ 1. Accountants can generally delegate their duties without consulting the client.

_____ 2. A creditor who was harmed by misstatements made by an accountant about the debtor's financial statements must prove that the accountant acted with scienter in order to prove that the accountant committed fraud.

_____ 3. Acting with reckless disregard of the truth is sufficient *scienter* to support a charge of fraud against an accountant.

_____ 4. Accountants are liable to investors of securities if the investors relied upon the defective registration statement in making their investment.

_____ 5. An accountant who violates a state or federal statute may be liable to injured clients under negligence per se theory.

_____ 6. In order for accountants to be held liable under Rule 10b-5, an investor in securities traditionally must rely on misstatements or omissions of material facts made by the accountant.

_____ 7. Working papers made by an accountant in auditing a client's books belong to the client.

_____ 8. A number of courts today will hold an accountant liable to non-clients in a negligence action, if the accountant knew that a client would be furnishing a copy of the accountant's work to the nonclients.

_____ 9. In order to establish that an accountant committed fraud, proof that the accountant merely failed to comply with GAAP and GAAS will normally be insufficient.

_____ 10. Accountants are usually criminally liable for negligently preparing tax returns.

Multiple Choice

1. Joyce is a CPA. She performs an audit for Rice Co. She issues an opinion letter stating that Rice Co. is in compliance with GAAS and GAAP. This is an example of a (n):
   a. Adverse opinion
   b. Unqualified opinion
   c. Qualified opinion
   d. Disclaimer

2. First Bank decides to loan money to Crummy Construction Co. partly due to Crummy's financial statements and accounting records, which have been audited by Ace Accounting. Crummy becomes insolvent and First Bank believes that Ace was negligent in performing its audit of the Crummy books and that the financial statements misrepresent the true financial condition of Crummy. Which of the following judicial approaches would probably give First Bank the least chance of winning a negligence suit against Ace?
   a. The Balancing Approach
   b. The Reasonably Foreseeable Users Approach
   c. The Ultramares Approach
   d. The Restatement Approach

3. Suppose in # 2 above, that an investor purchased Crummy stock based on the misleading financial statements that had been negligently audited by Ace. Which judicial approach would probably give the investor the best chance of winning a negligence suit against Ace?
   a. Restatement Approach
   b. Reasonably Foreseeable Users Approach
   c. Ultramares Approach
   d. Near Privity Approach

4. Which of the following statements concerning an accountant's liability is true?
   a. Accountants found liable for fraud may be liable to the client for punitive damages.
   b. Accountants who are found liable to their client for negligence may be liable for punitive damages.
   c. Accountants who follow GAAP and GAAS standards are never liable to clients for negligence.
   d. Most courts readily apply the defense of contributory negligence for accountants who are being sued for negligence.

5. Les Scruem, a certified public accountant, certified a client's financial statement because he believed it was accurate based on standard auditing and accounting practices. Later, he discovered information that indicated the financial statement he had certified was misleading. Scruem:
   a. Has a duty of loyalty to his client that prevents him from revealing to third parties the unreliability of the financial statement.
   b. Cannot be liable to a third party for failing to reveal the unreliability of the statement because he had reason to believe it was accurate when he certified it.
   c. Has a duty to inform the client but no duty to inform any third parties.
   d. Must disclose the unreliability of the statement to any third party he knows is relying on it.

6. Which of the following is a factor in applying the balancing approach?
   a. The extent to which the transaction was intended to affect the plaintiff.
   b. The moral blame attached to the defendant's conduct.
   c. The policy of preventing future harm.
   d. All of the above.

7. Dullard & Denson, a CPA firm, negligently certified a balance sheet of Shaky Corp. This balance sheet, which made Shaky look far more financially stable than it really was, served as the major factor in Insolvent Savings & Loan's decision to make a substantial loan to Shaky. Shaky later defaulted on the loan and filed for bankruptcy, making the loan effectively not collectible. Insolvent has sued Dullard & Denson for negligence. Applicable state law adheres to the Ultramares approach. Who will win the suit?

   a. Insolvent, because Dullard & Denson's negligence caused it to make a loan it would not have made had it known the truth about Shaky.

   b. Dullard & Denson, because the Ultramares approach allows only fraud as a basis of liability of an accountant to any party.

   c. Dullard & Denson, because it and Insolvent were not in privity.

   d. Insolvent, because Dullard & Denson is responsible for the fraud of Shaky.

8. Which of the following statements is not true regarding an accountant's liability?

   a. An omission by an accountant in a registration statement could cause the accountant to be held criminally liable under the 1933 and 1934 Securities Acts.

   b. Nerdly, an accountant, does not get around to filing Vicki's tax return until after the deadline. As a result, Vicki owes a penalty and interest. Nerdly can be held liable to Vicki for these amounts.

   c. The SEC bars Simpson from practicing accounting because of Simpson's violations of the federal securities acts. The SEC's decision is final and cannot be appealed.

   d. At one time, state accounting licensing boards tightly regulated an accountant's right to advertise their services to the public.

9. Incomp & Inepped (I&I), a CPA firm, negligently certified the balance sheet of Schlemiel Corp. The balance sheet made Schlemiel look quite solid financially even though it was not. I&I did not know that Schlemiel's officers would be showing the balance sheet to Local National Bank in an effort to obtain a loan, but I&I did know that Schlemiel had frequent borrowing needs. After relying heavily on what the balance sheet appeared to indicate, Local National made a loan to Schlemiel. Schlemiel later went "belly-up," without repaying the loan. Local National has sued I&I for negligence. Local National:

   a. Should win the suit if applicable state law follows the Ultramares approach.

   b. Could win the suit if applicable state law follows the reasonably foreseeable users approach.

   c. Should win the suit if applicable state law follows the Restatement approach.

   d. Could win the suit if applicable state law adheres to any one of the approaches referred to in answers a, b, and c.

10. Sandy is an accountant who audits Johnson's books. While conducting the audit, Sandy uncovers some information that causes her to doubt the accuracy of Johnson's books and financial statements. Which of the following alternatives would be Sandy's best choice to avoid liability?

   a. Issue an adverse opinion.

   b. Issue a disclaimer.

   c. Issue a qualified opinion.

   d. Issue an unqualified opinion.

Short Essay

1. Tina is a CPA who prepares Foster's tax returns. Foster is in trouble with the IRS and the case goes to court. Can the IRS require Tina to make her working papers involving Foster available? Can Tina be required to testify about Foster's records and conversations with the client?

2.   Briefly discuss three <u>statutory</u> bases of accountant liability to third persons.

3.   Dewey, Cheatem & Howe (DCH), a CPA firm, was hired by Dolt Corp. to audit financial statements that will be included in a Securities Act registration statement. DCH failed to discover that year-end inventory for 1989 was overstated by 85 percent. As a result, earnings for 1989 were overstated by 62 percent. DCH failed to discover the overstated inventory and earnings, because it never did a physical check of the inventory. Instead, it accepted as truthful whatever employees of Dolt stated. Horace bought preferred shares issued pursuant to the defective registration statement. Dolt went bankrupt within three months. Horace has sued DCH for damages under Securities Act Section 11. Will Horace win and why?

4.   Victor is an investor in Balcon Co. Victor is upset with Sanderson Accountants because he feels that they misstated some facts in the registration statement. What must Victor show in order to hold Sanderson liable under Rule 10b-5?

5.   Thomas agrees to perform an audit for Smith by no later than March 1. Smith's bank has set this deadline in processing Smith's loan application. Thomas fails to complete the audit by March 1 and Smith's loan application is rejected. How is Thomas liable to Smith?

6. Davis agrees to audit Howard's books. During the audit, Davis discovers some suspicious information. What would be the reasonable thing for Davis to do?

7. Why would the Restatement Approach to third-party negligence suits against accountants not be the best approach for an investor who relied on erroneous financial statements in investing in a company?

CHAPTER 32
PERSONAL PROPERTY AND BAILMENTS

Outline

I.   Nature of property.

    A. Ownership in property may be defined as a bundle of legal rights in relationship to property. Property is either <u>real</u> or <u>personal</u>.

    B. Personal property includes all objects other than the earth's crust and things firmly attached to it.

        1. Tangible property has a physical existence.

        2. Intangible property has no such existence. For example, a patent right or a security is intangible.

II. Acquiring ownership of personal property.

    A. Ownership of unowned property results from taking possession of it. Some states have estray statutes, which allow finders of property clear title to the property.

    B. A finder of lost property must return it to the owner if he knows who the owner is. All states have statutes of limitations protecting finders of lost or unclaimed property.

        Example: <u>Corliss v. Wenner and Anderson</u>: The court awarded found property to the owner of the land on which it was found.

    C. If property is mislaid, this may result in a bailment.

    D. A gift requires proof that the donor intended to make the gift, made delivery of the gift, and the donee accepted the gift.

        1. A gift *causa mortis* is a gift made in contemplation of death, and is a conditional gift.

        2. A conditional gift may be revoked before the donee complies with conditions of the gift.

            Example: <u>Lindh v. Surman</u>: When the donor of an engagement ring broke off the engagement and requested the return of the ring, the majority of the court adopted a no-fault rule for conditional gifts given in contemplation of marriage and held that the donor was entitled to the return of the ring. The dissent argued that the court was not on good grounds departing from the traditional rule in which fault was a consideration and that if the donor of the ring broke off the engagement, he should not be entitled to receive the ring back. The court noted that courts commonly have to sort through facts and determine fault in a wide variety of cases.

            Example: <u>Kenyon v. Abel</u>: The court found that the Salvation Army had no title to a painting it sold at a thrift shop to a third party. The painting was mistakenly picked up by the Salvation Army along with other items that the owner intended to donate. The original owner of the painting could recover it from the third party because the owner had never intended to make a gift of the painting to the Salvation Army. Therefore, the Salvation Army did not have title to the painting and is liable for conversion for selling it at a thrift store.

    E. Uniform Gifts to Minors Act provides a method for making gifts to minors.

    F. Confusion results in each person owning a proportionate share of the entire quantity of personal property; title to personal property can also be obtained by accession.

        Example: <u>Ballard v. Wetzel</u>: Wetzel became the owner of Ballard's wrecked corvette by accession.

III. Co-Ownership includes joint tenancy, tenancy in common, tenancy by the entirety, and community property.

A. Tenancy in common entitles a co-tenant to divide the property.

B. Rights of use, possession, contribution, and partition of joint tenants are the same as those of tenants in common, but upon the death of one joint tenant, that person's interest passes to the surviving joint tenant(s).

IV. Nature of a bailment.

A. The delivery of personal property by a bailor to another person (bailee), who accepts it and is required to return it, is a bailment.

B. A bailment is created by expressed or implied contract.

Example: <u>Detroit Institute of Arts v. Rose and Smith</u>: No bailment was found to exist.

C. There is a distinction between delivering possession of goods and merely giving custody of goods.

V. Rights and duties of bailor/bailee.

A. The duty of care may depend on who benefits from the bailment. There are three types of bailments:

1. Bailment for the benefit of the bailor;

2. Bailment for the benefit of the bailee;

3. Bailment for mutual benefit.

B. The bailee has a duty to take reasonable care of the property and return the property at the termination of the bailment.

Example: <u>Institute of London Underwriters v. Eagle Boats, Ltd.</u>: The duty of a bailee to use ordinary care to protect the bailment includes the theft of a motorboat.

C. The bailee must return the goods to the bailor in an undamaged condition; failure to do so results in the presumption (rebuttable) of negligence.

D. Limitations or disclaimers of liability are often unenforceable because they violate public policy.

Example: <u>Jasphy v. Osinsky</u>: A document entitled "fur storage sales receipt" that was signed by a customer contained a clause on the opposite which attempted to limit the bailee's liability to $1 per garment unless a higher value was declared. There was no place to indicate a higher value on the receipt and the clause was not called to the bailor's attention, therefore the contractual provision was not enforceable when the bailor's establishment was destroyed by fire along with furs that had been left by the bailor/customer.

E. A bailee has the right to compensation; further, a bailor makes an implied warranty that there are no hidden defects in the property making it unsafe for use.

F. When personal property is rented or loaned, the bailor makes an implied warranty that there are no hidden defects in the property that make it unsafe.

VI. Special bailment situations.

A. Common carriers are held to a higher level of responsibility than private carriers.

B. Hotelkeepers are held to a higher standard of care than the ordinary bailee, but are protected under the laws of most states

C. In the case of safe-deposit boxes, the Bank is generally held to be bailee but is not an insurer of the contents of the box. It is obligated to use due care in maintaining and protecting the box.

Learning Objectives

1. You should understand the difference between personal and real property.

2. You should understand the ways in which a person acquires ownership of personal property.

3. You should understand the meaning of the terms "property," and "ownership."

4. You should understand the difference between lost, mislaid, and abandoned property.

5. You should understand the requirements for making a valid gift.

6. You should be familiar with the various kinds of personal property.

7. You should know the circumstances under which a person can become owner of personal property by possession of the property, including accession and confusion.

8. You should know what differences there are between a gift *inter vivos* and a gift *causa mortis*.

9. You should know the legal status of a conditional gift.

10. You should be able to describe the major features of the Uniform Gifts to Minors Act.

11. You should understand the rights and duties of a bailor and bailee as a result of a bailment.

12. You should understand the effectiveness of disclaimers of liability in a bailment situation.

13. You should know what a bailment is and what its essential elements are.

14. You should be able to describe the distinguishing features of the three different types of bailments.

15. You should know the factors that will be considered in determining the bailee's duty of care toward the bailed goods.

16. You should know how the bailee's duty of care toward the goods differs according to the type of bailment involved.

17. You should be able to discuss the bailor's liability for defects in the bailed property, and should know how this liability differs according to the type of bailment involved.

18. You should be able to describe the respective liabilities of special bailees such as common carriers, hotelkeepers, and banks that rent safety deposit boxes.

Learning Hints

1. Ownership is defined as a "bundle of rights" in personal or real property. Sometimes, a person may have less than all the sticks in that bundle. For example, a tenant acquires certain rights of possession in real property, but the lessor retains the right of ownership.

2. The law treats ownership rights differently in cases of abandoned, lost, and mislaid property. Generally, if a person finds lost property, he has an obligation to return it to the true owner, and, if he knows who the owner is, to notify the owner.

3. In order to make an effective gift, a person must complete delivery of the gift. This means that a gift is generally revocable at any time prior to delivery. Some courts have created exceptions in cases where a donee justifiably relies on the promise to make a gift, and suffers loss as a result of that reliance.

4. A person may obtain ownership of personal property by mere possession, but only in cases in which the property is unowned because it is wild or has been abandoned by its previous owner.

5. If A makes a gift to B, B becomes the owner of the property and has better rights in that property than anyone in the world--even better than the original owner. A has no right to demand the property back.

6. Gifts *inter vivos* ("during life") cannot be revoked once the donor has satisfied the three requirements of a gift stated above. Gifts *causa mortis* (in contemplation of death) are gifts made conditional on the donor's death. Unlike the *inter vivos* gift, the donor can revoke the gift *causa mortis* after delivery.

7. Confusion occurs when property belonging to two or more owners is mixed in a way that makes it difficult to separate the property. In cases of good faith confusion, courts give each person his or her proportionate share. Accession means increasing the value of property by adding materials or labor. It is similar to confusion in that both involve the combination of property originally belonging to two different owners. However, accession involves a supplementation of the original property with new and different parts or labor, whereas confusion involves a mixing up of two or more kinds of indistinguishable property. Where there has been bad faith accession, the original owner gets to keep the

improved property without reimbursing the person who improved it. Where the accession has been done in good faith, however, the person who improved the property will have some right to reimbursement or rights in the property.

8. The distinction between lost property and mislaid property is that with lost property, the owner did not intend to put the property in the place where it was found, whereas in the case of mislaid property, the owner intentionally put the property in a certain place and then forgot about it. The distinction between lost and mislaid property and abandoned property is that the former owner of abandoned property intentionally placed the property somewhere and did not want it back, whereas the owners of lost and mislaid property will want the property back.

True-False

In the blank provided, put "**T**" if the statement is True or "**F**" if the statement is False.

_____   1. The finder of abandoned property becomes the owner of the property.

_____   2. Accession is the intentional intermixing of goods belonging to different owners in such a way that the goods cannot be separated.

_____   3. Renting a car from Avis is an example of a mutual benefit bailment.

_____   4. Confusion is a legal term describing the relationship between tenants in common.

_____   5. Patent rights constitute tangible property.

_____   6. The donor can revoke a gift *causa mortis* before he dies.

_____   7. You park your car in a parking garage and keep your keys. This is an example of a mutual benefit bailment.

_____   8. A bailee will have a higher degree of care in a bailment for the sole benefit of the bailee.

_____   9. Common carriers may avoid liability for damage to goods in their possession if they can show that the damage resulted from the inherent nature of the goods.

_____   10. In some instances, the bailee may have a lien on the bailed property to secure payment of the reasonable value of the bailee's services.

Multiple Choice

Circle the best answer.

1. The Simpson family checks in to a hotel in Dallas. The family discovers some new clothing in the dresser drawers. Which of the following statements is true?
    a. Finders, keepers. The Simpsons are now the owners of the clothes.
    b. The Simpsons may become the owners of the clothes if the true owners cannot be located.
    c. The hotel will own the clothes if the true owners cannot be found.
    d. This is an example of lost property.

2. Sarah is told she has a few days to live. During this time, she tells Andrea that she wants her to have her new car when she dies. Which of the following statements is false?
    a. If Sarah recovers, there is no gift of the car to Andrea.
    b. Sarah could change her mind the next day and revoke the gift to Andrea.
    c. This is an example of a gift *causa mortis*.
    d. This is an example of an *inter vivos* gift.

3. Tom goes on Jim's land without permission, cuts down some trees, and hauls the logs off to his own property. Tom sells some of the wood to Fred, who knows nothing of how Tom acquired the wood. Fred makes furniture from the wood. Jim learns about this and demands that Fred return the finished furniture to him. Which of the following is true?

   a. Fred must give the furniture to Jim.

   b. Jim can obtain the furniture from Fred, but pay Fred for the improvements to the original wood.

   c. Fred can keep the furniture, but pay Jim for the reasonable value of the wood.

   d. Both c and d.

4. Grace pulls into a parking garage. The attendant gives Grace a ticket, parks the car for her, and keeps the keys. The garage has signs saying in large print that the garage is not liable for damages to cars parked there. Several hours later, Grace returns for her car. When the attendant brings the car to Grace, there is a large dent in the fender that was not there earlier. Under these circumstances:

   a. The garage is not liable to Grace because the signs disclaimed any liability on the part of the garage.

   b. This is a mutual benefit bailment, so the garage needs to show that it was not negligent in causing the fender to be dented.

   c. This is not a bailment, so the garage does not owe Grace any reasonable care of her car.

   d. None of the above is correct.

5. Amy rents a car from Hertz. While driving the car, Amy is injured when the brakes failed. Which of the following statements is most correct?

   a. Hertz is not liable to Amy if they told her about the bad brakes in advance and Amy still chose to drive the car.

   b. Hertz is liable to Amy if the defective brakes could have been discovered by a reasonable inspection.

   c. Hertz is liable to Amy because the car was not fit to drive.

   d. Both c and d.

6. Which of the following is not a special bailment situation?

   a. Grain elevator

   b. Hotelkeeper

   c. Common carrier

   d. Safe deposit box

7. Darlene agrees to watch Brandon's dog at her house while Brandon goes on vacation. This is an example of:

   a. A mutual benefit bailment.

   b. A bailment for the sole benefit of the bailor.

   c. A bailment for the sole benefit of the bailee.

   d. This is not a bailment.

8. In which of the following relationships does each person have the same undivided interest in property?

   a. Finder and loser of property.

   b. Tenancy in common.

   c. Person who finds mislaid property and owner of place where property was mislaid.

   d. Tenant and landlord.

9. The Uniform Gifts to Minors Act:
   a. Has only been adopted in a few states.
   b. Provides a simple and flexible method for making gifts of money to minors.
   c. Prohibits making gifts of securities to a minor through a trustee.
   d. Substantially limits the discretion of the custodian's discretion to use the gift for the minor's benefit.

10. In a situation where a business leases goods to consumers, for example "U-Rent-It," and the consumer is injured as result of a hidden defect in the goods:
    a. States do not impose strict liability in such cases because the property was rented rather than purchased.
    b. Because the bailment is a mutual benefit bailment, the bailor is only liable for disclosing defects that it knew existed.
    c. Because the bailment is a mutual benefit bailment, the bailor is probably liable for breach of a duty to exercise reasonable care.
    d. The fact that the bailor is a commercial lessor does not result in imposition of a higher standard of legal responsibility in this case.

Short Essay

1. Andersen Windows manufactures windows that leave the factory and are shipped to Lowes. Jill buys the windows from Lowes. They are delivered to her house and then installed. Describe the type of property that the window is from the time it leaves the factory to when it is installed in Jill's house.

2. Briefly distinguish among abandoned property, lost property, and mislaid property. Include in your discussion the status of the person who finds the property in each of these situations.

3.	Orville is an elderly man who has no family. The Johnsons live next door to Orville and they have been very nice to him over the years. Orville is very fond of the two Johnson children, Janice and Johnny. Orville tells the kids that he is going to give them each a large check. Orville writes checks to Janice and Johnny for $10,000 each and puts them in his dresser drawer. That same night, Orville dies suddenly of a heart attack. Discuss who has ownership of the checks.

4.	Tanya takes her car to Herb's garage for repairs. Herb repairs Tanya's car and charges her $200. Tanya tells Herb that the fee is outrageous and refuses to pay him. What can Herb do?

5.	Phil hunts on Roger's property without his knowledge or permission. Phil kills a deer on Roger's property. Phil has the deer stuffed and displays it in his home. Roger learns about Phil's hunting adventure and demands that Phil give the stuffed deer to him. What logic would a court likely use in this case?

6.	Abe, Bill, Carl, and Dave, owned property as joint tenants. Abe died, leaving his wife Shirley as his sole heir. Bill died one week later, leaving no heirs. Who owns the property and in what proportion?

7. Vicky went to a local department store to purchase a new purse. She laid her old one on the counter and, forgetting it was there, left the store. Wilma found the purse. What are the relative rights of Vicky, the store, and Wilma?

8. Aunt Sally promised little Lucy her diamond ring when Lucy reached the age of 16. Sally put the ring in her bank deposit box with a note "for Lucy." Only Sally had the key to the box. Sally dies before Lucy reaches the age of 16. Who owns the ring, Lucy or Sally's estate?

CHAPTER 33
REAL PROPERTY

Outline

I.   The nature of fixtures.

   A.   A fixture is personal property that is so attached to or used with real property that it legally is considered part of real property.

   B.   The test is the <u>intent</u> of the parties; a court will consider an express and agreement by the parties, attachment and use in determining whether an item is a fixture.

   C.   Additions by tenants for business purposes remain personal property of the tenant under the <u>trade fixture</u> doctrine.

   Example: <u>Rottermich v. Union Planters National Bank</u>: Pin spotters in a bowling alley were considered not intended to be fixtures based on the intent of the parties.

II. Rights and interests in real property.

   A.   There are different possible ownership interests in real property. These include fee simple (basic ownership interest), life estates, leasehold estates, and easements.

   B.   An easement is a right to use or enjoy the land of another person. An easement can also be established by adverse possession.

   Example: <u>Lee v. Lozier</u>: Neighbors obtained an easement by prescription.

   C.   Other interests in land include a license and private restrictions enforceable by parties to the agreement.

   Example: <u>Mains Farm Homeowners Association v. Worthington</u>: Worthington's use of her property as an adult home business should be enjoined as a violation of a neighborhood restrictive covenant.

III. Co-ownership of real property.

   A.   Different kinds of co-ownership discussed in Chapter 33 include tenancy in common, joint tenancy, tenancy by the entirety, and community property.

   Example: <u>Frank v. Frank</u>: The rights of use, possession, contribution, and partition of joint tenants are the same as those of tenants in common.

   B.   Condominium ownership gives the purchaser title to the unit she occupies; in a cooperative, the entire building is owned by a group of people and the buyer holds his unit under a long-term renewable lease.

IV. Acquisition of real property.

   A.   Real property may be acquired through purchase, gift, inheritance, tax sale, or adverse possession.

   B.   To acquire title by adverse possession, a person must possess land that belongs to another in such a way that the claim is hostile, open, and continuous for the statutory period of time.

   Example: <u>Vezev v. Green</u>: A woman acquired land by adverse possession when she was given the land by her grandparents, possessed it, built a seasonal home there and possessed the property for the statutory period of 10 years. Her use of the property was continuous, open and notorious, exclusive, and hostile to the true owner.

   C.   Brokers assist sellers in the sale and purchase of real property. Generally, they are entitled to a commission if they produce a "ready, willing, and able buyer."

D. There are several federal laws designed to protect purchasers of real estate. These include the Real Estate Settlement Procedures Act (RESPA) and the Interstate Land Sales Full Disclosure Act. The Fair Housing Act is designed to prevent discrimination in the housing market.

E. Real property is transferred by deed. There are different kinds of deeds, but the two most common are the general warranty deed and the quitclaim deed. In the latter case, the grantor makes no warranty of title in the conveyance.

F. A purchaser should be certain he can obtain good title to the property. Different means of assessing title include a certified abstract of title, title insurance, and certificate of title under a Torrens system.

G. Common law contract rules apply in sales of real property. Today, most states recognize an implied warranty of habitability in the sale of new homes by a builder/vendor. One issue arising in sales of new homes is whether this implied warranty may be disclaimed. Another is whether the warranty runs to subsequent purchasers.

Example: Hershey v. Rich Rosen Construction Company: In this case an implied warranty of habitability ran to subsequent purchaser.

V. Public controls.

A. Nuisance may be private or public. Under common law, a court may enjoin an activity that is a nuisance.

Example: United States v. Wade: Disorderly houses may be closed as public nuisances.

B. Zoning ordinances are an exercise of municipal power to regulate use of property.

C. The constitution permits the taking of private property for public use, but such taking must be compensated. Particular problems arise in determining when a regulation so impacts the use or value of property that it becomes a "taking."

Example: Dolan v. City of Tigard: City placed several conditions on granting plaintiff's permit to redevelop a site; Supreme Court held that these conditions constituted an unconstitutional taking of Dolan's property for public purposes without payment of just compensation.

Learning Objectives

1. You should understand when personal property may be treated as real property, and the tests courts use for determining when an item of personal property becomes a fixture.

2. You should understand the kinds of interests a person may acquire in real property, and the differences between those interests.

3. You should note the different ways a person may acquire an interest in real property.

4. You should be familiar with the different steps required to acquire real property by purchase.

5. You should be familiar with various controls that society places on a person's ability to use her property-- for example, public nuisance laws and zoning ordinances.

6. You should know what a trade fixture is and should know the special rules governing trade fixtures.

7. You should be able to describe the different kinds of easements.

8. You should know the distinguishing features of the different forms of co-ownership of real property.

9. You should know what is necessary to make a gift of real property.

10. You should know the meaning of the term "adverse possession" and what is necessary to acquire ownership of land by adverse possession.

11. You should know the general rights and obligations of real estate brokers.

12. You should know the various ways of discovering and protecting against defects in title to real property: title opinion based on abstract of title, title insurance, and the Torrens system.

13. You should know what the implied warranty of habitability is and should know the other duties a seller of residential real estate has with respect to defects in the property.

14. You should know what eminent domain is.

Learning Hints

1. It is not always easy to distinguish an item of personal property from a fixture. Generally, courts attempt to determine the intention of the parties, and consider different factors, such as the use of the item and the degree of annexation to the property, in making this determination.

2. Ownership of property actually consists of a bundle of rights with respect to property. The most complete ownership interest is called a fee simple. A life estate is less than complete ownership because the interest terminates on the death of the holder and thus cannot be devised (that is, inherited by an heir).

3. Some interests in real property are less than ownership interests. For example, the right to use but not possess the land of another (affirmative easement) or to prevent the other person from doing something on his land that he would otherwise have the right to do (negative easement) is called an easement. An example of a negative easement would be one in which your neighbor agreed not to build a second story on his house so that he would not block sunlight to your solar collector.

4. There are different ways to acquire real property. The most common is by sale or purchase, and the transfer of ownership in property is accomplished through a deed.

5. Today, most courts recognize an implied warranty of habitability in the sale of a new home by a builder-vendor. This is one example of the erosion of the traditional common law doctrine of *caveat emptor*, ("Buyer beware"). Today, the rule *caveat venditor* ("Seller beware") is more common, especially in sales of new residential property.

6. A license is temporary and limited permission to enter upon or use another person's land. When you invite a friend over for dinner, you give that person a license to enter your land. That means she can enter the land without liability for trespass.

7. Real property is capable of a number of forms of joint ownership, some traditional and some fairly modern. Among the traditional forms of co-ownership, an important distinction between the joint tenancy and the tenancy by the entirety and the tenancy in common is that the first two include the right of survivorship. This means that the share owned by a tenant who dies automatically passes to the surviving co-tenant(s) rather than to the deceased tenant's heirs. In a tenancy in common, the deceased tenant's share is distributed to his heirs rather than to the surviving co-tenant.

8. The difference between a cooperative and a condominium is that when you own a condominium, you own your individual unit in fee simple (or some other form of ownership) and you own your fractional share of the common elements of the condominium as tenants in common with all the other unit owners, whereas if you "own" a cooperative apartment, you really own stock in a corporation that owns the building. Technically, you do not have an ownership interest in real estate, but rather an ownership interest in a corporation. The "owner" of a cooperative gets a long-term lease of the unit she occupies.

9. Adverse possession is like "squatter's rights" with certain technical requirements. It means possessing land in such a way and for such a length of time that the possessor gets better rights to the land than the title owner.

10. To remember the requirements for adverse possession, think of the acronym POACH. P=possession for the statutory period, O=open and notorious, A=actual possession, C=continuous, and H=hostile to the real owner's title. Add to that the requirement in some states that the adverse possessor pay taxes on the land. By the way, "hostile" does not mean that there must be malice toward the owner. It means that the adverse possessor's use contradicts the owner's ownership. In other words, the adverse possessor is using the property without the owner's permission or after the owner has ordered the adverse possessor to leave.

True-False

In the blank provided, put "**T**" if the statement is True or "**F**" if the statement is False.

_____ 1. Storm windows installed on a house are considered fixtures.

_____ 2. Alisa leases an office from Chris. Both Alisa and Chris have the right to terminate the lease at any time. This is an example of tenancy at will.

_____ 3. A temporary right to use another person's land for a limited and specific purpose is called a restrictive covenant.

_____ 4. Acquiring title through adverse possession is illegal in most states today.

_____ 5. Harold owns 180 acres of farm land. A rural water district asks Harold for permission to run a water line across his land. This is an example of a negative easement.

_____ 6. The federal Real Estate Settlement Procedures Act (RESPA) requires that a buyer receive advance disclosure of the settlement costs that will be incurred in a settlement.

_____ 7. Willis and Hill develop real estate. They own several properties as tenants in common. If Hill dies, his interest in the properties passes automatically to Willis.

_____ 8. The U.S. Constitution allows the government to take property from private persons without paying for it, so long as the government uses the property for the public's benefit.

_____ 9. Title to property can be obtained through adverse possession by using the property for 20 years with the permission of the owner.

_____ 10. Bob and Francis Smith own real estate as tenants by the entirety. Upon Bob's death, Francis automatically becomes the owner of the property.

Multiple Choice

Circle the best answer.

1. A person who has a legal right to drive across another person's property most likely possesses:
   a. A fee simple estate.
   b. A life estate.
   c. An affirmative easement.
   d. A tenancy at will.

2. Jackson owns a lot that borders on property owned by Hart. Jackson installs a fence and builds a shed that actually sits on some of Hart's property. If Hart never objects to the fence and the shed, Jackson could become the owner of this property by:
   a. Gift.
   b. Adverse possession.
   c. Purchase.
   d. Tax sale.

3. A restrictive covenant:

   a. Is an easement of necessity.

   b. Generally "runs with the land."

   c. Is created by special warranty deed.

   d. Only applies to leases and subleases of property.

4. Todd sells his house to Drake. Todd conveys title to Drake and guarantees to make good any defects in the title he conveys to Drake. The document that Todd is using to convey title to Drake is called a:

   a. Warranty deed.

   b. Title.

   c. Quitclaim deed.

   d. Special warranty deed.

5. Fisher owns a house and land in fee simple. Fisher has a certificate of title to the property. Fisher sells the property to West and delivers the certificate of title and a deed to West. West takes the deed and certificate of title to the appropriate government office and receives a new certificate of title that assures her that the title to the property is good, except for any liens mentioned on it. This is an example of:

   a. Title insurance.

   b. Abstract of title.

   c. Warranty deed.

   d. Torrens system.

6. Which of the following is an example of a restraint on Lisa's ability to use her property as she wishes?

   a. Her neighbors consider Lisa's pit bulls to be a nuisance.

   b. The city wants to exercise its right of eminent domain and buy Lisa's property so that a speedway and tourist area can be built.

   c. Subdivision ordinances require Lisa's house to be at least 2,500 square feet. Ordinances also prevent her from building a privacy fence.

   d. All of the above.

7. Hogan, Burns, and Smith own some real estate. Hogan dies and his wife now owns the property with Burns and Smith. This is an example of:

   a. Joint tenancy with rights of survivorship.

   b. Tenancy in common.

   c. Tenancy by the entirety.

   d. Community property.

8. Nash owned a commercial building that he leased for three years to Stickells for use as a restaurant. During the first winter of Stickells' lease, Stickells complained to Nash that the heating was inadequate. Stickells purchased an electric space heater, which he installed by bolting it to the ceiling. In the second year of Stickells' lease, Nash sold the building to Hopkins. In the third year of the lease Stickells decided to seek a larger space and elected not to renew the lease. A dispute arose between Stickells and Hopkins over the space heater. Which of the following is true?

    a. The space heater is a trade fixture, which Stickells is free to remove at any time, even after the leasehold has ended.

    b. The space heater is a fixture in the building that belongs to Hopkins by virtue of his purchase of the building from Nash.

    c. The space heater is a trade fixture, which Stickells may remove so long as he does so before his leasehold terminates.

    d. Stickells may remove the space heater and take it with him even if removing the heater would damage the building.

9. Kramer is a farmer. Dodd works as a hired hand for Kramer. Dodd has an agreement with Kramer to live in a small farmhouse on the Kramer farm for the rest of Dodd's life. This arrangement is called:

    a. Tenancy at will.

    b. Fee simple.

    c. Life estate.

    d. Easement.

10. Blake and his daughter Amanda own Blake's house as joint tenants. Which of the following statements concerning this relationship is not true?

    a. Blake can effectively transfer ownership of the house upon his death to a charity by naming the charity in his will.

    b. Amanda will become the sole owner of the house upon Blake's death even if Blake does not have a will that stipulates that this is his intent.

    c. The rights of use, possession, contribution, and partition in this ownership relationship are the same as in tenancy in common.

    d. Blake could mortgage the property during his lifetime.

Short Essay

1. The Smiths purchased a new home from JC Construction in Sunnyvale subdivision. They signed a standard purchase agreement that stated in boilerplate language that there were no warranties, express or implied, in the sale of the home. One year after they moved into the home, the basement began to flood as a result of substantial defects in the construction of the basement. It will cost the Smiths $10,000 to repair the basement. Is JC liable for that cost? Why or why not?

2. Dawn buys a house on some acreage. Describe the ownership interest Dawn more than likely has in this property.

3. Suppose Dawn in the above case installs an above-ground swimming pool on her property. Describe Dawn's potential premises liability. What would be some things Dawn could do to exercise reasonable care in regard to her swimming pool?

4. Describe how zoning ordinances and the power of eminent domain could affect Dawn's right to enjoy her property.

5. Troy buys a convenience store in an older neighborhood that has some problems with crime. Describe Troy's reasonable care and duty to provide a safe environment for his customers.

6. Dixon owns a minor league baseball team. Dixon builds a beautiful stadium for his team. Describe how the ADA may affect Dixon's design of his stadium.

7. Briefly describe *caveat venditor* and the implied warranty of habitability.

CHAPTER 34
LANDLORD AND TENANT

Outline

I.   Nature of leases.

    A. A lease is a contract for possession of property. A tenancy may be fixed, periodic, at will, or at sufferance.

    Example: <u>Schultz v. Wurdlow</u>: A tenancy at will was created where there was no valid written lease but the tenant took possession of the property.

II. Rights and duties of the landlord.

    A. The landlord impliedly warrants that the tenant will have quiet possession; in most states, a residential lease also carries with it an implied warranty of quality or habitability.

    B. Housing codes and other legislation may impose other duties on the owner of leased property.

    C. Landlord's liability for injuries: a number of courts impose on landlords the duty to reasonable care in maintenance of leased property.

    Example: <u>Brooks v. Lewin Realty III, Inc.</u>: The court found that it was not necessary to show that a landlord had actual notice of a violation of the housing code in order for it to constitute a breach of duty where the City Housing Code provided that rental dwellings be kept in good repair and in a safe condition, including free of loose and peeling paint and that new paint be lead free, and also provides that the landlord has the right to make inspections and to have access to make repairs.

    D. A landlord may be liable for negligently failing to protect a tenant from the criminal acts of third parties.

    Example: <u>Morgan v. 253 East Delaware Condominium Association</u>: The court held that Association had not breached a duty to plaintiff who was attacked by gunman.

III. Rights and duties of tenant.

    A. Tenant has the right of possession and duty to pay rent and not to commit waste.

    B. The lease may generally be assigned; a subleasing occurs when the tenant transfers less than complete rights to possession to a third person.

IV. Assignment and subleasing: Assignment occurs when the landlord or tenant transfers all rights under the lease to another. Subleasing occurs when the tenant transfers some but not all of his right to possess the property to another.

V.   Termination.

    A. Constructive eviction occurs when a tenant vacates after giving the landlord a reasonable opportunity to cure a defect and he fails to do so.

    Example: <u>Weingarden v. Eagle Ridge Condominiums</u>: A wet basement was sufficient to create constructive eviction of the tenant.

    B. Today, many states require the landlord to attempt to mitigate damages if the tenant abandons the premises.

    Example: <u>Stonehedge Square Limited Partnership v. Movie Merchants, Inc.</u>: A tenant may not avoid paying rent by leaving the property and sending the landord the key.

    C. The landlord should be careful to comply with all applicable laws governing evictions.

Learning Objectives

1. You should understand when leases have to be in writing and when oral leases are effective.

2. You should understand the rights, duties, and liabilities of the landlord and tenant as a result of a lease agreement.

3. You should know the meaning of the implied warranty of habitability.

4. You should understand the circumstances under which a landlord may be liable for failing to protect tenants against criminal conduct of third parties.

5. You should understand the difference between an assignment and sublease.

6. You should know the difference between a periodic tenancy, a tenancy at will, a lease for a definite period of time, and a tenancy at sufferance.

7. You should know when a landlord is liable for injuries caused by dangerous conditions on the leased premises.

8. You should know the different ways in which a tenancy can be terminated.

Learning Hints

1. A lease is a contract, and thus is subject to the requirements of the statute of frauds. Generally, an oral short-term lease is enforceable.

2. As in the case of contract law in general, there has been an erosion of the traditional doctrine of "caveat emptor" in landlord-tenant disputes. Today, many courts and legislation protect tenants by imposing upon the landlord an implied warranty of habitability in leased premises. Further, many states regulate by statute provisions for lease termination and other lease provisions.

3. In leasing real property, a landlord and tenant will often agree that the tenancy is to last for a specified period of time. For example, a student signs a lease for nine months on an apartment in a college town. The lease will automatically expire at the end of the period specified in the lease. Also, neither party, acting alone, can terminate the tenancy during the lease period.

4. In other situations, the parties do not specify how long the tenancy will last, but they agree that the tenant is to pay rent at regular intervals of time: monthly, weekly, or even yearly. These are called periodic tenancies. They continue until one of the parties gives advance notice to the other party that he or she wants to terminate the tenancy.

5. If the landlord agrees that someone else may live on or otherwise possess the landlord's property but the parties do not have an understanding about how long the tenancy will last or at what intervals the tenant is to pay rent, a tenancy at will exists. For example, a father permits his son and his son's wife to live in the apartment above the father's garage. Such tenancies last until either party terminates them. Most states require the landlord to give some advance notice of termination.

6. A tenant who has retained possession of the leased property after his lease has expired is called a tenant at sufferance. For example, George signs a 9-month lease on an apartment until May 10. George does not move out on May 10, however, and stays in possession. George's landlord has two choices now. He can treat George as a trespasser and evict him, or he can accept rent from George and treat George as a periodic tenant or a tenant for a specified term. In the period between the time George holds over and the time the landlord takes action (either rejecting or accepting George as a continued tenant), George is a tenant at sufferance.

7. Although a tenant may often assign or sublease leased property, assignment or subleasing does not permit the tenant to escape his legal obligations under the lease. If the subtenant does not pay rent during the period covered by the lease, for example, the landlord can go after the tenant for payment.

8. A tenant who abandons leased property (moves out before the lease term has elapsed) breaches his legal obligations to the landlord. The tenant cannot escape the obligation to pay rent merely by moving out. However, many states now place the obligation on the landlord to make reasonable efforts to re-rent the property.

9. Constructive eviction is a doctrine that developed in the days when tenants had no legal protection with respect to the quality and safety of the leased property. If the leased premises (generally residential premises) became uninhabitable because of the landlord's act or failure to act, the tenant could move out without incurring liability for rent for the remainder of the lease term. The idea was that he had been forced to leave by the condition of the property. For the doctrine to apply, there must be some serious defect in the property such as rodent infestation or inoperative plumbing—a Jacuzzi on the blink would not be enough. After giving the landlord a reasonable opportunity to fix the problem, the tenant must move out within a reasonable time in order to claim constructive eviction.

True-False

In the blank provided, put "**T**" if the statement is True or "**F**" if the statement is False.

_____ 1. Today a landlord is more likely to be responsible for injuries caused to a tenant by a defect in the premises than in the past.

_____ 2. A tenancy at will exists when property is leased for an indefinite period of time and either party can terminate the lease anytime.

_____ 3. The implied warranty of habitability applies to landlords of both commercial and residential properties.

_____ 4. In most states, a lease for less than one year must be in writing to be enforceable.

_____ 5. The landlord retains the right of possession in a lease agreement.

_____ 6. A lease can be created without an explicit agreement between landlord and tenant as to how long the lease will last.

_____ 7. A landlord is liable for all injuries suffered on leased premises.

_____ 8. A tenant may vacate a property without further rent obligation under the doctrine of constructive eviction.

_____ 9. Today, a landlord is generally not liable to a tenant for defects in her apartment that result from the landlord's failure to make the necessary repairs.

_____ 10. A tenant has the right to exclusive possession and quiet enjoyment of the leased property.

Multiple Choice

Circle the best answer.

1. The implied warranty of quiet possession:
   a. Means that a landlord warrants the condition of leased premises.
   b. Means that the landlord impliedly warrants the quality of leased premises.
   c. Means that the landlord has no right to enter the premises during the term of the lease.
   d. Means that the landlord may evict tenants who do not pay rent as agreed.

2.   Mark rents a duplex from Jill. Mark pays his rent monthly. The lease does not specify a timeframe. This lease appears to be an example of:
     a.   Periodic tenancy.
     b.   Tenancy at will.
     c.   Tenancy for a term.
     d.   Tenancy at sufferance.

3.   Eileen rents a house from Hugh. The lease expires at the end of one year and Eileen continues living in the house. Hugh can have Eileen ejected or he may allow her to continue living in the house as a tenant. This situation is an example of:
     a.   Tenancy at will.
     b.   Tenancy at sufferance.
     c.   Tenancy for a term.
     d.   Periodic tenancy.

4.   Which of the following statements concerning the landlord's duties to the tenant is not true?
     a.   Landlords made implied warranties about the condition of leased property under common law.
     b.   The Fair Housing Act requires landlords to permit a handicapped tenant to make reasonable modifications to the property at her own expense.
     c.   Landlords make an implied warranty of possession to tenants.
     d.   Landlords make an implied warranty of quiet enjoyment to tenants.

5.   Which of the following statements concerning housing codes is not correct?
     a.   Many cities and states have enacted housing codes that can be the basis of a lawsuit for a landlord's breach of duty under the code.
     b.   Failure to comply with a housing code can result in the landlord's loss of rent.
     c.   Landlords may be subject to fines or penalties for breach of housing code provisions.
     d.   Housing code provisions are only effective if included in the terms of the lease agreement.

6.   Nancy rents a house from George. The house is in terrible condition and Nancy decides to seek remedies from George for breach of the implied warranty of habitability. Which of the following remedies is not available to Nancy?
     a.   Nancy may be able to withhold part of the rent for the period of time George is in breach.
     b.   Nancy may be able to have repairs made to the property and then deduct the repair costs from the rent she pays to George.
     c.   Nancy may be able to recover damages from George.
     d.   Nancy may terminate the lease even if the breach was not considered to be material.

7.   Which of the following would create a periodic tenancy?
     a.   A lease for a period of 9 months, from August 1, 2002 to May 1, 2003.
     b.   Rental of a furnished apartment on a weekly basis.
     c.   A tenant stays in possession after the expiration of a one-year lease and Landlord elects to treat him as a trespasser.
     d.   A father allows his son and daughter-in-law to live in a cabin on his land indefinitely, without any agreement about paying rent or the length of time that they will remain there.

8. Which of the following is not one of the traditional exceptions to the no-liability rule for landlords?
   a. The landlord must disclose hidden defects in the property to tenants.
   b. Landlords must maintain furnished dwellings.
   c. Landlords are liable for defects in the tenant's property that resulted from the landlord's failure to repair the defects.
   d. The landlord must use reasonable care in performing repairs to the property.

9. Which of the following is true concerning termination of leases?
   a. Most states allow landlords to have liens on the tenant's personal property.
   b. Most states today require the landlord to mitigate damages by attempting to rent the property to another tenant.
   c. The landlord is obligated to mitigate damages under common law.
   d. Local regulations generally allow a landlord forcible entry to change locks.

10. Which of the following statements is true concerning the tenant's rights and duties under a lease?
    a. A tenant is generally not allowed to assign the remainder of her lease to another person.
    b. A sub-lessee acquires rights and duties under the lease between the landlord and the original tenant.
    c. The original tenant remains liable to the landlord under both an assignment and a sublease.
    d. Cotenants are only jointly liable on a lease.

Short Essay

1. Delbert rented an apartment for one year from Property Plus and paid a $250 deposit. At the end of the year, Property Plus refused to return the deposit because it maintained that Delbert ruined the wallpaper in the apartment by printing the words "Delbert loves Millie" all over the walls. If it will cost $500 to replace the wallpaper, may Property Plus apply the security deposit to this cost?

2. Bo rents a house on a one year lease from Jo. Briefly describe three ways that this lease could be terminated.

3. Adam leased an apartment from Phillips for a period of one year beginning April 1, 1983. On April 30 1983, Phillips entered the apartment using a passkey while Adam was at work so that he could se whether Adam was keeping the apartment clean. Adam came home from work and found Phillips in th apartment. Does Adam have a suit against Phillips? Why or why not?

4. Linda rents an apartment in the Paradise Cove apartment complex. When returning to her apartment from work one evening, Linda is attacked by someone who was hiding in the bushes next to the building. Could Linda recover damages from the landlord in this situation?

5. Brad rents an apartment at Shady Lane Apartments. When Brad signed the lease, he noticed that i contained an exculpatory clause. Discuss the legality of an exculpatory clause in a lease.

6. Harvey rents houses to tenants. Briefly describe Harvey's duties to his tenants under the implied warranty of habitability.

7. Phil rents an apartment from Dana. Phil cannot sleep at night because of the loud music that is playing in apartments adjacent to his apartment. What duty may Dana be breaching in his lease with Phil?

8. Ms. Sallie Doright owns and operates a ten-unit apartment complex in Tulsa, OK. She has strict personal moral views and seeks to set that tone in her properties. Last week, a young man and woman applied to rent an apartment from Ms. Doright. They financially qualified but failed to pass Ms Doright's marriage test, i.e., they were "living in sin" without benefit of clergy. The couple claims that is discriminatory and sue Me. Doright. Who wins?

9. Jerry and Linda lease an apartment in a college community. They want to hold on to the apartment for the next two years when they both plan to finish their graduate studies. They do, however, also want to spend their summers out of town. They seek to find a subtenant for the summer, but the landlord does not want subtenants under any circumstances. Can the landlord do this?

CHAPTER 35
ESTATES AND TRUSTS

Outline

I. Disposition of property by will.

    A. A will disposes only of property belonging to the testator at his/her death.

        1. Requires capacity and legal age.

        2. Must meet statutory requirements. Some states recognize handwritten wills (holographic wills).

            Example: <u>Estate of Rowell v. Hollingsworth</u>: The handwritten will not be valid because a testator did not execute it.

        3. An oral will (nuncupative) will is only valid in some states and only under limited circumstances.

        4. There are limitations on disposition by will under state statutes.

            Example: <u>Estate of Jennie Nicole Gonzalez</u>: A father, who had abandoned his daughter and failed to provide for her during her life, was found by the court to not be entitled to take an intestate share of his daughter's estate or to share in any wrongful death recovery following her death in the World Trade Center terrorist attack in 2001.

        5. All wills are revocable.

        6. A living will is a document in which a person states his intention to forgo extraordinary medical procedures. In some cases, a person may protect that interest by giving another a durable power of attorney.

            Example: <u>Cruzan v. Director, Missouri Department of Health</u>: The court held that it was appropriate for a state to recognize that under certain circumstances a surrogate may act for a patient to forgo hydration and nutrition, but in doing so the state should establish procedural safeguards.

        7. A durable power of attorney gives another person the legal authority to act for another in the case of mental or physical incapacity.

II. Intestate succession.

    A. Intestate succession (disposition of property in cases where person dies without a will) differs from state to state.

    B. Under a "uniform simultaneous death act" property of husband and wife may be distributed as if each survived the other.

III. Administration of estates.

    A. The will must be proven (probated), and an administrator of the estate.

        Example: <u>Probate Proceedings, Will of Doris Duke, Deceased</u>: The coexecutors of a will should be removed for waste of assets.

IV. A trust is a legal relationship in which a person holds property for the use and benefit of another.

    A. Creation of an express trust requires that the donor have legal capacity, intention to create the trust, specific property, and identification of the beneficiary, as well as compliance with trust laws. Special rules govern the establishment of charitable trusts.

    B. The law recognizes resulting trusts, based on presumed intention of donor. A constructive trusts\ arises by operation of law.

Example: <u>Pagliai v. Del Re</u>: A constructive trust was imposed in favor of Pagliai for the value of a painting.

C. The trustee owes a fiduciary duty to the beneficiaries of a trust.

D. Some trusts contain spendthrift clauses, which restrict the transfer of a beneficiary's interest.

E. A trustee has certain duties, such as the duty of loyalty and the duty to avoid conflicts of interest.

Learning Objectives

1. You should understand the laws governing distribution of assets upon death of a person who has no will.

2. You should know the requirements for executing a valid will.

3. You should recognize the most common grounds for challenging wills.

4. You should know under what circumstances oral wills or documents not formally complying with requirements of a valid will will be recognized.

5. You should know the limitations on disposition of property by will.

6. You should know the meaning of the word "intestate."

7. You should be able to describe the typical steps in the administration of estates.

8. You should know what a trust is and what the requirements are for the creation of an express trust.

9. You should know how resulting trusts and constructive trusts are created.

10. You should know what a spendthrift clause is, as well as the situations in which creditors or assignees may have claims to such a trust.

Learning Hints

1. The laws governing intestate succession and requirements for a valid will are state laws. Consequently, these requirements will vary from state to state.

2. It is extremely important that a person comply strictly with the requirements for executing a valid will. If a person fails to so comply, the will may be invalid. In such cases, the laws of intestate succession of the state may apply, and the person's wishes for disposition of his/her property upon death may not be met.

3. People who are of legal age and have sufficient mental capacity may dictate who get their property at death by making wills that will comply with all the formalities required by state law.

4. If a person dies without a valid will in effect, she is said to have died intestate. The property she owned at death will be divided according to the standards provided by her state's law of intestate succession (also called "descent and distribution"). An administrator will be appointed at administer the estate.

5. Generally, wills must be in writing, signed and acknowledged by the testator, and witnessed by a certain number of disinterested witnesses. Some, but not all, states recognize the validity of less formal wills, known as nuncupative and holographic wills. A nuncupative will is an oral will, whereas a holographic will is written and signed in the testator's own handwriting, but is not properly witnessed and not in compliance with other statutory requirements.

6. A person who makes a will is called a "testator" or "testatrix." Testators and testatrixes are free to revoke wills, even up to the moment immediately preceding death. A person who is named as a beneficiary in a will has no interest in the testator's/testatrix's property before the testator's/testatrix's death because the testator/testatrix could always change his/her mind and revoke or change the will.

7.	If the testator/testatrix wants to modify the will without executing an entirely new will, he/she can execute a codicil amending some provision of the will. The codicil must meet the same formal requirements mandated by statute for the execution of wills.

8.	Many states now recognize, by statute, "living wills" or "durable power of attorney" by which a person may indicate his/her wish that extreme unusual medical care not be administered if that person is close to death and otherwise not able to make those wishes known.

9.	A trust exists when a person who has some legal right to property also has the obligation to hold the property for the benefit of someone else. For example, Robert deeds property to a bank as trustee of a trust created to benefit Robert's wife, children, and grandchildren. The bank has legal title to the property, but also has the legal obligation to administer the property for the beneficiaries named by Robert.

10.	The "settlor" or "donor" is the person who creates the trust. (In the example above, Robert is the settlor.) A trust that goes into effect during the settlor's life is called an inter vivos trust. A trust that is established by a will and goes into effect on the settlor's death is called a testamentary trust. Express trusts are usually quite detailed about the identity of the beneficiaries, the duties of the trustee, and the terms of the trust.

11.	In some situations, trusts can be imposed by law to effectuate the intent of the settlor (resulting trust) or to avoid injustice (constructive trust).

True-False

In the blank provided, put "**T**" if the statement is True or "**F**" if the statement is False.

_____	1.	A person who makes a will is called the settlor.

_____	2.	Porter's will passes her house to her grandchild. This is called a devise.

_____	3.	State law normally requires that a will be witnessed by two or three disinterested parties and that it be signed by the testator.

_____	4.	Uniform federal law governs the execution of a will in all states.

_____	5.	A holographic will is entirely written and signed by the testator.

_____	6.	All states recognize a holographic will.

_____	7.	The personal representative named by the probate court to administer the estate of a person who died without a will is called an executor.

_____	8.	Generally, the beneficiary of a trust may assign, to another person, the beneficiary's right to the principal or income of a trust.

_____	9.	Publication of a will is a declaration by the testator, at the time of signing the will, that the instrument being signed is in fact his will.

_____	10.	Ed deposits money in First Bank in trust for his son, Jim. Ed is the trustee and he may revoke the trust anytime. This is a spendthrift trust.

Multiple Choice

Circle the best answer.

1. Which of the following restricts the ability of a beneficiary of a trust to transfer his interest to another?
   a. Spendthrift clause.
   b. Cy pres.
   c. Rule against perpetuities.
   d. Constructive trust.

2. A codicil:
   a. Is a testamentary trust.
   b. Can be created by merely striking out objectionable provisions of a will and inserting new provisions.
   c. Need not be signed.
   d. Is an amendment of a will.

3. Smith transfers property to Jones as trustee for Smith's daughter Jody. Jody dies before Smith. Jones now holds the trust property for Smith and Smith's heirs. This is an example of a:
   a. Resulting trust.
   b. Constructive trust.
   c. Testamentary trust.
   d. Totten trust.

4. Which of the following situations involving trusts does not meet the requirements for an express trust?
   a. Tim and Tina Johnson set up a trust for their children, Tom and Tammy. They both are of sound mind and legal age.
   b. Gary and Margaret set up a trust naming their children, Ying and Yang, as beneficiaries.
   c. The Wilsons transfer property in trust for their children to Davis as trustee. Davis signs the trust instrument.
   d. Doug talks with his bank about setting up a trust, but he cannot decide whether to fund the trust with stocks, mutual funds, or certificates of deposit.

5. A Totten trust:
   a. Is illegal in all states.
   b. Is a deposit in trust by the settlor of his own money for the benefit of another.
   c. Is not revocable during the settlor's lifetime.
   d. Is a trust that prohibits use of trust funds by the settlor for his own benefit.

6. Andy is the personal representative for his father's estate. Which of the following is a responsibility Andy must fulfill in discharging his duties as executor?
   a. He must give notice to creditors so that they can file their claims.
   b. Andy must make sure that the funeral expenses are paid.
   c. Andy must make sure that the estate tax return is filed in a timely manner.
   d. All of the above.

7. Mike and Carol Brady are married and have six children. Mike dies and all of their property now belongs to Carol. Carol later dies. Which of the following is true?

   a. The house that is owned jointly with rights of survivorship by Carol and the children is part of her probate estate.

   b. The proceeds of Carol's life insurance policy that names the children as beneficiaries is part of Carol's probate estate.

   c. Carol's pension benefits that are payable to the children are part of her probate estate.

   d. Carol's car titled just in her name is part of her probate estate.

8. Which of the following statements is true concerning Martha who dies without a will?

   a. Martha's personal representative named by the court is called an executor.

   b. Martha's illegitimate daughter, Marci, is not entitled to inherit anything.

   c. If Martha dies leaving no surviving relatives, her property escheats to the state.

   d. Martha lived in Iowa. She owned a vacation home in Florida. The vacation house will be distributed according to the intestacy statutes of Iowa.

9. Which of the following statements is true concerning Betty, an elderly woman who is in the early stages of Alzheimer's disease?

   a. Several years ago, Betty gave her son Rod ordinary power of attorney. Rod still has power of attorney now that his mother has Alzheimer's.

   b. Betty had given Rod the durable power of attorney several years ago. Rod's ability to conduct his mother's affairs is not affected by Betty's health condition.

   c. Rod has durable power of attorney for health care. Betty still retains the ability to make her own health care decisions.

   d. The durable power of attorney for health care is irrevocable.

10. Which of the following statements is not true?

    a. Living wills must follow all terms and conditions of the applicable state statute.

    b. Lois wants to make sure that she will never be kept on life support when there is no chance of recovery. Lois puts this in writing. This is an example of an advance directive.

    c. A later will always serves to revoke an earlier will.

    d. Children born after the testator made a will are called pretermitted children and they have a right to share in the testator's estate.

Short Essay

1. Seth is a single soldier serving in Iraq. The night before a dangerous mission is to begin, Seth makes a nuncupative will to his chaplain. Is this will valid?

2. Charles was beneficiary of his grandfather's trust. The trust contained a spendthrift provision prohibiting the voluntary or involuntary transfer of a beneficiary's interest. A doctor who has provided necessary medical care for Charles has been unsuccessful in collecting the debt. Will the spendthrift clause prevent the doctor from compelling the trustee of the trust to recognize his claim? Explain.

3. Lola, an elderly woman, knew that she was dying. She took out a pen and paper and scrawled these words: "I give all my property to my brother, Lamoine." She signed the paper, using her full legal name. Is this an enforceable will? Explain your answer.

4. Dora has four children: Sue, Stan, Steve, and Shelly. Sue has one child, Vern. Stan has two children, Bob and Barb. Shelly has two children, Adam and Ava. Steve has no children. Sue, Stan, and Steve predecease Dora. Dora's will states that the residuary of her estate, $300,000 should go to her descendants *per stirpes*. How much will each of the heirs receive?

5. After 50 years of marriage, Harold is sick of Connie's nagging. Harold wants to write a will that leaves nothing to Connie. Can he do that? Explain.

6. Earl owns his house and car in joint tenancy with his daughter, Maxine. Maxine is also a joint owner on all of Earl's stock, mutual funds, and other investments. Earl also named Maxine as beneficiary on a $100,000 insurance policy. Maxine will also be entitled to receive payments from Earl's pension plan. Do any of these assets of Earl's pass through probate?

7. Howie wants to set up a charitable trust. Is Howie required to name a specific charity in order to effectively set up a charitable trust?

CHAPTER 36
INSURANCE

Outline

I.   Life insurance contracts.

    A. The insurance contract is a valued policy (requiring the insurer to pay a fixed amount).

        1. A whole life policy creates a cash surrender value if the policy is terminated.

        2. Term life creates no cash surrender value.

    B. Property insurance contracts are indemnity contracts.

        1. Insurers usually specify certain covered perils and excluded perils

            Example: State Mutual Automobile Insurance Company v. Kastner: Kastner was abducted in a parking lot and driven, in her car, to an isolated area where she was robbed and sexually attacked. The court held that her personal injuries were not covered by her automobile insurance policy because, at the time of her injuries, the car was not being used in a manner that she anticipated at the time she procured the insurance policy.

            Example: America Online v. St. Paul Mercury Insurance Company: AOL's Version 5.0 access software caused damages to users' computer systems and pre-existing software. The court ruled that AOL's insurance company did not have to defend and indemnify AOL because the policy only covered property damage. It did not believe that damage to software was physical damage to tangible property, which was covered by the policy. The court believed the damage was to data and software, which was not covered.

        2. Insurance can also cover personal property--for example, comprehensive and collision sections of automobile policies provide coverage for personal property.

        3. Some property insurance policies are valued policies; most policies are open policies.

    C. A coinsurance clause may limit the insured's right to recovery.

    D. A pro rata clause determines the liability of a particular insurer in proportion to the total amount of insurance covering property.

    E. Liability insurance policies cover sums for which the insured becomes legally obligated to pay to another person.

        1. Personal liability insurance contracts often restrict coverage to bodily injury and property damages;

        2. Business liability policies often provide broader coverage.

            Example: Belt Painting v. Tig Insurance Company: Belt Painting's liability insurance policy had an exclusion for bodily injury or property damage caused by the discharge of pollutants. The exclusion did not apply to personal injuries suffered by someone who had inhaled paint fumes in an office building where Belt Painting was working. The court did not believe that ordinary paint fumes are discharged.

        3. Liability insurance providers have a duty to defend the insured, and a duty to pay within the coverage provisions of the policy.

    F. Health insurance contracts provide coverage for medical expenses

        1. Insurance provided by employers or other organizations are generally group insurance.

            Example: Phillips v. Saratoga Harness Racing, Inc.: The employer should have advised Melody Phillips of her right to continue health coverage under COBRA.

2. The deductible is the amount the insurer must pay before the insurer's payment obligation begins.

II. Contract law applicable in insurance cases.

A. General contract rules of offer and acceptance apply; a binder is an agreement for temporary insurance pending the insurer's decision to accept or reject the risk.

Example: <u>SR International Business Insurance v. World Trade Center Properties</u>: An insurer argued that, under the terms of its insurance policy, the terrorist attacks on the World Trade Center on September 11 constituted a single occurrence. The court agreed, concluding that the definition of "occurrence" in the company's binder controlled and that definition treated both plane crashes as a single occurrence.

B. Misrepresentation by insured or agent may be basis for rescission or damages.

Example: <u>Amex Life Assurance Co. v. Superior Court</u>: This case illustrates how an insurer is liable under an incontestability clause.

C. Warranties are express terms in the policy that operate as conditions on which insurer liability is based. Most states require life insurance contracts to be in writing. Ambiguities are generally construed against the insurer.

D. Life insurance policies are assignable because the identity of the insured remains unchanged; fire insurance policies are generally not assignable.

E. A person must have an insurable interest in the life or property being insured.

Example: <u>Mayo v. Hartfield Life Insurance Company</u>: Wal-Mart purchased life insurance policies on all of its employees, naming itself as beneficiary. The court held that Wal-Mart did not have an insurable interest in the lives of its employees, therefore it could not purchase insurance on its employees.

III. Other provisions.

A. Notice and proof of loss are required to recover benefits under an insurance policy. Under the right of subrogation, an insurer obtains all of the insurer's rights to pursue legal remedies against a third party who may have caused the loss.

B. Cancellation of lapse of the policy will terminate the policy.

Learning Objectives

1. You should understand the contractual rules governing the creation of the insurance relationship.

2. You should be able to explain how courts assess the liability of insurers.

3. You should understand when and how an insurer may cancel an insurance policy.

4. You should know the basic differences between whole life and term insurance policies, and should become aware of the advantages and disadvantages of each type of policy.

5. You should understand what an indemnity contract is.

6. You should become familiar with the types of fire insurance policies and should know the differences among them.

7. You should understand what a coinsurance clause is and how it may be applied.

8. You should understand how a pro rata clause in a fire insurance policy may operate when the insured has in force more than one insurance policy that would apply to a loss.

9. You should be aware of what constitutes <u>acceptance</u> in the context of an insurance contract, and should comprehend why courts might construe insurance contracts in ways other than was specifically intended by the insurer.

10. You should understand how courts will handle misrepresentations by the insured, and should be able to distinguish between representations and warranties.

11. You should be aware of the insurance contracts that can be assigned to a third party, as well as why those contracts are assignable and why others are not assignable.

12. You should understand what constitutes an insurable interest and should know why the insurable interest is a necessary element of an insurance contract.

Learning Hints

1. An insurance policy is essentially a contract between the company and the insured. As such, common law rules of contract law, such as offer and acceptance, and rules of contract interpretation apply. However, many states have adopted statutes regulating insurance contracts, and these may override common law rules.

2. A life insurance contract differs from a fire or casualty insurance policy in that the insurer is bound to pay a certain sum when the death of the insured occurs. Unlike most fire insurance policies, a life insurance policy is a valued policy with a face value.

3. Most fire insurance policies are open policies, permitting the insured to recover the fair market value of the property at the time it was destroyed, up to the policy limit.

4. It is important to remember that insurance law, like contract law in general, is in a state of flux. Its rules are taking on more and more of an equitable flavor in situations involving one party's possessing superior knowledge or bargaining strength. This is especially the case in most insurance contracts, because the insurer dominates the contracting process.

5. Insurance contracts are of special interest to the courts because of the weak bargaining position of the beneficiary after the insured's death or disability. The courts are aware of the fact that many insureds trust the company's representative as their agent, when in reality what resembles an arm's length transaction may have taken place. Further, some litigation has involved alleged strategies on the part of insurance companies to intentionally refuse payment on meritorious claims. Such strategies assume that the beneficiary will settle for a lesser amount or drop the claim entirely. In cases in which such strategies on the part of the insurer have been proved, the courts have been willing to award punitive damages against the insurer for its bad faith conduct.

6. Note that the law's treatment of misrepresentation by the insured resembles ordinary contract law's treatment of misrepresentation by a party to a contract. However, in some cases the law will not allow the insurer to avoid the contract, despite the misrepresentation. There is a presumption that the insurer would be willing to insure the insured person in most instances; the only question is the amount of the premium. Therefore, instead of rescinding a contract that has been in effect for some time, it is considered more reasonable to reform the agreement in a manner that avoids rewarding the insured for the misrepresentation. To totally invalidate the contract might reward insurance companies that ignore misrepresentations until the time when the benefits are due.

7. The policy of construing ambiguities in insurance contracts against the author (which in most cases will be the insurer) is consistent with the approach generally taken in contract law. It avoids rewarding a party for having confused the other contracting party.

8. The requirement of an insurable interest may be important in protecting against widespread destruction and even murder. The persons who qualify as possessing the interest fit within a group whose members should be less likely to injure the person or property that is the subject of the insurance contract. In a sense, those with an insurable interest merely are being compensated for the loss they have suffered. Persons who do not have an insurable interest might have fewer reservations about doing away with the insured person or about damaging the insured property.

True-False

In the blank provided, put "**T**" if the statement is True or "**F**" if the statement is False.

_____   1. Term insurance policies build cash value that the insured can recover if she cancels the policy.

_____   2. Norma's house is severely damaged from a flood. Norma's homeowner's insurance policy will likely not cover this loss.

_____   3. Property insurance contracts are indemnity contracts.

_____   4. Under a valued policy, an insured can recover the fair market value of the property at the time it was destroyed, up to the face amount of the policy.

_____   5. The insurance relationship is basically contractual in nature.

_____   6. Health insurance policies typically do not cover pre-existing health conditions.

_____   7. A fire that begins as a friendly fire may become a hostile fire, for purposes of determining whether a loss is covered by a fire insurance policy.

_____   8. A typical misstatement of age clause will operate to invalidate the policy if the insured misrepresented his or her age in the application for insurance.

_____   9. Chip and Sue Lay bought a new car for $25,000. The Lays borrowed $20,000 from 2nd Bank. The bank has an insurable interest in the Lay's automobile and it can require the Lays to purchase insurance that adequately covers the vehicle.

_____   10. Without an insurable interest on the part of the purchaser, an insurance contract would be an illegal wagering contract.

Multiple Choice

Circle the best answer.

1.   Liability insurance policies:

    a. Furnish coverage for the insured's intentional torts.

    b. Usually do not cover an insured's negligent action or omission.

    c. Typically do not require the insurer to defend the insured against liability claims.

    d. Usually do not cover punitive damages assessed against the insured.

2.   Which of the following statements concerning life insurance is not true?

    a. Bob's life insurance coverage lapses when he fails to pay his premiums.

    b. Bob may have a grace period that gives him about 30 days to pay his past due premium so that his policy will not lapse.

    c. Bob's policy may contain a reinstatement clause that allows him to pay all past-due premiums and reinstate his coverage.

    d. If Bob allows his cash value policy to lapse, he loses his rights in the cash value.

3. If a fire occurs following submission of the application for fire insurance but prior to delivery of the policy, what result and why?

    a. There is no effective policy because there was no insurable interest.

    b. There is no effective policy because there was no acceptance of the offer until delivery of the policy to the insured.

    c. There is an effective policy because a binder is an agreement for temporary insurance pending the insurer's decision to accept or reject the risk.

    d. There is an effective policy because submission of the application to the agent generally constitutes acceptance in insurance cases.

4. Ken's car is a total loss after he was hit by a juvenile delinquent who had stolen a car from a dealer. Since the juvenile was driving a stolen car, his parents' car insurance would not cover Ken's loss. Ken's collision insurance policy covers his loss. The insurance company then sues the juvenile and his parents to recover the amount paid to Ken. The insurance company is exercising its right of:

    a. Reimbursement.

    b. Cancellation.

    c. Subrogation.

    d. Collection.

5. Which of the following statements regarding insurable interest is not correct?

    a. Jim, Jane, and John are partners in a business. The partners most likely have an insurable interest in each other's lives.

    b. When a person purchases an insurance policy who does not have an insurable interest in the property or person insured, this is an illegal wagering contract.

    c. An insurable interest in life insurance contracts must exist at the time the loss occurs.

    d. An insurable interest in property must exist at the time the loss occurs.

6. Which of the following statements is not true concerning insurance?

    a. Courts will likely interpret ambiguities in insurance contracts against the insured.

    b. Life insurance contracts can generally be assigned.

    c. Dad buys a life insurance policy on young Daughter. This policy is not voidable even though Daughter is a minor.

    d. Statements made by Applicant on his life insurance policy application are treated as representations and not as warranties.

7. Smith's house has a fair market value of $100,000. Smith insures it for $60,000. Lightening causes a fire at Smith's home that does $30,000 of damage. Which of the following statements is true?

    a. Smith's $30,000 loss is totally covered by his insurance policy.

    b. The insurance company will reimburse Smith $22,500 for the fire loss.

    c. Since Smith did not meet coinsurance requirements of insuring his house for 80% of the fair market value, Smith's loss is not covered at all by insurance.

    d. The insurance company will pay Smith $60,000 for his fire loss.

8. In the question above, suppose Smith had his home insured for $80,000. How much would the insurance company pay Smith if the fire caused a total loss?

    a. Since Smith meets the coinsurance requirement of 80%, the loss is fully covered by the insurance company.

    b. The insurance company would reimburse Smith for $80,000, the amount of coverage on the house.

    c. Since Smith did not carry insurance for the full market value of the house, the loss is not covered at all.

    d. The insurance company will pay Smith $22,500 for the loss.

9. Which of the following statements concerning insurance is not true?

    a. Most people have health insurance through group policies.

    b. Insurance companies have a duty to pay an insured's liability claim to a third party.

    c. Generally, an insurer's delay in accepting a property insurance application constitutes an acceptance of the application.

    d. Insurance companies have a duty to defend an insured against legal claims filed by a third party.

10. At the time she purchased her home, Gabrielle purchased (from Heartless Insurance Co.) a fire insurance policy covering the home. The policy was a valued policy with a face amount of $113,000 – the amount Gabrielle had paid for the property. Two years after the policy went into effect, the home was totally destroyed by fire. At the time of the fire, Gabrielle's home had a fair market value of $99,000 because of declining property values in the area where it was located. On these facts, how much must Heartless pay Gabrielle?

    a. $99,000.

    b. $99,000 plus interest at the legal rate.

    c. $113,000.

    d. $106,000.

Short Essay

1. Tina is a youthful looking 30-year-old woman. Tina applies for a $100,000 life insurance policy and states her age as 21. The insurance company issues a policy. Tina's premium would have purchased $75,000 of coverage for a 30-year-old. Tina dies 50 years after purchasing the policy. How much will the insurance company pay to Tina's beneficiary at the time of Tina's death?

2. Reese purchases a $100,000 life insurance policy. On the application, Reese states that he does not and has never used illegal drugs. Three years after purchasing the policy, Reese dies of a drug overdose. Will the insurance company pay the claim to Reese's beneficiary?

3.　Briefly describe two features commonly found in health insurance policies that help reduce the cost of the insurance for the insured.

4.　Beverly is a gynecologist. She delivers a large number of babies each year. What type of insurance coverage would Beverly be wise to purchase?

5.　Describe some perils that are often not covered by insurance.

6.　Mark has a health care policy with Yellow Cross and Yellow Shield Insurance Co. This policy has been in effect for over five years, and Mark has been fortunate in that he has not had to file any claims under the policy. His luck turned bad when he was admitted to a hospital emergency room last week because of an auto accident. His luck got even worse when he was told by the hospital that his insurance had lapsed because of nonpayment of premiums. It turned out that Mark's insurance agent had converted Mark's premium payments to his own use in order to pay gambling debts. What can Mark do?

7. Normally, most states require a certain period of time to pass before a missing person is declared deceased for insurance purposes. But, these are not normal times. Several hundred missing people were never found out of the area known as "ground zero" in the terrorist attack on the World Trade Center. What can a state do to speed up the payment of much-needed insurance monies to the surviving families of those missing persons?

CHAPTER 37
NEGOTIABLE INSTRUMENTS

Outline

I. Nature of negotiable instruments.

    A. Commercial paper is a contract for payment of money: promises to pay and orders to pay are two basic types.

        1. Notes and certificates of deposit are promises to pay; drafts and checks are orders to pay.

    B. Articles 3 and 4 of the Uniform Commercial Code govern the law of commercial paper.

    C. A negotiable instrument is a special kind of paper because it can be accepted in place of money. There are two basic types: promises to pay money and orders to pay money.

II. Kinds of negotiable instruments.

    A. A promissory note is primarily a credit instrument

    B. A certificate of deposit is an instrument containing (1) an acknowledgement by a bank that it has received a deposit of money, and (2) a promise by the bank to repay the sum of money.

    C. A draft is an order to pay money rather than a promise to pay money. The most common example of a draft is a check.

    D. A check is a draft payable on demand and drawn on a bank.

III. Benefits of negotiable instruments.

    A. If the holder of a negotiable instrument is a holder in due course, he takes the instrument free of all defenses and claims to the instrument except those that concern its validity.

    The Federal Trade Commission has adopted a regulation that alters the rights of a holder in due course in consumer purchase transactions.

    B. Formal Requirements for Negotiability.

        1. There are different requirements for a note or check to be negotiable. If the instrument does not satisfy these formal requirements, it is nonnegotiable.

    C. The instrument must be in writing and signed.

    D. It must contain and unconditional promise or order, and must be to pay a sum certain in money.

    Example: <u>Interbank of New York v. Fleet Bank</u>: An agreement between a bank and its depositor where withdrawals from the customer's account were verbally authorized by the depositor was considered by the court to serve as the depositor's signature.

    E. The instrument must be payable on demand or at a specified time, and be payable to order or bearer.

    Example: <u>Chung v. New York Racing Association</u>: Vouchers issued by the New y\York racing Association were "bearer paper" under the UCC.

    F. Not state any other undertaking or instruction to do any act in addition to the payment of money.

        1. However, the instrument may includes clauses concerning giving, maintaining, or protecting collateral, an authorization to confess judgment or to realize on or dispose of collateral, and waiving the benefit of any law intended for the protection or benefit of any person obligated on the instrument.

        2. Where a conflict or an ambiguous term exists, general rules of interpretation are applied.

    Example: <u>Galatia Community State Bank v. Kindy</u>: The amount in figures imprinted by a checking writing machine controls over the amount written in hand figures.

Learning Objectives

1. You should understand the special qualities and benefits of negotiable instruments.
2. You should be familiar with the basic types of commercial paper.
3. You should know the formal requirements that must be met for instruments to qualify as negotiable instruments.
4. You should understand what happens when you receive a check in which there is a conflict between the amount set forth in figures and the one written out in words.
5. You should be able to distinguish the rights of an assignee of an ordinary contract from the rights of a holder in due course of a negotiable instrument.
6. You should know what promises or orders are conditional and, therefore, make a contract to pay money in which they are included nonnegotiable.
7. You should know the effect of acceleration and extension clauses on the negotiability of a contract to pay money.
8. You should know what *order language* is and what *bearer language* is, and whether an instrument contains order or bearer language.
9. You should have an awareness of e-checks and e-payments.

Learning Hints

1. There are two basic kinds of commercial paper: promises to pay money and orders to pay money.
2. The promissory note and certificate of deposit are promises to pay money; drafts and checks are orders to pay money.
3. The significance of a negotiable instrument is that an assignee can obtain greater rights than the assignor. If a person qualifies as a "holder in due course," he takes the instrument free of all defenses and claims to the instrument except those that concern its validity.
4. Try to think of all the situations in which you have used negotiable instruments. You may have purchased groceries with a check, and you may have purchased a stereo on credit by signing a promissory note. You may have signed a promissory note with a bank to obtain money to pay your college tuition. You may have received a payroll check from an employer.
5. Note why negotiable instruments were used in these situations. They were used as substitutes for money because you did not have enough money or because it was too inconvenient or risky to carry large amounts of money with you. These examples explain why the law created negotiable instruments: to create a substitute for money. Negotiable instruments are not perfect substitutes for money, but they are as much like money as is consistent with our society's notions of fairness.
6. A promissory note is a two-party instrument. The maker promises to pay the payee.
7. A draft is a three-party instrument. The drawer orders the drawee to pay the payee.
8. A negotiable instrument is merely a special type of contract to pay money, one that a HDC may enforce despite any personal defenses the maker or drawer may have against the payee. Preventing a maker or drawer from asserting personal defenses to payment of a negotiable instrument works a hardship on the maker or drawer. Therefore, the law will not impose such a hardship unless the maker or drawer has issued a contract that is a negotiable instrument.
9. For a contract to be a negotiable instrument, it must meet each of the six requirements listed in the book. If any one of the requirements is not satisfied, the contract is not a negotiable instrument and assignees take the contract subject to all defenses. If all the elements of negotiability are met, the contract is a negotiable instrument and a HDC can hold it and enforce it free of personal defenses.

10. Note that a draft is an order to pay. That is, the drawer orders or commands the drawee to pay the payee. The order (or command) is the word "Pay" in "Pay to the order of Joe." This is the first of three uses of the word "order" in negotiable instrument law. To avoid confusion it is important that you understand these three uses of the word "order." The other two uses of the word "order" are discussed in Learning Hints 12 and 13 below.

11. If a promise or order to pay is conditional, the contract to pay money is nonnegotiable even if the condition is fulfilled. For example, a note says "Pay only if John delivers the goods." Even after John delivers the goods, the note is nonnegotiable. Why? Because the note is not like money. The note will not be easily transferred, because the condition included in the note requires a person to determine whether the condition has been satisfied. Such a determination is unnecessary when one takes money.

12. Likewise, if one cannot calculate the value of the instrument by merely looking at the instrument, it is not like money and is therefore not negotiable. However, a statement requiring the payment of attorney fees or the calculation of interest "at the judgment rate" does not make the instrument nonnegotiable.

13. For the instrument to be payable on demand or at a definite time, one must be able, by looking only at the instrument itself, to determine the latest date payment must be made or can be demanded. "On demand" means that payment must be made when a holder demands payment from the maker or drawee.

Acceleration clauses never prevent an instrument from being negotiable. Such clauses merely allow the holder to be paid earlier. One can calculate the latest date payment must be made.

Extension clauses will destroy the negotiability of an instrument if the payment date is extended at the option of the maker for an unlimited time. This is because the maker may choose never to pay the instrument. However, any extension at the option of a holder will not destroy negotiability, because the effect is the same as having it payable on demand. Giving a drawer any option to extend the payment date will make the draft nonnegotiable.

Extension clauses that delay payment for a definite time upon the maker's option do not destroy negotiability. This is because even if the extension is made, one can calculate the latest date that the instrument must be paid.

14. Every negotiable instrument must have order or bearer language. Order language usually includes the word "order," such as "Pay to the order of Joe." The order language is the word "order." This is the second use of the word "order" in negotiable instrument law. The first was discussed above in Learning Hint 8. Bearer language usually includes the word "bearer."

15. The third use of the word "order" in negotiable instrument law is its use in distinguishing order paper from bearer paper. This third use of the word order is discussed in Learning Hint 3 of Chapter 40.

16. When we decide a contract is a negotiable instrument, we mean that a HDC may enforce it free of personal defenses. A negotiable instrument is not necessarily enforceable or collectible. Real defenses may be asserted by the maker or drawer against a HDC, or the maker or drawer may have no money to pay the HDC.

When we decide a contract is nonnegotiable, we mean that it is an ordinary contract, that it cannot be held by a HDC, and that all defenses are good against the person seeking payment or performance. "Nonnegotiable" does not mean there is no contract. It does not mean that the contract is unenforceable or uncollectible. It means that the instrument is merely an ordinary contract.

True-False

In the blank provided, put "**T**" if the statement is True or "**F**" if the statement is False.

_____ 1. A note is an example of a promise to pay money.

_____ 2. The drawee of a check is always a bank.

_____ 3. Glen borrows money from Sam. Glen issues a note to Sam that says, "I promise to pay to Sam $1,000 at 8% interest for 90 days." This note is negotiable.

_____ 4. A non-negotiable note is not valid or collectible.

_____ 5. Under the UCC, words control figures if there is a conflict between numbers and written words on a check.

_____ 6. A bank may properly ay a postdated check.

_____ 7. A draft is a form of commercial paper that involves an order to pay money rather than a promise to pay money.

_____ 8. A note payable "30 days after sight" is not negotiable.

_____ 9. A payroll check with a stamped signature of the drawer is negotiable.

_____ 10. A promissory note written on a cocktail napkin can be negotiable.

Multiple Choice

Circle the best answer.

1. Farmer gave Grocer an otherwise negotiable note promising "to pay to Grocer's order ten bushels of apples". Which of these is true?
   a. This is a negotiable instrument.
   b. This is not a negotiable instrument because it is not payable in money.
   c. This is not a negotiable instrument because it is not payable to the order of Grocer.
   d. This is not a negotiable instrument because it is not payable to bearer.

2. Which of the following is a promissory instrument?
   a. A certificate of deposit.
   b. A draft.
   c. A check.
   d. A cashier's check.

3. Which of the following would be non-negotiable?
   a. A promissory note written on construction paper.
   b. A promissory note for $10,000 payable in money or stock.
   c. A check payable to Jane Smith or Herb Jones.
   d. A promissory note for $10,000 at 6% for 60 days.

4. An instrument that is payable to the order of Betty Nelson, and is charged to the account of Acme Co. and signed by Bert Thomas is most likely:
   a. A promissory note.
   b. A check.
   c. A draft.
   d. A cashier's check.

5. Which of the following instruments would be non-negotiable?
    a. A promissory note that mentions the collateral that secures the loan.
    b. A promissory note that has an acceleration clause in the event of default.
    c. A promissory note that contains a confession of judgment clause.
    d. A promissory note that states, "I owe you $1,000, signed Bill Grant."

6. Which of the following is negotiable?
    a. A check with a notation in the memo line that the funds for the check are to be taken from the travel budget of the drawer company.
    b. A promissory note that is payable in money or property.
    c. A verbal promise to pay Sue Stone $1,000 plus interest of 5% for 30 days.
    d. A promissory note that says, "I promise to pay Jim Jones $5,000 at 8% interest for 60 days."

7. Which of the following is not a requirement for negotiability?
    a. The instrument must be in writing of some form.
    b. The instrument must be signed by the maker or drawer of the instrument.
    c. The instrument is valid and collectible.
    d. The instrument must be payable to bearer or to order.

8. Stella Starr is nicknamed "Kitty" by her friends. Which of the following is a valid signature for her for purposes of negotiability?
    a. Stella Starr.
    b. S. Starr.
    c. Kitty.
    d. All of the above.

9. Which of the following is true concerning ambiguous terms on a check or a promissory note?
    a. Printed terms prevail over typewritten terms.
    b. Words control numbers.
    c. Typewritten terms prevail over handwritten terms.
    d. Numbers control words.

10. Jim Smith gave Freda Field a piece of paper with the following writing on it. "I promise to pay $50 to Freda. /Signed/ Jim."
    a. This is a negotiable instrument.
    b. This is not a negotiable instrument because there is no payment date.
    c. This is not a negotiable instrument because it is not payable to order or to bearer.
    d. This is not a negotiable instrument because Jim's signature is invalid.

Short Essay

1. Joe issues a promissory note to Jane, promising to pay Jane $1,000 at 6% interest in 90 days. Before the note matures, Jane sells the note to Don. When Don presents the note for payment, Joe tells Don that he does not have the money, but would give Don furniture instead. Don agrees. If the holder of the instrument accepts something other than money, is the note non-negotiable?

2. Roy and Dale are cowboys. Dale agrees to sell 50 cattle to Roy. Roy gives Dale a note promising "to pay to the order of Dale $25,000 on June 1, 1983, unless Dale fails to deliver the cattle." Dale signs the note. Is this a negotiable instrument?

3. Lester sold Tammy a new car. Tammy did not have enough money to buy the car, so she gave Lester a note promising "to pay to the order of Lester $3,500 and to give to Lester or bearer my 1956 Volkswagen." Is this a negotiable instrument?

4. Grandpa gives Danny a promissory note that says, "I promise to pay to Danny $5,000 on June 1, 2007 if he graduates from college with honors." Is this note negotiable? Why or why not?

5. Under the new Article 3, a check that reads "Pay John Doe" is negotiable even though it obviously is not payable to bearer and doesn't appear to be payable to John's order. Why does the new Article 3 permit this deviation from the general rule?

6. June borrowed $10,000 at Mayfield State Bank to buy a car. June signs a promissory note as maker. On the back of the note is a clause that says, "If the maker of this note defaults on one payment, the entire balance of the loan plus interest is immediately due and payable." Does this clause make the note non-negotiable? Why or why not?

7. Describe how promissory notes containing variable interest rates can still meet the fixed amount requirement and be negotiable.

8. Why is an IOU note non-negotiable? What is the word (or words) on a check that meets the requirement of an order to pay?

CHAPTER 38
NEGOTIATION AND HOLDER IN DUE COURSE

Outline

I. Nature of negotiation.

    A. Negotiation is the transfer of an instrument to a holder

    B. Formal requirements are simple: If it is order paper, it can be negotiated by delivery after necessary indorsements. If it is bearer paper, no indorsement is necessary.

    C. Indorsement is necessary to negotiate an instrument payable to the order of someone; second, indorsement generally makes a person liable on the instrument.

        Under revised Article 3, if a check is deposited in a depositary bank without indorsement, the depositary bank becomes a holder if the customer at the time of delivery qualified as a holder.

    D. Kinds of Indorsement: special, blank, restrictive, and qualified

        Example: <u>Lehigh Presbytery v. Merchants Bancorp, Inc.</u>: The bank is legally bound to follow restrictive indorsements.

    E. Under revised Article 3, some indorsements are no longer considered restrictive.

II. Holder in due course.

    A. A holder in due course (HDC) takes a negotiable instrument free of all personal defenses. A holder must have possession of an instrument issued to him or her or indorsed and delivered to him or her.

    B. A HDC must have a complete chain of authorized indorsements.

        Example: <u>Golden Years Nursing Home, Inc., v. Gabbard</u>: Once a payee indorses a check in blank it becomes bearer paper.

    C. A HDC must give value and take it in good faith. To be a holder in due course, a person not only must take a negotiable instrument before he has notice that it is overdue but also before it has been dishonored. A holder who has notice that an instrument has been altered cannot qualify as a HDC, nor can a person who is on notice of an adverse claim.

    D. To qualify as a HDC, a person almost must acquire the instrument without notice that any party has defenses or claims in recoupment.

    E. A person cannot be a HDC if the instrument is irregular or incomplete.

    F. Any person who can trace his title to an instrument back to a holder in due course receives the same rights as the holder in due course under the "shelter provision" of the UCC.

III. Rights of a holder in due course.

    A. HDC is not subject to any personal defenses; however, the HDC is subject to real defenses (defenses which go to the validity of the instrument).

        Example: <u>Triffin v. Dillabough</u>: A holder in due course may enforce the instruments according to the original tenor, and when an incomplete instrument has been completed, he may enforce it as completed.

    B. Revised Article 3 establishes four categories of claims and defenses.

    C. Real defenses can be asserted against any holder including a holder in due course.

        Example: <u>General Credit Corp. v. New York Linen Co., Inc.</u>: A check issued by the drawer to the payee was negotiated to a holder in due course. A personal defense the drawer had against the payee could not be used against the holder in due course.

    D. A HDC is not subject to any personal defenses or claims between original parties to the instrument.

E. For purposes of Revised Article 3, a HDC takes free of claims that arose before he became a holder, but is subject to those arising when or after he becomes a HDC.

F. A claim in recoupment is an offset to liability.

G. Some states have limited the HDC doctrine, particularly as it affects consumers. The FTC also protects consumers by requiring a notice in the note or contract making the potential holder subject to all claims and defenses of the consumer.

Example: Music Acceptance Corporation v. Lofing: Breach of warranty relieves the promissor of his duty to pay the consumer note for his Steinway piano.

Learning Objectives

1. You should understand the requirements for negotiating a check to someone else.

2. You should understand the circumstances under which someone may cash a lost instrument.

3. You should understand the different kinds of indorsements and their effect.

4. You should know the requirements for a holder in due course.

5. You should understand the defenses that may be asserted against the holder in due course, and those defenses that may not be asserted against the holder in due course.

6. You should know how a person becomes a holder of an instrument.

7. You should know how to negotiate order and bearer paper.

8. You should know what is meant by irregular paper.

9. You should be able to distinguish real defenses from personal defenses.

10. You should know what changes in the holder in due course doctrine the FTC and the states have made.

Learning Hints

1. Negotiation is the transfer of an instrument in such a way that the person who receives it becomes a holder in due course. A holder acquires certain benefits in that he takes the instrument free of personal defenses that could have been asserted against the maker.

2. An indorsement is necessary in order for there to be a negotiation of an instrument payable to the order of someone else.

3. There are different kinds of indorsements with different effects. A special indorsement is the signature of the indorser along with words indicating to whom or to whose order the instrument is payable. An indorser who merely signs his name and does not specify to whom the instrument is payable is payable to the bearer.

5. Do not confuse the terms "negotiable" and "negotiation." Negotiable means that the instrument meets the six requirements of negotiability and can therefore be held by a holder in due course. Negotiation is the process by which a person becomes a holder of a negotiable instrument. Contracts become negotiable by complying with the requirements for negotiability. The process of negotiation negotiates negotiable instruments.

6. Order paper is the third use of the word "order" in negotiable instrument law. (Refer to Learning Hints 8 and 12 in Chapter 39.) Since order paper is payable to a specific person, that person's indorsement and delivery are necessary for negotiation; that is, necessary to make the next possessor of the instrument a holder. Bearer paper is negotiated by delivery alone.

7. Note that an instrument may be issued as order paper (to a specific person), be indorsed in blank (to no specific person), and thereby become bearer paper. It can then be indorsed specially (to a specific person) and thereby become order paper again. Therefore, it is possible that one instrument at different times in its life can be bearer paper or order paper. Note also that the word "order" need not appear in the special indorsement. "Pay to Alex" is a special indorsement and the instrument is order paper. It is order paper because it is payable to Alex.

8. Note that a restrictive indorsement, even though conditional, does not destroy the negotiability of an instrument. An indorsement never affects the negotiability of an instrument.

9. A qualified indorsement is designated as such because it qualifies the indorser's liability by eliminating his liability as an indorser and limiting his liability as a transferor.

10. You must understand completely what a holder in due course (HDC) is and why the law allows such a person to exist. The HDC is the most important person in all of negotiable instrument law. By allowing a HDC to take a negotiable instrument free of personal defenses, the law has created a substitute for money.

    Negotiable instruments are like money in that money is perfectly negotiable. If you receive money from Todd that Todd received from Jane, you do not need to worry about whether Todd cheated Jane when Jane gave the money to Todd. In fact, even if Todd stole the money from Jane, you receive clear ownership (title) to the money despite any defense Jane may have against Todd. This is the key aspect of money: it is transferred free of any defenses. This aspect is essential. Would a person be as willing to accept money if she took it subject to defenses a third party (Jane) had against her transferor (Todd)? Of course not.

    A negotiable instrument is as perfect a substitute for money as is consistent with our society's notions of fairness. If a person is a HDC, he takes the instrument free of personal defenses, but not real defenses. Our law states, in effect, that it is unfair for a person to be prevented from asserting a real defense against anyone. Real defenses are too important. Personal defenses are not so important, and the person who has the personal defense can always assert it against the person who harmed him. He merely cannot assert the personal defense against a third person not involved in creating the defense who is a HDC.

    Because the law allows a HDC to take a negotiable instrument free of personal defenses, people are more willing to accept negotiable instruments in commercial transactions. Less cash need be used. The result is safer commercial transactions and lower cost of credit, merchandise, and services.

11. Here is a handy formula to remember what value is:

    Value = consideration + antecedent claims - executory promises

    In contract law you learned that past consideration is not consideration. In negotiable instrument law, past consideration is value. If someone has owed you $5000 for two years and gives you a $5000 check today, you have given value for the check, because of your antecedent claim against the drawer.

    Executory promises, while consideration, are not value. Executory promises are unperformed promises. If you merely promise to do something, you have not given value. Once you perform the promise you have given value.

12. A person is a HDC only to the extent she has given the value she has agreed to give. So if you promise to give $5000 for a $6000 note but have given only $2500 so far, you are a HDC for only $2500. The other $2500 is an executory promise, not value. However, once you have given all the value you have agreed to give, you are HDC for the entire amount of the note. So if you gave $5000 cash for the $6000 note, you would be a HDC for $6000, unless the discount was too large to establish your good faith.

13. Note that all five requirements of a HDC must be met. If a person obtains notice of any defense (real or personal) before she becomes a holder or before she pays value, she is not a HDC. For example, you forget to indorse a note payable to your order and sell it to me for $1000 cash. A week later I discover a defense against the note. The next day you indorse the note. I am not a HDC, because I had notice of the defense before I became a holder.

14. To help you understand the distinction between real and personal defenses, think of the importance of the real defenses. These defenses exist because people are incapable of protecting themselves due to age or mental condition. It would be unfair to allow anyone to enforce a negotiable instrument against a minor, a drunk, or any insane person. Personal defenses are not so important, because the person could have better protected himself, but the young, the drunk, the insane, the unduly influenced, and those not given an opportunity to see what they are signing (as in fraud in the essence) cannot protect themselves.

15. Many consumers sign negotiable notes without knowing the effect of what they are signing: they cannot assert their personal defenses against a HDC. This ignorance explains why most states and the FTC have eliminated the HDC doctrine in most consumer transactions.

True-False

In the blank provided, put "T" if the statement is True or "F" if the statement is False.

_____ 1. A note payable to X's order requires X's indorsement for its negotiation.

_____ 2. A blank indorsement converts order paper to bearer paper.

_____ 3. Indorsing an instrument "without recourse" makes the instrument non-negotiable.

_____ 4. An instrument that is indorsed with a special indorsement becomes bearer paper.

_____ 5. An order instrument can be negotiated by just delivering the instrument.

_____ 6. A note payable "to the order of Jonathan" is order paper.

_____ 7. A note with the payee's name misspelled must be indorsed with the payee's signature misspelled.

_____ 8. A customer's bank could supply a customer's missing indorsement on a check the customer deposits at the bank under original Article 3.

_____ 9. A maker of a note can use his bankruptcy as a real defense against a holder in due course.

_____ 10. A maker of a promissory note can use alteration as a real defense against a holder in due course. The maker will not be required to pay anything on the altered note to the holder in due course.

Multiple Choice

Circle the best answer.

1. Which of the following is order paper?
   a. A check indorsed "pay to John".
   b. A check payable to the order of John and indorsed in blank.
   c. A check payable to the order of cash.
   d. A note payable to bearer.

2. Pam buys a used car from Acme Motors. Acme arranges the financing and the note is sold to Last National Bank, which qualifies as a holder in due course. The note contains the FTC Rule clause. Pam discovers that Acme lied to her about the history of the car and refuses to pay Bank on the loan. Bank sues Pam for payment. Which of the following statement is true?

    a. Bank will prevail because Pam has only a personal defense.

    b. Pam will win because she has a real defense.

    c. Pam will win because the FTC Rule states that the holder is subject to all defenses that Pam could assert

    d. This is an example of fraud in the essence.

3. Which of the following is not a requirement to be a holder in due course?

    a. The holder must give value for the instrument.

    b. The instrument must not have been dishonored.

    c. The holder must take the instrument in good faith.

    d. The holder must have no notice that the instrument is overdue.

4. Which of the following is a real defense?

    a. Fraud in the inducement.

    b. Duress that makes the contract voidable.

    c. Non-issuance of the instrument.

    d. Fraud in the essence.

5. A check that is indorsed "For deposit only in account # 32453" is an example of:

    a. A special indorsement.

    b. A blank indorsement.

    c. A restrictive indorsement.

    d. A qualified indorsement.

6. Which of the following would prevent further negotiation of an instrument?

    a. Pay to Helen Crump only.

    b. Without recourse to me, Andy Taylor.

    c. Pay to Floyd Lawson only if he cuts my hair by June 1st, Barney Fife.

    d. Indorsements do not affect further negotiation of an instrument.

7. Which of the following is bearer paper?

    a. A check payable "to order of bearer".

    b. A check payable "to the order of Jim".

    c. A check indorsed "to Jim".

    d. A check payable "to Jim's order".

8. A law firm bought office furniture at Nebraska Furniture Mart and financed the purchase at the store. The Mart later sells the paper to Commercial Bank, which qualifies as a holder in due course. Which of the following could the law firm raise as a valid defense against the Mart?

    a. Fraud in the essence.

    b. Modification of the obligation by a separate agreement.

    c. Duress that makes the contract voidable.

    d. Failure of consideration.

9. Barb borrowed money from Green and issued a promissory note to Green. Green sold the note to Smith who gave value for the instrument. Smith gives the note to his son. Which of the following is true?

   a. Son does not have the rights of a holder in due course since he did not give value for the note.

   b. Son has only the rights of an ordinary holder.

   c. Son has the rights of a holder in due course under the shelter provision.

   d. Son is a holder in due course.

10. Shana purchases a $7,000 used truck to use in her lawn care business. She gives her seller, Truck Sales Inc., a negotiable note for $7,000 due in six months. Truck Sales sells the note to Talbott Factors, holder in due course. Talbott agrees to pay Truck Sales $6,800 for the note, $800 in cash immediately and $6000 in four months. In one month the truck proves to be defective and Truck Sales refuses to repair it, despite the existence of an express warranty covering the defect. Shana tells Talbott that she will refuse to pay the note when it is due because of the unrepaired defect. Nevertheless, three months later Talbott pays Truck Sales the remaining $6000. On the note's due date Talbott demands payment but Shana refuses. Which of the following is correct?

   a. Talbott cannot collect anything from Shana.

   b. Talbott can collect only $800 from Shana.

   c. Talbott can collect only $6,800 from Shana.

   d. Talbott can collect $7,000 from Shana.

Short Essay

1. Is the following writing a negotiable instrument? Decide and discuss.

   "Santa Rosa, California, May 1, 1993.

   I promise to pay to the order of Grace Hamilton the sum of $1,000 out of the proceeds of the sale of my 1986 Camarro.

   "(Signed) Fronzel Pool."

2. Terry belongs to a national college accounting teachers organization. At the next conference in New York, Terry has volunteered to take checks from members from around the country who want to go as a group to a New York Yankees game. Most of the members are just making the checks out to Terry, who will then deposit them in an association bank account. Since Terry knows virtually none of the members, what would be the best way for him to indorse the checks?

3. John issues a promissory note to Judy. Judy indorses the note by signing her name and sells it to Jane. Jane sells it to Stan without indorsing it. Stan sells it to Bob, writes "pay to Bob" on the note and signs it. Bob then sells the note to Larry and gives it to Larry without signing it. Is Larry the holder of the note?

4. Jones buys a computer from Computer Geeks. Jones signs a $3,000 note due in six months. Jones soon discovers that the computer is not as warranted and seeks a breach of warranty claim against Geeks. Geeks sells the note to State Street Bank, which is aware of the warranty claim. Can State Street qualify as a holder in due course?

5. Marty Minor wants to take out a loan to buy a car. Acme Motors is willing to sell Marty a car and arrange financing through Fidelity Bank. What is the risk for Fidelity Bank to make Marty the loan? What would the bank likely demand from Marty before it would make a loan to him?

6. Distinguish between void and voidable contracts and how these are related to real and personal defenses. Discuss how fraud, incapacity, and duress could be either real or personal defenses.

7. Describe the implications for both consumers and holders of the FTC Rules.

8. Uncle Fred writes a check to his favorite nephew, Ted, as a birthday present. This check is a gift for which Ted is grateful, and he tells his uncle he intends to use it to get some really high-grade crack. Uncle Fred objects to Ted's intended use of the money and orders a stop payment on the check. Ted claims that the bank must cash it because he is a holder in due course. Who wins?

9. Why do you think some businesses refuse to take checks that have special indorsements?

CHAPTER 39
LIABILITY OF PARTIES

Outline

I. Liability on negotiable instruments flows from signatures as well as actions concerning them.

    A. Contractual liability on the instrument depends on the capacity in which the person signed. Article 3 of the UCC provides the terms of the contract.

        1. A person may be primarily or secondarily liable.

        2. The maker of a promissory note is primarily liable for payment of it.

        3. The acceptor of a draft is obligated to pay the drafter according to the terms at the time of acceptance.

        4. At the time a check or draft is written, no party is primarily liable. If the drawee bank certifies the check, it becomes primarily liable.

        Example: American Federal Bank, FSB v. Parker: A subsequent holder in due course may enforce an incomplete instrument as completed.

        5. The drawer of a check is secondarily liable unless she disclaims liability by drawing "without recourse."

        6. A person who indorses a negotiable instrument is usually secondarily liable unless the indorsement is qualified.

        7. An accommodation party is a person who signs a negotiable instrument for the purposes of lending her credit to another party to the instrument.

    B. No person is contractually liable unless his signature appears on the instrument. An authorized agent can sign the instrument.

    Example: Packaging Materials & Supply Company, Inc. v. Prater: An individual who signs a check drawn on a corporate account without indicating he is signing in a representative capacity is not personally liable on the instrument.

    C. If a person's signature was unauthorized, the person is not bound.

II. Contractual liability in operation.

    A. The instrument must be presented. A note is presented to the maker when due. A check or draft is presented to the drawee.

    B. A person who transfers an instrument or presents it may incur liability on the basis of certain implied warranties, called transferor's warranties and presentment warranties.

    C. Other liability rules include common law negligence rules.

    Example: Gulf States Section, PGA, Inc., v. Whitney National Bank of New Orleans: A bank may prevent a customer whose check has been forged from recovery if the account has been negligently handled.

    D. The Code establishes special rules for checks made payable to impostors and fictitious persons.

    Example: C & N Contractors v. Community Bankshares, Inc.: Community Bankshares, the depositary bank, was not liable to the drawer for conversion because it accepted checks containing forged payee indorsements.

E. A bank that pays a check that contains a forged indorsement may become liable for conversion.

    Example: <u>Lawyers Fund for Client Protection of the State of New York v. Bank Leumi Trust Co. of New York</u>: A payee has a claim for conversion when an instrument is paid to someone else with his indorsement.

III. Discharge of negotiable instruments.

    A. Payment by the person primarily liable discharges all parties to the instrument.

    B. Discharge may also occur through cancellation or by alteration of the instrument.

Learning Objectives

1. You should understand the liability a person assumes when she indorses a check.

2. You should understand the warranties made when a check is presented to a drawee bank for payment.

3. You should understand the liability of a drawee bank to its customer if the check contains a forged signature.

4. You should know whether the drawee bank bears the loss if an imposter presented a check for payment.

5. You should understand the affect of materially altering a negotiable instrument.

6. You should be familiar with the ways that liability on a negotiable instrument may be discharged.

7. You should be able to distinguish primary liability from secondary liability.

8. You should know the effects of the certification of a check.

9. You should be able to determine the contractual liability of an accommodation party.

10. You should know what is meant by presentment, dishonor, and notice of dishonor.

11. You should know who makes which transferor's warranties, and to whom.

12. You should know who makes which presentment warranties, and to whom.

13. You should know the effect of a maker or drawer's negligent execution of a negotiable instrument.

14. You should be familiar with fictitious payees. You should know the special rule concerning forged indorsements when an imposter or fictitious payee exists.

15. You should know the extent of a drawee bank's liability for conversion when it pays a check with a forged indorsement.

Learning Hints

1. This chapter examines how a person becomes liable on a negotiable instrument and the nature of the liability incurred. Basically, liability may be based on the fact a person signed the instrument. In such cases, liability depends on the capacity in which the person signed the instrument.

2. Liability on a negotiable instrument can also be based on breach of warranty, improper payment, negligence, or conversion.

3. When a person signs a negotiable instrument, he generally becomes contractually liable on the instrument. That liability may be primary or secondary.

4. Note that the only way a person may become contractually liable on a negotiable instrument is to sign it. This explains why the forgery of your signature on a check does not make you liable, but makes the forger liable. Of course, your agent may sign for you and make you liable.

5.   To aid your understanding of contractual liability, address each type of negotiable instrument separately. For example, a note has a maker, payee, indorser, and perhaps accommodation parties. What is the contractual liability of each? An uncertified check has a drawer, drawee, payee, indorser, and perhaps accommodation parties. What is the contractual liability of each? Do the same for certified checks, drafts, and accepted drafts.

6.   Note that "accommodation" means help. This is why an accommodation maker has the liability of a maker, because the accommodation maker has helped the maker obtain credit.

      Note that an accommodation maker is primarily liable. This means that the holder of the note can obtain payment from the accommodation maker before trying to obtain payment from the maker. As far as the holder is concerned, the accommodation maker is like any other maker.

      That a person is an accommodation maker is important only between the accommodation maker and the maker. If the accommodation maker pays, she can recover the payment from the maker.

      The above analysis also applies to accommodation drawers and indorser, except that in these situations, the liability is secondary.

7.   Note that no one is primarily liable on an uncertified check or unaccepted draft. The drawee has no contractual liability, because the drawee has not signed the check or draft. The drawer has only secondary liability, because the drawer promises to pay only if the drawee does not pay.

8.   Transferor's warranties arise because a person transfers an instrument. A person may have no contractual liability, yet have a transferor's warranty liability. A person may have both contractual liability and transferor's liability.

9.   Transferor's warranties are based upon reasonable expectations. A person who receives a negotiable instrument expects five things to be true, because he expects to receive something very much like money. These five things are the five transferor's warranties. You must memorize them.

10.   To help you understand transferor's warranties, make a chart setting forth the transferor's warranties made by the nonindorsing transferor, the indorser, and the qualified indorser, and to whom each of these parties makes transferor's warranties.

11.   Presentment warranties are also based upon the reasonable expectations of the person who pays for the instrument.

12.   It is easier to understand how contractual and warranty liability operate if you make a diagram of the transfer of the instrument. These schematics help you to see who held the instrument, and in what order. You can put notes next to each person's name indicating whether, for instance, he was a thief and whether he signed the instrument. Schematics also illustrate how the instrument eventually returns to its issuer.

13.   The liability rules regarding negligence, impostors, and fictitious payees make good sense. The negligence rule places liability on the person who was negligent. Good examples of negligence are leaving unfilled spaces on the payee and amount lines of a check. A dishonest person could easily and skillfully raise the amount of the check and change the payee's name. The imposter rule places liability on the maker or drawer who failed to ascertain the true identity of the person to whom the instrument was written. It is fairer to impose liability on the drawer who dealt with the imposter than to impose it upon a holder who never met the imposter. The fictitious payee rule places liability upon the employer who should have better supervised the employee who made out the payroll checks to the fictitious payee. It is fairer to impose liability on the employer whose unsupervised employee did the wrong than to impose it upon a holder who was not aware of the fiction.

True-False

In the blank provided, put "T" if the statement is True or "F" if the statement is False.

_____ 1. The drawee bank has primary liability on a normal check.

_____ 2. When a maker dishonors a note, the holder should give timely notice to any indorsers.

_____ 3. A person who indorses a negotiable instrument usually is secondarily liable.

_____ 4. The maker of a note is secondarily liable on the note.

_____ 5. Maker makes a note payable to payee's order; payee indorses and negotiates the note to First, who in turn indorses and negotiates the note to Second. If Second cannot recover from maker, he can successfully sue either Payee, or First on their secondary indorser's liability.

_____ 6. Sheila issues a promissory note to Tim. Tim indorses it over to Carl. Carl indorses it over to Rodney. Tim makes a warranty to Rodney that all signatures on the instrument are genuine.

_____ 7. In question # 6, Rodney makes a warranty to Sheila that all signatures are genuine.

_____ 8. The drawer of a forged check is liable for the check if the fictitious payee rule applies.

_____ 9. An accommodation maker is secondarily liable.

_____ 10. Notice of dishonor may be made orally or in writing to hold a drawer liable on a draft.

Multiple Choice

Circle the best answer.

1. The party who is primarily liable on a check or a draft is called:
    a. The drawee.
    b. The acceptor.
    c. The payee.
    d. The maker.

2. Who is primarily liable on a check at the time it is written?
    a. The payee.
    b. The drawer.
    c. The drawee bank.
    d. No one.

3. Which of the following always blocks recovery on any transfer warranty?
    a. That the instrument has not been negotiated to the transferee.
    b. That the transferor did not indorse the instrument.
    c. That the transferor is a holder in due course.
    d. That the transferor received no consideration for the transfer.

4. Which of the following may avoid the indorser's secondary liability on a dishonored instrument?
    a. A qualified indorsement.
    b. A restrictive indorsement.
    c. A blank indorsement.
    d. A special indorsement.

5. Which of the following is not a reasonable request of a maker upon presentment of the instrument?
   a. Ask to see the note.
   b. Ask for a signed receipt.
   c. Require surrender of the note.
   d. None of the above.

6. Liz writes a check drawn on 1st State Bank to pay Phil for mowing her lawn. Which of the following statements is true?
   a. 1St State Bank is primarily liable on the check.
   b. Liz is primarily liable on the check.
   c. 1st State Bank is primarily liable on the check if the bank certifies the check.
   d. Liz has no liability on the instrument.

7. How should Abby Alston, president of Astra Corporation, sign checks on behalf of Astra, if her signature as an agent is required on the checks?
   a. Astra Corporation by Abby Alston, President.
   b. Abby Alston, President.
   c. Astra Corporation.
   d. Abby Alston.

8. Tad issues a promissory note to Ann, who indorses it to Steve. Steve negotiates it to Gail without indorsing it. Gail indorses it to Henry, who presents the instrument to Tad for payment. Which of the following is not true?
   a. Henry makes a warranty to Tad that he had no knowledge of Tad's signature being unauthorized.
   b. Steve makes a warranty to Henry that the instrument is not altered.
   c. Steve makes a warranty to Gail that all signatures are authentic.
   d. Ann makes a warranty to Steve that she has no knowledge of any insolvency proceedings against Tad.

9. Arnie issues a note to Carol for $1,000. Arnie was negligent in making the note and allowed a lot of blank spaces on it. Carol was able to alter the instrument to $10,000 and sold it to Frank, who qualifies as a holder in due course. Frank presents the note to Arnie. Which of the following is true?
   a. Arnie will not be required to pay on the note due to the alteration.
   b. Arnie will only be required to pay the original amount of $1,000.
   c. Arnie will be required to pay $10,000 due to his negligence in drafting the note.
   d. Arnie is not allowed to seek damages from Carol.

10. Milt works in the accounting department for Franks, Inc. Milt creates a false invoice to Smith Co. A check is drawn on Fidelity Bank. Milt forges Smith's indorsement and cashes the check. Which of the following is true?
    a. The bank is liable for paying on a forged instrument.
    b. Franks is not liable on the check due to the forgery.
    c. Milt is not liable for the forgery.
    d. Franks is liable on the check under the fictitious payee rule.

Short Essay

1. Amy issued his negotiable promissory note payable to the order of Buddy. Buddy indorsed the note, "Without recourse, Buddy," and negotiated it to Second Bank. At the time Buddy negotiated the note, Amy was insolvent but this was unknown to Buddy. The note was not paid. Is Buddy liable to the Bank on his indorsement?

2. Rose is the president of ABC Beverage and has the authority to sign negotiable instruments for ABC. Rose common signs the checks "Rose Red" on the signature line below where "ABC" is printed. Supply Company takes a check signed as above by Rose. The drawee bank dishonored the check because there were insufficient funds in the account. If Supply Company sues ABC and Rose to make the check good, is Rose personally liable to Supply Company?

3. Ernie steals a car from Al. Ernie takes the car to Honest Hollie's Used Cars and sells it to Hollie. Hollie writes a check drawn on People's Bank to Al, thinking that Ernie is Al. Ernie then forges the check and cashes it. Who is liable for this forged check? Why?

4. Valerie steals some checks from Roni. She then buys some goods from Dollar Mart by forging Roni's signature on a check. The checks are drawn on State Bank. Who is liable for the forged checks?

5. Laura applies for a loan at Farmer's Bank. Laura's credit history is a bit weak, so the bank asks for an accommodation party to sign with Laura. What type of accommodation party is the bank likely to require for Laura's loan? Why?

6. Describe the liability of the parties involved in a check. Distinguish an ordinary check from a certified check.

7. Tom pays his 60-day note plus interest to April on time. Greg issued a promissory note to Gina. Gina negotiated the note by indorsement to Buddy. Buddy decides to forgive Greg's debt and destroys the note. Describe the liabilities in each of these situations.

8. Helen is vice president of finance for Coffee Enterprises, Inc. She does all the bookkeeping and check distribution for the company. One of their suppliers is Margaux Café Products. Helen has set up an account at her company's bank named Margaux Coffee, with Helen as its sole proprietor. Over a period of time, Helen signed a number of company checks made out to "Margaux" and proceeded to direct them into her own account. Coffee Enterprises finds out about this embezzlement and sues its own bank for wrongfully honoring the checks that went to Margaux Coffee. Is the bank liable?

CHAPTER 40
CHECKS AND ELECTRONIC FUNDS TRANSFERS

Outline

I. The drawer/drawee.

    A. The bank has a duty to pay as drawee if the check is properly drawn and there are sufficient funds in the account.

    B. The drawee bank has the right to charge a properly payable check to the customer's account. It does not owe a duty to pay checks out of the account that are more than six months old.

    Example: RPM Pizza, Inc. v. Bank One-Cambridge: The bank did not violate a duty to customer when it paid a check that was more than six months old.

    C. The bank's right or duty to pay a check or charge the depositor's account may be terminated or modified by a "stop payment" order. This must be given to the bank within reasonable time for it to comply. It is valid for only 14 days if oral unless confirmed in writing.

    D. Under revised Articles 3 and 4, a postdated check that is presented for payment before the date on the check may be paid unless the customer has given notice to the bank.

    E. While a stop-payment order is in effect, the drawee bank is liable to the drawer of a check that it pays for any loss that the drawer suffers as a result.

    Example: Seigel v. Merrill, Lynch, Pierce, Fenner & Smith, Inc.: The drawer was not entitled to have his account recredited for checks paid over his stop-payment order because he was unable to demonstrate he suffered any loss because of the bank's failure to honor the stop-payment order.

    F. When a drawee bank certifies a check, it substitutes its promise to pay the check for the drawer's undertaking and becomes obligated to pay the check.

    G. A cashier's check is a check on which a bank is both the drawer and the drawee.

    H. Bank has the right to pay the checks of an incompetent person until notice, and for a period of 10 days after the customer's death.

    I. A forged check is generally not properly chargeable to the customer's account. The customer has a duty to report forgeries to the bank under UCC rule.

    Example: American Airlines Employees Federal Credit Union v. Martin: Martin could recover unauthorized withdrawals made to his account, which were not reported to the Credit Union within 60 days after the statement documenting them was made available to him since the time period is reasonable and not unconscionable.

II. Electronic banking.

    A. Electronic Funds Transfer Act of 1978 provides a basic framework establishing the rights and responsibilities of participants in such systems.

    B. EFT systems include automated teller machines, point of sale terminals, preauthorized payments, and telephone transfers.

    Example: Kruser v. Bank of America NT & SA: Failure to notify the bank in a timely fashion of the first unauthorized use of a bankcard relieved the bank of liability for subsequent unauthorized transfers of funds.

Learning Objectives

1. You should know what happens if your bank refuses to pay a check even though you have sufficient funds in your account.

2. You should know whether your bank can create an overdraft in your account by paying an otherwise properly payable check.

3. You should know your rights and the bank's obligation if you stop payment on a check.

4. You should understand the right and liabilities that arise if the payee on a check has it certified.

5. You should know the difference between a certified check and a cashier's check.

6. You should know the duties a drawee bank owes to its customer.

7. You should know what constitutes wrongful dishonor.

8. You should understand why a drawee bank has no liability to the drawer for disobeying a stop payment order when the drawee bank pays a person against whom the drawer has no defense to payment.

9. You should know the effect of a drawee bank's attempt to disclaim or limit its liability for disobeying a customer's instructions.

10. You should know when a drawee bank has the right to pay a check, especially forged and altered checks.

11. You should know when a drawee bank has the right to refuse to pay a stale check.

12. You should know the effect of certification on the liability of the drawer, the drawee bank, and the indorsers.

13. You should know the drawee bank's duty to report forgeries and alterations.

14. You should have an awareness of e-checks.

Learning Hints

1. The person who deposits money in a bank account becomes a creditor of the bank and the bank becomes that person's debtor. The bank also becomes an agent of the person who owns the checking account.

2. The Uniform Commercial Code (Article 4) established the obligations of the bank under banking law.

3. A drawee bank may incur liability for wrongfully failing to honor a check drawn on a drawer's account.

4. A customer may order the drawee bank to "stop payment" on a check. The bank is under the obligation to follow the order if reasonable and it has time to comply. Note, however, that a stop payment order does not necessarily relieve the customer of liability to a holder in due course.

5. Note that on an uncertified check, the drawee bank has no liability of any kind to anyone, except the bank's customer, the drawer. This means that when a drawee bank refuses to pay or to certify an uncertified check, the holder of the check who refuses to pay or to certify the check cannot successfully sue the drawee bank.

6. The drawee bank's only liability with respect to an uncertified check is to the customer-drawer. The basis of the drawee bank's liability to its customer-drawer is that the bank failed to follow the customer-drawer's instructions. As we saw in agency, so we see in banking law: the drawee bank, as an agent, must obey the instructions of the customer-drawer, the principal.

7. The two ways a drawee bank disobeys a customer-drawer's instructions are by paying a check when the bank should not pay the check and by not paying a check when it should. You should be able to organize the rules concerning wrongful dishonor, stop payment orders, stale checks, properly drawn checks, forged checks, and altered checks under these two categories.

8. Note why a bank need not recredit the customer's account when the bank disobeys a stop payment order and pays a holder against whom the customer does not have a good defense: the holder paid would have been able to collect on the check from the customer if the bank had obeyed the stop payment order. Either way, the drawer loses her money and the holder gets paid.

9. Understanding why certification at the request of a holder releases prior indorsers and the drawer from contractual liability is easier when you are aware of the reason for the rule: the holder is impliedly looking to the bank only for payment. When the drawer requests the certification, the holder makes no such choice. Hence, only the prior indorsers are discharged when the drawer requests certification.

10. Do not confuse cashier's checks and certified checks. Bank cashiers draw cashier's checks. The bank is a drawer and drawee. The bank certifies certified checks.. The bank is only a drawee.

11. To help the bank pay only properly drawn and indorsed checks, the customer owes the bank the duty not to assist a forgery or alteration by negligently drawing the check. Also the customer will help the bank reduce its loss if the customer quickly gives the bank notice of an altered or forged check the bank has paid. If given timely notice, the bank may be able to collect its loss from the forger or alterer. This explains why the customer will not be able to require the bank to recredit the customer's account when the customer negligently draws a check or fails to notify the bank of an alteration or forgery within a reasonable time.

True-False

In the blank provided, put "**T**" if the statement is True or "**F**" if the statement is False.

_____ 1. If a bank wrongfully dishonors a check, it is liable for both actual and consequential damages caused to the drawer by the dishonor.

_____ 2. Angie writes a check to Dottie drawn on 1st Bank. 1st Bank makes a mistake and dishonors the check. Dottie can recover from 1st Bank.

_____ 3. If a bank pays a skillfully altered check in good faith and while observing reasonable commercial standards, it may charge the customer's account for the amount of the check as altered, even though the customer was not negligent in filling out the check.

_____ 4. The bank does not have the right to pay on a check that creates an overdraft in a customer's account.

_____ 5. A bank may in good faith pay a stale check.

_____ 6. A bank may not be liable to a customer for paying on a check over a stop payment order.

_____ 7. A written stop payment order is valid for six months.

_____ 8. A bank can pay on a deceased customer's account until the bank is given notice of the customer's death.

_____ 9. A drawer has no contractual liability after the bank has certified the check at the request of the drawer.

_____ 10. A bank has the right to pay the checks of a deceased customer until the bank has notice that the customer is deceased or for 10 days after the death, whichever is later.

Multiple Choice

Circle the best answer.

1. Which of the following statements concerning "stale checks" is correct?

   a. The bank may not pay a check that is more than six months old without authorization of the customer.

   b. A stale check is any check that is more than three months old.

   c. The bank may pay a stale check out of a customer's account and charge it to the customer's account.

   d. Both (b) and (c) are correct.

2. A personal check on which the bank guarantees payment is called a:

   a. Certified check.

   b. Cashier's check.

   c. Teller's check.

   d. Stale check.

3. Steve orally stopped payment on a check made payable to Eleanor because she failed to deliver goods he had purchased from her. In the meantime, Eleanor negotiated the check to Hannah, who took it as a holder in due course. Steve's bank then paid Hannah despite the stop-payment order. Must the bank recredit Steve's account for the amount of the check?

   a. No, because the stop-payment order was oral.

   b. No because Steve suffered no loss by the bank's paying Hannah.

   c. Yes, because Steve had a good defense against Hannah.

   d. Yes, because the stop payment order was in effect.

4. Natalie is a bookkeeper for Judy. In April, Natalie forges three of Judy's checks drawn on Second Bank. This is the first time Natalie had forged any checks. On May 5th, Judy receives a bank statement with the three forged checks. During May, Natalie forges four more checks. Natalie forges ten more checks later in June and July. Finally, Judy discovers the forgeries and demands that the bank credit her account for the amount of the forged instruments. Which of the following is true?

   a. Second Bank is liable for all of the forged checks.

   b. Judy is liable for all of the forged checks.

   c. Judy is liable for the first 7 forged checks.

   d. Second Bank is liable for the first 7 checks.

5. Which of the following is not an EFT system?

   a. Automated teller machines.

   b. Point of sale terminals or debit cards.

   c. Credit cards.

   d. Telephone transfers.

6. Dan has $1,000 in his checking account at First Bank. Dan gives Paula a check for $50. When Paula presents the check for payment at First Bank, First Bank refuses to pay Paula and marks the check "N.S.F." First Bank has:

   a. Issued a stop payment order.

   b. Wrongfully dishonored the check.

   c. Improperly debited Dan's account.

   d. Done all of the above.

7. Tina skillfully alters a check drawn by Art on Security Bank. The check was originally written for $500, but Tina changed it to $5,000. Security Bank pays $5,000 to Tina. Which of the following is true?

    a. Art is discharged from all liability on the check.

    b. Art is liable for the full $5,000 since the check was skillfully altered.

    c. Security Bank is liable for $4,500.

    d. Tina has no liability for the instrument.

8. Arnold takes his car to EZ Paint to have it painted. Arnold pays EZ with a check. After driving his car home, Arnold discovers that the paint job is poorly done. Arnold calls State Bank and stops payment on the check. The bank makes a mistake and pays the check over the stop payment order. Which of the following is true?

    a. The bank is liable to Arnold for acting in bad faith.

    b. The bank is not liable to Arnold because his personal defense is not good against a holder in due course.

    c. The bank is liable to Arnold because he had a real defense.

    d. The bank is liable to Arnold because he could prove he suffered loss with a personal defense he could hold against EZ.

9. Bill notifies Harvest Bank about a postdated check he wrote to Cardinal. Harvest Bank pays the postdated check to Cardinal before the date on the check. As a result, Bill's account is overdrawn. Which of the following is most true?

    a. Harvest Bank is within its rights to pay postdated checks.

    b. A bank can never pay a postdated check before the date, so the bank is liable.

    c. Harvest Bank may be liable to Bill for damages as a result of paying on the postdated check.

    d. None of the above.

10. For which of the following situations would the bank be liable?

    a. Bank pays a check 8 days after the drawer's death.

    b. Bank pays a check that was forged.

    c. Bank in good faith pays an incomplete check that has been completed.

    d. Bank pays a check forged by an imposter of the payee.

Short Answer

1. Bob requested that his bank certify his $100 check payable to Bob's father. Is bank required to certify the check? What is the result if it does so?

2. Harley writes a postdated check to Johnson. Harley's bank pays the check before the date on the check. Is the bank liable for paying the postdated check?

3. Tom bought a used car for $1000 from Acme Motors, paying by check. Tom soon discovered that the car was a lemon, so he telephoned his bank to stop payment on August 1. Shortly thereafter, Acme negotiated the check to Smith, who is a holder but not a holder in due course. On August 20, Smith presented the check for payment to Tom's bank, and the bank paid it. Tom wants the bank to recredit his account. Is the bank obligated to do so?

4. Describe similarities between certified checks and cashier's checks. Also discuss how these two types of checks are different from each other.

5. Bryant, an employee of ABC Manufacturing, forged a series of checks on the ABC account at First Bank over a period of two years. When ABC discovered the forged checks, it requested the Bank to recredit its account for the total amount of the forged checks. Can ABC require the bank to recredit the account? Explain the rules governing your answer.

6. Terry buys a car from Harry. Harry misrepresents facts about the car. Terry pays for the car with a check. Terry soon discovers problems with the car and stops payment on the check. If the bank does not honor the stop payment order, is it liable to Terry?

7.	Assume the same facts in the case above, but suppose Harry negotiates the check to Barry, who qualifies as a holder in due course. If the bank does not honor Terry's stop payment order in this case, is the bank liable to Terry?

8.	If the bank in the case above did honor the stop payment order and did not pay on the check to Barry, is Terry still liable for payment to Barry?

9.	Why are there exceptions to the general rule on forgeries with the Imposter Rule and the Fictitious Payee Rule?

10.	Toby forged 150 checks of his employer over a span of two years. Discuss the liability of the drawer and the drawee bank on these 150 checks.

CHAPTER 41

INTRODUCTION TO SECURITY

Outline

I. Credit.

    A. Credit may be defined as a transaction where one party is obligated to pay consideration for the bargain at some future date.

    B. Many transactions are based on unsecured credit.

    C. In other cases, the creditor requires the debtor to convey a security interest on the debtor's property to secure payment.

        1. A surety is a person who is liable for the payment of another's debt. The surety joins with the person who is primarily liable. A guarantor makes a separate promise agreeing to be liable on the happening of a certain event.

        2. A surety can use any defenses against the creditor that the primary debtor has; other defenses include lack of consideration, fraud or duress in inducement of the contract, and breach of contract by the other party.

        3. The creditor is required to disclose material facts affecting risk to the surety.

        Example: <u>Camp v. First Financial Federal Savings and Loan Association</u>: The surety was relieved of his obligation by bank's failure to disclose material facts.

        4. A surety acquires rights of subrogation upon performance of the principal's obligation; if the surety performs the obligation, the surety has the right to reimbursement from the principal.

II. Liens.

    A. Liens on Personal Property.

        1. Under common law, artisans improving property acquire a lien on the property until paid. Many states today recognize these liens by statute.

        2. Possessory liens permit a lien holder to keep possession of the property until paid.

        Example: <u>National Union v. Eland Motors</u>: An automotive repair shop was entitled to a priority garage keeper's lien on vehicles in its possession that it had repaired.

    B. Security Interests in Real Property.

        1. A mortgage is a security interest in real property. Foreclose is the process of terminating rights of the mortgagor in the property.

        2. Other security interests include the deed of trust and land contracts.

        Example: <u>Bennett v. Galindo</u>: Even though they defaulted and were in breaches, the Galindos are entitled to by statutes a six month period to redeem the contract

    C. All states provide for mechanics liens to protect persons who furnish labor or materials to improve real estate.

    Example: <u>Mutual Savings Association v. Res/Com Properties, LLC</u>: The court ruled that mechanic's liens related to work done after the mortgages were filed take priority over those mortgages under state law that allow mechanic's liens to relate back to the earliest mechanic's lien. In this case, the first mechanic's lien took place prior to the filing of the mortgages.

Learning Objectives

1. You should understand the difference between secured and unsecured credit, and the importance of that difference.

2. You should know different ways a creditor can obtain security in personal or real property.

3. You should be familiar with common law and statutory liens protecting artisans or trade people, innkeepers, and common carriers.

4. You should know what a mechanic's or materialman's lien is and how it protects laborers or suppliers of materials to the property.

5. You should understand the risks that attend unsecured credit, as far as creditors are concerned, and should recognize how difficult it is to recover from an unwilling or destitute debtor.

6. You should be aware of how secured credit minimizes the risks of loss in credit transactions.

7. You should be familiar, in the context of surety and guarantor relationships, with what are personal defenses and what are defenses going to the merits, as well as with the significance of distinguishing between the two.

8. You should understand the duties the creditor owes the surety, along with the rights of the surety.

9. You should understand the mortgage relationship, as well as the rights of the parties upon default.

10. You should understand the importance of recording the mortgage.

11. You should be able to compare and contrast the deed of trust and the mortgage, and should understand why a deed of trust might be employed.

12. You should be able to compare and contrast the land contract and the mortgage, as well as the land contract and the deed of trust.

13. You should have an awareness of real estate financing on the internet.

Learning Hints

1. Understanding the nature of a credit transaction is increasingly important for business people. In the event unsecured credit is extended to a debtor, for example, and the debtor fails to pay the debt, the creditor may be unable to recover the debt. For this reason, to minimize credit risk, a creditor can contract for security. In a secured credit situation, if the debtor defaults on the debt, the creditor may be able to foreclose his lien on the real or personal property of the debtor and recover some, if not all, of his loss.

2. There is a difference between a surety and a guarantor, but their rights and liabilities are very similar. A surety joins with the person who is primarily liable in promising to make payment or perform the duty, while a guarantor makes a separate promise agreeing to be liable on the happening of a certain event.

3. The rights and obligations of the surety or guarantor are easy to understand if one remembers that the relationship is basically contractual. Therefore, when the parties materially alter the terms without the surety's consent, one would expect the surety's performance to be excused. This also explains why defenses that go to the merits will excuse performance while the principal's personal defenses will not. Likewise, if the principal and the creditor do anything to increase the surety's risk, the surety's performance should be excused because the contract has been materially altered.

4. Notice that frequently a surety's right of subrogation will make the surety an unsecured creditor of the principal. However, the surety will be a secured creditor if property was also used to secure the original debt or the surety's promise.

5. The greatest weakness of the common law and statutory liens, from the standpoint of the creditor, is that they generally require the creditor to maintain possession of the security. Such a requirement does not necessarily facilitate smooth completion of the vast majority of consumer and commercial transactions that occur today.

6. Remember that foreclosure cannot take place without notice being given to the debtor and to the public before a sale is made. Notice to the debtor is essential in affording the debtor an opportunity to redeem by satisfying the debt. Notice to the public helps ensure that the creditor will receive the highest possible price at the foreclosure sale. The creditor's receiving the highest possible price works in favor of the debtor also because the debtor could still be liable for any deficiency still owed after the foreclosure sale.

7. Recording a mortgage performs the role possession plays in the common law lien context. Third persons would often not be aware of security interests in property and might purchase from the debtor, since possession generally signifies ownership. Thus, in the common law lien situation, the creditor maintains possession in order to avoid the hardships that might arise if an unwitting buyer bought from the debtor. With real property, it is not practical for the creditor to take possession, because doing so would effectively deny the debtor use of the property. The recording statutes were designed to allow prospective buyers and prospective creditors to discover encumbrances on real estate before they purchase it or extend credit in reliance on it.

8. The debtor's right to redeem is his or her last chance to maintain possession of the property securing the debt. In order to redeem and thereby avoid sale of the property, the debtor must pay the debt and any costs or penalties in full.

9. All states have statutes protecting materialmen or mechanics who improve real property. The procedure for obtaining and foreclosing such liens varies from state to state. It is important to note, however, that a valid mechanic's lien may take priority over other lien-holders. No one should purchase real property without making a title search (search of title records) to determine the existence of liens on the property.

10. Even though a land sales contract may not expressly create a security interest in real property, some courts have held that the legal effect of such contracts is to convey equitable title in the property to the purchaser, with the seller retaining a security interest in the property. The practical effect of that holding is to require the seller to foreclose his or her security interest upon default by the purchaser, and to give the buyer rights to redeem the property in certain cases.

True-False

In the blank provided, put "**T**" if the statement is True or "**F**" if the statement is False.

_____ 1. A MasterCard account is an example of a credit account that is unsecured.

_____ 2. A parent who cosigns on a promissory note for a child is an example of an accommodation surety.

_____ 3. A surety can utilize the defense of lack of capacity to contract by the principal.

_____ 4. Al's Garage does $250 of repairs on Amy's car. Amy asks Al to bill her for the repairs and drives away. Al has a lien on the car for the amount of the repairs.

_____ 5. A creditor is not required to disclose any material facts about the risk involved to the surety.

_____ 6. Tony buys a home by assuming a mortgage. In case of a default, the property is liable for the debt and the property can be sold to satisfy the debt.

_____ 7. The owner of mortgaged property ordinarily cannot sell the property without the consent of the mortgagee.

_____ 8. The owner of real estate who sells her property in a land contract maintains title to the property until the buyer pays the full purchase price.

_____ 9. The creditor has a right to a deficiency under strict foreclosure.

_____ 10. A surety may use a breach of warranty defense against a creditor of the principal.

Multiple Choice

Circle the best answer.

1. A common law lien is lost:
    a. If the debt if paid.
    b. If the lien holder gives up possession (unless the debtor regains possession by fraud).
    c. Both a and b are correct.
    d. If the debtor gains possession by fraud.

2. Alice charged a $5,000 wedding dress on her Visa credit card. If she fails to pay the account:
    a. Visa is a secured creditor.
    b. Visa has a common law lien on the dress.
    c. Visa has no lien because this is an unsecured account.
    d. Alice is guilty of violating the state mechanic's lien statute.

3. Which of the following is a possible remedy for an unsecured creditor in the event of default by the debtor?
    a. Repossession of the property.
    b. Lawsuit against the debtor.
    c. Garnishment.
    d. Both b and c.

4. Which of the following defenses could not be used by a surety?
    a. Minority of principal party.
    b. Lack of consideration.
    c. Breach of contract by the dealer.
    d. Breach of warranty by the dealer.

5. Brenda signs a note as surety for Carla. Carla defaults on the instrument and Brenda pays the bank for the amount of the note plus interest. Brenda now as the right to pursue any remedies against Carla that the bank would have had. This is called the:
    a. Right to reimbursement.
    b. Right of contribution.
    c. Right of subrogation.
    d. Right of foreclosure.

6. Alf and Biff were co-sureties of their friend, Chloe, on a certain obligation on which Chloe was the principal. When Chloe defaulted, Biff paid the entire obligation. After having done so, Biff:
    a. Was automatically relieved from any liability for any other obligations on which he was a surety and Chloe was the principal.
    b. Acquired all rights the creditor had against Chloe.
    c. Acquired the right to call upon Alf to reimburse him for Alf's share of the obligation.
    d. Acquired the rights referred to in answers b and c.

7. Ernie and Ethel Ray buy a new home. The Rays go to Friendly Bank and borrow the money to purchase the home. The Rays sign an agreement promising to pay the debt plus interest each month for the next 30 years. This security device is called a:

    a. Land contract.

    b. Mortgage.

    c. Deed of trust.

    d. Possessory lien.

8. Which of the following situations does not create a possessory lien?

    a. Rob takes his car to Ed for repairs. Ed does the work and demands payment.

    b. Stella drops her watch off at Diamond Jewelers for repairs. Diamond does the agreed work on the watch.

    c. Tom goes to Kathy's house and fixes her television set.

    d. John takes Paula's computer to his shop for repairs and does the work.

9. Which real estate security device has a third party who holds legal title to the property so that the security can be more easily liquidated in the event of default?

    a. Deed of trust.

    b. Mortgage.

    c. Land contract.

    d. Mechanic's lien on real estate.

10. Which of the following is not true concerning mortgages?

    a. A mortgage should be properly recorded to protect the mortgagee's rights.

    b. If foreclosed property sells for more than the amount of the debt, the debtor is generally entitled to the surplus.

    c. A purchaser who buys subject to the mortgage is personally liable for any deficiency.

    d. An owner may be able to redeem the property up to six months after foreclosure.

Short Essay

1. Nancy buys a house from Ginger. Nancy will pay Ginger monthly payments and she will also pay the taxes and insurance on the house. Describe this situation. Who has title to the house?

2. Lowes sells replacement windows for Bates' house on credit. The total cost of the windows is $20,000. What rights does Lowes have against Bates?

3. Bart purchased a home for $99,000. He paid $10,000 down and financed the rest through Solvent Savings & Loan, which obtained a mortgage on the property to secure payment of the debt. Because of a Solvent employee's error, Solvent failed to record its mortgage interest. Several years later, Bart sold the house to Seretha, who paid him $118,000. At the time of the sale to Seretha, Bart still owed Solvent $81,000. When Bart failed to make his monthly payment for the second consecutive month, Solvent discovered the sale to Seretha. After learning that Bart had squandered the $118,000 in Las Vegas, Solvent instituted proceedings to gain possession of the property from Seretha. Seretha defended on the ground that she was not aware of the prior security interest and was therefore the sole owner of the home. Discuss the strength, or lack of strength, of Solvent's position.

4. Rhonda is a loan officer at a bank. Darla is a customer who has had some problems paying back a loan. Glen is a surety on Darla's current loan at the bank. Darla approaches Rhonda about an extension of her loan. Discuss the impact of a formal extension of time on Glen's obligation as a surety. What will the impact be on Glen if Rhonda just tells Darla she can have another ten days to make a payment?

5. Greg assumes Todd's mortgage and buys Todd's house. Discuss the impact of an assumption on Todd's potential liability for the debt.

6.   EZ Credit Union is considering making an unsecured loan to Kara. EZ is also considering making a car loan to Brent. Discuss the credit union's recourse on both of these loans in the event of a default. Also discuss the risks involved in each loan and which loan the credit union would like charge the higher interest rate.

7.   Some states use a subrogation rule regarding the payment of contractors for liens owed to subcontractors. Under those rules, if the general contractor is paid, but fails to pay the subcontractors, the property owner has a defense in having paid the contractor, i.e., the subcontractor's remedies are to go against only the general contractor. Most states do not follow this rule. What can you do to assure yourself that the general contractor has paid his/her subcontractors?

CHAPTER 42

SECURITY INTERESTS IN PERSONAL PROPERTY

Outline

I. Security interests in general.

    A. Article 9 of the Uniform Commercial Code governs security interests in personal property or fixtures.

    B. Security interests under the UCC include a broad class of interests.

    C. Obtaining an interest: attachment and perfection

II. Attachment is legal rather than physical. It requires a security agreement, for value, and an underlying debt.

    A. The agreement must be in writing and signed by the debtor.

    Example: In re Shirel: Information contained in a credit application did not meet the requirements for a security agreement.

    B. The agreement may cover future advances, after-acquired property, and proceeds of the collateral.

    C. Waiver of defenses clauses in consumer contracts has been severely limited. Thus, an assignee of the contract will be subject to claims or defenses of the buyer-debtor.

III. Perfecting the interest.

    A. Attachment gives rights to the creditor vis a vis the debtor; perfection protects the creditor against other creditors.

    Example: In re Rainer, In re Hovland, Horowitz v. Green Tree Financial Corp.: Green Tree was not required to file financing statements covering the vehicles in order to prevail against another creditor.

    B. There are three ways to perfect the interest under the UCC: filing public notice, taking possession, or automatic perfection in certain transactions.

    1. A creditor who sells goods to a consumer on credit has a purchase money security interest in those consumer goods, and no filing is required.

    2. If state law requires a certificate of title for motor vehicles, the security interest must be noted on the title.

    3. The retailer who would otherwise hold a perfected security interest by attachment does not have priority over the "BFP" (Bona Fide Purchaser).

IV. Priorities.

    A. Problems arise when different creditors claim a security interest in the same collateral. The UCC establishes rules for determining which interest takes priority.

    B. Basic rule is that the first interest to be perfected takes priority.

    C. There are exceptions--for example, a perfected purchase money security interest in inventory takes priority in some cases.

    Example: In re McAllister: A purchase money security interest has priority over an earlier filed competing security interest if the purchase money security interest is perfected at the time the debtor receives possession of the collateral or within 20 days thereafter.

    D. A buyer in the ordinary course of business takes free from the security interest.

    Example: DBC Capital Fund, Inc. v. Snodgrass: A buyer in the ordinary course of business defeats the priority rule.

E. A retailer of consumer goods does not have priority over a bona fide purchaser unless it files a security interest.

F. Special rules govern the priority of fixtures.

Example: Capital Federal Savings & Loan Ass'n v. Hoger: A furnace and air conditioner installed in a home became fixtures; in dispute between creditor and mortgagee, however, the security interest was limited to the fixtures themselves and did not extend beyond that to an interest in the real property.

V. Default and foreclosure.

A. The secured creditor may, on default, sue on the debt, repossess the collateral and keep it in satisfaction of the debt, or repossess and foreclose on the collateral.

Example: Giles v. First Virginia Credit Services, Inc.: A creditor was not in breach of the peace when repossessing a debtor's automobile from his driveway in the early morning hours.

B. Method of disposal of the collateral must be commercially reasonable. Creditor must comply with Article 9 requirements.

C. The Code sets out the order in which proceeds of sale of collateral are to be distributed.

Learning Objectives

1. You should understand how creditors and suppliers of businesses can obtain security for the credit they extend.

2. You should know the steps that creditors must take to obtain maximum protection against the debtor and other creditors.

3. You should know the relative rights of creditors regarding each other in the event the debtor defaults.

4. You should know the rights of creditors regarding someone who buys from the business in the ordinary course of business.

5. You should remember that the creditor will usually lose her protection as a secured creditor under Article 9 if she does not conform strictly to the procedures established in Article 9.

6. You should understand the meaning and significance of attachment, the purpose of perfection, and the difference between attachment and perfection.

7. You should become familiar with the respective meanings of the terms future advances, after-acquired property, and proceeds, and should understand why they are important to the creditor and the debtor.

8. You should become able to recognize the various classifications of collateral and should know how they differ in their treatment by Article 9.

10. You should become familiar with the ways in which perfection occurs, and should understand not only why some security interests are perfected under one means as opposed to another, but also what the strengths and weaknesses of each method of perfecting are.

11. You should become familiar with the importance of priority, in the context of competing security interests, and should understand the basic priority rule and the exceptions to it.

12. You should know what a buyer in the ordinary course is, and should understand why the buyer in ordinary course concept is significant with regard to secured commercial transactions.

13. You should understand the special procedures that pertain to security interests in fixtures, and should know why fixtures are given special treatment.

14. You should understand the various paths open to the creditor upon default by the debtor, as well as why the creditor might choose one path over another.

15. You should know the various procedures the creditor must follow in order to protect not only his interests, but also the debtor's interests, when the debtor sells collateral after default.

16. You should have an awareness of click-through secured transactions.

Learning Hints

1. In many credit transactions, a creditor will take a security interest or lien in personal property belonging to the debtor. The law covering security interests in person property is contained in Article 9 of the Uniform Commercial Code.

2. There are many different kinds of collateral recognized by Article 9. Two important concepts underlie effectively securing transactions under Article 9: attachment, and perfection. Attachment is required to secure a lien against the debtor; perfection gives the creditor priority over other creditors.

3. The security interest is a matter of concern, initially, to the debtor and the creditor. It is an acknowledgement that the debtor has given the creditor certain rights in the property of the debtor. The security interest is also of concern to third persons, however, as they may wish to buy or extend credit on the same property. Article 9, therefore, serves to help coordinate the rights of all of these potential parties in the property.

4. Attachment is important to the debtor and the creditor. It is an acknowledgement of the debt and the creditor's interest in the collateral. A security agreement generally is in writing; the only other way for attachment to be effective is for the creditor to take possession of the collateral. Sometimes it is not possible for the creditor to take possession (as with accounts receivable, for example) and frequently it is not acceptable to the debtor for the creditor to take possession.

5. The attachment and perfection rules for personal property are generally dependent upon the classification of the collateral. The classification into which the property falls is generally determined by the debtor's intended use at the time the security agreement is drafted. Some courts, however, classify the property on the basis of its actual use.

6. Proceeds are what the debtor has acquired in return for a sale or exchange of the collateral. Proceeds take the form of money most of the time, although proceeds may take the form of other kinds of property. In a sense, the debtor transforms the collateral into money if it is sold for cash, or the debtor transforms the collateral into a car if it is traded for another car. With after-acquired property, however, the debtor has gained something in addition to the original collateral. This gives the creditor extra collateral, whereas with proceeds, only the form of the collateral has changed.

7. Notice that perfection is of significance as between the creditor and third persons who might wish to purchase an interest in the debtor's property. Filing of a financing statement and possession by the creditor are clear ways of informing third persons of the creditor's superior interest in the property. Remember, however, that automatic perfection is allowed for purchase money security interests in consumer goods. Many, if not most, holders of purchase money security interests in consumer goods are sellers who sell their own goods on credit. If these sellers were required to file financing statements on their own goods that were sold on credit, the filing system would be overwhelmed and the cost of credit would likely rise.

8. Note the problems that can arise when the debtor removes the collateral from the state. Because each state has its own filing system, there is no easy way to discover whether property has been secured in another state. A diligent creditor will check the new debtor's prior address to determine if it was an out-of-state address and, after making a loan or credit sale, will attempt to monitor the account to discover an interstate move as quickly as possible. Creditors must be wary when dealing with a debtor new to the state, because a prior creditor who has perfected in the debtor's former state could have a "hidden lien" for four months.

9.	The basic priority rule is "first in time--first in right." This means that the first creditor to perfect generally has the superior security interest. After perfection, all later creditors should have been placed on notice of the prior encumbrance. You may note that it is possible to file a financing statement prior to the actual attachment of the security interest. In this way, a creditor can protect his or her interest while the parties are still negotiating the precise terms of the agreement.

10.	A purchase money security interest arises when a seller/creditor retains a security interest in goods that the buyer/debtor has bought on time. However, a creditor may also possess a purchase money security interest when it loans the debtor money to buy certain goods. If the creditor wishes to have the benefit of a purchase money security interest, the creditor must be certain that the very money it loans is used to buy the goods. Therefore, to protect itself, the creditor loaning purchase money to the debtor may wish to make the loan in the form of a check payable to the seller.

11.	A buyer in the ordinary course of business takes free and clear of an encumbrance on the seller's inventory. The seller's creditor anticipates that sales will be made and expects to be paid with the proceeds of such sales.

12.	An exception to the basic priority rule is given to perfected security interests in fixtures. This poses no real hardship to a mortgagee, because the mortgagee's interest attached to the real property before the addition of the fixtures. It would be a windfall to the mortgagee if he or she also gained superior rights over the fixture.

13.	Artisans' liens are given a special priority because it is not believed that doing so will impose any additional burdens on the prior secured creditors. The artisan has enhanced the value of the goods by making the repairs. In theory, the other secured creditors' liens are improved in the sense that the liens cover property that now has greater value than it did before. Not to give the artisan a special priority would be to give the creditor a windfall and greatly curtail the performance of repairs that could not be paid for immediately with cash.

14.	When the debtor has paid more than 60 percent of the purchase price or debt owed on consumer goods in which the creditor has a security interest, the assumption is that there would be a surplus if the goods were sold at a repossession sale. Therefore, the creditor cannot have a strict foreclosure in such a situation unless the debtor agrees to it in writing after the default. Otherwise, the chances would be great that the creditor could pocket a large surplus whenever the debtor defaulted in such a situation. Imagine, for instance, a creditor's making a strict foreclosure on a relatively new car when the balance of the loan was only a few hundred dollars. When the debtor has paid less than 60 percent of the purchase price or debt owned on consumer goods in which the creditor has a security interest, the chances of such an unconscionable result are lessened greatly. Note, however, that even in this latter case, the debtor can avoid the strict foreclosure by making a proper written objection to the creditor's proposal of a strict foreclosure.

True-False

In the blank provided, put "**T**" if the statement is True or "**F**" if the statement is False.

_____	1.	A security agreement that covers after-acquired property is not enforceable.

_____	2.	Goods held for sale or lease or to be used under contracts of service are called "fixtures."

_____	3.	Bank has a security interest in Anderson's inventory. When Anderson sells inventory, the bank automatically has a security interest in the proceeds of the sale.

_____	4.	Generally, oral security agreements are enforceable.

_____	5.	A security agreement may be drafted to grant a creditor a security interest in after-acquired property of the debtor.

_____ 6. Idaho Furniture Mart sells office furniture to Legal Eagles law offices on credit. Mart can perfect its interest in the furniture by attachment of its security interest.

_____ 7. Even if he or she is actually aware of a prior recorded security interest in inventory, a buyer in the ordinary course will defeat such a security interest when buying from the dealer/debtor.

_____ 8. Credit Union makes a loan to Ivy secured by Yahoo stock owned by Ivy. A good way for the credit union to perfect its interest in the stock is to take possession of the stock certificates.

_____ 9. Bank A and Bank B both have security interests in Lana's furniture. Bank A completed a security agreement covering the furniture on October 3. Bank B completed a security agreement and filed a financial statement on October 10. Bank B's security interest has priority over Bank A's interest because Bank B filed a financing statement and Bank A did not.

_____ 10. The debtor who has defaulted necessarily loses the right to redeem the collateral.

Multiple Choice

Circle the best answer.

1. Commercial Bank perfects a security interest in all present and after-acquired inventory of Ace Sports. Ace now wants to buy a large quantity of inventory from Nike. What can Nike do to have a priority claim over Commercial on the inventory it sells to Ace?

   a. File a financing statement before the goods reach Ace and notify Commercial Bank of its purchase money security interest before it ships the goods to Ace.

   b. File a financing statement before the goods arrive or within 20 days of delivery.

   c. A security agreement is all that is needed for perfection in this case.

   d. File a financing statement before the goods arrive.

2. Mike purchased a new Toyota truck. He financed it through Bank Three. In a state which issues certificates of title for motor vehicles:

   a. The Bank must file a notice of its security interest with the Department of Motor Vehicles of the state.

   b. The Bank must note the security interest on the title.

   c. The Bank may perfect its interest either by (a) or (b) above.

   d. Nothing—the Bank perfects its security interest by attachment in such cases.

3. Security Bank perfects a security interest in the inventory of Quality Motors. Jim Bob buys a new car from Quality. Which of the following is true?

   a. Security Bank still has a security interest in the automobile Jim Bob purchased from Quality Motors.

   b. The bank has a priority claim over Jim Bob's interest in the car.

   c. Security Bank can repossess the car from Jim Bob if Quality Motors defaults on its loan.

   d. Jim Bob is a buyer in the ordinary course of business and takes the car free of Quality Motors' security interest.

4. Article 9 does not recognize which of the following as collateral?

   a. Documents of title.

   b. Chattel paper.

   c. Transcripts of university students who are indebted to the university.

   d. Article 9 recognizes all of the above as collateral.

5. Tara buys furniture on credit for her home from Rhoades. Rhoades obtains Tara's signature on a security agreement. Which of the following is true?

    a. The security agreement give Rhoades a perfected security interest in consumer goods that is superior to any other claims on the furniture.

    b. Rhoades must file a financing statement in order to have a perfected security interest in the furniture.

    c. Rhoades' security interest in the furniture can be defeated if Tara sells the furniture to Jane, who is a bona fide good faith purchaser.

    d. A security agreement alone never can serve as a way to perfect a security interest.

6. Exchange Bank takes and perfects a security interest on all present and after-acquired property of Bob's IGA grocery store. XYZ Co. sells new freezers to Bob's IGA on credit. XYZ files a financing statement. Which of the following is true?

    a. Exchange Bank will have a priority claim over XYZ Co. because they perfected their security interest in Bob's property before XYZ perfected its interest in the freezers.

    b. XYZ has a priority claim to the freezers because it filed a financing statement.

    c. XYZ only needs attachment to perfect its interest in the freezers.

    d. XYZ can have priority claim to the freezers if it did a fixtures filing before the freezers became fixtures or within 20 days after the freezers became fixtures.

7. Of the following statements concerning proceeds, which is/are correct?

    a. If the creditor's security interest is to extend to proceeds, the creditor and debtor must enter into a special security agreement that is separate from the security agreement dealing with the primary collateral.

    b. No proceeds are generated if the debtor transfers collateral to another party in exchange for property other than money.

    c. Under the 1972 amendments to Article 9, proceeds automatically are covered by a security agreement unless the security agreement specifically states to the contrary.

    d. Both b and c.

8. Don finances a new car with a $20,000 loan at Fidelity Bank. After Don has paid back $15,000 he has some financial difficulties and can no longer make payments on the car loan. Which of the following is not true?

    a. Fidelity Bank can repossess the car and just keep it in satisfaction of the debt.

    b. Fidelity Bank can forget the collateral and sue Don for defaulting on the loan.

    c. Repossess the car, sell it for $4,000 and seek a deficiency judgment against Don.

    d. Repossess the car, sell it for $6,500 and refund Don the surplus.

9. Which of the following is not true concerning security agreements?

    a. A security agreement may cover future advances of credit.

    b. A security agreement prefects a security interest in inventory.

    c. A security agreement may cover after-acquired property.

    d. A security agreement automatically covers proceeds from the sale of the collateral.

10. Mindy buys a new car and finances it at City Bank. Which of the following is most likely the best and most practical way for the bank to protect its interest in Mindy's car?

    a. Have its security interest noted on Mindy's title to the car.

    b. File a financing statement.

    c. Execute a security agreement.

    d. Keep the car until receiving final payment from Mindy.

Short Essay

1. Rod is driving down the road when a car comes up on his left and forces him off the road. Rod is past due on car payments to EZ Finance and it is EZ employees who force him off the road and drive his car away. Edna is also past due on car payments to EZ Finance. While Edna is sleeping, EZ employees have her car towed away from her driveway. Discuss the rights of the parties in both of these situations.

2. Hal bought a camera on credit from Bloom's Department Store. The store took a security interest in the camera. Later, Hal took the camera to Sonny's Repair Shop, which repaired the camera for $55.

   Hal failed to pay Sonny and later defaulted on her debt to Bloom's. As between Bloom's and Sonny, who has priority against the camera? Would your answer change if Bloom's had filed a financing statement on the camera? Why or why not.

3. Ned is past due on truck payments to Texas Bank. The bank sends two employees to Waco to repossess the truck. The employees have the truck towed away from Ned's residence and eventually one of the employees drives his truck back to Dallas. The bank employees have lunch in Waco and fill the two vehicles with gas. Ned owes the bank $6,000 on the truck, but the repossession costs, legal fees, and sales fees total $1,000. The bank is able to sell the truck for $6,500. Discuss the rights of the parties in this case. Are the rights of the parties affected if Ned had installed a fancy CD player and wheel covers on the truck? What if Ned had a tool box with work tools in it attached to the bed of the truck?

4. Alaska Furniture Mart sells living room furniture to Jensen on credit. AFM has Jensen sign a security agreement, which describes the collateral. Jensen later goes to Friendly Finance and borrows money using the furniture as collateral. Friendly attempts to file a financing statement. Between AFM and Friendly, who has the greater rights in Jensen's furniture?

5. Suppose in the above case, Jensen bought the furniture but shortly after the purchase, he sold it to his neighbor, Hartley. Who has greater rights to the furniture, AFM or Hartley? What should AFM have done to protect itself in this situation?

6. Bill and Jane are avid art collectors. They usually finance their purchases through a lay-a-way arrangement where the gallery holds the art while they pay for it. No financing statement is filed because the retained possession of the artwork perfects the security interest of the gallery. After having paid off 65 percent of the value of the art, Bill and Jane cannot continue the payments. What are the respective rights of the parties in this artwork?

7. Security Bank loans Hallie a large amount of money to start her business. The bank perfects its security interest in Hallie's property. An after-acquired clause is included in the contract. Later, Hallie wants to purchase a large quantity of merchandise from Standard Co. What could Standard do to protect its security interest in inventory it sells to Hallie?

CHAPTER 43
BANKRUPTCY

Outline

I.   Bankruptcy proceedings.

    A. The Bankruptcy Act covers several different types of proceedings.

    B. Liquidations are called "straight bankruptcies." At the end of the proceedings, the petitioner's debts are discharged.

    C. Other types of proceedings include reorganizations, family farms, and consumer debt adjustments.

II.   Liquidation proceedings (Chapter 7).

    A. Either a voluntary or involuntary petition may be filed. The filing of the petition operates as an automatic stay of various actions against the debtor or his property.

    B. The trustee takes possession of the property and presides over the meeting of creditors.

    C. Certain property is exempt from creditors' claims under state law or federal law.

        Example: In Re Kyllogen: Kyllogen was not entitled to claim the full 10 acres of her homestead on the grounds that it was an agricultural operation.

        A debtor is also permitted to void certain liens against exempt property.

    D. The trustee may recover preferential payments made by the bankrupt person—those payments made within 90 days of filing of the bankruptcy petition are preferential payments. Likewise, a trustee may negate a preferential lien or fraudulent transfer.

        Example: Trujillo v. Grimmett: Transfers of autos and houses may be avoided as fraudulent if they meet the test.

    E. Creditors must file proof of claim. Certain claims have priority over other claims. At the end of the proceedings, the bankrupt's debts are discharged. Some debts, however, are not dischargeable in bankruptcy.

        Example: In re Gerhardt: A debtor was denied discharge of student loans because of hardship because the debtor had the potential to secure better paying employment opportunities.

    F. The law permits a debtor to reaffirm a debt, but the reaffirmation is subject to court review.

    G. Bankruptcy courts may dismiss cases there determine are a substantial abuse of the process.

        Example: In Re Huckfeldt: This case illustrates situation in which the court concluded that a petition in bankruptcy had been filed in bad faith.

III. Chapter 11 reorganizations.

    A. Intended primarily for use by businesses, this proceeding requires the business to file a reorganization plan that is submitted to the creditors for approval.

        Example: In re Made in Detroit, Inc.: A reorganization plan proposed by a debtor was not approved, and the plan submitted by the creditors committee was approved, on the grounds that the debtor's plan was not realistic; it was contingent on exit funding from a third party, and there was little or no chance that the conditions for obtaining it would be met or that it would ever materialize.

    B. Amendments to the law address concerns that some companies were using Chapter 11 to avoid collective bargaining agreements.

IV.   Other provisions of the Bankruptcy Code.

    A. Chapter 12 establishes special rules for relief for family farms

    B. Chapter 13 provides for adjustment of consumer debt for individuals. It is similar to Chapter 11 in that the debtor submits a plan of payment that is submitted to the secured creditors for acceptance.

Example: <u>In the Matter of Kelly</u>: A Chapter 13 reorganization must be proposed in good faith.

Learning Objectives

1. You should understand how the federal Bankruptcy Act provides an organized procedure for dealing with the problems of insolvent debtors.

2. You should know the different kinds of proceedings available to debtors under the Bankruptcy Act.

3. You should understand provisions of the Act that protect creditors against potentially unfair actions by the debtors and other creditors.

4. You should understand the significance of a discharge in bankruptcy, and the requirements for reaffirmation of debt.

5. You should be able to distinguish among liquidations, reorganizations, and consumer debt adjustments.

6. You should understand, with regard to liquidation proceedings, the difference between voluntary and involuntary proceedings, as well as the procedural safeguards that accompany each.

7. You should understand the duties of the trustee in a liquidation proceeding.

8. You should become familiar with the categories of property that are exempted by federal law in a bankruptcy proceeding, and should be aware of the kinds of property that may be exempted by applicable state law.

9. You should be familiar with the priority of claims in a straight bankruptcy, and should understand why it is so important, from the individual creditor's standpoint, to be a secured creditor.

10. You should be able to recognize a preferential payment and a preferential lien, and should know why the preferential payment and preferential lien provisions are in the Bankruptcy Act.

11. You should know and be able to recognize the types of debts that are not dischargeable, and should understand the responsibilities of the debtor for such debts even after a discharge in bankruptcy.

12. You should understand why a debtor may wish to pursue reorganization instead of liquidation, and should be familiar with the administrative procedures that govern reorganization.

13. You should understand why a debtor may wish to secure a consumer debt adjustment, and should become familiar with what the prerequisites for a consumer debt adjustment are.

Learning Hints

1. Bankruptcy law is a matter of federal law, although the exemptions available to a debtor may be determined under state law.

2. The most common kind of individual bankruptcy is the Chapter 7 or "liquidation" proceeding. Under Chapter 7, a debtor is entitled to discharge debts and get a "fresh start."

3. Note that some kinds of debts are not dischargeable in bankruptcy. For example, child support payments and taxes are not dischargeable. Congress recently amended the law to provide that student loans are not exempt in bankruptcy proceedings.

4. Business reorganization plans are filed under Chapter 11. Under this chapter, a business may continue operating (and thus bring in money to pay creditors) while staying legal action against it by creditors. The plan is submitted to a trustee, who submits it to the creditors for their approval.

5. Recognize how the procedures governing an involuntary petition in bankruptcy are designed to protect the debtor from unfair treatment by an over-anxious creditor. If the debtor has many creditors, it will take more than one to start the bankruptcy forces in motion. If the debtor has a few creditors, only one or more creditors with a sizeable amount of unsecured claims cam impose an involuntary petition.

6. You should note the protection accorded the creditors in a bankruptcy proceeding. They select the bankruptcy trustee. This is important, because the trustee will be attempting to challenge the secured claims against the estate and thereby enlarge the pool of property available to the unsecured creditors. When voting among creditors takes place, the creditors' vote is determined both by their absolute numbers and by the amount of claims that each possesses.

7. This chapter should impress upon the student the importance of being a secured creditor. In a bankruptcy proceeding, the secured property is immediately separated from the property available to the general unsecured creditors. (Exempt property is also separated from the pool of unsecured property.) Secured property will only be available to satisfy the claims of unsecured creditors if a surplus exists after the secured creditor is paid (assuming that the "excess" portion of the secured property is not otherwise exempt). Secured creditors, on the other hand, can share in the pool of unsecured property if the secured property is insufficient to satisfy their claims against the debtor.

8. The exemption policy of the new Bankruptcy Act may be somewhat confusing. The list of federal exemptions is available to the debtor unless the debtor's state has prohibited use of the federal exemptions. In some instances, a state may permit the debtor to elect either the federal exemptions or a separate list drafted by the state. Hence, in terms of exemptions, debtors will not be treated the same from state to state.

9. Preferential payments and preferential liens are prohibited by the bankruptcy laws because of their generally unfair impact on the creditors who did not receive the benefit of the preferential treatment. By transferring large amounts of property for little or no consideration within 90 days of bankruptcy, the debtor removes property that might have been used to satisfy the claims of unsecured creditors. Likewise, by giving an unsecured creditor a lien immediately prior to bankruptcy, the debtor ensures that a favored creditor will receive a greater proportionate return than the other unsecured creditors. In such situations, the appearance of impropriety is so great that the transfer or lien is likely to be invalidated, so as to treat the other creditors more fairly.

10. Concern over debtor abuse of the bankruptcy privilege lies at the heart of the Bankruptcy Act's provisions making certain debts nondischargeable and the Act's provisions concerning actions that may prevent a debtor from obtaining a discharge. It would not be sound public policy to allow debtors to discharge any and all debts, regardless of nature or type, or to allow debtors who have been dishonest or have engaged in other reprehensible behavior to obtain the relief bankruptcy may afford.

True-False

In the blank provided, put "**T**" if the statement is True or "**F**" if the statement is False.

_____ 1. Archie has ten creditors. Archie owes First State Bank $5,000 on an unsecured loan. First State could file an involuntary petition to have Archie declared bankrupt.

_____ 2. Lenders will not likely loan customers money secured with used furniture because this is a lien that could be avoided in the event the debtor declares bankruptcy.

_____ 3. Michaels Furnishings files for bankruptcy. Michaels owes Brad, an employee, $3,000 in wages he earned in the last month. Michaels also owes Best Buy $10,000 for computers it purchased. The computers were used to secure the debt. Brad has a priority claim over Best Buy.

_____ 4. Harold owes alimony to his ex-wife Paula. Harold can avoid paying the alimony by filing for bankruptcy.

_____ 5. April files for bankruptcy. April owes Angela $15,000 in unsecured debt. Angela could begin Chapter 13 proceedings against April by filing an involuntary petition.

_____ 6. A farmer may obtain relief under Chapter 12 of the Bankruptcy Act regardless of whether he has regular income.

_____ 7. Secured creditors must file a proof of claim in a bankruptcy proceeding, but unsecured creditors need not do so in order to protect their rights to a distribution of assets.

_____ 8. In order to be able to file a voluntary petition in bankruptcy, the debtor must be insolvent.

_____ 9. In a bankruptcy proceeding, the debtor may be permitted to void certain liens against exempt property if the liens impair his exemptions.

_____ 10. The obligation to repay certain educational loans will not be affected by a discharge in bankruptcy.

Multiple Choice

Circle the best answer.

1. A voluntary petition in straight bankruptcy cannot be filed by:
   a. Municipal corporations.
   b. Railroads.
   c. Insurance corporations.
   d. All of the above.

2. Which of the following statements is not true?
   a. A reaffirmation agreement must be made before discharge in bankruptcy.
   b. A discharge may be barred if the bankrupt person destroyed financial records.
   c. All education loans are discharged in bankruptcy.
   d. Secured creditors are paid before priority claims are paid.

3. Jerry wants to file bankruptcy but is concerned that he will lose the following assets: a car worth $1,000, an heirloom ring worth $300, assorted clothing worth less than $50 per item, and $800 in cash. Under these circumstances:
   a. He will lose all these assets in a Chapter 7 bankruptcy.
   b. He will lose everything but the clothing.
   c. He can keep the clothing and the ring.
   d. All the property falls within legal exemptions and thus he may keep everything listed above.

4. Nine months before Connie filed for bankruptcy, she paid her parents back the $10,000 she owed them. Which of the following statements is most accurate?
   a. The trustee can recover the payment made to the parents because it is preferential.
   b. The payment made to Connie's parents is not preferential because it was not made within 90 days of the filing of the petition.
   c. This is a preferential lien.
   d. This is a fraudulent transfer.

5. Which of the following is true?
   a. Credit Union can continue efforts to collect from Bill on a loan after Bill files a bankruptcy petition.
   b. Sarah owes Bob $3,500 in unsecured debt. Sarah has four other creditors, all of whom are secured. Bob could successfully file an involuntary bankruptcy petition against Sarah.
   c. Debts incurred to pay taxes to the United States are dischargeable in bankruptcy.
   d. A debtor in Chapter 13 bankruptcy may seek a composition of debts.

6. The petitioner in bankruptcy is permitted to exempt in bankruptcy:
   a. Property exempted by state law.
   b. Property exempted by federal law.
   c. Either property exempted under state or federal law, at the petitioner's election.
   d. Both property exempted by state and federal law.

7. Which of the following is not true concerning Chapter 11 bankruptcy?
   a. Chapter 11 is only available to corporations.
   b. The plan must divide the creditors into classes.
   c. A two-thirds majority of creditors in dollar amount and a one-half majority in number in each class must approve the plan.
   d. The bankruptcy court will do careful analysis before approving any reorganization plan that modifies a collective bargaining agreement.

8. Which of the following is not true?
   a. A person who anticipates filing a bankruptcy petition could successfully move money into life insurance policies.
   b. The owner of a bankrupt grocery store could continue to purchase equipment on credit.
   c. A person who anticipates filing a bankruptcy petition could successfully sell a valuable painting to his parents for $5.
   d. Child support is a non-dischargeable debt.

9. Which of the following is not a priority claim in bankruptcy?
   a. Taxes owed to the government.
   b. Unsecured claims for wages up to $4,300 per person earned within 90 days of the filing of the petition.
   c. Secured debt on a car loan at Fidelity Bank.
   d. Contributions up to $4,300 per person made to employee benefit plans.

10. Which of the following is a major purpose of the Bankruptcy Act?
    a. To protect creditors from other creditors of the debtor.
    b. To protect creditors from actions of the debtor.
    c. To protect the debtors from actions of the creditors.
    d. All of the above.

Short Essay

1. John and Marcia filed a joint petition for bankruptcy under Chapter 7. In their state, they were entitled to exempt $7500 each for real property and $5000 each for personal property. They listed their assets as follows:

   Home valued at $70,000. (Property encumbered by a mortgage of $50,000.) Personal property, including automobile, furniture, and $500 in bank account valued at $12,000.

   They listed debts as follows: $100,000 to the Valley Hospital; $50,000 in various credit card debts; $25,000 to Marcia's father Bill, and $15,000 in property taxes on the residence. Only the mortgage debt to the bank is secured. Which of these debts are dischargeable? What assets are available for distribution to the creditors? Discuss.

2. School Employees Credit Union has a policy of not loaning money secured by used furniture and appliances. Discuss why the credit union has such a policy.

3. School Employees Credit Union made a loan to Fran that is secured by Fran's jewelry. The credit union took possession of the jewelry. Fran defaults on the loan and files for bankruptcy. Can Fran void this lien?

4. Smith files for bankruptcy. Six months before filing the petition, Smith paid his mother $5,000 to pay off a loan. Smith also sold a late model car to his father for $10 three months prior to filing the petition. A month before filing the petition, Smith bought furniture on credit from Ethan Allen. Three weeks before filing the petition, Smith bought a fur coat for his wife for $5,000 on credit at Alaskan Furs. Discuss the rights of the parties in these situations.

5. A number of high profile corporations have recently filed for Chapter 11 bankruptcy reorganization. Any number of economic factors can be blamed, such as the burst of the dot.com bubble and deregulation of the energy markets. Many find these bankruptcies disturbing because of the high dollar bonuses, stock options, and executive pay packages given to key executives just before the filing for bankruptcy. Can these payments be brought back into the bankrupt's estate?

6. Why would a debtor possibly prefer to file for Chapter 13 bankruptcy instead of Chapter 7? Why would a creditor perhaps prefer this as well?

CHAPTER 44
THE ANTITRUST LAWS

Outline

I. The Sherman Act.

    A. The Sherman Act prohibits contracts in restraint of trade and monopolization.

        Example: <u>F. Hoffman-Laroche, Ltd. v. Empagran S.A.</u>: The court dismissed this antitrust lawsuit, concluding that it lacked subject matter jurisdiction. U.S. antitrust laws do not reach overseas activities unless they adversely affect domestic commerce, imports to the United States, or exporting activities by U.S. businesses. This lawsuit arose out of foreign injury.

    B. Private plaintiffs may be entitled to treble damages under the act.

    C. Section I of the Act prohibits contracts in restraint of trade.

        1. One problem is determining whether there was an agreement--that is whether there was "joint action" rather than "unilateral action."

          Example: <u>Blomkest Fertilizer v. Potash Corporation of Saskatchewan</u>: The court dismissed the claim as a matter of law because there was no proof of joint action.

        2. In finding joint action, courts determine whether the action was *per se* or a *rule of reason* violation.

          Example: <u>State Oil Company v. Khan</u>: State Oil's restraint of trade was not unreasonable.

          Example: <u>Continental Airlines Inc. v. United Air Lines, Inc.</u>: The court should not grant Continental a summary judgment under a "quick look" analysis.

        3. Price-fixing is prohibited by Section I of the Act.

        4. Rule of reason trials involves complex attempts by the courts to balance anticompetitive effects of the defendants' acts against competitive justifications for their behavior.

        5. Joint ventures and strategic alliances are protected under the National Cooperative Research Act.

    D. Section 2 of the Act.

        1. The government or plaintiff must show not only that the defendant has monopoly power, but also intent to monopolize.

          Example: <u>Morris Communications v. PGA Tour, Inc.</u>: The court ruled that the PGA did not violate Section 2 of the Sherman Act by restricting the resale of its real time golf scores because there was no valid business justification for not sharing its product with rivals, even if the PGA had monopoly power.

        2. Joint action is <u>not</u> necessary to show violation of this section.

        3. In order to determine monopolization (70% or more of the relevant market), courts must determine geographic and product market.

II. The Clayton Act.

    A. Supplements the Sherman Act by preventing monopolies. There is no criminal liability, but treble damages are available.

    B. Section 3 addresses anticompetitive behavior: tie-in contracts, exclusive dealing contracts, and requirements contracts involving commodities.

        1. Exclusive dealing and requirements contracts require courts to look at percentage share of relevant market foreclosed to competition.

C. Section 7 addresses horizontal, vertical, and conglomerate mergers.

III. The Robinson-Patman Act prohibits discrimination in price between different purchasers.

A. Defenses include sellers who can cost-justify its discriminatory prices, changing conditions, and meeting competitive demands in good faith.

Example: <u>Hoover Color Corp. v. Bayer Corp.</u>: Bayer's motive of meeting general competition in the marketplace was not sufficient to trigger the meeting competition defense.

IV. Limits of Anti-Trust

A. The Parker Doctrine (State action exemption) exempts actions of state officials under authority of state law and actions of private firms or individuals under state official supervision.

B. The Noeer Doctrine permits joint lobbying by business.

Example: <u>A.D. Bedell Wholesale Co. v. Philip Morris Inc.</u>: The major tobacco companies are immune from antitrust prosecution under the Noerr doctrine.

C. International limitations include the sovereign immunity doctrine, act of state doctrine, and sovereign compulsion defense.

D. Substantive coverage of the European Community Competition Law is similar to that of the U.S. antitrust laws.

Learning Objectives

1. You should understand the kinds of behavior that the antitrust laws prohibit, and the harmful consequences flowing from the anti-trust regulatory scheme.

2. You should be familiar with the defenses that businesses may raise to protect them from antitrust liability.

3. You should understand international aspects of anti-trust legislation, including defenses and the recently enacted European Community Competition Law.

4. You should understand the ongoing debate between the Chicago School advocates and those who advocate traditional antitrust policy, and should become familiar with the basic tenets of each of the two views concerning the direction antitrust law should take.

5. You should know and understand the basic prerequisites to liability under Section 1 of the Sherman Act, and should remain conscious of the necessity of joint action in order for there to have been a violation of such section.

6. You should become familiar with the alleged violations of Sherman Act Section 1 that will be considered per se violations, as well as with the alleged violations that will be considered under a rule of reason analysis.

7. You should be able to distinguish the proscriptions of Section 2 of the Sherman Act from those of Section 1, and should understand the test used by the courts in determining whether Section 2 has been violated.

8. You should understand how the Clayton Act is designed to remedy some of the perceived shortcomings of the Sherman Act, as well as what the procedural differences between the two acts are.

9. You should become familiar with the kinds of activities reached by Section 3 of the Clayton Act, and should become able to compare the Clayton Act's treatment of such activities to the way they would be handled under Section 1 of the Sherman Act.

10. You should know the various types of mergers and how Section 7 of the Clayton Act deals with them.

11. You should understand the operation of the Robinson-Patman Act, along with understanding the three levels of price discrimination and the defenses to a price discrimination charge.

12. You should become aware of the various exceptions to the antitrust laws and the reasons that support each of the exemptions.

Learning Hints

1. Public outcries for legislation designed to preserve competitive market structures and to prevent accumulation of economic power in the hands of a few resulted in the passage of the Sherman Act in 1890, later supplemented by the Clayton and Robinson-Patman Acts.

2. The Sherman Act makes contracts in restraint of trade and monopolization illegal and provides criminal penalties and civil damages for violations. The Clayton Act supplements the Sherman Act by prohibiting certain practices that monopolists had used to gain monopoly power. The Robinson-Patman Act prohibits price discrimination between different purchasers of commodities of like grade and quality.

3. The Chicago School of economics is a major force in current antitrust law. This approach gives little regard to the desirability of any antitrust provisions other than Sections 1 and 2 of the Sherman Act. Further, within Section 1, it would greatly expand the vitality of rule of reason analysis, considering it applicable for all but horizontal restraints.

4. When an activity is *per se* unlawful, the courts will not allow the defendant to offer any excuse or economic justification for the restraint. It automatically will be prohibited. Horizontal activities nearly always fall into this category because the courts can think of no reason for their use other than to limit competition. Vertical restraints, on the other hand, may have effects that actually increase competition at the interbrand level despite their limitation of competition at the intrabrand (dealer) level. If interbrand competition is enhanced by the intrabrand restraint, the courts are likely to allow the activity. You should read carefully the Sylvania decision, which appears in the text, in order to understand this discussion.

5. Oligopolies are largely beyond the reach of the Sherman Act. They never have to actually meet in order to engage in parallel behavior. Most of them are so large that they can regularly determine what the others are doing by following the newspapers. When a major steel producer raises prices, it is national news. If the other companies do not follow suit, it can roll back the price. This parallel behavior is also beyond the reach of Section 2 of the Sherman Act, because no one of the companies possesses monopoly power. Attempts to create antitrust violations for conscious parallelism have not been successful.

6. The inquiry into geographic scope and product line that is required by Section 2 of the Sherman Act is necessary to determine whether the defendant possesses monopoly power. If a seller has this power, the buyer will have no choice but to pay the seller's price or do without the product. Therefore, analysis is necessary in order to determine the seller's control of the product and all its substitutes in the area where the buyer could be expected to go in search of an alternate supplier.

7. Horizontal mergers are more likely to be proscribed than are vertical mergers, because invariably the former tend to limit competition by reducing the number of competitors. Vertical mergers, on the other hand, following the logic of Sylvania, may well enhance competition, because it may be less costly to produce and market a product through a single entity than it is for producers to sell the product to independent dealers who, in turn, sell it to the consumers.

8. Some observers have criticized the Robinson-Patman Act as being contrary to the spirit of antitrust, because (in their view) the act merely protects small competitors rather than truly furthering competition. Note how the defense of meeting the low bid of a competitor in order to retain a current customer may tend to stabilize prices rather than lower them.

9. The Parker doctrine allows the states to exempt certain activities from the federal antitrust laws if the state intends to replace competition with regulation and if the state actually regulates the activity. The Noerr doctrine exempts lobbying efforts, even though they may have an anticompetitive intent or result. Combined, the two allow special interests to shield themselves from the rigors of competition by resorting to the regulatory processes of the state governments.

True-False

In the blank provided, put "**T**" if the statement is True or "**F**" if the statement is False.

_____ 1. The Sherman Act provides for both civil and criminal penalties for violation of the provisions of the Act.

_____ 2. Indirect purchasers have a standing to sue due to a defendant seller's claimed antitrust violations.

_____ 3. A manufacturer seller who consigns goods to dealers, and who fixes the prices of those goods, is in violation of Section 1 of the Sherman Act.

_____ 4. Unlike the Sherman Act, the Clayton Act contains no criminal penalties for violation of its provisions.

_____ 5. Under the Sherman Act, courts do not have the power to order companies to divest themselves of the stock or assets of other companies.

_____ 6. Competitors who attempt to control market prices of their goods are engaging in horizontal price-fixing, which is illegal *per se* under Section 1 of the Sherman Act.

_____ 7. The quick-look form of *rule of reason* focuses on pro-competitive justifications of the restraint of trade.

_____ 8. In a case arising under Section 2 of the Sherman Act, the courts look to see how the defendant acquired monopoly power.

_____ 9. Joint action is a requirement for violations of Section 2 of the Sherman Act.

_____ 10. The Robinson-Patman Act, like the Clayton Act, only requires that there be a probable anticompetitive effect in order for there to be a violation.

Multiple Choice

Circle the best answer.

1. Which of the following statements is true?

   a. Under FISA, commercial activities of foreign sovereigns are exempt from antitrust liability because of the sovereign immunity doctrine.

   b. Professional licensing requirements that have non-competitive effects are not allowed under the Parker Doctrine.

   c. The Noerr Doctrine allows lobbying of government officials even thought the effects may be anti-competitive.

   d. Under the act of state doctrine, a U.S. court can legally adjudicate a politically sensitive dispute that would require the court to determine the legality of a sovereign act of a sovereign nation.

2. Which of the following statements is not true regarding the Robinson-Patman Act?

   a. The Robinson-Patman Act requires only that price discrimination have a probably anticompetitive effect.

   b. A good defense under Section 2(a) of the act is for the seller to show that the difference in price results from lower production costs.

   c. A seller is not in violation of Section 2(a) if she lowers her price of goods to meet a competitor's offer to the buyer.

   d. Under Section 2(d) of the act, sellers can generally discriminate in the services they provide to competing customers.

3. Which of the following statements concerning the Clayton Act is not true?

   a. The purpose of the act was to nip monopolies in the bud.

   b. A party who is harmed resulting from an exclusive dealing contract of services may bring action under Section 3 of the act.

   c. Section 3 of the act does not apply to true consignment contracts.

   d. Section 3 of the act applies to the sale or lease of commodities.

4. Which of the following statements concerning the Clayton Act is not true?

   a. Under Section 7 of the Clayton Act, the Supreme Court will look at whether a contested merger will have a negative impact on competition.

   b. Proposed mergers of a certain size that impact U.S. commerce must be reported to the Federal Trade Commission and to the Department of Justice.

   c. Conglomerate mergers that create potential for reciprocal dealing are covered under Section 7 of the act.

   d. All of the above.

5. Schlemiel Co. manufactures fertilizer spreaders. It has entered into distribution agreements with various retail dealers of Schlemiel spreaders. Under these agreements, each dealer has its own sales territory. Each dealer has agreed (with Schlemiel) that he will stay within his sales territory and will respect the sales territories of the other Schlemiel dealers. If a proper plaintiff brings a civil suit against Schlemiel on the theory that these agreements violated Section 1 of the Sherman Act:

   a. The court will give the agreements rule of reason treatment, meaning that Schlemiel will not necessarily be held to have violated Section 1.

   b. Proof that the agreements existed will be enough to establish liability on Schlemiel's part, because of the per se treatment given to agreements of this nature.

   c. Schlemiel may be forced to pay a fine of as much as $1 million to the government.

   d. Both b and c are accurate.

6. Recent decisions by the courts have expanded rule of reason analysis to include:

   a. Horizontal price restraints.

   b. Vertical non-price restraints.

   c. Unilateral refusals to deal.

   d. None of the above.

7. Which of the following situations would not be a *per se* violation under Section 1 of the Sherman Act?

   a. Distributor D persuades manufacturer M to refuse to do business with D's competitor, Distributor E.

   b. Competing firms X, Y, and Z come up with a plan that divides the country into exclusive territories for each of the three businesses.

   c. Manufacturer M decides it will only sell its products through distributor D.

   d. Competitors A, B, and C agree on the prices of their products.

8. Which of the following situations would least likely be analyzed under the *rule of reason*?

   a. Licensing arrangements.

   b. Joint ventures involving research and development of products.

   c. A manufacturer requires a dealer to refuse to sell to customers outside their assigned territory.

   d. An agreement between a manufacturer and a dealer that sets the prices of the manufacturer's products.

9. Which of the following factors would be considered under Section 2 of the Sherman Act in determining whether monopoly power exists?

    a. The relevant product market.

    b. A firm controls 70% or more of the relevant market.

    c. The geographic market.

    d. All of the above.

10. Marginal Co. and Average, Inc. were competitors in the retail sale of televisions. They set the prices of their televisions that within a range that included both an agreed minimum price and an agreed maximum price. Both parties abided by the agreement. Which of the following statements is/are accurate?

    a. Marginal and Average committed a per se violation of Section 1 of the Sherman Act.

    b. Only that part of the parties' agreement concerning minimum prices was a per se violation of Section 1 of the Sherman Act.

    c. The portion of the parties' agreement that fixed maximum prices did not violate Section 1 of the Sherman Act because consumers are benefited by agreements on maximum prices.

    d. Both b and c.

Short Essay

1. Recent investigative news programs have claimed that Wal-Mart frequently tells suppliers of its merchandise what price they can sell their products for in Wal-Mart stores. Discuss this situation. Do you think Wal-Mart is in violation of any of the antitrust laws?

2. Swineco, Inc. supplies pickled pigs' feet (in jars) to numerous grocery stores across the country. The normal price is $2.19 per jar. In some circumstances, however, Swineco will give a 20 percent discount to stores that are able to sell in excess of 100 cans per month as an inducement to push the product during times of economic uncertainty. Discuss the antitrust aspects of Swineco's actions.

3. GM has a contract with Heaters R Us to provide heater core units for all of its vehicles. Is this contract a violation of the Clayton Act?

4. ABC Co. is the largest producer of black tea and controls over 50 percent of that market. XYZ Co. is the largest producer of herb teas and controls over 50 percent of that market. These two tea companies decide to merge because of the synergies that will come from the two of them bringing their respective expertise to a combined company. NOM Co. is a smaller tea company that produces both black and herb teas, and it objects to that merger. What would be its best strategy for blocking the merger?

5. Perry starts a franchised law firm called Legal Eagles. His idea is to have law offices across the country that will provide legal services to clients at fixed prices. Is this kind of an arrangement in violation of Section 3 of the Clayton Act?

6. Most new automobiles on dealer lots have stickers with the manufacturer's suggested retail price. Is this a violation of the antitrust laws?

CHAPTER 45
CONSUMER PROTECTION LAWS

Outline

I.   The Federal Trade Act is the grandfather of consumer protection legislation.

    A. The FTC (Federal Trade Commission) has power to establish rules and enforce consumer protection laws under this Act.

       Example: <u>Federal Trade Commission v. Zuccarini</u>: The court ruled that Zuccarini was improperly redirecting customers from their intended destinations on the internet to his Web sites.

    B. Consumer Credit Laws: The Truth in Lending Act protects consumers by requiring lenders to advise them of important terms of their credit transactions.

       Example: <u>Roberts v. Fleet Bank</u>: The court found that the bank was in violation of the Truth-in-Lending Act because its introductory letters contained offers that were confusing to consumers.

    C. Fair Credit Reporting Act ensures that information about a person's credit background is accurate and current.

       Example: <u>TRW Inc. v. Andrews</u>: The two year statute of limitations period is strictly construed and does not begin when the consumer discovers the problem. This case emphasizes the importance of checking one's credit report regularly.

    D. Consumer Leasing Act requires the creditor to disclose the costs of leasing goods.

    E. Fair Credit Billing Act provides protections for users of credit cards.

    F. Equal Credit Opportunity Act prohibits discrimination in credit transactions.

    G. Fair Debt Collection Practices Act regulates debt collection practices.

       Example: <u>Chuway v. National Action Financial Services, Inc.</u>: The court found that a collection letter sent by an agency was in violation of the Fair Debt Collection Practices Act because it did not clearly state the amount of the debt that the collector was trying to collect.

    H. The FTC holder in due course rule: This rule preserves a consumer's claims and defenses against a holder in due course.

II.   Consumer Product Safety

    A. The Consumer Product Safety Commission has authority to promote product safety in consumer products under the Consumer Product Safety Act.

    B. A majority of states have now passed "lemon laws" designed to protect consumers from defects in motor vehicles.

       Example: <u>Cannon v. Newmar Corp.</u>: The Cannons were entitled to summary judgment because Newmar violated New York's Lemon Law because he failed to correct several defects in the automobile during the appropriate timeframe.

Learning Objectives

1.   As society has changed, so has the law has changed. In the past, the law reflected the position of *caveat emptor* (let the buyer beware) because the purchaser and seller were more often than not in an equal bargaining position with respect to goods and could more freely negotiate the terms of their contracts. Today, the law is more protective of the consumer/purchaser. You should be familiar with important federal legislation designed to protect consumer interests that reflect this change in the law.

2. Just as Congress has passed several laws protecting consumers, so many states have adopted consumer protection legislation. You should be familiar with some examples of such legislation—for example, state "lemon laws."

3. You should be familiar with the broad reach of the Federal Trade Commission Act, as well as with the numerous functions served by the Federal Trade Commission.

4. You should understand the purposes and provisions of the Truth-in-Lending Act, and should know how its provisions implement the purposes.

5. You should understand, with regard to the Fair Credit Reporting Act, the aims of the Act, along with the rights of a consumer who contests information in a credit report and the limitations the Act imposes on credit reporting agencies.

6. You should become familiar with the rights of the consumer under the Fair Credit Billing Act and with the procedures established by the Act for instances in which the consumer disputes the accuracy of a billing statement.

7. You should know the classes of persons protected by the Equal Credit Opportunity Act, and should understand when and why the law will sometimes allow a creditor to ask for the applicant's marital status.

8. You should become aware of the protections provided to debtors by the Fair Debt Collection Practices Act.

9. You should understand the rights and responsibilities of the debtor, the seller, and the holder in due course in situations to which the FTC holder in due course rule applies.

10. You should become familiar with the essential provisions of the Consumer Product Safety Act and should know the functions served by the Consumer Product Safety Commission.

Learning Hints

1. The Federal Trade Commission Act established the Federal Trade Commission (FTC) in 1914 that has authority to adopt rules and enforce federal consumer protection laws and regulations discussed in this chapter. Some have suggested that the importance and influence of the FTC has diminished in the last decade during the administrations of Reagan and Bush.

2. In order to better understand the powers and authority of the Federal Trade Commission, you may wish to review the portion of Chapter 46 that discusses the FTC.

3. The Truth in Lending Act (TILA) requires disclosure of all of the terms of credit transactions at or before the time the credit contract is signed.

4. You should note the correct application of the three-day "cooling off" period provided by the Truth-in-Lending Act. Most persons mistakenly believe that this right of rescission has a broader application than it actually has. Note that it applies only when the creditor, as part of the credit transaction, secures a lien on the debtor's home (other than a first mortgage to finance the purchase or construction of the home).

5. The provisions of the Equal Credit Opportunity Act closely mirror the provisions and underlying assumptions of the anti-discrimination legislation that exists in the employment area. These laws are designed to prevent creditors and employers from rejecting certain applicants simply because they are members of a certain class concerning which the creditors or employers have generalized preconceived notions. Instead, the laws seek to force such decision-makers to examine the qualifications of each person individually, erasing the stereotypical assumptions that have developed over time.

6. Remember that the Fair Credit Reporting Act's provisions apply only in the consumer context, and do not apply in a situation involving an applicant's request for commercial credit or commercial insurance. Similarly, the FTC holder in due course rule applies only in the consumer credit setting, and not in the commercial credit context.

7. The FTC Holder in Due Course Rule is an important protection for consumers because it preserves their right to use claims and defenses against a holder in due course. Because credit contracts are often sold to third parties, without this rule the consumer would frequently be unable to assert a defense such as breach of warranty against the holder of the paper.

8. Laws of the sort discussed in this chapter tend to be restricted to the consumer setting because lawmakers often regard consumers as more vulnerable and more subject to being taken advantage of by creditors than are seekers of commercial credit. Debtors and potential debtors in the commercial arena are likely to have more sophistication and experience in the securing of credit, making them better able (at least in theory) to protect themselves.

True-False

In the blank provided, put "**T**" if the statement is True or "**F**" if the statement is False.

1. The Truth-in-Lending Act requires lenders to disclose the interest rate as an annual percentage rate.

2. The Truth-in-Lending Act applies to credit advertising.

3. Under the FTC holder in due course rule, a consumer is permitted to assert contract defenses against a holder in due course.

4. Carla receives her credit card statement in the mail and she is sure that one of the charges shown is in error. Carla should contact the creditor in writing about the error within 60 days of the time the statement was mailed.

5. The Federal Trade Commission Act was the first consumer protection legislation passed in this century.

6. Tim and Marci filed for bankruptcy this year. The credit bureau can report this information for seven years.

7. Bill and Beverly are a married couple. Both Bill and Beverly work. Beverly applies for a credit card in her own name. The creditor can require that the card must be issued in Bill's name.

8. Under the Equal Credit Opportunity Act, the creditor must approve or reject a credit applicant within 30 days after the application is submitted.

9. Hal is a collector for Farmer's Bank. The Fair Debt Collection Practices Act covers what Hal can legally do in collecting on past due loans.

10. The right of rescission contained in the Truth-in-Lending Act applies to transactions in which the creditor supplying financing for the purchase or construction of a home acquires a first mortgage on the home.

Multiple Choice

Circle the best answer.

1. Arnold bought a car from Honest Motors. Arnold financed the car through the dealer. Honest Motors sells the note to 1st Bank. The note contains the FTC statement. Honest Motors lied to Arnold about the mileage on the car. Arnold refuses to pay 1st Bank on the note. Which of the following statements is true?

    a. Arnold must pay 1st Bank because it is a holder in due course.

    b. Arnold can hold the defense of fraud against 1st Bank and refuse to pay them.

    c. Arnold is protected under the Truth-in-Lending Act.

    d. Arnold is protected under the Fair Debt Collection Practices Act.

2. The Wilsons apply for a credit card from Dears. Dears turns them down and tells the Wilsons that the reason for the rejection is a bad credit report. Which of the following laws give the Wilsons the right to prove that the information contained in their credit file is wrong and the opportunity to have this wrong information deleted from their credit file?

    a. The Fair Credit Reporting Act.

    b. The Equal Credit Opportunity Act.

    c. The Fair Debt Collections Practices Act.

    d. The Truth-in-Lending Act.

3. Which of the following is covered under the Fair and Accurate Credit Transactions Act of 2003?

    a. Merchants must delete all but the last five digits of a customer's credit card number on store receipts.

    b. Consumers may receive one free copy of their credit report per year.

    c. The law creates a national fraud detection system that tracks identity theft earlier.

    d. All of the above.

4. Which of the following situations is covered under the Equal Credit Opportunity Act?

    a. The credit history on a mortgage loan made to Ken and Kendra Kendall must be reported in both names.

    b. Information about Ken and Kendra's vacation loan can be reported for seven years.

    c. The rate on Ken and Kendra's mortgage must be expressed as an annual percentage rate.

    d. Ken and Kendra have 60 days to report errors on their credit card statements.

5. Leasing of goods:

    a. Is not governed by any federal consumer protection laws.

    b. Is governed by the Consumer Leasing Act.

    c. Is governed by the Truth in Lending Act.

    d. Is governed by both (b) and (c).

6. Bobby is bothered and befuddled when he learns that he mistakenly left his credit card at Bed, Bath and Beyond. Brett found Bobby's card and bought $2,000 in merchandise with it. Bobby's maximum liability on the card is $50 under what law?

    a. Fair Credit Reporting Act.

    b. Fair Credit Billing Act.

    c. Truth-in-Lending Act.

    d. Equal Credit Opportunity Act.

7. The Federal Trade Commission Act gives the FTC authority to:
   a. Decide whether specific sales practices are unfair.
   b. Establish rules governing industry conduct.
   c. Require corrective advertisements to offset the impact of deceptive advertisements.
   d. Do all of the above.

8. Under the terms of the Consumer Leasing Act:
   a. The lease agreement must define the consumer's liability at the end of the lease term.
   b. The creditor must disclose the aggregate costs of the lease for all consumer leases, regardless of the duration of the lease.
   c. The creditor must disclose the aggregate costs of the lease for all consumer leases, regardless of the dollar amount of the obligation.
   d. All of the above are true.

9. Marge is furious that sales people call her during the dinner hour in efforts to sell everything from magazines to aluminum siding. What law gives Marge the ability to place her phone number on a national do-not-call registry?
   a. FTC Holder in Due Course Rule.
   b. Gramm-Leach Bliley Act.
   c. Telemarketing and Consumer Fraud and Abuse Prevention Act.
   d. Consumer Product Safety Act.

10. Even works for a collection agency. Which of the following collection practices used by Eve is acceptable under the Fair Debt Collection Practices Act?
    a. Eve loves to call debtors at work.
    b. Eve finds that she is more successful at collecting on debts when she yells profanities at debtors on the phone.
    c. Eve calls relatives of debtors in an effort to collect on debts.
    d. Eve calls Bob about a debt at 1:00 a.m., shortly after Bob arrives home from the night shift at work.

Short Essay

1. Theresa buys a new car from a dealer. Even though the car is new, the engine has serious problems. Within a year of purchasing the car, Theresa has taken it to the dealer four times to be fixed, but the dealer cannot seem to fix the problem. Assuming Theresa lives in a state with a lemon law that allows four attempts to fix defects in cars, what can she now do?

2. Roy is a 65-year-old teacher who plans to retire in two years. Roy already receives retirement benefits from the military and he will receive a pension from his school also. Roy decides to buy a home in Arizona. Can a lender refuse to make Roy a 30-year mortgage because of his age and the fact that he will retire soon?

3. Joan went to her dentist for some major work on her teeth. The dentist hurt Joan and did an overall lousy job on her teeth. Joan refuses to pay the $200 fee. The dentist reports Joan as non-pay to the credit bureau. What could Joan do?

4. The Adams family obtains a home equity loan in order to buy siding for their home. What rights do the Adams family have under the Truth-in-Lending Act?

5. Reckless Toy Co. came out with a new product, which is a toy shaped like a small metal-tipped spear. The idea is to toss this projectile into a ring set at the other side of the yard. The toy is market to children aged 6-12. A number of children have been severally injured from being "speared" by this toy. What can the Consumer Product Safety Commission do in this case?

6. Telemarketing has caused widespread anger among consumers throughout the United States. It is estimated that over 16 million such calls are made each night. The use of random dial codes has allowed these calls to go through even if the consumer has an unlisted number. The states are seeking to respond to consumer complaints. What are some typical measures being taken by the states (in addition to the Federal Telemarketing and Consumer Fraud Abuse Prevention Act)?

7. Shirley receives her credit card statement and she knows that some of the information is incorrect. Describe the process of disputing bills under the Fair Credit Billing Act.

CHAPTER 46
ENVIRONMENTAL REGULATION

Outline

I. Historically, environmental protection issues were addressed through common law nuisance law.

II. The Environmental Protection Agency (EPA).

    A. Created in 1970 with responsibilities for administering provisions of various federal environmental laws.

    B. The National Environmental Policy Act requires an environmental impact statement be prepared for every major federal action significantly affecting the quality of the environment.

III. Air pollution.

    A. The Clean Air Act of 1963, amended in 1965 and 1967, and comprehensive legislation passed in 1970, amended in 1977 and 1990, is the basis for federal regulation of air pollution.

        1. The EPA sets national ambient air quality standards: (1) primary standards and (2) secondary standards.

        2. Each region of the country is required to adopt an implementation plan (SIP).

        3. Specific provisions were added in 1990 to address acid rain, and to add regulations for emission of toxic air pollutants.

        4. The Clean Air Act also requires EPA to regulate the emission of toxic air pollutants.

            Example: United States v. Ohio Edison Company: The court found that construction projects at Ohio Edison constituted "modifications" that would subject the plant to preconstruction review and permitting requirements and more stringent pollution control standards under the Clean Air Act.

    B. New stationary sources must install the best available technology (BAT) under the Act; the 1990 amendments also expanded the permit system for all sources.

    C. The Act also mandates air pollution controls on transportation sources such as automobiles.

    D. Other issues include international pollution and indoor air pollution.

    E. The Nuclear Regulatory Commission generally addresses radiation control issues.

IV. Water pollution.

    A. Amendments to the Federal Water Pollution Control Act, especially the 1972 amendments known as the Clean Water Act, comprise the federal legislative scheme for addressing problems of water pollution.

    B. The law set water quality standards and requires dischargers to obtain permits; Any citizen or group of citizens with adversely affected interests may bring a court action to enforce provisions under the CWA.

        Example: United States v. Hopkins: A knowing violation of the CWA occurs when the actor intentionally acts without knowing the precise legal prescription.

    C. The Act also protects wetlands.

        Example: Bersani v. U.S. Environmental Protection Agency: A developer was not permitted to drain and fill a wetland in order to build a shopping center.

    D. The Marine Protection, Research, and Sanctuaries Act regulates the dumping of materials into ocean waters.

    E. The Safe Drinking Water Act protects the quality of drinking water.

V. Waste disposal.

    A. The Resource Conservation and Recovery Act (RCRA) governs the generation, treatment, storage, and disposal of hazardous waste "from cradle to grave," and specifically includes underground storage tanks. The Act also provides for civil and criminal penalties.

       Example: United States v. Dean: The employee of a company that disposed of hazardous waste without a RCRA permit was held criminally liable.

    B. The U.S. Supreme Court has struck down states' attempts to prohibit the importation of solid waste originating outside the state.

       Example: Fort Gratiot Sanitary Landfill, Inc. v. Michigan Department of Natural Resources: Michigan waste import restrictions held unconstitutional because it discriminated against interstate commerce.

    C. The Comprehensive Environmental Response Compensation and Liability Act (CERCLA or Superfund) establishes a scheme for cleaning up hazardous wastes sites throughout the nation. The 1986 amendments to Superfund (SARA) also include "community right to know" provisions.

       Example: United States v. Lombardi Realty: A purchaser of land that was contaminated and was to be cleaned up by the EPA under the Superfund program did not make adequate inquiries about the environmental status of the land before purchasing it and therefore was not considered an innocent landowner and was required to share in the cost of the cleanup with the previous owner of the property.

       1. Part of the 1986 amendments to Superfund contain "Community Right to Know" provisions and a provision for emergency cleanup.

VI. Regulation of toxic chemicals.

    A. The Federal Insecticide, Fungicide, and Rodenticide Act (FIFRA) and Toxic Substances Control Act (TSCA) regulate new and existing chemicals.

    B. Under FIFRA, the EPA has the authority to register pesticides before they may be sold, and to suspend or cancel registration to protect the public from an imminent hazard.

    C. Under the Toxic Substances Control Act, or TSCA, the EPA may regulate chemicals that present an unreasonable risk of injury to health or the environment.

       1. Biotechnology issues are addressed in TSCA.

Learning Objectives

1. You should understand the historical background and the evolution of government regulation of business activities affecting the environment.

2. You should be familiar with legislative controls on the emission of chemicals and other pollutants into the atmosphere.

3. You should be familiar with legislative controls on the emission of chemicals and other pollutants into rivers, streams, and lakes.

4. You should understand the legislative controls on the manufacture, storage, and disposal of toxic chemicals.

5. You should understand legislation addressing the cleanup of hazardous waste sites that exist as a result of past manufacturing or industrial activity.

6. You should come to recognize that for many businesses, compliance with environmental statutes and regulations is an expensive and time-consuming process that cannot be ignored.

Learning Hints

1. The scope of environmental regulation has increased drastically in the past quarter-century. Environmental notions are now firmly entrenched in the legal scene and are not about to disappear. Therefore, prudent businesspersons cannot afford to be indifferent to and unaware of the major provisions of environmental law.

2. In studying what the text has to say about the National Environmental Policy Act and its requirements concerning environmental impact statements for federal projects, do not forget that various state and local governments have passed their own NEPA-like laws that also require environmental impact statements for major public and private projects.

3. Note that under the Clean Air Act, both the federal government and the state governments have enforcement roles. The federal government (through the EPA) sets the relevant air quality standards. The states have the primary responsibility for enforcing these standards, but the federal government has the authority to enforce them when the states have failed to do so. In a sense, private citizens may also have a role in enforcement as well. Private citizens may file suits to force industry or the government to comply fully with the Clean Air Act's provisions.

4. Note how the Clean Water Act's provisions on wetlands may significantly limit the uses to which a property owner may put his, her, or its property.

5. The Resource Conservation and Recovery Act (RCRA) and the Superfund legislation were products of a growing awareness during the past two decades of the potentially devastating problems associated with hazardous waste disposal and abandoned or uncontrolled hazardous waste sites. In studying your text's treatment of these statutes, note their differing functions. RCRA is proactive in the sense that it is designed to minimize the likelihood that environmental disasters involving hazardous wastes will occur. Superfund, on the other hand, is reactive, in that it provides a mechanism for dealing with an environmental problem that has already occurred—In the form of an abandoned or uncontrolled hazardous waste site--but is certain to become worse if ignored.

6. As you consider the various legislative attempts to address the problems of industrial pollution, you should consider the following questions: What is (are) the problems the legislation attempts to address? What is (are) the method(s) by which the legislation addresses those problems? (Note, many of these federal laws are "command and control" legislation--that is, they do not rely on economic incentives to accomplish their goals). How successful is the legislation in meeting those goals? In what ways might business and industry better address the problems of industrial pollution utilizing a "cost-benefit" approach?

True-False

In the blank provided, put "T" if the statement is True or "F" if the statement is False.

_____ 1. In recent years, the federal government has made an effort to move from command and control regulations in dealing with environmental problems to a system of economic incentives and voluntary action.

_____ 2. The EPA has the authority to register pesticides before they can be sold.

_____ 3. Violators of the RCRA are subject to civil, but not criminal, penalties.

_____ 4. Under the Clean Water Act, the federal government has the primary responsibility of preventing, reducing, and eliminating water pollution.

_____ 5. The Safe Drinking Water Act addresses the problem of acid rain.

_____ 6. Up to this time, federal and state regulatory efforts have dealt only with outdoor air pollution; indoor air pollution is as yet unregulated.

_____ 7. The Clean Water Act regulates dredging or filling in wetlands, except when the wetlands are privately owned and the activity is being carried out by the landowner.

_____ 8. Persons who dispose of hazardous waste in violation of the Resource Conservation and Recovery Act may be criminally, as well as civilly, liable.

_____ 9. A state must decide which activities must be regulated or curtailed so that air pollution emissions for a given air quality region do not exceed national ambient air quality standards.

_____ 10. The EPA has the authority to order automobile manufacturers to recall and repair vehicles that exceed emission standards.

Multiple Choice

Circle the best answer.

1. Environmental impact statements must:
   a. Discuss impacts that cannot be avoided.
   b. Discuss alternatives to the proposed action.
   c. Describe the environmental impact of the proposed action.
   d. All of the above.

2. Which of the following statements about the Clean Water Act is correct? The Clean Water Act:
   a. Requires that all industrial dischargers but not municipal discharges to obtain permits to discharge any pollutants.
   b. Requires all dischargers to keep records and install and maintain monitoring equipment.
   c. Does not permit citizens to sue anyone violating an effluent standard under the Act.
   d. Gives the federal government the primary responsibility for preventing water pollution.

3. Which of the following statements is not true?
   a. The EPA is required to set national ambient air quality standards.
   b. The EPA develops plans for each state to meet national ambient air quality standards.
   c. Primary standards are designed to protect the public's health from harm.
   d. Secondary standards are designed to protect vegetation, climate, etc.

4. Which of the following statements is not true concerning the Clean Air Act?
   a. Most electric-generating utilities are required to install scrubbers.
   b. The EPA regulates the emission of toxic air pollutants.
   c. The Clean Air Act requires new factories to install the best available technology for reducing air pollution.
   d. The primary responsibility for enforcing the Clean Air Act belongs to the EPA.

5. Which of the following statements is not true concerning the Clean Water Act?
   a. All municipal and industrial dischargers must obtain permits.
   b. Dischargers who are in violation of the law may be fined, but not sent to prison.
   c. The states have the main responsibility of preventing, reducing, and eliminating water pollution.
   d. Anyone dredging in a wetland requires a permit from the Army Corps of Engineers.

6. Which federal environmental statute does not permit private citizen lawsuits?
   a. Resource Conservation and Recovery Act.
   b. Clean Air Act.
   c. Clean Water Act.
   d. None of the above.

7. Which of the following statements is true concerning the Resource, Conservation and Recovery Act?
   a. Anyone who generates, treats, stores, or transports hazardous waste must obtain an ID number from the EPA, follow procedures for handling the hazardous waste, and keep records.
   b. Operators of land disposal facilities must meet financial responsibility requirements.
   c. The EPA regulates underground product storage tanks and can order owners of these tanks to upgrade or replace them.
   d. All of the above.

8. Which of the following statements is not true?
   a. The RCRA Authorized the EPA to set minimum standards for waste disposal.
   b. The not-in-my-backyard syndrome is a major obstacle in finding sites for new waste facilities.
   c. State and local governments have the primary responsibility for waste sites and their regulation.
   d. The EPA bears sole responsibility for the costs incurred in cleanups of hazardous waste sites.

9. The Superfund legislation requires:
   a. That a state prevents future environmental problems on sites that have been cleaned up.
   b. That responsible parties reimburse the EPA for its costs of cleaning up a hazardous waste site.
   c. That those responsible for contaminating a site be jointly and severally liable for the cost of cleanup.
   d. All of the above.

10. Which of the following statements is not true?
    a. Chemicals must be tested by manufacturers before placing them on the market.
    b. The EPA has the authority to regulate chemical substances that pose an unreasonable risk of injury to health or the environment.
    c. Regulation of research and use of biotechnology is the sole responsibility of the FDA.
    d. The EPA can suspend registration of a pesticide if there is reason to believe that it poses an imminent hazard.

Short Essay

1. The City of Lawrence would like to build a by-pass to circle around the city. Part of it would be built near a wetlands area. Describe the process the city would need to follow under the National Environmental Policy Act.

2. Briefly describe some of the main features of the Clean Air Act.

3. Briefly describe the three federal laws that protect water quality.

4. Beth and Ernie have just moved into their new home built by Rusty's Fast House Inc. After living in the home for just a few weeks, both Beth and Ernie have had symptoms of difficulty breathing and other respiratory problems. They hire a building inspector to do an environmental audit of their home, and she finds that the house is creating a "sick building syndrome." What can Beth and Ernie do?

5. After the Exxon Valdez disaster, a number of measures were taken to prevent a recurrence of that environmental tragedy. What do you think some of these measures might be?

6. The federal government is in the process of cleaning up one of the highest concentrations of nuclear waste in the US: the Rocky Flats Nuclear Arsenal. The plant was used to make atomic warheads during the Cold War era. It has been decommissioned, and the waste is being shipped to various locations for treatment and storage. One such place is South Carolina where the governor seeks to stop shipments of this waste into his state. Can he do that?

7. What agency is responsible for enforcing the Federal Insecticide, Fungicide, and Rodenticide Act? Describe some of the actions this agency can take in enforcing the law.